GIDE'S
BENT

IDEOLOGIES OF DESIRE

David M. Halperin
Series Editor

The Female Thermometer
Eighteenth-Century Culture and the Invention of the Uncanny
TERRY CASTLE

Gide's Bent
Sexuality, Politics, Writing
MICHAEL LUCEY

GIDE'S BENT

Sexuality
Politics
Writing

MICHAEL LUCEY

New York Oxford
OXFORD UNIVERSITY PRESS
1995

Oxford University Press

Oxford   New York
Athens   Auckland   Bangkok   Bombay
Calcutta   Cape Town   Dar es Salaam   Delhi
Florence   Hong Kong   Istanbul   Karachi
Kuala Lumpur   Madras   Madrid   Melbourne
Mexico City   Nairobi   Paris   Singapore
Taipei   Tokyo   Toronto

and associated companies in
Berlin   Ibadan

Copyright © 1995 by Oxford University Press, Inc.

Published by Oxford University Press, Inc.,
200 Madison Avenue, New York, New York 10016

Oxford is a registered trademark of Oxford University Press

Library of Congress Cataloging-in-Publication Data
Lucey, Michael, 1960–
Gide's bent : sexuality, politics, writing / Michael Lucey.
    p.   cm. — (Ideologies of desire)
Includes bibliographical references and index.
ISBN 0-19-508086-6. — ISBN 0-19-508087-4 (pbk.)
1. Gide, André, 1869–1951—Criticism and interpretation.
2. Homosexuality and literature—France—History—20th century.
3. Politics and literature—France—History—20th century.   4. Gay
men in literature.   5. Utopias in literature.   6. Sex in literature.
I. Title.   II. Series.
PQ2613.I2Z6534   1995
848'.91209—dc20   94-23094

A version of chapter 1 originally appeared in *The Yale Journal of Criticism* 4 (Fall 1990): 174–92. A version of
chapter 2 first appeared in *Qui Parle?* 4 (Spring 1991): 23–42. My thanks to the editors at both journals for
their help.

9 8 7 6 5 4 3 2 1

Printed in the United States of America
on acid-free paper

ACKNOWLEDGMENTS

It is only because of the growth of queer studies over a number of decades that I can write a book such as this now. I am grateful for the very existence of the intellectual space in which I found myself writing this book, grateful to all those who have contributed to its development. Specific intellectual debts will be acknowledged at appropriate points in the book, but here I offer a general and necessary thanks.

Berkeley has been a pleasant and challenging place to work on this book. It is a great pleasure to mention, first of all, Timothy Hampton, Leslie Kurke, Celeste Langan, and Lydia Liu, who make up a formidable reading group. Their friendly comments have enriched this project as well as my intellectual life more generally. I would also like to thank my colleagues Leo Bersani, Walter E. Rex, and Ann Smock for their encouragement and for the generous amounts of time they have spent reading my work. Thanks, as well, to Francine Masiello and William Nestrick for their help. Jon Lang provided a critical eye and helpful conversation on several occasions. I am also grateful to those graduate students who read and wrote on Gide with me. Lincoln Shlensky, David Copenhafer, and Yuji Oniki provided invaluable assistance with the final preparation of the manuscript. Grants from the Committee on Research of the University of California at Berkeley supported this work.

I am grateful to David M. Halperin, who both took an early interest in this project and undertook a painstaking and helpful reading of the completed manuscript, resulting in improvements I would never have discovered on my own. Further thanks are due to the two readers engaged by Oxford University Press, and to Liz Maguire, my editor, all of whose comments led to further material improvements.

I suspect that my family awaits the publication of this book—which has been "in the air" for so long—with bemused and enduring curiosity. Their love and material support has been an important contribution to it.

Yopie Prins has been a sympathetic reader and friend for a long time, as well as a constant voice of encouragement from the earliest stages of this project. I am glad to be able to say here how important the conversation and friendship of Carolyn Dinshaw have been to me. David Price was present at the writing of many of these pages and is necessarily intertwined with much of the thinking that went into them; that fact is also a pleasure to acknowledge. Finally, a heartfelt thanks to Christopher Palacios for his curiosity, provocations, love, and company. Friends such as these make possible and sustain intellectual projects in multiform ways we only half suspect and acknowledge as best we can.

ACKNOWLEDGMENTS

It is only because of the growth of queer studies over a number of decades that I can write a book such as this now. I am grateful for the very existence of the intellectual space in which I found myself writing this book, grateful to all those who have contributed to its development. Specific intellectual debts will be acknowledged at appropriate points in the book, but here I offer a general and necessary thanks.

Berkeley has been a pleasant and challenging place to work on this book. It is a great pleasure to mention, first of all, Timothy Hampton, Leslie Kurke, Celeste Langan, and Lydia Liu, who make up a formidable reading group. Their friendly comments have enriched this project as well as my intellectual life more generally. I would also like to thank my colleagues Leo Bersani, Walter E. Rex, and Ann Smock for their encouragement and for the generous amounts of time they have spent reading my work. Thanks, as well, to Francine Masiello and William Nestrick for their help. Jon Lang provided a critical eye and helpful conversation on several occasions. I am also grateful to those graduate students who read and wrote on Gide with me. Lincoln Shlensky, David Copenhafer, and Yuji Oniki provided invaluable assistance with the final preparation of the manuscript. Grants from the Committee on Research of the University of California at Berkeley supported this work.

I am grateful to David M. Halperin, who both took an early interest in this project and undertook a painstaking and helpful reading of the completed manuscript, resulting in improvements I would never have discovered on my own. Further thanks are due to the two readers engaged by Oxford University Press, and to Liz Maguire, my editor, all of whose comments led to further material improvements.

I suspect that my family awaits the publication of this book—which has been "in the air" for so long—with bemused and enduring curiosity. Their love and material support has been an important contribution to it.

Yopie Prins has been a sympathetic reader and friend for a long time, as well as a constant voice of encouragement from the earliest stages of this project. I am glad to be able to say here how important the conversation and friendship of Carolyn Dinshaw have been to me. David Price was present at the writing of many of these pages and is necessarily intertwined with much of the thinking that went into them; that fact is also a pleasure to acknowledge. Finally, a heartfelt thanks to Christopher Palacios for his curiosity, provocations, love, and company. Friends such as these make possible and sustain intellectual projects in multiform ways we only half suspect and acknowledge as best we can.

CONTENTS

Note on Translation, ix

Introduction, 3

1. Watching Sex in *Si le grain ne meurt,* 21

2. The Place of the Oedipal: Writing Home from North Africa, 42

3. *Corydon* and *L'Ecole des femmes:* Mimesis, the Mantis, the Gynaeceum, 68

4. Without Delay: *Les Faux-Monnayeurs,* Lacan, and the Onset of Sexuality, 108

5. *Gribouille en Afrique:* Gide's *Voyage au Congo,* 143

6. Sexuality, Politics and Culture: Gide's Trip to the Soviet Union, 181

Epilogue: Queer Tears, 217

Works Cited, 223

Index, 231

NOTE ON TRANSLATION

I have made a point of citing Gide's writings in both French and English on almost every occasion. I sometimes do this for other writers as well, where the French text seems to me of especial import. Where no English translation for a text is given in the Works Cited section, the translation is my own. When a published translation is cited, I have frequently modified that translation for the sake of accuracy, or to bring out a particular nuance. When two page numbers are given within the same parentheses, the first refers to the English and the second to the French edition.

GIDE'S
BENT

INTRODUCTION

In the early 1920s André Gide, by then in his fifties and one of the most well established literary figures in France, began publishing writings that insisted on his homosexuality. (Earlier writings such as *L'Immoraliste* [1902] or *Les Caves du Vatican* [1914] had hinted at this aspect of his life but stopped well short of the explicitness he aimed at in the 1920s and thereafter.) In addition, throughout the 1920s and 1930s Gide increasingly advocated a variety of left-wing causes, declaring his allegiance to communism in the early 1930s and visiting the Soviet Union in 1936.

Gide's sexuality continually troubles discussions of his work, even when those discussions consciously avoid mentioning it. If, for many commentators, Gide's explicitly *political* interests of the 1920s and 1930s—in anticolonialist struggles, feminism, communism, and the Soviet Union—represent a decline in his "literary" interest or value, for many others his *sexuality* lessens not only his "literary" value but his political reliability as well. These kinds of judgments are, as we will see, sometimes explicit, sometimes discreetly implied. The alliance of politics, sexuality, and literature in Gide's case almost inevitably has a discomfiting effect. That effect is the subject of this book.

My effort will be not so much to explicate, justify, or admire Gide's politics or his sexuality[1] as to trace the contours of a writing practice that insistently imbricates psychic and political crises. Gide's texts refuse to separate personal expression from social thought, sexuality from politics, the shape of one's sexual subjectivity from that of one's political subjectivity. Such a practice of writing illuminates the traversal of the personal by the social; it exhibits an awareness that the psychic and the social realms are contiguous and interpenetrating, that personal acts (and, in particular, the acts that delimit sexualities) are politically and socially structured. That particular awareness is somewhat difficult to assign to a place (this or that text, this or that moment in a text), or a person (André Gide). In this light, writing

1. There are, in fact, many unadmirable things about Gide's politics, notably a current of antisemitism that is prominently displayed in a troubling review of Céline's *Bagatelles pour un massacre* from 1938 ("Les Juifs, Céline et Maritain") and resurfaces in a joke told in *Ainsi soit-il* (58–59/1189). See Jeffrey Mehlman, "'Jewish Literature' and the Art of André Gide," on this question. See also Alice Yaeger Kaplan, *Reproductions of Banality: Fascism, Literature, and French Intellectual Life*, 48–50. As for his sexuality, as we will see, even within his advocacy of certain forms of homosexuality there will be ample space for expressions of homophobia.

and sexuality might be said to be similar; they are both often expressive in their own right, beyond any intention of the writing or the sexual subject in question. Writing and sexuality could be said to *pre*occupy Gide: they preoccupy the person he knew himself to be and the expressive acts he undertook.

At times, in the readings that make up this book, it will seem as if Gide is aiding and abetting those aspects of his sexuality that are finding expression in his writing; indeed, at times it will seem that Gide *intends* to express most of the ideas about sexuality I will be investigating. Yet, sometimes certain things will seem to find expression without Gide's knowledge, or even despite his stated intention. This odd effect is not one Gide particularly minded. Indeed, he can be said to have cultivated it, often to have chosen to write *sous le coup de la sexualité,* that is, under the influence of sexuality.

I will be concentrating on a small number of Gide's texts, often focusing on the precise details of selected passages from those texts. My hope is that Gide's careful writing will offer a series of instructive examples of how, through a writerly attention to precision of expression and style, one can, in fact, open oneself to express more than one *knows.* Gide consistently—both willingly and unwillingly —expresses more than he knows about his sexuality, the sources of his political commitments, and the forms of his pleasures and of his desires. Through those pleasures, desires, and commitments he finds himself woven into his particular social fabric, unsure how much of the weaving he might have done himself. Much as I have occasionally felt, as I wrote these chapters, that I disliked this or that trait of the man in question (this may be especially apparent in chapter 3), I have found that the honesty or the strange expressivity he achieved through his rigorous insistence that his writing practice somehow exceed who he thought himself to be, are an honesty and an expressivity that, despite their contradictions—even *because* of their contradictions—I admire.

I trace this contradictory honesty across a series of texts published during the period roughly between 1920 and 1940, but my effort is not to be comprehensive, either biographically or in the sense of providing "complete" readings of the texts I consider. In the remainder of this introduction, and occasionally in the chapters that follow, I will sketch in some of the historical context of Gide's writings from this period, but my main interest is not so much in providing information about Gide's life and work as in investigating the ways he tried, through his writing, to understand and express his own bent. I hope to bring into focus the shape of his writing practice, his political commitments, and his sexuality—interwoven shapes inevitably elusive to him even as he came to understand them and to act them out.

To understand the interweaving of sexuality and politics involves many things, as the politics of sexuality is necessarily related to the politics of class, colonialism, gender, or race. But these particular intersections will not exhaust the political content of any given form of sexual expression. Of all the political overdeterminations of sexual acts, that part which seems related to sexuality "it-self" often seems most elusive analytically, especially as, in the case of homosexuality, political commentators have formed a tradition of denying that very overdetermination any import. It is not clear to me that any particular set of analytical tools provides the best access to that political material, nor is it certain that I have always managed to keep it in focus throughout this book. The gesture of calling the book *Gide's Bent* is an effort to remind myself of that most elusive political potential hidden in sexuality. The undeniable presence of some writings by Lacan in chapters 4 and 5 will indicate to the reader that I have found in Lacan's writing some analytical provocation to thinking in detail about the political material of sexuality. (This is not to say that I feel that a certain "Lacanian conceptual structure," as it is so often invoked in current academic discourse, should be understood as inevitably useful to queer theory. To the extent that I invoke that structure, I nonetheless remain suspicious of it. Rather, my interest is drawn to certain specific passages in the Lacanian text that provide complications to the effort to read sexuality.)

The writings by Gide I will consider here vary widely in form: autobiographical writings, letters, novels, travel journals, philosophical dialogues. In each of these texts sexuality and politics place themselves or are placed differently. In an effort to respect differences in the sexual and political bent of these texts, and to allow the variegated contours of Gide's bent to be revealed as complexly as possible, I will not develop here, nor have I fully developed elsewhere, *the* theoretical framework (should there be one) that determines my reading. Such determinations seem to me, when presented, necessarily riddled with ignorance and forgetfulness precisely because one's theoretical bent, like one's sexual bent, is never fully apparent to oneself.

Blasphemy and Vice

> I didn't apply myself to English until very late. . . . "I can't speak English" was for a long time the only sentence I could utter. I first had occasion to use it during the first and very short trip I made to London with our minister M. Allégret, to whom my mother had entrusted me. He took me to hear a preacher named Spurgeon, famous then, who, after the sermon, used to baptize adults in an *ad hoc* pool. . . . After the service, when everyone was leaving, a very seemly young lady came up to me at the door and said a few words in the sweetest voice, to which I smilingly protested: "No, thank you" (*that* I knew how to say), thinking that she was offering to do me some service or other. She immediately drew herself up, and from her hurt manner I suspected that that was not what I should have answered. M. Allégret had heard everything. "She was asking you if you wanted to be saved," he explained. The rest of the trip I prudently remained mute. (*So Be It*, 61–62)[2]

2. Je ne me suis mis à l'anglais que très tard . . . *I can't speak english* est la seule phrase que durant longtemps je pus dire et dont j'eus pour la première fois l'occasion de me servir durant le premier et très court voyage que je fis à Londres avec le pasteur Allégret, à qui m'avait confié ma mère. Il me mena entendre un prédicateur, célèbre en ce temps, Spurgeon, qui baptisait, après le sermon, des adultes dans une piscine *ad hoc* . . . Après le service, comme tout le monde se retirait, une très décente jeune dame vint à ma rencontre près de la sortie et me dit quelques mots

One of the headlines on the front page of the *New York Times* of June 1, 1952, read: VATICAN BANS ALL WRITINGS OF GIDE; BLASPHEMY AND VICE ARE CHARGED. André Gide had died on February 19, 1951, at the age of eighty-one, and most of his writings had been around long enough that the Vatican could easily have decided to ban them earlier. It would appear that the posthumously published *Ainsi soit-il (So Be It)*, a series of intimate reflections dating from the last months of his life, was deemed so egregious by the Sacred Congregation of the Holy Office that it resolved on a posthumous ban as a necessary symbolic gesture, even though nothing in *Ainsi soit-il* would have surprised anyone who had been reading Gide throughout his long career. In its article the *New York Times* quoted from the Vatican newspaper *L'Osservatore romano:*

> "The church, as his dearest friends, waited to the very end for the prodigal son to return. He did not return. Let at least his place in the Catholic lineup be marked among the enemies and corruptors—among the followers of the adversary. . . ."
>
> His "taste for profanation" was "carried as far as blasphemy," the newspaper declared, saying that the last pages he had written before his death were "filled with bitter negations of Christ as well as with vice and ugly references to Catholics."[3]

Crudely put, but to some extent true, one has to admit. In *Ainsi soit-il,* Gide makes a few derisive remarks about his erstwhile friend Paul Claudel, for example, who, according to Gide, accused the Nobel Prize committee of being a "clique protestante" for awarding Gide the prize for literature in 1947 (*So Be It,* 129; *Ainsi soit-il,* 1224).[4] In that same text Gide also made light fun of a number of his Catholic friends (Francis Jammes, Paul Claudel, Charles du Bos) and of their various attempts to convert and save him.

More to the point, in *Ainsi soit-il* Gide continued to be uncompromisingly explicit about his homosexuality, providing new details about sexual encounters during his trips to the Soviet Union in 1936 and to Africa in 1925. "Little do I care," he writes, speaking of the boy whom he had met during the African trip, "if these words should shock some, who will consider them impious." Indeed, the scandalous nature of those words was carefully calculated: "Sweet little Mala! On my deathbed it is your amused laugh and your joy that I should most like to see again" (126/1223). To announce that while waiting to die you would most like to remember the joyous face of a young African boy with whom you had just shared

---

d'une voix des plus suaves; à quoi je protestai en souriant : *No, thank you* (ça je savais le dire), croyant qu'elle se proposait à me rendre je ne sais quel service. Elle se redressa aussitôt et je me doutai, à son air cabré, que ce n'est pas du tout cela que j'aurais dû lui répondre. Le pasteur Allégret avait tout entendu. « Elle te demandait si tu voulais être sauvé », m'expliquait-il. Le reste du voyage s'effectua prudemment à la muette (*Ainsi soit-il,* 1190–91).

    3. The text of the Vatican condemnation and of the *Osservatore romano* article reporting it can be found in David Littlejohn, ed., *Gide: A Collection of Critical Essays,* 30–35.

    4. An anecdote recorded by George D. Painter in his biography of Gide indicates the state of affairs between these two literary figures: "Claudel, for the last quarter of a century, had remained implacable. 'That,' he gleefully exclaimed one day at lunch, at the sight of a pancake cooking in flaming brandy, 'is how Gide's soul will burn in hell!' Gide particularly enjoyed this anecdote of the *crêpe flambée*" (Painter, 131).

your bed—such resolutely pagan writing is meant to be provoking, and, as far as the Vatican was concerned, it apparently succeeded.

Gide then goes on to link his observations about Mala to a lifetime of sensual experience about which he had had much practice writing:

> But I should like to protest also against any excessive limitation one might be tempted to see in this profession of materialism. I do not intend thereby to confine myself to mere carnal pleasure; it invites me to melt into and merge with surrounding nature. This is why my most perfect memories of sensual pleasure are those enveloped in a landscape which absorbs it and in which I seem to be swallowed up. (126–27)[5]

Sexual experience, Gide claims, is more than just physical pleasure. As an experience, it challenges the boundaries of the self; it furthers an understanding of how those boundaries are drawn and redrawn. From at least as early as his *Nourritures terrestres* (*Fruits of the Earth*, 1897), through his autobiography *Si le grain ne meurt* (*If It Die*, 1926), through the travel journal of his trip to equatorial Africa, *Voyage au Congo* (*Travels in the Congo*, 1927), on to at least his *Nouvelles Nourritures* (*Later Fruits of the Earth*, 1935), a text infused with his communist enthusiasms of the 1930s, Gide's writings on sexuality and sexual experience consistently investigate sexuality's challenges to the boundaries of a self and consistently invoke a pagan frame of reference to do so.[6]

One salient example of this kind of writing would be the following passage from *Si le grain ne meurt*, where Gide reports a bit of advice he was once given by a doctor:

> "Every time," said he, "you see a piece of water into which you can dive, do so without hesitation."
> And so I did. O you foaming torrents! you waterfalls, and icy lakes! how your coolness tempts me! And then how sweet to rest on the yellow sand beside the backward curl of the waves! For it was not the bath alone that I loved, but afterwards the expectant, the mythological waiting for the god's naked and enfolding flame. My body, shot through with rays, seemed to enjoy some chemical benefaction; with my garments I laid aside anxieties, constraints, worries, and as my will evaporated, I felt myself becoming porous as a beehive, and let my sensations secretly distil the honey that flowed into the pages of my *Nourritures*. (264)[7]

5. Mais je voudrais aussi bien protester contre une limitation excessive que l'on serait tenté de voir dans cette profession de matérialisme; je ne m'y cantonne pas dans la seule jouissance charnelle : celle-ci m'invite à me fondre et confondre dans la nature environnante. C'est bien aussi pourquoi mes souvenirs de volupté les plus parfaits sont ceux qu'accompagne l'enveloppement d'un paysage qui l'absorbe et où je me paraisse me résorber (1223).

6. Emily S. Apter's "Homotextual Counter-Codes : André Gide and the Poetics of Engagement" helpfully analyzes the early, sensual *Nourritures terrestres* in light of Gide's later political interests.

7. — Chaque fois, me disait-il, que vous voyez une eau où pouvoir vous plonger, n'hésitez pas.
Ainsi fis-je. O torrents écumeux! cascades, lacs glacés, ruisseaux ombragés, sources limpides, transparents palais de la mer, votre fraîcheur m'attire; puis, sur le sable blond, le doux repos près du repliement de la vague. Car ce n'était pas seulement le bain, que j'aimais, mais la mythologique attente, ensuite, de l'enveloppement nu du dieu; en mon corps pénétré de rayons, il me semblait goûter je ne sais quel bienfait chimique; j'oubliais avec mes vêtements, tourments, contraintes, sollicitudes, et, tandis que se volatilisait tout vouloir, je laissais les sensations, en moi poreux comme une ruche, secrètement distiller ce miel qui coula dans mes *Nourritures* (318).

Gide understands sexuality as a force both interior and exterior to his identity that finds expression in his writing, but not a force that he necessarily controls as he gives it expression. The sensational honey of his writings comes from a porous subjectivity that wills its will away in order to experience the pleasure around which it nonetheless seems somehow to take shape. It is part of Gide's writing practice, from *Les Nourritures terrestres* onward, to experiment with this predicament. And as the reference to Apollo in this passage suggests, it is not just any sexuality that Gide writes about, but homosexuality—the "vice" that so exercised Claudel and the Vatican.

Les Nourritures terrestres and its sensuality could perhaps sneak by the censors, as the rapturous prose never pauses to make absolutely clear the type of sexual adventure being pursued. Later Gide leaves little doubt in this regard, and the clearer it becomes that he is writing specifically about (his) *homo*sexual experience, the more focused the attacks against him become. The more effort, too, that certain critics would have to exert in order to ignore what Gide was striving to force on their attention.

Out

> Dear friend, how painful it is to me to have spoken so much about myself, when it is you that I think of ceaselessly. My self is really hateful and I am furious that I spoke of myself. I shall calm down by thinking of you, of my tenderness, my admiration for you.[8]
> —Marcel Proust to André Gide, November 21, 1918

I have proceeded a bit anecdotally, and indeed it has seemed for some time now that Gide's place in literary history might be reduced to the anecdotal. Already in 1965 Paul de Man could observe that "it has almost become a commonplace of today's criticism to state that André Gide's work had begun to fade away even before the author's death in 1951" (de Man, "Whatever Happened to André Gide?", 130). Gide would be remembered, it has seemed, as much or more for those strange conjunctures of literary history in which he participated—his meetings with Oscar Wilde in Paris and Algeria or his decision to turn down Proust's *Du côté de chez Swann* for publication by Gallimard (and his subsequent efforts to undo this wrong and win the rest of the manuscript back for Gallimard)—as for anything he might have written.[9]

---

8. Cher ami, qu'il m'est pénible de vous avoir tant parlé de moi, alors que c'est à vous que je pense sans cesse. Mon moi m'est bien haïssable et je suis excédé d'avoir parlé de moi. Je vais me reposer en pensant à vous, à ma tendresse, à mon admiration pour vous.

9. For information on Gide and Wilde, see Jonathan Dollimore, 3–18, and Richard Ellmann, "Corydon and Ménalque." For information on Gide and Proust, see Proust's *Lettres à André Gide*.

This tendency to view Gide anecdotally might be seen as related to his openness about his (homo)sexuality. Gide would remember conversations with both Proust and Wilde about being public and about the relationship between literature and sexuality. Gide visited Wilde shortly after Wilde arrived in France, having been recently released from prison in England. Among the books Wilde had with him was Gide's recently published *Nourritures terrestres*. Gide tells us that he remembers Wilde counseling him at the very end of the visit:

> "Listen, dear, now you must make me a promise. Your *Nourritures terrestres* is fine . . . very fine, even. . . . But dear, from now on never again write 'I'."
>
> And as I didn't seem to understand him fully enough, he went on: "In art, you see, there is no *first* person." (*Oscar Wilde*, 46)[10]

Doubtless the particularities of the enforcements on gay men of the distinction between public and private realms, the forms of the closet, are in both minds here. Gide's retrospective essay on Wilde, for example, itself constitutes an attempt on Gide's part to understand one particular side of the phenomenon of Wilde's personality—to understand why Wilde would have let himself be trapped into a court case that used his homosexuality to send him to prison. A consideration of the complexities and particularities of the social forces that attempt to dictate the public/private behaviors of gay men is thus perhaps *the* essential part of Gide's attempt to understand Wilde. In writing about Wilde, about sexuality—specifically about homosexuality—Gide negotiates the same issues for himself.

In a journal entry from 1921 Gide recounts a similar conversation during an evening spent with Marcel Proust.

> I am taking him *Corydon*, of which he promises not to speak to anyone; and when I say a word or two about my Memoirs:
>
> "You can relate anything," he cries; "but on condition that you never say: *I*." But that won't suit me.
>
> Far from denying or hiding his uranism, he exhibits it, and I could almost say boasts of it. . . . He tells me his conviction that Baudelaire was a uranist. . . .
>
> "In any case, if he was a uranist, it was almost without his knowing it; and you don't believe that he ever practiced. . . ."
>
> "What!" he cries. "I am convinced of the opposite; how can you doubt that he practiced? He, Baudelaire!" (*Journals*, 2:265)[11]

---

10. « Ecoutez, dear, il faut maintenant que vous me fassiez une promesse. Les *Nourritures terrestres*, c'est bien . . . c'est très bien . . . Mais, dear, promettez-moi : maintenant n'écrivez plus jamais JE ».

Et comme je paraissais ne pas suffisamment comprendre, il reprenait : — « En art, voyez-vous, il n'y a pas de *première* personne ».

⋯

Gide returns to these reflections in his journal entry for October 1, 1927. See Jonathan Dollimore's discussion, 74–75.

11. Je lui apporte *Corydon* dont il me promet de ne parler à personne; et comme je lui dis quelques mots de mes Mémoires :

« Vous pouvez tout raconter, s'écrie-t-il; mais à condition de ne jamais dire : *Je* ». Ce qui ne fait pas mon affaire.

Some complications are noteworthy here. Gide brings Proust a clandestine copy of *Corydon* (four dialogues on homosexuality he would publish openly in 1924). Proust promises to keep it secret but recommends a more "literary" form of secrecy, the same one Wilde had recommended several decades earlier. Don't say I. Such advice is not to Gide's taste. He wishes, whatever his understanding of the relationship between sexuality and self, to attach a first person to his homosexuality. (The pronominal strategies of *Corydon* are in fact more complicated than this, as we will see in chapter 3.) The memoirs he tells Proust about, *Si le grain ne meurt*, are notably explicit in this regard, yet notably slippery in the way they trace a self's relation to its sexuality.

Proust cries out against the idea of a first person and then cries again in dismay at Gide's resistance to the idea of Baudelaire as a practicing homosexual. Gide, for the time being, keeps *Corydon* a secret, and keeps relatively secret as well early versions of his first-person memoirs. Proust's way of vaunting, of bragging about his (and others') "uranism" remains slightly distasteful to him.[12] This turmoil around the question of the first person could well be recast in contemporary terms as a question about "outing,"[13] or about coming out of the closet. Eve Kosofsky Sedgwick, in *Epistemology of the Closet*, has shown skillfully how in Proust (and in Wilde) a strange written ballet is performed, so that knowledge about the writer's sexuality seems always on the verge of being proffered, so that the writer seems to some readers to exist almost simultaneously inside and outside of the closet.[14] Gide was to be much more *out*, both in public life and in his writings, than either Proust or Wilde, and this has had certain consequences in the reception of his work. Such consequences began much earlier than the posthumous condemnation by the Vatican.

If in the 1921 encounter with Proust Gide was still only tentatively out, pondering exactly what form that outness would take, by 1926 its contours would

---

Loin de nier ou de cacher son uranisme, il l'expose, et je pourrais presque dire : s'en targue . . . Il me dit la conviction où il est que Baudelaire était uraniste . . .

— En tout cas, s'il était uraniste, c'était à son insu presque; et vous ne pouvez penser qu'il ait jamais pratiqué . . .

— Comment donc! s'écrie-t-il. Je suis convaincu du contraire; comment pouvez-vous douter qu'il pratiquât? lui, Baudelaire? (*Journal, 1889–1939*, 692).

12. As one might expect, Gide found Proust's *Sodome et Gomorrhe* dishonest. Reading an installment of it in *La Nouvelle Revue Française* a few months later (December 1921), Gide reports a "sursaut d'indignation": "I have read Proust's latest pages (December issue of the N.R.F.) with, at first, a shock of indignation. Knowing what he thinks, what he is, it is hard for me to see in them anything but a pretense, a desire to protect himself, a camouflage of the cleverest sort, for it can be to no one's advantage to denounce him" (*Journals*, 2:276). [Connaissant ce qu'il pense, ce qu'il est, il m'est difficile de voir là autre chose qu'une feinte, qu'un désir de se protéger, qu'un camouflage, on ne peut plus habile, car il ne peut être de l'avantage de personne de le dénoncer (*Journal, 1889–1939*, 705]. Gide is offended by the extent to which the queers Proust portrays correspond to the "invert" model, a model he feels will confirm straight peoples' repugnance and be of little interest to homosexuals of Gide's sort. I note this prejudice of Gide's in both chapters 1 and 3.

13. For useful discussions of the coining, usage, and cultural significance of this term, see Michelangelo Signorile's *Queer in America: Sex, the Media, and the Closets of Power*, esp. the Preface, Introduction, and chapter 5.

14. See *Epistemology of the Closet*, esp. chapters 2, 3, and 5.

be more clear. *Corydon* and *Si le grain ne meurt* would be published, along with *Les Faux-Monnayeurs* (*The Counterfeiters*), a novel whose central character, a middle-aged male novelist, has a clear sexual interest in young men. But even in 1914, with the publication of *Les Caves du Vatican* (variously titled in translation *Lafcadio's Adventures*, *The Vatican Swindle*, or *the Vatican Cellars*), Gide had a tussle with Claudel, Francis Jammes, and Charles du Bos, over a scene with pederastic implications.[15] At more or less the same moment Gide was striving for a reconciliation with Proust over the rejection of *Du côté de chez Swann* and trying to obtain sections of the second volume of Proust's *Recherche* for publication in *La Nouvelle Revue Française*. Proust was himself at the time reading *Les Caves du Vatican* in monthly installments in *La Nouvelle Revue Française* and lauded in a roundabout way the homosexual overtones in the character of Lafcadio: "But in the creation of Cadio, no one has been objective with that much perversity since Balzac and *Splendeurs et misères*. All the more so, it seems to me, since Balzac was aided in inventing Lucien de Rubempré, by a certain personal vulgarity" (*Lettres à André Gide*, 24–25).[16] Proust seems once again to out a nineteenth-century author while claiming that author's novel, *Splendeurs et misères des courtisanes,* and its protagonist, Lucien de Rubempré, as precursors in a gay tradition that includes both himself and Gide. Gide would spend the next decade explicitly stepping into that tradition, experimenting with ways of saying "I"—and with the consequences of such an act—in ways contrary to the aesthetic and political advice of Wilde and Proust.[17]

15. For an account of the details, see "Orage sur Sodome," 302–52, in Auguste Anglès, *André Gide et le premier groupe de "La Nouvelle Revue Française,"* vol. 3.

16. Proust's and Gide's texts would often find themselves neighbors in the pages of *La Nouvelle Revue Française* in the years ahead. *Le Temps retrouvé,* for example, ran posthumously in the journal from January to September 1927, overlapping with the journal's publication of Gide's *Voyage au Congo.* In September 1928 the journal published the initial exchange of letters between the two authors, discussing the contretemps around Gide's rejection of Proust's manuscript.

17. Jonathan Dollimore begins his book *Sexual Dissidence* by contrasting Gide and Wilde, who have, he asserts, two different ways of conceptualizing identity: essentialist and antiessentialist, respectively, Dollimore calls them. Dollimore's book describes these two positions in complex ways; ultimately, in his analysis, Wilde and the antiessentialists are the unquestionable heroes.

To my mind such a way of proceeding leaves unanswered questions about the usefulness of general categories such as essentialist/antiessentialist for specific cultural analyses. Dollimore suggests that his book is an exercise in "reading culture," which he says "involves trying to read the historical process within the social process, and in a way adequately aware of the complexity and discrimination of both" (24). Yet, the categorization he gives of Gide and Wilde in his opening discussion seems limited in complexity and discrimination precisely because of the way large categories are invoked. That is, demonstrations of the presence of antiessentialist or essentialist rhetorics in various writings take the place of, and even cloud, discussions of the complex social fields in which writings take effect, in which lives take shape.

Dollimore writes: "For Gide transgression is in the name of a desire and identity rooted in the natural, the sincere, and the authentic; Wilde's transgressive aesthetic is the reverse: insincerity, inauthenticity, and unnaturalness . . . decentered identity and desire" (14). Later: "Someone like Gide seeks to partake in the dominant term rather than the inferior one ('we're natural too'); this involves a struggle for inclusion *within* the very concepts which exclude the subordinate" (226). Something almost suggested by Dollimore's argument is that it is *because* Wilde was an antiessentialist and Gide was not that Wilde provoked his society to more violence against him than did Gide. Yet, both Wilde's and Gide's cases pose complex questions about the relationship between on the one hand an essentialist/antiessentialist position given voice in a particular piece of writing and on the other the acts that make up a life, between a rhetorical position and the shape of a life—in sum, the way a life takes and receives effects from its world.

In 1918 a deep personal crisis in Gide's life occurred that many see as a crucial turning point, one that enabled him to become outspoken about his homosexuality and to turn toward political activity as well. In 1895 Gide had married his cousin, Madeleine Rondeaux. Their marriage apparently remained unconsummated. Gide considered it a deep spiritual commitment, yet one that did not preclude sexual encounters elsewhere. This dispensation seemed to work as long as those sexual encounters remained physical and fleeting. But around 1917–18 Gide formed an abiding attachment to Marc Allégret, son of the minister who had taken the young Gide to England and to Spurgeon's church.[18] In 1918 Gide took Marc with him to spend the summer in England, and Madeleine apparently took this as a breach of their unspoken contract. As a response to this betrayal, she reread and then burned all the letters Gide had ever written her, letters Gide had imagined her carefully preserving for posterity as one aspect of his ongoing self-portraiture. The discovery of her act threw Gide into a deep depression, the recovery from which apparently encouraged a radical reimagining of himself that would allow for all the changes he would pursue in the 1920s.[19]

Gide turned fifty in 1919 and might have chosen to work to consolidate his position as a preeminent French literary figure, a master of the *récit*, of a rigorously classical French prose, a successor to the long tradition of French moralists. But already that claim to a place in the tradition of French moralists had come under attack, especially in the Catholic press. One could use the dubious pages from *Les Caves du Vatican*, the fact that Gide had known and written about Oscar Wilde, the frank sensuality of texts such as *Les Nourritures terrestres*, to spin a web of innuendoes that left little open to doubt. Henri Massis, a prominent Catholic

---

Dollimore seems to suggest that Wilde was being put into prison *both* for being an antiessentialist *and* a sodomite: "In the first of the three trials involving Wilde in 1895, he was cross-examined on his *Phrases and Philosophies* . . . the implication of opposing counsel being that its elegant binary inversions, along with *Dorian Gray*, were 'calculated to subvert morality and encourage unnatural vice.' There is a sense in which evidence cannot get more material than this" (67). No doubt the evidence is material, but perhaps it is not sufficiently interpreted. The trial in question was one brought by Wilde for libel against the father of his lover Alfred Douglas. Wilde's failure to establish that calling him a "somdomite" [sic] was libel enabled his own subsequent prosecution. Wilde's peers were able to exercise their violence against him in a legal forum thanks to a conjuncture of circumstances that include, beyond Wilde's stated aesthetic, his conscious and unconscious efforts to shape his life, his reputation, his rapport with his family, and with his lover Douglas. The circumstances include as well his conception of the extent to which he was "out" and the relation between that necessarily political conception and his aesthetics. (See, on this subject, Neil Bartlett's *Who Was That Man? A Present for Mr Oscar Wilde*, esp. chapter 5.) How does an antiessentialist commitment (if it could ever be established that Wilde conceived one) inflect this conjuncture, these efforts?

Both Gide and Wilde operate within contexts of power relations and personal desires in which essentialist and antiessentialist rhetorics occur and have effects but do not seem to me sufficiently explanatory or determining of the differences, aesthetic and political, between them.

18. Whether the attachment had a sexual component is a question that has vexed many critics. See, for example, Daniel Durosay's introduction to Allégret's *Carnets du Congo: Voyage arec Gide*, 11, 39–40, 50. Many of Gide's critics have a tendency to believe that for a relationship between two men to be serious or mature, there can be no sex and to feel honor-bound to reclaim certain of Gide's companions for heterosexuality. Aside from Allégret, attention is often directed in this regard to Gide's relationship with Athman, from *Si le grain ne meurt* (see chapter 2).

19. The story of this crisis has been told from many points of view. See, for example, Gide, *Et nunc manet in te* (English-language translation, *Madeleine*): Jean Schlumberger, *Madeleine et André Gide*; D. A. Steel, "Escape and Aftermath: Gide in Cambridge, 1918."

critic, spun such webs aggressively. Massis was also fascinated by Gide's vaunted classicism, a style apparently as given to innuendo as was Massis himself. Thus, in an article by Massis from November 1921 entitled "L'Influence de M. André Gide," we find the following remarkable passage, entirely permeated by Gide's own sly lexicon of "délices," "traverses," "détours," and "inquiétantes sincérités":

> That classicism, of which he claims to be the "best representative," is useful to him in making himself less accessible, in furthering his dissimulations. . . . He doesn't want to be an open book: he needs an austere exterior, one in no way particular. His perversity is too conscious, too critical, not to have chosen an art that knows not to say everything, one where his troubling sincerities can find the right kind of shelter. Classical art, in effect, demands a kind of collaboration on the part of the reader that provides Mr. Gide with his most secret delights. For Gide does not permit one to find one's way immediately to his private quarters. He prefers us intelligent and attentive to his subterfuges—thus all those euphemisms, that reserve, all those obstacles that he carefully arranges, the better to extricate himself later. (Massis, 508).[20]

By the mid-1920s, though Gide will continue to use his classical "traverses" and "détours," certain public avowals will have made impossible any attempt to "se mieux dégager" and will consequently force his critics into further contortions when they wish to avoid the embarrassment of being explicit, to remain on the level of discreet innuendo. Often resisting any frankness themselves, critics will nonetheless take Gide's frankness, just as they took his dissimulations, as a failing, as if there were in fact no interesting way for a literary figure to say "I" when speaking of homosexuality. We can perceive here a dissymmetry with which some of us might be familiar: one might be more easily taken seriously saying "I" in relation to heterosexuality. That seriousness often seems harder to come by when homosexuality is in question. That Gide, speaking as a "homosexual," might choose to say "I" and nonetheless produce writings that reflect subtly the complex encounters of a self and its sexuality is a possibility critics do not often entertain.[21]

Mixing in Politics

The sudden openness about his sexuality is not the only new departure in Gide's life. In 1926 he sets out on a long voyage through the French colonies in equatorial Africa. Upon his return the following year, he publishes his travel journals, deeply

20. Ce classicisme, dont il affirme qu'il est aujourd'hui « le meilleur représentant », lui sert à rendre son accès plus difficile, à mieux dissimuler . . . Il ne se veut pas tout livré : il a besoin d'un extérieur austère que rien ne singularise. Sa perversité est trop consciente, trop critique, pour n'avoir pas élu un art qui sait ne pas tout dire et où ses inquiétantes sincérités puissent s'abriter davantage. L'art classique exige, en effet, cette collaboration du lecteur où M. Gide trouve ses plus secrètes délices; car Gide n'admet pas qu'on pénètre d'un coup vers ses étages privés; il nous veut intelligents, attentifs à ses détours; d'où ces demi-mots, ces réserves, toutes ces traverses qu'il dispose savamment pour se mieux dégager plus tard.

21. There are important exceptions. Recent writings on Gide by Emily Apter, Jonathan Dollimore, Eric Marty, and Jeffrey Mehlman, for example, are instances of more seriously speculative works on Gide, sexuality, and politics. They have been influential throughout my writing of this book.

critical of the exploitation of the colonies by the concessionary companies operating under governmental license. The journals created a notable political stir in France. They were an embarrassment to the government then in power and marked the opening of a new period of political engagement in Gide's life. In subsequent years he would become a fellow traveler, write a didactic play, a "feminist" series of novels, and, in 1936 visit the Soviet Union as a guest of its government. The travel journal from that trip, *Retour de l'U.R.S.S,* a best-seller when published, is a text of political disillusionment, a recognition that whatever radicalism Gide felt committed to, his dreams were not being realized under Stalin.

The political feel of the *Retour de l'U.R.S.S.* differs substantially from that of the *Voyage au Congo,* not only because of Gide's accumulation of experience in left-wing causes in the intervening years,[22] but also because Gide manages to insist subtly on his homosexuality throughout the *Retour de l'U.R.S.S.,* slyly mixing it in with political observations in a way not found in the *Voyage au Congo.* The passage about Mala from *Ainsi soit-il,* touching on the sexual encounters he avoids mentioning in the *Voyage au Congo,* reveals again how difficult a calculus there is in Gide's writing between reticence and explicitness. Thus, as I hope to establish in chapter 5, the *Voyage au Congo* does contain complex reflections on sexual impulses and political impulses and their relations within a colonial context, but Gide's homosexuality will be less thematized there than in many others from this period—*Si le grain ne meurt,* for example, with its explicit descriptions of sexual encounters with North African youths.

The reticence of the *Voyage au Congo* might seem a bit unnecessary, given the texts Gide had already published or was about to. *Corydon,* for example, had appeared before Gide left on the African trip, and *Les Faux-Monnayeurs* appeared while he was there. But such reticence perhaps dissipates fitfully and threatens to recur in ever-new forms. In this regard one further event from this period deserves notice.

In April 1925 a few months before setting out for the Congo, Gide put up for public auction 405 items from his personal library: first editions, his own manuscripts, and, most scandalously, a large number of books from friends that had been personally dedicated to him. The *Mercure de France,* publishers of Henri de Régnier, one of Gide's targets in the sale, rose to de Régnier's defense, telling of his noble response:

> Mr. Henri de Régnier, in addressing his latest work, *Proses datées,* to André Gide on April 27, 1925, added this witty dedication in his handsome, aristocratic hand:
>
> To Monsieur André Gide,
> to add to his sale.
> H. DE REGNIER

22. For brief rundowns of his activities in these years, see Herbert Lottman, *The Left Bank,* and Shattuck, "Having Congress." See also Daniel Moutote, *André Gide: L'Engagement, 1926–1939.*

R. de Dury, the critic for the *Mercure de France* writing this *fait divers*, then adds his own comment: "What seems to me most immoral, under the circumstances, is the huge sum represented by the sale of these books, once graciously offered, books 'garnished' with letters and signatures, now converted into government notes or railroad bonds."[23]

The "official" story Gide gave out is that he was selling these books to raise money for his impending trip to Africa and that he was ridding himself of some burdensome earthly possessions. In fact, Gide was financially not in the least needy. But he willingly displayed in a public sale and the accompanying catalogue, his friends' books and their intimate dedications. He wrote the following in the preface to the catalogue of the sale: "A hankering after property has never been strong in me. . . . Moreover, little given to taking care, I am constantly worried that the objects I hold on to are going to deteriorate; that they might deteriorate even more if, going on a trip, I leave them behind."[24] Gide barely hints in the preface that some of the books he had kept only so long as "they only brought to my mind memories of friendship." The rumors circulating were that one of the things Gide was doing was selling off books by people who had attacked *Corydon*. Gide later (in 1949) confirmed these rumors in one of a series of interviews with Jean Amrouche. When asked if the publication of *Corydon* hadn't caused a rift between him and certain friends, Gide responded that of course it had.

> The disapproval of some friends was so violent that I nearly broke with them, and that's what brought about, at a particular moment, the book sale from my library, books by those who had repudiated me. . . . I had originally written a preface giving the reasons why this or that friend of mine had repudiated me, and Champion, who was in charge of the sale, said to me: "But this is a massacre!" And he completely altered the preface. I was a bit sorry that happened. (Marty, *André Gide*, 292).[25]

The book sale is perhaps a typically Gidean *détour,* classically elegant, slightly secretive, slightly malicious, willing to give a certain amount of offense. Yet, the preface to the sale catalogue is sufficiently marked by evasion so as to ensure that what is most importantly going on stays behind the scenes.[26]

23. R. de Dury, "Revue de la Quinzaine : Les Journaux," *Mercure de France,* 180, June 15, 1925, 794. Other articles on the subject include: "La Vente Gide," *Chronique des lettres françaises,* no. 16, July –August 1925, 569–71; R. Maran, "André Gide et son vilain geste," *Le Journal littéraire,* April 25, 1925, 2; Gérard Bauër, "Un Ecrivain vend ses livres," *L'Echo de Paris,* April 23, 1925. A bibliography helpful for finding some of these articles is to be found in Pierre Lafille, *André Gide romancier* (Paris: Hachette, 1954).

24. Le goût de la propriété n'a, chez moi, jamais été bien vif . . . Au surplus, peu soigneux, j'ai sans cesse la crainte que les objets que je détiens ainsi ne s'abîment; qu'ils ne s'abîment davantage encore si, partant en voyage, je les abandonne.

25. Des amis m'ont désapprouvé si violemment que j'ai presque rompu avec eux, et c'est ce qui a amené, à un certain moment d'ailleurs, la vente de livres que j'ai faite de ma bibliothèque, de ceux qui m'avaient renié . . . J'avais d'abord écrit une préface donnant les raisons pour lesquelles tel ou tel de mes amis m'avait renié et Champion, qui avait présidé la vente, m'a dit : « Mais, c'est un massacre! » Et il m'avait complètement changé ma préface. Je l'ai un peu regretté.

26. One might also remark that, as the people he intended to offend were those who had criticized *Corydon,* the sale also constitutes one of the earliest examples of an assertion Gide would make repeatedly in years to come: that *Corydon* (along with the *Retour de l'U.R.S.S.*) was in his eyes one of his centrally important books. (See, for example, *Ainsi soit-il,* 1231–32; *So Be It,* 143–44.) Such an assertion has not been given much support by people writing on

In its mixture of reticence and public insult, this book sale remains a rather oblique way of indicating the importance Gide was learning to place on public acknowledgment of his sexuality. His regret at the softening of the wording of his preface to the sale's catalogue betokens the more assertive statements he was making in certain writings and would continue to make in the years ahead. Ongoing revelations about his sexuality, descriptions of his sexual activities, statements as to *Corydon*'s importance in his eyes—all these could be read in his *Journal,* whose slow publication began in 1932 with the appearance of a multivolume *Œuvres complètes,* which included pages from his *Journal* in chronological order along with the rest of his writings.[27] The project of publishing his *Journal,* and thereby consolidating the public nature of his sexuality, continued in regular installments in the pages of the *Nouvelle Revue Française* and in book form for the rest of his life. The *Journal,* published in two volumes in Gallimard's Pléiade series (the first of them, *Journal, 1889–1939* [1939], being the Pléiade's first publication of a living author), constitutes a carefully constructed "private space made public." Eric Marty, in *L'Ecriture du jour,* his study of the *Journal,* comments: "Through the general tendency of the *Journal* to reduce public events to their private repercussions, we find here a will, or at least a desire, to *subvert* what is public using the private order to do so" (136). The strategically organized *publication* of this private space suggests that the *Journal* also envisions a symmetrical subversion to the one Marty is describing: to exhibit in public what is usually lived in private, to insist on the public importance of private repercussions. This project is of a piece with Gide's general project of these years: to use writing as an experimental realm in which to understand how his politics and his sexuality interrelate, how they play themselves out on a stage where nothing is purely public, nothing purely private.

The six chapters that follow concentrate on texts published mainly in this period of sexual openness and political activity, a period not often treated carefully in writing about Gide, perhaps out of embarrassment about his militancy on the question of homosexuality, perhaps out of distrust of what is perceived as a certain facileness in his political commitments, perhaps out of what is perceived as a diminution in the literary quality of his writings. It seems to me that these writings

---

Gide, who tend to see precisely these two books as his most nugatory. I will try to find reasons for this contradiction in the chapters ahead.

27. The editor of the 1930s *Œuvres complètes* was to be Louis Martin-Chauffier. As of 1926 this might have seemed a somewhat odd choice. Proust's *Sodome et Gomorrhe* had appeared in 1921, Gide's *Corydon* in 1924. In 1926 the journal *Les Marges* decided to publish the thoughts of various figures in the world of letters on the subject "L'homosexualité en littérature." Martin-Chauffier commented there: "We are surrounded by inverts; and these inverts no longer bother to hide themselves; the secret taint now flaunts itself [la tare secrète commence à s'afficher]. . . . One final audacity remained: writing." As of 1932 Martin-Chauffier would apparently have done enough of a turnabout to be editorially abetting that audacity. For commentary on the literary atmosphere of the time and on the inquiry in *Les Marges* in particular, and for one of the better portraits of the French gay world of the 1920s, see Gilles Barbedette and Michel Carassou, *Paris Gay 1925.* My thanks to Amy Lyford for bringing this book to my attention.

are, in fact, literarily extremely complicated, and what I propose to examine are precisely the links one can trace between Gide's literary techniques, his portrayal of his own homosexuality, his discussions of sexuality more generally, and his involvement in and writing about politics. The six chapters are grouped as pairs, resulting in three parts. The first part is, in large measure, about Gide's memoir *Si le grain ne meurt*. In the first chapter I analyze the way the language and style of the presentation of sexual encounters raise certain questions about the nature of Gide's sexual identity and political position. The second chapter extends these analyses into a consideration of how Gide traced his development of a particular sexual identity in relation to his mother (and to female sexuality generally), to his social location, and to his development as a political subject within France and its colonies.

Gide's long literary career was dotted with trips to Africa. The most obvious way of describing his African career would be to say that he began simply as a rich European tourist looking for an escape into exoticism as well as for erotic adventure, but that a gradually dawning political consciousness led him to a more critical stance as regards his relationship to Africa. Finally, once his awareness of the French colonialist machinery had become sufficiently acute, this way of describing things would have it, Gide was led to a firmly anticolonialist position. Such a narrative seems acceptable as a starting place from which to ask more complicated questions about both the effects of Africa on Gide's self-formation and formal problems that developed as he tried to give literary expression to his thoughts about Africa. Texts such as Gide's *Voyage au Congo* and *Le Retour du Tchad* seem to demonstrate a more explicit political awareness than, say, the letters Gide wrote home to his mother from North Africa in the 1880s and 1890s, more awareness perhaps than even the retelling of those early trips to North Africa in *Si le grain ne meurt*. Nonetheless, I prefer to resist a narrative that traces a growing politicization across Gide's writing about or from Africa—resist it just enough to insist that the politics is inevitable and legible from the start. The clear thematicization of politics in the *Voyage au Congo* should not stand in the way of a reading of the earlier texts as equally, if not explicitly, political.

The second part of the book deals with *Corydon, L'Ecole des femmes,* and *Les Faux-Monnayeurs,* investigating the ideological consequences of different ways of conceptualizing and narrativizing a homosexual aetiology and a homosexual identity. The homophobia of Gide's critics and, indeed, his own homophobia will be scrutinized here. Particularly in the two sections of chapter 3 (on *Corydon* and then on *L'Ecole des femmes*) I will be tracing the analytic links between the homophobia and misogyny of certain of Gide's writings and trying to contrast this particular conceptual construct with a more inchoate sense in other Gidean texts (especially those discussed in chapter 2) of the productive possibilities of queer allegiances between Gide's sexuality and the sexuality he sees in certain women.

I will also attempt to situate Gide's arguments about the nature of homosexu-

ality and his creation of gay characters within the psychiatric debates about homosexuality in his lifetime and after. Those debates and their idiosyncrasies, for
example, deeply influence one of the most imposing portrayals of the early part of
Gide's life, Jean Delay's two-volume study *La Jeunesse d'André Gide,* a psychobiography whose inadequacies to the complexities of Gide's own writing I hope to
point out.[28] In an effort to characterize in some detail the effect of sexuality on
Gide's writing, I will be looking at some of Lacan's ideas about sexuality, both in
his essay on Gide (and Delay's biography) and in his *Four Fundamental Concepts of
Psychoanalysis.*

In particular, chapter 4 represents an effort to displace dominant ways of
reading *Les Faux-Monnayeurs.* I trace the categories usually invoked in analyses of
the novel (sincerity, morality, deficit, fakery, etc.) and critique the readings that
arise from a too heavy dependence on them. I suggest that finding a different way
of conceptualizing sexuality from that usually used by critics of the novel would be
the key to displacing these readings. To develop that different conceptualization, I
contrast two ways of understanding sexuality, one of which insists on sexuality as
an irrevocably forward-moving and developmental concept, the other of which
understands sexuality as a pulsative, intermittently observable experience that
cannot be successfully captured by any narrative model. Throughout the chapter I
point to instances within *Les Faux-Monnayeurs* of sleeping, or of being between
sleeping and waking, and use these instances to develop this second understanding
of sexuality and its relation to subjectivity. At a certain point I turn to a long
discussion of passages in Lacan that have to do with this question of the pulsative
nature of sexuality and of the ways the interface between sleeping and waking
proves revelatory for an understanding of sexuality's challenge to the boundaries of
any given subjectivity. The final implications of this alternate way of reading *Les
Faux-Monnayeurs* are revealed in a reading of Boris' suicide, the concluding event
of the novel. I am interested in how that suicide can be understood through the
competing notions of sexuality at work in the novel, thereby further revealing what
has been at stake in the contrast between a disciplined, narrative construal of
sexuality and a construal of sexuality as related to the dispossession experienced in
somnolence.

The final part of my book contains chapters on Gide's *Voyage au Congo* and
his *Retour de l'U.R.S.S.* The two central concepts that I use in chapter 5 to link the

---

28. In general, critics tend to treat Delay's imposing tomes with a bit too much respect. One interesting
exception would be Daniel Guérin, who, in his essay "André Gide et l'amour," comments that Delay takes on Gide's
homosexuality "in a spirit of total incomprehension, of belligerent and outdated partiality. . . . His views on homosexuality are as out-of-date as those of the pedants who stubbornly defended the immutability of the species even after
Darwin's work had been published" (58). Guérin's career as a homosexual, an anarcho-socialist, and a political
activist could be interestingly juxtaposed with Gide's (I do not have the space to undertake that project here). See Peter
Sedgwick, "Out of Hiding: The Comradeships of Daniel Guérin," for an introduction to Guérin's life and work that
clearly indicates his proximity to Gide.

experience of sexual with the experience of political subjectivity are *frustration*, a concept I develop in relation to Gide's problems "seeing" Africa, and *alienation*, a concept whose particular usage I borrow from Lacan. I am particularly interested in a well-known passage from Lacan in which he narrates his own alienation upon sighting a sardine can floating in the ocean. The sardine can passage is used by Lacan as an exemplary instance of the ways the experience of political subjectivity and sexual subjectivity can be understood through similar conceptual categories. Lacan and Gide are remarkably similar in their experience and analysis of the frustration and alienation attendant on a forced confrontation with the necessary limits of one's own subjectivity, political and sexual. The sardine can passage is particularly revealing in its raw politicality, unusual for Lacan, but finally un-surprising given the implications of his conceptual schema as I elaborate it throughout chapters 4 and 5. That passage also opens new possibilities for under-standing some of the psychic discomfort and, in particular, the fantasies of death and disappearance that punctuate Gide's *Voyage au Congo*.

In chapter 6 my intent is once again to clarify the complicated negotiations to which Gide subjected himself as he tried to determine the kinds of control he might exercise over the public/private nature of his sexuality—and of other parts of his persona. These Gidean negotiations were necessarily complex and ongoing, as his *Retour de l'U.R.S.S.* reveals. Gide is not as forthright about his sexuality in this text as he is in many. But it is not difficult to show to what extent Gide's sexuality was "in the air," not only in his text but also in most discussions of his communist commitment. I use the word *sly* to describe Gide's way of bringing up sexuality in the text of the *Retour de l'U.R.S.S.*: in the references he encodes in his opening retelling of the Demeter myth, in his appendix on the *besprizornis*, in his astonishingly artful way of citing the Persian proverb: "*women for duty, boys for pleasure, melons for delight*," in his casual footnote to the legal oppression of homosexuality by the Stalinist regime. In this chapter I also continue the analysis of the common frustration Gide felt in the experience not only of his sexuality but also of his politicality. The frustration might be seen as aggravated by those dominant forms of political analysis that could only cast a negative valence on the politics of sexuality "itself"—especially homosexuality. In what way would it be possible, I would like to ask, for Gide to affirm *his* sense of the politicality of his sexuality, faced with the antihomosexual discourse surrounding him? Thus, a major portion of the chapter is concerned with his vexed experience of himself not only as homosexual but also as a highly cultured Westerner in a society that in complicated ways was refusing to value that culture. The chapter thereby investi-gates the complex matrices of forces in which Gide was obliged to move both in France and in the Soviet Union, in which being openly homosexual, being com-munist, and being a cultured Westerner became at times an almost incomprehen-sible mix.

The two concluding chapters (and the short epilogue) thus continue to trace Gide's portrait of himself as a developing political subject, showing how that portrait is consistently inflected by his perception of himself as a sexual subject, how utopian political imaginings and utopian sexual imaginings are constantly linked in a fashion that troubled and offended his contemporaries and that, needless to say, continues to trouble Gide's readers today—whatever their bent.

CHAPTER 1

WATCHING SEX IN
SI LE GRAIN NE MEURT

> At the time, it seemed to me I could only write—and I was about to say, think—in front of this small mirror; to become conscious of my own excitement, my own thoughts, I felt I had to read them first, in my eyes. Like Narcissus I would lean over my image; all the sentences I wrote then thus remain somewhat bent.[1]
>
> —Gide, *Si le grain ne meurt*

Writing disdainfully about "sex as self-hyperbole," Leo Bersani, in his article "Is the Rectum a Grave?" deplores our attempts to believe that sex makes us feel bigger and better about ourselves. He calls this "the phallicization of the ego" in sex. Bersani would have us confront the possibility that sexual acts might instead lead to self-loss. As soon as we assume the stability, or even the reinforcement, of our sense of self through sex, we lose our critical edge. Our analytic insightfulness fails, and we fall back inevitably into the perennial and hackneyed realm of sexual warfare: "As soon as persons are posited, the war begins. It is the self that swells with excitement at the idea of being on top, the self that makes of the inevitable play of thrusts and relinquishments in sex an argument for the natural authority of one sex over the other" (Bersani, 218). Not selves, Bersani recommends: just sex.

Just Sex

I begin here by asking what "just sex" might be, and where we might find it. I will be looking for it primarily in two places: in Bersani's essay and in André

---

1. En ce temps, je ne pouvais écrire, et j'allais presque dire : penser, me semblait-il, qu'en face de ce petit miroir; pour prendre connaissance de mon émoi, de ma pensée, il me semblait que, dans mes yeux, il me fallait d'abord les lire. Comme Narcisse, je me penchais sur mon image; toutes les phrases que j'écrivais alors en restent quelque peu courbées.

Gide's memoirs, *Si le grain ne meurt* (*If It Die*). This is a way of opening one of the central problems of this book. For Gide and Bersani are in one way or another each interested in trying to answer the question, Which comes first, sex or politics? Bersani's article will be helpful in understanding what Gide is up to in his descriptions of sex between men, in his search for a context in which that sex could be pure, "as if the sexual . . . could somehow be conceived of apart from all relations of power, were, so to speak, belatedly contaminated by power from elsewhere" (221), says Bersani in another context. The nature of Gide's virtuoso squirmings in the face of scorn such as Bersani's might in turn help us to delineate some of the perhaps equally suspicious longings in Bersani's essay.

At certain points, for both Gide and Bersani, the question of the relation of sexuality to politics is rendered acute by a consideration of the specific case of anal intercourse. By the end of this chapter, I hope we will not be surprised as to why the question, Which came first, sodomy or politics?[2] produces writing of such great interest. I hope that we will no longer be surprised either that that writing cannot provide us with a satisfactory answer to the question it poses for itself— which is not quite the same as saying that the question is unanswerable. At least three answers are immediately available: that sodomy as a concept can come first, or that politics must, or that both will inevitably be conceptualized at the same moment. I suppose I would choose the last one if I had to; but I would finally like to end up insisting here that when one writes in order to answer such a question, one cannot find a position from which to write an answer that carries any authority.

I do not want to be understood as saying that there is no use in writing about a question when one is bound only to write oneself into a corner. That corner, whose complex boundaries are under investigation here, is now more than ever a place where much living and dying happens. The more one calls attention to it, then, the better. Bersani's critical attack on those who indulge in "a certain refusal to speak frankly about gay sex" (221) is one I sympathize with, and I am consequently after a certain *franchise* in the performance of this chapter. But Bersani's claim that *jouissance* could somehow represent the true *nostos*, the "hygienic" return to selfless sensation, is a claim whose particular rhetorical structure needs close scrutiny. It is with an eye to that end that I turn to the strategies and problems of describing sex.

I cannot, of course, examine this kind of representation without indulging in it myself, forcibly recontextualizing in my own writing the explicit passages that catch my eye elsewhere. The heavy burden of citation is part of the point: the context seems always to be interfering with the possibility that sex could merely be sex. This predicament makes itself felt quite often these days: by, for example, the cultural activists collectively called Boy with Arms Akimbo, whose *Just Sex/Sex Is* posters (see figure) a few years ago made their mark in San Francisco, Berkeley,

---

2. On the historical vagaries in the usage of "sodomy," see, for instance, chapter 16 of Jonathan Dollimore's *Sexual Dissidence*, esp. pp. 236–40.

Just Sex. Boy with Arms Akimbo, San Francisco. 1989. (Courtesy of Boy with Arms Akimbo.)

New Haven, and elsewhere, proffering a message their very presence inevitably, and doubtless intentionally, contradicted.[3] In the course of this chapter, at least, sex will never quite manage to be *just* sex, nor will it ever be something we can just watch. Sex will here always be imbricated with memory, with class and race, and, given that we will be watching gay sex, with homophobia.

3. See, for example, the article in the *New York Times* of November 2, 1989, "Yale Advocates of Gay Rights Protest Arrests," about the furor caused by posters put up during a Gay Studies conference at Yale: "The confrontation began when a participant in the conference, William Dobbs, a New York lawyer, was arrested by Yale police officers about 9:30 P.M. Friday after he put up a sexually explicit poster in the law school, the police said. The poster is one of a series made by a group of San Francisco artists known as Boy with Arms Akimbo that show men posing in the nude. They also contain the phrase "Sex Is" or "Just Sex." The police became involved after a female law professor working in the building called them. . . . Mr. Schmidt said the incident appeared to focus on two issues: Whether the

"l'un près de l'autre"

Si le grain ne meurt, Gide's memoirs, begins with the traditional narrative sign of reasonably absolute origin: "I was born on November 22, 1869." Never able to bear a single tradition for long, however, Gide rapidly, in only the second paragraph, moves to a discussion of the complexity of a different kind of origin, the origin of sexual knowledge, and involves us immediately in that topsy-turvy kind of temporality we have come to know under the Freudian rubric *Nachträglichkeit* ("l'après-coup" in French, "deferred action" in English):

> I look back and see a fairly large table, the dining-room table, no doubt, covered with a low-falling tablecloth, under which I would slip with the son of the concierge, a kid of about my own age who sometimes came to play with me.
> "What are you two getting up to under there?" my nurse would call out.
> "Nothing. We're just playing."
> Then we'd shake some toys about noisily, toys we had brought along for show. In truth we were amusing ourselves otherwise: the one next to the other, but not, however, one with the other, we were indulging in what I later learned one calls "nasty habits."
> Which of the two of us had taught them to the other? And who had this first one learned them from? I don't know. You may just have to admit that sometimes a child invents them from scratch. As for me, I can't say if someone taught me or how I discovered pleasure, but no matter how far back my memory pushes, it is there. (9)[4]

Let us begin with the tablecloth in this opening scene. We might notice, in this scene and in others that follow, that Gide is perfectly happy to watch himself and to

---

Boy with Arms Akimbo/Girl with Arms Akimbo explain the poster series as follows: "*Just Sex/Sex Is* uses texts and images—often in a deliberately ambiguous, absurd, or disturbing fashion—to demonstrate the constructed nature of sexuality and to challenge viewers to deconstruct their own sexual ideology. This action subverts the broad concepts of sexual regulation, 'natural/unnatural' dichotomies, and propriety of discourse that frequently motivate efforts at censorship and other restrictions on self-determination in American society." (From the collective's catalogue of projects: "Boy with Arms Akimbo/Girl with Arms Akimbo: An Introduction," dated March 20, 1990.)

For a trenchant analysis of the collective's work and the Yale incident, see Douglas Crimp, "The Boys in My Bedroom."

4. Je revois aussi une assez grande table, celle de la salle à manger sans doute, recouverte d'un tapis bas tombant; au-dessous de quoi je me glissais avec le fils de la concierge, un bambin de mon âge qui venait parfois me retrouver.
— Qu'est-ce que vous fabriquez là-dessous? criait ma bonne.
— Rien. Nous jouons.

Et l'on agitait bruyamment quelques jouets qu'on avait emportés pour la frime. En vérité nous nous amusions autrement : l'un près de l'autre, mais non l'un avec l'autre pourtant, nous avions ce que j'ai su plus tard qu'on appelait « de mauvaises habitudes ».

Qui de nous deux en avait instruit l'autre? et de qui le premier les tenait-il? Je ne sais. Il faut bien admettre qu'un enfant parfois à nouveau les invente. Pour moi je ne puis dire si quelqu'un m'enseigna ou comment je découvris le plaisir; mais, aussi loin que ma mémoire remonte en arrière, il est là (9–10).

· · ·

For a helpful discussion of these opening paragraphs, see Eric Marty, *André Gide: Qui êtes-vous?*, 13–19. See also his fine discussion of the erotic attractions of North Africa for Gide, pp. 53–65. Philippe Lejeune in his book *Exercices d'ambiguïté*, pp. 18–39, offers close readings of passages from *Si le grain ne meurt.* Many of his analyses have been suggestive to me and are relevant to what I discuss here.

watch others having sex, but he is not enthusiastic about being watched himself. This is not (or not only) due to some easily dismissed prudery. I would like to suggest that for Gide the acknowledged presence of a third person (such as his maid) during sex would threaten, through something called *Nachträglichkeit*, to introduce politics into the sexual moment itself, to deny that moment the purity of its sensation. For doubtless the memory of that moment overwrites it with considerations that would corrode any hypothetically pure sensual content it could have had. But the intervening voice of the maid suggests that *the moment itself* may never have had any such purity (or only in a way too fleeting to grasp), may already have been marked by a social ordering in which that sensuality is framed, with which the sensuality is complicit.

Nachträglichkeit is the process of assigning importance to a memory after the fact, a memory of a moment that may not even be remembered or important until something else happens later in life. Was it important to those two boys at that childhood moment that they were only near each other, not actually doing it to each other, or does this fact become significant only on later reflection, after some other event has intervened? Was it important to those two boys that one was from a wealthy family with servants, the other the son of the concierge, or is this, too, only retrospectively significant? Temporal questions also lurk behind the assigning of a name in this passage: the very young Gide might not yet have learned the name of what he was doing, "de mauvaises habitudes," but he does seem already to have learned that these were nasty habits, to be practiced in hiding, and the two boys were savvy enough to bring along a couple toys, "pour la frime," although from our perspective, their way of noisily shaking their toys is inevitably metonymically associated with their masturbation, and their "nous jouons" ("we were playing") echoes slightly with a "nous jouissons" (we were coming), another word that they might not quite yet have learned. The passage reveals the imbrication of several moments in the life, the sexual development, of someone named André Gide, reveals the necessity of a chain of moments and a complexly woven social context in order for any particular scene to become crucial.

Now this is clearly not the first, initial, primal scene in the back-and-forth temporal motion necessary to describe the historical development of a sexual practice. Gide makes a quick bow to this problem with the rather feeble "Il faut bien admettre qu'un enfant parfois à nouveau les invente." Whenever these nasty habits were invented, it clearly wasn't in this particular scene beneath the table, which is, moreover, only one of a series: "un bambin de mon âge qui venait *parfois* me retrouver." And in any case, to posit a sui generis arrival of autoeroticism (but is that what this is?) is really not, I think, what Gide is attempting here. He is much more interested, on the one hand, in the possibility that sexual practices are contagious, and, on the other hand, in the difficulty of establishing the moment at which they were caught, a difficulty that would be occluded were he really to accept that they were merely "invented."

In their essay on *Nachträglichkeit*, Jean Laplanche and Jean-Bertrand Pontalis suggest a helpful distinction between the way scenes such as the Gidean one we are considering might exist in the unconscious and the way they are brought into conscious memory or into daydreams. The distinction depends on the ego's ability, in the second case, to associate itself with a particular fixed role in a given daydream or memory.

> In daydreaming, the scenario is basically in the first person, and the subject's place clear and invariable. The organisation is stabilized by the secondary process, weighted by the ego: the subject, it is said, *lives out* his reverie. But the original fantasy, on the other hand, is characterized by the absence of subjectivization even as the subject is present *in* the scene: the child, for instance, is any character amongst the many in the fantasy "a child is beaten." Freud insisted on this visualization of the subject on the same level as the other protagonists, and in this sense the screen memory would have a profound structural relationship with original fantasies. (Laplanche and Pontalis, 22)

Laplanche and Pontalis make this distinction even clearer toward the end of their essay, where they characterize in more detail the relation between desubjectivization and "original fantasy":

> Fantasy . . . is not the object of desire, but its setting. In fantasy the subject does not pursue the object or its sign: he appears caught up himself in the sequence of images. He forms no representation of the desired object, but is himself represented as participating in the scene, although, in the earliest forms of fantasy, he cannot be assigned any fixed place in it. . . . As a result, the subject, although always present in the fantasy, may be so in a desubjectivized form, that is to say, in the very syntax of the sequence in question. (26)

One can see the traces of both of these stages (daydream or conscious fantasy versus original fantasy) in the Gide passage in the way the strong "Je revois" of the first sentence gradually dissolves back into a series of "nous," "l'on," and "l'un/l'autre." The memory/fantasy also includes two children on the same level, at the same rank. It remains unclear at what temporal moment, at what point in the repetitions of this fantasy it might become significant that these are two boys from different classes messing about together, at which point it will become important who taught whom, at which point one of the two will become André Gide, the other the son of a concierge.

Two things will happen in similar scenarios in *Si le grain ne meurt* to bring politics into sex, to open the borders of this perfect egalitarian moment (where selves can fluctuate from position to position) to the influences of political culture: first, the posture in which sex is performed, and the nature of the sex act itself could change to bring in the concept of differing levels; second, a third person could be present.[5] In *Si le grain ne meurt* (as elsewhere in Gide), such an observer

---

5. In fact, the second case will for Gide be more crucially irreversible, since even in sexual scenarios *à deux* where power is unequally distributed, one can fantastically shift back and forth between the two roles. See Sigmund Freud, "A Child Is Being Beaten." But even in that shifting back and forth, there usually exists a denial of politics, since every

always somehow ruins the equal complicity of the two participants: the social or cultural discrepancy two people were ignoring will be made explicit by the presence of a third. The implied cultural proximity of the observer to one of the participants, on the one hand, and the concomitant cultural distance between the observer and the second participant on the other bring in a chilling dose of reality. Needless to say, there is a certain dishonesty here. If the politics is there, it is simply there, we might want to say. The third person surely doesn't bring it along him or herself. The problem is to find out when it arrived. In terms of the analyses I undertake in the next part of this chapter, the question is this: Is a private sexual encounter between a European and a North African any less political than an encounter between a European and a North African while another European looks on? Could privacy, consensuality, pleasure, positioning, could insisting on any of these things keep sex just sex or return it to that blissful state?

To the extent that we might successfully isolate some politics of sexuality "itself"—the political content of a sexual act that is not exhausted by other political categories such as gender, class, race, colonial positioning—that politics would seem to arise precisely out of this kind of questioning. The challenge of analyzing the question, Couldn't it just be sex? is in fact to go beyond merely noting the dishonesty and/or ideological blindness of various forms of nostalgia for pure sexual apoliticality to accept another provocation of that question, to notice an excess in any sexual encounter and its representation, an excess that cannot be tallied up by mentioning all the other political overdeterminations of the encounter and its representations. It is hard to imagine the success of an effort to pin down the arrival or departure of politics in sex, something that seems riddled with the same difficulties of temporality that render inconclusive attempts to pin down the arrival of sexual knowledge or the onset of a sexual inclination. Claims to establishing the moment of all such arrivals and onsets are necessarily rhetorically duplicitous.[6] In what follows in this chapter, I will be watching some of the consequences of imagining these political and sexual arrivals or trying to avoid them. In these very representational struggles perhaps we might find the lineaments of sexuality's particular elusive politicality.

Sexual Encounters

To begin examining the search for the arrival of politics into sexuality, I'd like to look at the relationship in Gide's work between homosexuality and luxury. One

participant nonetheless has a social history, be it in the future or the past. A Frenchman and a North African boy can do all the free-floating imagining that they want to—it won't affect their nationalities, their economic relations, or the social meanings attached, willy-nilly, to what they do. Gide would sometimes like to forget this, even as his writing insists on it.

6. The essay of Laplanche and Pontalis is convincing in this regard.

sometimes has the impression that in Gide's imagination the proper form of homosexuality follows a Spartan or ascetic code, including a renunciation of the trappings of a bourgeois existence. A possible way to politicize Gide's homosexuality would be to develop this particular chain of associations (and I am going to do so, but only for a moment) between homosexuality and antibourgeois asceticism. Emily Apter pursues this possibility in her article, "Homotextual Counter-Codes: André Gide and the Poetics of Engagement." At one point in that article, she is considering the concept of *dénuement,* of stripping away, a word that might apply as much to a homoerotic gaze as to a peeling off of worldly goods. Apter comments that "as one traces allusions to nakedness, in addition to finding it associated with the traditional prelapsarian ideals of spiritual purity, moral sincerity, and the innocent primitive, one also discovers it closely tied to the act of casting off clothes, money, worldly possessions and domestic obligations. Books, the clothing of the mind, are undressed, shed like the bark of a tree, rejected like the tenets of middle-class morality" (Apter, "Homotextual Counter-Codes," 79).

The salutary nature of nudity is something I will dwell on for a moment, although the full extent of its importance in the Gidean imagination won't become entirely obvious until we look at a scene late in *Si le grain ne meurt,* where Gide watches while a friend of his has sex with a North African boy without even undressing. Let's begin by looking ourselves at Gide's first sexual encounter with a North African boy, and, for all we know, his first homosexual encounter since those early trysts under the table. The boy's name is Ali, and late one day he and Gide walk out (alone) together into the dunes. Once they are a safe distance out, Ali throws himself down on his back in the sand and smiles at Gide: "I wasn't such a simpleton as to misunderstand his invitation. Still, I didn't respond immediately. I sat down, not far from him, but in any case not too close, and, pointedly staring at him in my turn, I waited, immensely curious to see what he was going to do" (248).[7] We see the opening under-the-table scene at work again, here. The "l'un près de l'autre, mais non l'un avec l'autre pourtant" of that scene lurks behind the "non loin de lui, mais pas trop près pourtant" of this one. And what is at stake is also the same, a desire that it be unclear with whom the sexual encounter originates, an uneasiness with the concept of seduction and the discrepancies in power it implies. How, Gide is wondering, is the difference between *moi* and *Ali* going to dissolve back into the "l'un l'autre" of the previous scene? That dissolve has become more difficult to achieve for at least two reasons: first because Ali's skin color is a much plainer mark of difference than was the more easily repressed fact of being the son of a concierge; second because Gide, well past adolescence, now knows in an unproblematic way a name for what he is about to do. Notice how the way Gide names but refuses to name his act here resembles his efforts in the earlier scene:

---

7. Je n'étais pas niais au point de ne comprendre pas son invite; toutefois je n'y répondis pas aussitôt. Je m'assis, non loin de lui, mais pas trop près pourtant, et, le regardant fixement à mon tour, j'attendis, fort curieux de ce qu'il allait faire (299).

But was it really curiosity that was holding me back? I no longer know. The secret motive for the things we do, and I mean the most decisive things, escapes us; and not only in the memory we keep of them, but even in the moment itself. On the threshold of what is called sin, was I still hesitating? No; I would have been too disappointed had the adventure been obliged to end in the triumph of my virtue—something that I had begun to despise, that I held in horror. No, it really is curiosity that made me wait. . . . And I saw his laughter slowly fade, his lips close over his white teeth; an expression of disappointment, of sadness darkened his charming face. Finally he got up:

"So, see you," he said.

But, seizing the hand he held out to me, I pulled him back down to the ground. At once he began laughing again. He didn't take long over the complicated knots in the laces that served him as a belt; pulling a little dagger out of his pocket, he sliced through the mess with a single blow. The garment fell; he threw his jacket far away, and stood up naked as a god. (248–49).[8]

What is curiosity? What is the difference between curiosity and sin? Does the pagan nakedness of Ali somehow outweigh the puritanical impulses behind the word *sin?*[9] As Ali throws off his own clothes, should we forget that his official role in this trip to the dunes is that of a porter, carrying Gide's extra clothes for him? The temporal confusions Gide plants in our path here show the work the writing undertakes in order to confound certain uncomfortable realities, to smooth certain sharp corners in an otherwise pleasurable fantasy. "Etait-ce bien la curiosité qui me retenait?" "*Was* it really curiosity that *was holding* me back?" Gide asks. "I no longer know," he would have us believe, as if true understanding belonged to an earlier time. "Our secret motivation for doing things . . . escapes us; and not only in the memory we keep of them, *but even at that very moment*" (my emphasis). So it's not even a question of no longer knowing: we didn't even know then; we never know, except through reconstructions pressured into inaccuracy by whatever impulse necessitates the reconstruction.

Having made this point, Gide nonetheless goes on to reconstruct, indulging himself in an apparently accurate self-examination. Perhaps curiosity had nothing to do with it. Perhaps Gide was still a bit afraid, really didn't want to commit a sin? A definitive answer presents itself: no, virtue no longer interested him. Therefore, we can conclude that "*c'est* bien la curiosité qui me faisait attendre." Notice the

---

8. Mais était-ce bien la curiosité qui me retenait? Je ne sais plus. Le motif secret de nos actes, et j'entends : des plus décisifs, nous échappe; et non seulement dans le souvenir que nous en gardons, mais bien au moment même. Sur le seuil de ce que l'on appelle : péché, hésitais-je encore? Non; j'eusse été trop déçu si l'aventure eût dû se terminer par le triomphe de ma vertu – que déja j'avais prise en dédain, en horreur. Non; c'est bien la curiosité qui me faisait attendre . . . Et je vis son rire lentement se faner, ses lèvres se refermer sur ses dents blanches; une expression de déconvenue, de tristesse assombrit son visage charmant. Enfin il se leva :

— Alors, adieu, dit-il.

Mais, saisissant la main qu'il me tendait, je le fis rouler à terre. Son rire aussitôt reparut. Il ne s'impatienta pas longtemps aux noeuds compliqués des lacets qui lui tenaient lieu de ceinture; sortant de sa poche un petit poignard, il en trancha d'un coup l'embrouillement. Le vêtement tomba; il rejeta au loin sa veste, et se dressa nu comme un dieu (299).

9. On the conflict between paganism and Christianity in *Si le grain ne meurt,* see Lejeune, *Exercices d'ambiguïté,* 95–102.

change in tenses from "*était-ce* bien la curiosité qui me retenait?" So why doesn't Gide just go all the way into the present and say, once and for all, "c'est bien la curiosité qui *me fait attendre?*"[10] Curiosity is meant to confuse who is inviting whom, or who invited whom. The sources of knowledge, corruption, or contamination cease momentarily to pertain. Furthermore, curiosity, whatever it is, is in the service of the capacity of fantasy to make "me" wait, to put the *moi* on hold, so to speak, to derail one's coherence by derailing memory—along with any other structure, any form of sociality, that really might put me in my place.[11]

For the structures that put "me" in "my" place are not solely temporal. By casting this scene in confused temporal terms, Gide manages (or fails) to cast out other, more brutally obvious terms—terms having to do with the French as the colonial masters of Algeria. These terms find their way into the scene anyway, in the question of who is up and who is down. "Upon arriving there, where the sand slopes, Ali throws down shawl and coat; he throws himself down, and, stretched out on his back, arms outflung, begins to look at me, laughing" (248).[12] Ali throws himself down on the bed he has made from Gide's clothes, the clothes he had been hired to carry during Gide's walk. Will Ali pull Gide down? No, Gide sits down himself. Perhaps, then, it is Gide, the European, who pulls Ali down? Not quite that either. Ali, the paid porter, ends up standing naked like a God, before passively, as if without agency, allowing himself to fall into Gide's arms ("puis, en riant, se laissa tomber contre moi"). The passage is a startling example of politics writing itself into a scene even as it is being effaced. Put another way, one could imagine the goal of the writing here being to show a sexual encounter that, in its pleasure and its laughter, would somehow exceed certain politics, escape their burden, and yet simultaneously fail to do so.[13]

In the subsequent sexual scenes of *Si le grain ne meurt*, the specifically colonial politics and the sex are both unavoidably explicit. This explicitness, along with the inability of the sexual act in such scenes to escape the political, will be the mark of Gide's disapproval. To prepare the ground for the analysis of those scenes,

10. This play of tenses, confusing the moment of the act of narration with the moment being narrated is more than frequent in *Si le grain ne meurt*. Lejeune comments on it in another context. See *Exercices d'ambiguïté*, 80–83.

11. Compare the famous passage from Foucault's introduction to *L'Usage des plaisirs* : "As for what motivated me, it is quite simple; I would hope that in the eyes of some people it might be sufficient in itself. It is curiosity—the only kind of curiosity, in any case, that is worth acting upon with a degree of obstinacy: not the curiosity that seeks to assimilate what is proper for one to know, but that which enables one to get free of oneself. After all, what would be the value of the passion for knowledge if it resulted only in a certain amount of knowledgeableness and not, in one way or another and to the extent possible, in the knower's straying afield of himself? (8)." [Quant au motif qui m'a poussé, il était fort simple. Aux yeux de certains, j'espère qu'il pourrait par lui-même suffire. C'est la curiosité, — la seule espèce de curiosité, en tout cas, qui vaille la peine d'être pratiquée avec un peu d'obstination : non pas celle qui cherche à s'assimiler ce qu'il convient de connaître, mais celle qui permet de se déprendre de soi-même. Que vaudrait l'acharnement du savoir s'il ne devait assurer que l'acquisition des connaissances, et non pas, d'une certaine façon et autant que faire se peut, l'égarement de celui qui connaît? (14).]

12. Sitôt arrivé là, sur le sable en pente, Ali jette châle et manteau; il s'y jette lui-même, et, tout étendu sur le dos, les bras en croix, commence à me regarder en riant (298–99).

13. The intriguing final chapter of Jonathan Dollimore's *Sexual Dissidence*, "Desire and Difference," addresses this topic in Gide's *Amyntas, Si le grain ne meurt*, and in the writings of several other authors.

I would like to return for a few pages to the question of homosexuality's relationship to *dénuement*, to the rejection of materialism.

One of the paradigmatic moments in Gide's *œuvre* for watching him weave his sexual concerns into his concern with an escape from the trappings of bourgeois culture is the famous paragraph from *Les Nourritures terrestres*, where Ménalque declares, "Familles, je vous hais!":

> At night, I would watch as, in unknown villages, families that had been dispersed during the day reformed themselves. The father would come home, tired from work; the children came back from school. The door to the house would half open for a second on a glimpse of welcoming light, warmth and laughter, and then would close again for the night. No vagabond thing could enter now, no blast of the shivering wind outside.—Families, I hate you! closed up homes, tightly shut doors, jealous possessions of happiness.—Sometimes, invisible in the night, I have stayed leaning towards a window, observing at length the customs of a house. The father was there near the lamp; the mother sat sewing; the grandfather's chair stood empty; near the father, a child was studying—and my heart swelled with the desire to take that boy away with me on the road. (67)[14]

This triangular scene (Ménalque—boy—parents/culture) is similar to one we have observed and others to come. Instead of a tablecloth, we have a window, and, unlike the maid's threatening but somewhat hindered gaze, Ménalque's glance has salvific pretensions. Ménalque's desire to spy, unlike the maid's is justified through the insistence that his gaze work to make obvious a smothering excess of cultural attachments and security. The gaze is meant to reveal a decadence that *dénuement* works against. Because there is, theoretically, no decadence involved when Gide himself has sex (instead there is that perfect equanimity that curiosity is meant to enable), any outside gaze would thus only risk introducing decadence into the scene.

Here is an example of a contrasting triangle, where decadence is again clearly present, though not, perhaps, in the place Gide would have liked it. This descendant of the passage from *Les Nourritures terrestres* comes from a book on Gide by Ramon Fernandez, published in 1931. It demonstrates precisely how unstable is the division advocated in *Les Nourritures terrestres* between luxury and ascetic male bonding:

> Whether he likes it or not, the heterosexual can only see the sexual fervor of the pederast at the moment when it descends and deforms itself in vice, whereas the pederast himself preserves the marvelous memory of his exaltation. And since our

---

14. Au soir, je regardais dans d'inconnus villages les foyers, dispersés durant le jour, se reformer. Le père rentrait, las de travail; les enfants revenaient de l'école. La porte de la maison s'entrouvrait un instant sur un accueil de lumière, de chaleur et de rire, et puis se refermait pour la nuit. Rien de toutes les choses vagabondes n'y pouvait plus rentrer, du vent grelottant du dehors. — Familles, je vous hais! foyers clos; portes refermées; possessions jalouses du bonheur. — Parfois, invisible de nuit, je suis resté penché vers une vitre, à longtemps regarder la coutume d'une maison. Le père était là, près de la lampe; la mère cousait; la place d'un aïeul restait vide; un enfant, près du père, étudiait; — et mon cœur se gonfla du désir de l'emmener avec moi sur les routes (69).

morality gives us any number of reasons to despise homosexuality, that morality therefore supplies the heterosexual with the confirmation of his nausea. He watches the pederasts the way one watches a ball from behind a thick glass window, and he forgets that these gestures, without the music, are unable to yield up their enchanting secret. This is the motivation which pushed Gide to write *Corydon*. It was for him a matter of defending this exquisite music to which the pederast owes the best, the keenest part of his sensibility, to say it all, the fire that keeps him warm. (Fernandez, 65).[15]

An exquisitely embarrassing passage to have written and to read, without a doubt. But it can serve to remind us of two things: most obviously it recalls that homosexuality is as often and as easily (or even more easily) associated with than dissociated from luxury (this is as true for Gide as for Fernandez, so hopeful that we will perceive his phobic reaction as involuntary). Less obviously, the passage poses again, and quite acutely, the relationship between an observer and a participant in any act; it underlines the fact that it is always the belief in some shared *culture* that will (seem to) allow one corner of one of these triangles to communicate his "mémoire émerveillée," his "musique exquise," or even his vagabondish desires to another one of the placeholders. The decision to label that communication-enabling shared culture "decadent" is ideological, depending precisely on the outsider's way of describing that act of communication.

The question of memory is not unrelated to the question of culture here. One is invariably, as we have seen, an observer of, no longer a participant in, one's own memories. Gide is at pains to deal with this problem, and it governs the way he writes about sex. For all his reputation, acquired through his later work (particularly *Si le grain ne meurt*) for explicitness in his presentation of his sexual penchant, he is in fact quite selective, almost chary about voyeuristically describing his own sexual practices, perhaps out of a fear that describing them would be precisely the same thing as submitting them to a culture that might give them a name (*vice, péché, mauvaise habitude*) other than the one he might choose. Gide saves his most telling voyeurism, for example, for the sexual practices of others. Let us look briefly at the central sex scene within *Si le grain ne meurt,* concerned with that most important night when Oscar Wilde procures for Gide the young Arab Mohammed.

The description of the sexual part of this particular evening is surrounded by two startling references to memory. Gide opens this description by commenting: "Since then, every time I've looked for pleasure, I have chased after the memory of that night" (283).[16] Before we get to the event, we are already past it. Gide's at-

---

15. Sans le vouloir, l'hétérosexuel ne peut percevoir l'élan sexuel du pédéraste qu'au moment où il retombe et se déforme en vice, alors que le pédéraste, lui, garde la mémoire émerveillée de son exaltation. Comme, d'autre part, nos mœurs nous fournissent toutes sortes de raisons de mépriser la pédérastie, elles fournissent par là même à l'hétérosexuel la confirmation de sa nausée. Il regarde les pédérastes comme on regarde un bal de derrière une vitre épaisse, et il oublie que ces gestes, sans la musique, ne sauraient livrer leur secret enchanteur. Tel est le mobile qui poussa Gide à écrire *Corydon*. Il s'agissait pour lui de défendre cette musique exquise auquel le pédéraste doit le meilleur, le plus vif de sa force sensible, et pour tout dire le feu qui entretient sa chaleur.

16. Depuis, chaque fois que j'ai cherché le plaisir, ce fut courir après le souvenir de cette nuit (342).

tempt to prioritize this moment as the most memorable of all his erotic encounters might best be viewed as a reminder that no matter what he says, the temporal situation of all these memories is more or less equivalent. All are striving to become in some future retelling the primordial past moment. Gide expresses his predicament well in the phrase: "Depuis, chaque fois . . . ce fut courir après le souvenir de cette nuit," where the abyssal nature of his temporal confusion is indicated in the plethora of past moments: the evening itself, the many past moments at which he has tried to catch the memory of the evening, the moment in which that "depuis" was itself inscribed, which is to say the latest renarration of the elusive memory itself, a renarration from which, for all Gide's efforts to write it without fixing it, the memorable moment will nonetheless continue to run.

Gide moves *from* the description of this capital night to the next section of his memoirs with a sentence that begins, "We left Algiers, Wilde and I, shortly after that memorable evening" (287).[17] However, the identity of "cette mémorable soirée" has, in the interim, become somewhat confused, because Gide has in fact described *two* evenings spent with Mohammed, evenings separated by two years. Wilde arranged the first; on the second Gide shared the young man with a friend named Daniel B. It is on the second of these evenings that Gide, as an observer, will assume a disgust like that displayed by Fernandez, and thereby insist on politics being present. In contrast, on the first of the two evenings, Gide and Mohammed are alone in a room (no observer), and this is the moment at which something seems about to happen:

> At present I was finally finding what was normal for me. Here there was no more constraint, nothing was precipitous, nothing doubtful; there is no unpleasant residue in the memory I keep. My joy was immense, and such that I cannot imagine it any fuller even if love had entered into it. How could it have been a question of love? How could I have let desire take over my heart? My pleasure was free from ulterior motives and was not to be followed by any remorse. But how should I name the transports with which I clasped in my naked arms this perfect little body, wild, ardent, sensual and dusky? . . . (284)[18]

Immediately upon this list of exoticizing adjectives from a lexicon for oriental things, there follow three discreet dots, and a new paragraph commences:

> I then stayed a long time, after Mohammed had left me, in a state of quivering jubilation, and even though I had already *near* him, achieved ecstasy five times, I revived it a number of times more, and once back in my hotel room, I prolonged its echoes all the way until morning. (284–85; my emphasis)[19]

17. Nous partîmes d'Alger, Wilde et moi, très peu de temps après cette mémorable soirée . . . (346).

18. A présent je trouvais enfin ma normale. Plus rien ici de contraint, de précipité, de douteux; rien de cendreux dans le souvenir que j'en garde. Ma joie fut immense et telle que je ne la puisse imaginer plus pleine si de l'amour s'y fût mêlé. Comment eût-il été question d'amour? Comment eussé-je laissé le désir disposer de mon cœur? Mon plaisir était sans arrière-pensée et ne devait être suivi d'aucun remords. Mais comment nommerai-je alors mes transports à serrer dans mes bras nus ce parfait petit corps sauvage, ardent, lascif, et ténébreux? . . . (343).

19. Je demeurai longtemps ensuite, après que Mohammed m'eut quitté, dans un état de jubilation frémissante, et bien qu'ayant déjà, près de lui {as usual}, cinq fois atteint la volupté, je ravivai nombre de fois encore mon extase et, rentré dans ma chambre d'hôtel, en prolongeai jusqu'au matin les échos. (343).

Already chasing after the brilliant memory on the very evening of its inception, Gide astonishes in his ability both to state and to deny the problems of memory he has been tracing for us. On the one hand, he insists on his ability to enter this perfect memory, one with no residue, and to dissolve successfully into his old self. On the other hand, he admits that this memory is like any other: inaccessible, inauthentic, contaminated by the culture time brings. We see the dissolving aspect in the again startling present/past mix of phrases such as "à présent je trouvais" and the insistence that "mon plaisir était sans arrière-pensée [i.e., no deferred action of memory and no awareness of politics within the scene itself] et ne devait être suivi d'aucun remords," the truth of which is confirmed by the present tense of "rien de cendreux dans le souvenir que j'en garde." The moment and the memory seem to have remained pure. There is no sour foretaste or aftertaste of *Nachträglichkeit.* Yet, we can read the contamination of this memory by culture in that strangely clumsy, exoticizing string of adjectives describing Mohammed: "sauvage, ardent, lascif, et ténébreux." We can also see the almost intentional lack of naturalness in the studied literary effect of a sentence such as, "Ma joie fut immense et telle que je ne la puisse imaginer plus pleine si de l'amour s'y fût mêlé." The insistent delicacy of the direct object before the auxiliary "je ne la puisse imaginer" and not "je ne puisse l'imaginer") and the choice (grammatically unusual but typically Gidean) to use the imperfect subjunctive in a "si" clause ("si de l'amour s'y fût mêlé") both mark this passage as a literary set piece, a stylistic showcase that may set off nicely Mohammed's "petit corps sauvage" but clearly separates an almost decadently stylistic Gide, remembered or remembering, from the young Arab.[20]

The point about memory's role can be refined by examining the way Gide uses past tenses in a few of these scenes. If we examine the opening paragraphs of *Si le grain ne meurt,* those dealing with Gide's "mauvaises habitudes," and the "Familles, je vous hais!" passage from *Les Nourritures terrestres,* we find the predominant past tense to be the imperfect, and this choice of tense allows these two scenes to float in the past in an indefinite way; it contributes to their archetypal nature, to their quality, precisely, as *scenes.* One might think, here, of Roland Barthes' definition of *souvenir* in *A Lover's Discourse:*

> Happy and/or heart-rending rememoration of an object, gesture or scene linked to the loved one and marked by the intrusion of the imperfect into the grammar of the lover's discourse. . . .

---

20. See Gide's comments about "si" clauses in *Ainsi soit-il :* "French, which seems so simple to us, is a very difficult language full of little pitfalls. I know foreigners who speak it wondrously well but who still stumble over the use of *si* with the indicative. I am ready to understand them; this is one of the anomalies of our language; the foreigner feels that *if* should be followed by the subjunctive, or at least the conditional" (60). [Le français, qui nous semble si simple, est une langue très difficile, pleine de menus traquenards. Je connais des étrangers qui le parlent à merveille, mais qui trébuchent encore devant l'emploi du *si* avec l'indicatif. Je suis prêt à les comprendre; c'est une anomalie de notre langue; l'étranger sent qu'il faudrait que suivît le subjonctif ou tout au moins le conditionnel (1190).]

> The imperfect is the tense of fascination: it seems to be alive and yet it doesn't move: imperfect presence, imperfect death; neither oblivion nor resurrection; simply the exhausting lure of memory. From the start, greedy to play a role, scenes take their position in memory: often I feel this, I foresee this, at the very moment when these scenes are forming. (217)

Barthes' description suits these two passages from Gide admirably. The scenes become objects of obsession for memory. They are not told, narrated, they are not chronologically fixed so much as they flicker constantly in memory—they occupy it.

For Gide the preoccupation inherent in scenes cast in the imperfect is discomfiting precisely because as they flicker about in memory, chronology becomes problematic. Thus, in the opening pages of *Si le grain ne meurt,* it is the imperfect cast of the scene that forces on Gide the question: "Qui de nous deux en avait instruit l'autre?," a question that would probably require an answer in the preterite, something like: "Un jour sous la table le fils de la concierge me *montra . . .*" (One day under the table the concierge's son *showed* me . . .). But Gide can admit no simple origin of sexual knowledge: "je ne puis dire si quelqu'un m'enseigna ou comment je découvris le plaisir." Thus, the complex double bind of the passage: it is the imperfect that emphasizes the possibility of a hazily remembered, retrospectively activated seduction. It is also the imperfect that will not allow the question to be definitively answered. A preterite would clear the air, but that might have its own dangers.

Nonetheless, in other scenes, Gide *will* choose the clarity of the preterite in an effort to prevent sexuality and its origins from becoming an obsession. He will find other techniques to ward off questions of seduction. The scenes we have just examined between Gide and Ali and between Gide and Mohammed, for example, do have as their primary tense the preterite, the tense of narration, of chronology, a tense that can get something out of the way. In the scene with Ali, as we have remarked, Gide *nearly* becomes preoccupied: "Sur le seuil de ce que l'on appelle : péché, *hésitais*-je encore? . . . c'est bien la curiosité qui me *faisait* attendre" (imperfects). But this preoccupation, this possibility of obsession with the temporality of memory and with corruption are quickly eliminated by a strong series of verbs in the preterite: "je *vis* son rire lentement se faner . . . il se *leva* . . . je le *fis* rouler à terre." In the scene with Mohammed, when Gide comments that there is "rien de cendreux" in the memory he keeps, might he not mean, by that claim for purity, merely that he is going to insist on writing in the preterite, as if the moments were safe from the increasingly problematic temporality of fantasy? Thus, when telling us of his prodigious masturbation after five previous orgasms with Mohammed, Gide insists on staying, in his writing, at least, in the realm of strict chronology, even as the fantasizing mind and hand stray into the realm of obsessive fascination: "je *ravivai* nombre de fois encore mon extase . . . *prolongeai* jusqu'au matin les échos." The verb *prolonger* encapsulates Gide's tension as it sits awkwardly in the preterite. For in its air of duration, it seems rather more suited to imperfect, obsessional, fantasmatic uses.

This tension between a clean preterite and an obsessive imperfect will reoccur in the final and most explicit passage from *Si le grain ne meurt,* where we will find that Mohammed has sadly become part of an obsessive fantasy, one of corruption, one that will threaten to contaminate all previous encounters. The first encounter between Gide and Mohammed may have been explicit enough for some (it is one of the passages left out of certain expurgated versions of the English translation), but Gide elevates the level of explicitness in the description of the second encounter, one he watches, but does not participate in. We see here in Gide the very hatred we saw in the shut-out observer Ménalque in *Les Nourritures terrestres,* the very disgust of Fernandez, outsider at the ball. Here also we see clearly that it is the third person in the tryst, Gide, in fact, whose way of construing his cultural proximity to his friend Daniel and concomitant distance from Mohammed forces the reading of this scene into one of colonial rape:

> Then, while I stayed seated near our half-emptied glasses, Daniel seized Mohammed in his arms and carried him over to the bed that occupied the back of the room. He laid him down on his back, right at the edge of the bed, across it; and soon I saw nothing but, on each side of Daniel, who was panting away, two slender legs hanging down. Daniel hadn't even taken off his cloak. Very tall, standing against the bed, badly lit, seen from behind, his face hidden by his long black curly hair, in this cloak that fell all the way to his feet, Daniel seemed gigantic, and, leaning over this little body which he covered up, one could have seen in him a huge vampire feeding upon a corpse. I could have screamed in horror. (286)[21]

The passage moves from narration to description. Narration: "Daniel saisit Mohammed . . . le porta . . . le coucha . . . je ne vis bientôt," but as the story turns to nightmare, action becomes obsessive, haunting (*déchirante,* Barthes would say) description, and we encounter a sentence in the imperfect, strangely overburdened with prepositioned descriptive fragments: "Très grand, debout contre le lit, mal éclairé, vu de dos, le visage caché . . . dans ce manteau . . . Daniel paraissait. . . ." The *cendreux* has returned, it would seem, with a vengeance, as Gide assumes the nausea, the self-divided homophobia, of Fernandez's heterosexual. The act itself has become part of a corrupt, decadent culture. Thus, the reference to vampires, to Daniel's well-coiffed curls and fashionable cloak (one might wonder if these aren't the physical accoutrements of a dandy who knows how to deploy his imperfect subjunctives), and thus also what Gide construes as Mohammed's

---

21. Puis, tandis que je restais assis près des verres à demi vidés, Daniel saisit Mohammed dans ses bras et le porta sur le lit qui occupait le fond de la pièce. Il le coucha sur le dos, tout au bord du lit, en travers; et je ne vis bientôt plus que, de chaque côte de Daniel ahanant, deux fines jambes pendantes. Daniel n'avait même pas enlevé son manteau. Très grand, debout contre le lit, mal éclairé, vu de dos, le visage caché par les boucles de ses longs cheveux noirs, dans ce manteau qui lui tombait aux pieds, Daniel paraissait gigantesque, et penché sur ce petit corps qu'il couvrait, on eût dit un immense vampire se repaître sur un cadavre. J'aurais crié d'horreur (345).

learned capacity to submit himself to this practice: "As for myself, who can only conceive pleasure face to face, reciprocal and without violence, and who, like Whitman, find satisfaction in the most furtive contact, I was horrified both by Daniel's way of going at it and by seeing Mohammed go along with it so complacently" (286).[22] The very first time he saw Mohammed again after the two-year interval, Gide had noticed this change, the new marks of corruption:

> His body had kept its grace, but his gaze was no longer so languorous; I sensed something hard, restless, degraded.
> "You've stopped smoking hashish?" I asked, knowing what his answer would be.
> "Yes," he said. "Now I drink absinthe."
> He was still attractive; what am I saying? He was more attractive than ever; but no longer seemed so much sensual as brazen. (285)[23]

The pattern is clear. Mohammed has given up his naturalness, his association with North Africa, its *kief* and its languor. He has entered the shadows of the imperfect tense, the tense representing the problems of memory that, for Gide, transform sexuality into corruption, the tense of obsessive fantasy, one in which Gide would like to refuse to acknowledge his own complicity. On a more explicit level, Gide is distressed because from his point of view Mohammed has accommodated himself to the European homosexual culture represented by Wilde, absinthe, impudence, and, of course, fucking.

Fucking represents an excess Gide's fantasy cannot absorb, a form of pleasure he will not imagine as just sexual; it must also be political. Fucking is decadent, he insists, as if that insistence were the only route by which he could save his own sexual practices (in North Africa and elsewhere) from contamination by politics, as if that insistence might keep his sex just sex, might keep in abeyance questions about the possible social provenance of his—of all—sexual practices, and all construals of those practices. His pagan sexuality could be learned from scratch, he seems to insist; decadent fucking is learned from someone else. In fact, the patent futility of these insistences should render all the more intense our scrutiny of the way in which his own writing might belie such phobic insistence. Would there be another route we could take that might permit us to see both the necessary political and social web into which every sexual act is woven, even as we perceive in sexuality's expression something the web does not catch?

22. Pour moi, qui ne comprends le plaisir que face à face, réciproque et sans violence, et que souvent, pareil à Whitman, le plus furtif contact satisfait, j'étais horrifié tout à la fois par le jeu de Daniel, et de voir s'y prêter aussi complaisamment Mohammed (346).

23. Son corps avait gardé sa grâce, mais son regard n'avait plus la même langueur; j'y sentais je ne sais quoi de dur, d'inquiet, d'avili.

— Tu ne fumes plus le kief? lui demandai-je, sûr de sa réponse.

— Non, me dit-il. A présent, je bois de l'absinthe.

Il était attrayant encore; que dis-je? plus attrayant que jamais; mais paraissait non plus tant lascif qu'effronté (344).

Just Sex II

> Sensuality, my dear friend, simply consists in *considering as an end and not as a means both the present object and the present minute.*[24]
>
> —Gide, *Prétextes*

A final leap seems necessary now, from *Si le grain ne meurt* back to the point in the article "Is the Rectum a Grave?" where Bersani raises "the question not of the reflection or expression of politics in sex, but rather of the extremely obscure process by which sexual pleasure *generates* politics" (208). It would appear that Bersani aims to shed light on the question of when politics enters the scene, and he might, therefore, help us to some conclusions about Gide. The exact passage in Bersani's article that first prompted me to read it alongside Gide's *Si le grain ne meurt* comes toward the end, when Bersani is discussing an interview given by Foucault and published in *Salmagundi* in 1982–83. The relevance of this passage to Gide should be clear:

> Thus in the *Salmagundi* interview to which I have already referred . . . [Foucault] delivers himself of the highly idiosyncratic opinions, first of all, that "for a homosexual, the best moment of love is likely to be when the lover leaves in the taxi" ("the homosexual imagination is for the most part concerned with reminiscing about the act rather than anticipating [or, presumably, enjoying] it") and, secondly, that the rituals of gay S & M are "the counterpart of the medieval courts where strict rules of proprietary courtship were defined." The first opinion is somewhat embarrassing; the second has a certain campy appeal. Both turn our attention away from the body—from the acts in which it engages, from the pain it inflicts and begs for— and directs [sic] our attention to the romances of memory and the idealizations of the presexual, the courting imagination. . . . Representation is displaced from the concrete practice of fellatio and sodomy to the melancholy charms of erotic memories and the cerebral tensions of courtship. (219–20; Bersani's bracketed interpolations)

Bersani is presenting an ethics of the present moment. He holds out to us the tantalizing possibility that if we could somehow control displacement, if we could describe, experience, or represent sex *presently,* we might redeem ourselves—or at least something—from past-oriented memories or future-oriented cerebrations, indulgences we have not noticed Gide trying to avoid.

Still, we might think that this idea of sex in a dissolving present sounds even a little bit like Gide—and I think there are some similarities but will insist on the differences first. Gide is not obviously a person who thinks, like Bersani, about the "obscure process by which sexual pleasure *generates* politics." Instead, he might seem, according to what we have read, to be one of those who think that there is

---

24. La sensualité, chère amie, consiste simplement à *considérer comme une fin et non comme un moyen l'objet présent et la minute présente.*

merely a "reflection or expression of politics in sex." Gide would thus participate in what Bersani scathingly calls the "pastoralizing project," that project engaged in by those who speak "as if the sexual—involving as it does the source and locus of every individual's original experience of power (and of powerlessness) in the world: the human body—could somehow be conceived of apart from all relations of power, were, so to speak, belatedly contaminated by power from elsewhere" (221).

A roundabout way of specifying what the pastoral is for Gide would be to imagine his answer to the question, Which came first, sodomy (or, more specifically, anal intercourse) or politics? It seems that Gide would want to answer: politics. First came the pastoral stage where sex was "face à face," "l'un près de l'autre, mais non l'un avec l'autre pourtant"; then came consumerism, dandyism, colonialism, decadence, differentiation, and sodomy tagged along. Bersani is asking the same question (which may go a long way toward explaining why they sometimes sound a bit similar), although his answer would probably be the opposite, namely, that sodomy precedes politics. There is, in fact, a fall from a primary sexual stage (that Bersani sometimes chooses to see as typified by anal intercourse[25]) into politics. Primary sexuality is not (for either Bersani or Gide) a realm in which selves exist coherently. Sexuality is something that has to do with the body, not the self. Sexuality shatters the self, and for Bersani it is when this self that sexuality threatens to destroy nonetheless insists on holding onto its coherence that sexuality falls into power:

> The self which the sexual shatters provides the basis on which sexuality is associated with power. It is possible to think of the sexual as, precisely, moving between a hyperbolic sense of self and a loss of consciousness of self. But sex as self-hyperbole is perhaps a repression of sex as self-abolition. . . . it is perhaps primarily *the degeneration of the sexual into a relationship that condemns sexuality to becoming a struggle for power.* (218; Bersani's emphasis)

It is not, Bersani insists, that there is something inherently ideological about sex. But there is something about "the relational," something about the number 2 and the power effects inherent merely in the number, something that has it that those effects "can perhaps most easily be exacerbated, and polarized into relations of mastery and subordination, in sex" (216). Why is this the case?

25. There are some good reasons for this typification, because as Bersani (and also Lee Edelman in a recent article) argues, anal intercourse is a crisis point of contemporary Western sexuality and continues to provoke enormous phobia and anxiety amongst "observers" of gay sexuality. (Edelman and Bersani both point to the ways *gay* anal intercourse challenges notions of what is active and what passive in our conceptions of sexual subjects.) Such phobic anxiety, for instance, is present in an editorial Edelman discusses. That editorial, from New Hampshire's *Manchester Union Leader,* exhibits the very nexus of concepts under scrutiny in this chapter: phobia, fascination with origins, fantasmatic constructions. The *Leader* writes, to its shame: "Homosexual intercourse is the genesis of every single case of AIDS in that every case is traceable—either directly or indirectly—to the practice. However the disease is transmitted, the sexual perversion that is anal intercourse by sodomites is the fundamental point of origin." See Lee Edelman, "The Mirror and the Tank," 14–15.

But see also the interesting comments by Tim Dean, in his article, "The Psychoanalysis of AIDS," as to "a certain heterosexist conflation in Bersani's argument of sex with fucking" (114).

The answer Bersani gives has to do with anatomy and posture ("positioning" is the word he uses). Interestingly for us, this involves us in another (and, for this chapter, final) reasonably explicit description of sex, and, almost inevitably, it would seem, involves us in the same temporal problems with which we are by now reasonably familiar. This is one of Bersani's most Gidean moments:

> Human bodies are constructed in such a way that it is, or at least has been, almost impossible not to associate mastery and subordination with the experience of our most intense pleasures. This is first of all a question of positioning. If the penetration necessary (until recently . . .) for the reproduction of the species has most generally been accomplished by the man's getting on top of the woman, it is also true that being on top can never be just a question of a physical position—either for the person on top or for the one on the bottom. (216)

To associate mastery and subordination with any particular sexual experience is surely at some level fantasmatic and somehow an act of reflection that would fill with content a remembered experience. The structure of *Nachträglichkeit* would seem to be in effect here as well. This is precisely why the use of the adverb "never" becomes so interesting: "being on top can *never* be just a question of a physical position.[n] No matter how far back we push our memories ("It seems to me I *do* remember, when I was very young and a position was just a position," we hear someone hopelessly lamenting in the background), no matter how far back we push, the very act of remembering, as we saw in Gide, tarnished our hopes for that pastoral moment, that half ironical, half hopeful "Il faut bien admettre qu'un enfant parfois à nouveau les invente." But Bersani's abyssal "never" here, which might seem to want to forbid an attempt at rememoration, nonetheless seems to be what has propelled both Bersani's and Gide's writing. (They are, needless to say, not alone.) It might therefore also seem by this very fact integrally related to that melancholy nostalgia for which Bersani was chastising Foucault. When one writes about sex it is not so easy, no matter how hard one wriggles, to distinguish between past, future, and present, between reminiscences, anticipation, and enjoyment. One could write for years about sex and never get to a pure present without politics. Bersani's shattering present is ultimately inseparable from and even indistinguishable from past and future. It carries with it the structure of its own nostalgia. This could be seen as nicely encapsulated in his final sentence: "Male homosexuality advertises the risk of the sexual itself as the risk of self-dismissal, of *losing sight* of the self, and in so doing it proposes and dangerously represents *jouissance* as a mode of ascesis" (222, Bersani's emphasis). The present participle of "losing sight" holds out the theoretical possibility of a sustained, consistently and constantly repeated, present moment in which sex could be just sex, perpetually evading any traps of temporality, any politics of relationality, any social construals. Yet the insistent nature of that present participle depends for its force on the Janus-faced other verbs of the passage. Present tense they may be ("advertises," "proposes," "represents"), but they subversively remind us that this present moment depends equally on the one hand on utopian, forward-looking promotion campaigns and, on the other, on efforts to hoist the once presented past wholesale and undamaged into the present of representation. Bersani advertises one male homosexuality, Gide another; they both strive to represent *jouissance* outside of memory. The failure of the representations (that is, on the one hand, the failure of both Bersani's and Gide's representations to *be* "male homosexuality" and, on the other, the failure of *jouissance* to be represented anywhere) is perhaps emblematic of the elusive excess of the politics of sexuality "itself." This may not be a situation one can write one's way out of. And in this regard, sex may not be that different from writing.

CHAPTER 2

-
-
-
-
-
-
-
-
-

THE PLACE OF THE

OEDIPAL: GIDE

WRITING HOME FROM

NORTH AFRICA

-
-
-
-
-
-
-
-
-
-
-
-
-

I would like to look more closely now at some of the problems Gide confronts in writing about his arrival at a queer identity, at the role narrativization plays for Gide in understanding and even undergoing this process. In particu-
lar, I will be observing Gide's relation to the oedipalizing narratives so familiar to
many "Freudian" accounts of the arrival at "homosexuality." My impression is that
Gide perceives many of the ways such narratives deny, or at least work to dampen,
many of the political complexities, much of the political potential, of sexuality; my
impression is also that the Gidean text struggles in various ways against this
dampening effect, against this possible denial. This struggle is what interests me in
this chapter. I will be building on some of the considerations as to the confused
temporality of sexuality from the last chapter; I will also be trying to elaborate the
discussion of Gide's relation to North Africa, though from a rather different angle.
The main new departure here, one that plays an important role in making the
analyses of future chapters possible, is my discussion of Gide's ambivalent relation
to female figures in the construction of his sexuality: ambivalent in that he finds
certain things he might feel loyal to in the marginal status of certain female
sexualities even as he feels an often violent urge to define himself over against the
feminine.

Plunging Necklines

> One has only to look at children to see how intense the impulse
> to bite is.
> —Karl Abraham, "The Influence of Oral Eroticism
> on Character Formation"

Si le grain ne meurt can be read as a form of self-analysis, a place in which Gide
tries to construct in narrative form an explanation of his own sexual development,
or perhaps we should say a place where he confronts the difficulties that kind of
explanatory effort inevitably involves. It is in the context of such difficulties, for
instance, that one feels drawn to read the following scene, described by Gide on
only the second or third page of his book. The Gides are on a visit to his father's
side of the family in Uzès, and on this particular day they are visiting "les cousins
de Flaux":

> My cousin was very beautiful, and she knew it. . . . I remember very well the
> dazzling brilliance of her skin—and I remember it especially well because the day I
> was taken to see her she was wearing a low-necked dress.
> "Go and give your cousin a kiss," said my mother, as I came into the drawing-
> room. (I couldn't have been much more than four years old—five, perhaps.) I
> moved forward. My cousin de Flaux drew me towards her, leaning over as she did so,
> which caused her shoulder to be revealed. Faced with the brilliance of that flesh,
> some strange vertigo seized me: instead of putting my lips to the cheek she offered
> me, fascinated by her stunning shoulder, I gave it a great bite with my teeth. My
> cousin screamed with pain and I with horror; then I spit, full of disgust. (10–11)[1]

Gide passes on immediately without comment, but the scene resonates with many
others in the book in which he writes as if to come to terms with his relationship to
female sexuality and to his mother in particular. I would like here to draw a group
of these scenes together in order to find out what precisely Gide thinks he can
explain about his homosexuality—his struggle to fix on, accept, and account for a
particular object choice—by writing (often very obliquely) about his mother's
sexuality and his own relationship to it. I would also like to begin to account for the
places Gide finds himself called upon to go to in order to come to terms with this
relationship—to Biskra, in Algeria, for instance, where Gide would flee in order to

---

1. Ma cousine était très belle et le savait . . . De l'éclat de cette peau, je me souviens très bien; je m'en souviens
d'autant mieux que, ce jour où je lui fus présenté, elle portait une robe largement échancrée.
— Va vite embrasser ta cousine, me dit ma mère lorsque j'entrai dans le salon. (Je ne devais avoir guère plus
de quatre ans; cinq peut-être). Je m'avançai. La cousine de Flaux m'attira contre elle en se baissant, ce qui découvrit
son épaule. Devant l'éclat de cette chair, je ne sais quel vertige me prit : au lieu de poser mes lèvres sur la joue qu'elle
me tendait, fasciné par l'épaule éblouissante, j'y allai d'un grand coup de dents. La cousine fit un cri de douleur; j'en
fis un d'horreur; puis je crachai, plein de dégoût (10–11).

be outside the borders of what he construed as his mother's sexual empire, only to find that by constructing a certain outside around his mother, he had already, so to speak, let her in.

To uncover some of the complexities, some of what is at stake, in the scene where Gide is sent by his mother to kiss his cousin, but bites her instead, one might choose to examine a few of Melanie Klein's writings about an infant's relationship to the mother. Klein theorized how, in early infancy, before entertaining the concept of a whole person, an infant relates to parts of persons—*partial objects*. The first and crucial partial object for the child would be the mother's breast, a source of nourishment, but a source of frustration as well, when it is withdrawn or fails to be present. Already in this early stage of development, Klein holds, the infant has the rudiments of an ego structure in place, and that structure establishes certain distinctions. As if provoked by a desire for the coherence those distinctions might provide, it splits its image of the breast into good and bad partial objects. Through this splitting, the infant would be enabled to direct feelings of aggression, anxiety, and frustration toward the "bad" breast, feelings of satisfaction, pleasure, and love toward the "good" breast, thereby laying the groundwork for future affective relation in an emotional field of some consistency. Only at a later moment would the acceptance of the mother as an entity, a whole object, necessitate the integration of these split representations into a unity, necessitate the conceptualization of an object as including, perhaps inconsistently, both pleasurable and unpleasurable, good and bad components. And even after the integration had been performed, with whatever degree of success, the moment or, to use Klein's term, the *position* from which the subject splits its partial objects into good and bad halves, would exist within the psyche, capable of being returned or regressed to, capable of being reenergized in moments of later crisis.

It was an important innovation in psychoanalytic theory to insist that the infant's relation to the mother's breast was the foundation on which all other relations to objects would be built. Access to the breast could provide feelings of satisfaction; loss or denial of the breast, feelings of frustration. A newborn, with little sense of the boundaries of its own body, but oscillating between feelings of frustration and satisfaction, would learn initial lessons of love and hate, adoration and aggression, all around this initial object. Unclear as to where the breast was, or even what "where" would mean, the infant's "placement" of the breast both inside and outside of itself would also be its first encounter with introjection and projection, the processes through which it would gradually build up its own psyche, its first lessons in establishing a place for itself and for the breast both in the hallucinatory world of its fantasies and in the "real" world it would have to grow up into.[2]

Klein thus takes a step back from a paternal oedipal realm to a maternal

2. For discussion of some of these issues, see Julia Kristeva, "Place Names."

preoedipal one and works to establish the origins for most all the important structures in the earlier moment:

> The first introjected object, the mother's breast, forms the basis of the super-ego. Just as the relation to the mother's breast precedes and strongly influences the relation to the father's penis, so the relation to the introjected mother affects in many ways the whole course of super-ego development. Some of the most important features of the super-ego, whether loving and protective or destructive and devouring, are derived from the early maternal component of the super-ego. ("The Oedipus Complex," 388).

There are important consequences to Klein's theoretical insistence on the primacy of the relation to the mother's breast, as Elizabeth Abel has pointed out. "Klein transfers the formation of the superego from the paternal prohibition that resolves the Oedipal situation to the earliest relation to the nursing mother's body. . . . The superego is divorced from any notion of acculturation as the passage through the castration complex into a symbolic register, and the father is displaced from his critical position as the cultural origin of the human subject" (Abel, 11).[3] The nucleus for the superego, Klein suggests, is the incorporated imago of the mother's breast. Such an imago could easily carry with it all the aggressive, punitive possibilities traditionally assigned to the superego. In a destructive mood, the infant might introject the maternal breast by way of the fantasy of devouring it. Confused as to where the breast belongs, unclear as to the difference between images of the breast and the body part itself, anxious about its own destructive impulses, the infant might assign equally destructive impulses to the incorporated breast. The infant thereby turns this imago of the maternal breast into a punishing force, imagining it as having the power to carry out the destructive desires the infant has experienced, so that instead of devouring the mother, the child fears being devoured by the mother/superego within.[4] Later processes of reparation and integration, Klein argues, will need to come into place in order to check and control the anxiety such an introjection creates. Such anxiety, Klein suggests, will remain present, however well controlled, and will be the reservoir on which any future anxiety will draw, revivifying the earlier scenes even as the anxiety takes on new forms.

I am interested by the Kleinian move, the "step-back" structure, an effort to push an origin back, to deny originary status to one even (say the Oedipus complex and its dissolution) by insisting that it be read as the rehearsal of an

---

3. For a helpful account of the Kleinian switch in emphasis and Lacan's important objections to it, see Juliet Mitchell's introduction to Jacques Lacan, *Feminine Sexuality*, 1–26.

4. See chapters 8 and 9 of Melanie Klein, *The Psycho-Analysis of Children*. See also Leo Bersani, "Death and Literary Authority: Marcel Proust and Melanie Klein," 19: "Klein traces the history of the infant's attempts to deal with the anxieties engendered by a sexuality that is *born as aggression*. This history begins at birth. A complex nonverbal syntax of fantasmatic introjections and projections constitutes the infantile ego's defenses against internal and external bad objects, against, perhaps most profoundly, its own impulses to destroy both itself and the objects it loves."

earlier scenario (say the preoedipal coming and going of the breast). The strategy is similar to one we will see in Gide, although with significant differences. Gide sometimes seems willfully to deny the existence of anything oedipal in his childhood, in his relation to the maternal instance. Every hint of oedipality must be analeptically rewritten as preoedipal. In the analyses that follow, my goal is not to take sides, to restore any particular Gidean moment to its true oedipality or preoedipality; rather, I watch the precariousness of the balancing act on the threshold between those realms, and I inquire as to why Gide might have gone on so carefully pursuing this balance. The threshold into oedipality is one Gide never wishes to cross fully, preferring that it move forward in time with him. To ensure that it will do so requires an effort of writing—an effort that can be seen particularly when he writes about his mother and also as he works to restructure dominant forms of social (in particular: colonial) myths.

More than Klein, I would argue, who steps back to the relation to the mother in order to establish a firm beginning from which sexuality moves forward, Gide's effort aims to resist a unidirectional narrative. Such a narrative forgets the extent to which it is itself a construction that retroactively justifies an end point in a particular (usually normative) sexuality. Gide's writing can help us to see what queer theory interested in psychoanalysis more and more realizes it must come to terms with: it will not suffice to valorize the preoedipal moment over heterosexualizing castration anxiety; nor will it suffice to rewrite castration so that some "boy" or "girl" can accede to it in some queer, redemptive fashion. Instead, one must always insist that no matter how the relation between preoedipal and oedipal moments is construed or how a given narrative deploys those moments, that very narrative temporality will necessarily—in its incipient orthodoxy, in its way of grounding both sexual difference and sexual object choice—betray the complexity of the sexuality that must exceed the narrative it has produced.[5] Gide's writing seems to narrrativize and to distrust the effect of narrativization at the same time, recogniz-

---

5. Here are a few examples of this kind of queer work on psychoanalysis: Judith Roof's critique of Kristeva in the second chapter of *A Lure of Knowledge*, where she comments: "This mirror stage point of beginning—a second origin—is actually in the middle of a chronology, though it is the point from which we are able to see the first origin. The mirror stage thus defies chronology and becomes the origin of the origin. Operating in a temporal dialectic, the infant anticipates a future wholeness that enables a recognition of a previous chaos and fragmentation *as* chaos and fragmentation. The celebrated preoedipal lack of differentiation is actually a perceptual product of differentiation, both sexual and individual" (p. 93). See also Lee Edelman's "The Mirror and the Tank": "Drawing upon Lacan's hypothesis of the mirror stage as both precipitate and prolepsis of the subject's self-constitution, [my] argument seeks to unfold the logic behind the derisive representation of gay men as narcissistically fixated and oriented toward the mother. It does so by considering the mirror stage and the castration crisis in relation to one another as the two determining moments in the formation of the heterosexual male subject that defensively *generate* the myth of that subject's unidirectional development (out of and away from identification with—and domination by—maternal power), precisely because each of those moments *refutes* such unidirectionality to the degree that its subject-shaping force depends upon its capacity to elicit *retroactively* the history from which the subject thereafter will be said to have emerged. The fact that the subject emerges, however, not from that history . . . but rather from the narrative that enables him to *posit* his emergence from that history, means that the *experience* of such a history is never, properly speaking, the subject's property" (18). See also Judith Butler, "The Lesbian Phallus and the Morphological Imaginary," esp. 155–56.

ing that whatever temporality sexuality seems to follow, no one narrative can capture it, can account for a fixed perception of both sexual difference and sexual object choice through a particular series of moments, a series in which any particular moment would come *first*. Gide thus writes his way out from under dominant (heterosexualizing) narrative patterns (specifically those that insist that all sexualities must be construed as having a *totalized* relation to, a *fundamental* origin in, castration anxiety). To do so he perhaps invokes other marginalizing narratives, even though those other narratives necessarily also fail to capture sexuality's queer way of escaping narrative explanation.

Decentering the Oedipal

On the day he bites her, Gide's cousin has put on a dress with a plunging neckline, knowing that this sets off her beauty. As she bends over to kiss her young cousin, the dress slips as if to reveal her breast. Overcome with vertigo when faced with this unexpected expanse of skin, Gide, seemingly possessed, loses control. "Fasciné par l'épaule éblouissante," he acts out an infant fantasy and indulges his teeth. Perhaps it is his cousin's implied vanity that marks her as the bad object, worthy of punishment. This scene could be read as emblematic of many things: a desire to separate his mother, "ordinarily so modest, so reserved" ("Ma mère," 33/1099), from his more sensuous and sexual cousin; a desire to perform sexually in front of his mother; perhaps a desire to make evident his rejection of women as sex objects; or, of course, a desire to spit out a too forcefully introjected mother.[6] Gide's mother pushes him away from her, toward a wider society of women. He tests the waters and returns, as if refusing to move from endogamy to exogamy, as if resisting a certain social contract about exchange. A refusal to bond with his cousin might count as a refusal either to leave or to sexualize his mother, just as it might seem to work (retrospectively) as an indicator of a dawning sexual inclination, one already construed as part of a resistant relation to certain social contracts. Tasting the future, the young Gide spits it out, almost admitting no knowledge of it, even though some knowledge might be deemed necessary to the declaration of the other allegiances he is beginning to stake out here.

This "early" moment is thus written so as to participate in any number of possible narratives of the onset of a sexual identity. Further, the writing suggests that the narrative significance of the scene is both available at the moment it takes

6. Compare this remark by Melanie Klein: "It does not seem clear why a child of, say, four years old should set up in his mind an unreal, phantastic image of parents who devour, cut and bite. But it *is* clear why in a child of about *one year* old the anxiety caused by the beginning of the Oedipus conflict takes the form of a dread of being devoured and destroyed. The child himself desires to destroy the libidinal object by biting, devouring and cutting it, which leads to anxiety, since awakening of the Oedipus tendencies is followed by introjection of the object, which then becomes one from which punishment is to be expected. The child then dreads a punishment corresponding to the offence: the super-ego becomes something which bites, devours and cuts" ("Early Stages of the Oedipus Conflict," 203).

place and yet to be written; it suggests *both* that it is clear from the scene what the future might hold *and* that the future is necessary to give this scene its import. To refuse oedipality with a prescient awareness of its consequences, such is the game Gide writes himself into as he writes about his childhood sexuality.

Gide's writing about masturbation is also central to this project. Autoeroticism plays a role in keeping Gide out of oedipal *triads* and in maternal *dyads*. Melanie Klein has commented on the dubious "auto" in "autoeroticism":

> For many years I have held the view that auto-erotism and narcissism are in the young infant contemporaneous with the first relation to objects—external and internalized. I shall briefly restate my hypothesis: auto-erotism and narcissism include the love for and relation with the internalized good object which in phantasy forms part of the loved body and self. It is to this internalized object that in auto-erotic gratification and narcissistic *states* a withdrawal takes place. . . . This hypothesis contradicts Freud's concept of auto-erotic and narcissistic *stages* which preclude an object-relation. ("The Origins of Transference," 51)

Masturbation itself, then, could play a role in slowly forming patterns of sexual allegiance and resistances. It would be no surprise that masturbation troubled Gide throughout his childhood and even his adult life. *Si le grain ne meurt* recounts the capital masturbatory scene of his childhood, and in the recounting we can easily observe the way Gide links his troubles to oral gratification, to what some might construe as a regression to an oral stage of sexuality. But we might also see not a *regression* but an effort to refuse a certain narrative of *progress* that fails to encompass enough of the elements of Gide's sexuality. Thus, Gide might be seen as resisting a totalizing oedipal insertion—even as the details of the scene itself (and its other participants) try to force an oedipal reading on him. Finally, of great interest is the way his resistance to that oedipal reading inserts Gide into a certain position as regards larger politicocultural fantasies and the way his efforts at a retention of his dyadic relationship to his mother can thereby be cast on to a larger historical stage.

Gide was nine years old and attending the Ecole Alsacienne when the following event took place:

> My parents had had a dinner-party the evening before; I had stuffed my pockets with the sweetmeats that had been left over from dessert, and that morning, while Monsieur Vedel was exerting himself at his desk, I sat on my bench, enjoying alternately my pleasure and my chocolates.
>   Suddenly I heard myself summoned.
>   "Gide! You look very red! Come here and speak to me a minute." (56)[7]

As if to confirm Klein's theory that autoerotic behavior is linked to internalized good objects, Gide incorporates pralines within his masturbatory practice. Now

---

7. Mes parents avaient donné la veille un dîner; j'avais bourré mes poches des friandises du dessert; et, ce matin-là, sur mon banc, tandis que s'évertuait M. Vedel, je faisais alterner le plaisir avec les pralines.

Tout à coup, je m'entendis interpeller:

— Gide! Il me semble que vous êtes bien rouge? Venez donc me dire deux mots (65).

surely being caught by a teacher red-faced and red-handed would be a perfect time for some sort of castration anxiety to set in. Gide seems to be about to describe the moment of an oedipal interpellation. Castration anxiety theoretically involves a relation to the father, an acquiescence to his authority out of anxiety as to one's own bodily coherence. Klein points out that the needed anxiety would be available from the previous relation to the mother, from previous struggles to comprehend one's own body. Fears as to a father's punitive potential rely on fears about the mother.

> There are good grounds for assuming that as soon as genital sensations are experienced, castration fear is activated. . . . In my view this fear is first of all experienced under the dominance of oral libido. The boy's oral-sadistic impulses towards his mother's breast are transferred to his father's penis. . . . This arouses his fear that his own genital will be bitten off by his father in retaliation. ("The Oedipus Complex," 382)

Castration anxiety would thus rehearse during the infant's genital phase the same scenario played out by the child with respect to the mother's breast during the oral phrase.

Gide resists writing any such rehearsal, resists a straightforward transferring of pride of place in his internal world from his mother to his father, from autoeroticism to fear of castration. One might say that he is resisting a narrative, insisting on multiple paths. Whatever step back Klein has added to the traditional Freudian progress toward adult sexuality, her construals of patterns of gender identification seem to remain based on traditional forms of narrative progress, thereby having little queer about them. Thus, Gide may find useful the elaboration of a preoedipal space in which to work out maternal allegiances, without finding it necessary or desirable to accept any fixed *narrative* relation between oedipal and preoedipal moments.

Reported to his chagrined parents, expelled from school, Gide finds himself taken to the doctor:

> My parents' doctor at that time was no less a person than Dr. Brouardel, who shortly after became celebrated as an expert in medical jurisprudence. . . .
> "I know all about it, my boy," he said, putting on a gruff voice, "and there's no need to examine or question you. But if your mother finds it necessary to bring you here again, that is, if you don't learn to behave, well then" (and his voice became truly terrible), "well then, *these* are the instruments we should have to use—the instruments with which little boys like you are operated on!" And he rolled his eyes at me ferociously as he pointed out a panoply of Tuareg spearheads hanging on the wall behind his chair.
> This threat was really too obvious for me to take it seriously. But my mother's apparent anxiety, and her admonishments, and then my father's silent distress, all at last penetrated my torpor. . . . (57)[8]

8. Le médecin de mes parents, dans ce temps, n'était autre que le docteur Brouardel, qui bientôt devait acquérir une grande autorité comme médecin légiste . . .
— Je sais ce dont il s'agit, dit-il en grossissant la voix, et n'ai besoin, mon petit, ni de t'examiner ni de

Gide's abrupt and anticlimactic refusal to be affected by the threat of castration, presented in such detail, his insistence on worrying mostly about his mother, his careful placement of his father's distress second to his mother's, these maneuvers are perhaps as suspiciously obvious as the doctor's threats. As Gide perches on the threshold of the new oedipal realm, and hears the call to enter, he seems already knowledgeable enough, prescient enough, to comprehend the call, and sure enough of himself to close his ears, avert his gaze, turn his back—as if preparing always to remain within earshot of both realms, as if to be a denizen of both simultaneously.

Tuareg Spears

One odd detail from this scene in Brouardel's office seems to demand particular scrutiny: the "panoplie de lances touareg." What precisely would a display of Tuareg spears be doing on the walls of a doctor who caters to respectable Parisian clients? What cultural fantasies would make the doctor think of using them as a threat? Could the young Gide in 1878 (the year he was caught playing with himself in the classroom), himself label these spears as coming from the Tuareg, or is that later information helpfully—even creatively—added by the older narrator?

From 1881 onward the Tuareg of the Sahara would occupy a major place in the popular French imagination. In 1881 some of the Tuareg killed most of the members of a French expedition into their lands, an expedition led by a soldier named Flatters. The deaths, the efforts of the survivors to flee, the cannibalism they resorted to as they tried to return on foot across the Sahara, were all reported in detail in the French press. Flatters had set out from Algeria on a mapping mission, as part of a growing French effort to plan a route for and then to build the Trans-Saharan Railway that was to link Algeria by rail with French interests in West Africa. The Tuareg resisted ruthlessly French advances into their territory. In 1894 French troops, arriving from the west, defeated the Tuareg at Timbuctoo. In 1898–99 the Foureau-Lamy Saharan Mission set out from Algeria and this time marched forcefully and successfully through the Tuareg territory. Thus, from the early 1880s onward, a display of Tuareg spears would count as a trophy of war, wrested from a resilient enemy of France in Africa, an enemy difficult to reach, and consistently portrayed in the press and other accounts as the pinnacle of barbarism and deceitfulness.[9] In 1878, when the young Gide was threatened in Brouardel's

---

t'interroger aujourd'hui. Mais si ta mère d'ici quelque temps, voyait qu'il est nécessaire de te ramener, c'est-à-dire si tu ne t'étais pas corrigé, eh bien (et ici sa voix se faisait terrible) voici les instruments auxquels il nous faudrait recourir, ceux avec lesquels on opère les petits garçons dans ton cas! — Et sans me quitter des yeux, qu'il roulait sous ses sourcils froncés, il indiquait, à bout de bras, derrière son fauteuil, une panoplie de lances touareg.

L'invention était trop apparente pour que je prisse cette menace au sérieux. Mais le souci que je voyais qu'avait ma mère, mais ses objurgations, mais le chagrin silencieux de mon père, pénétrèrent enfin ma torpeur (66–67).

9. See, for example, William H. Schneider, *An Empire for the Masses*, esp. 113–24. For an account of the Flatters Mission from the period, see Fr. Desplantes, *Les Explorateurs français du continent noir*, 200–26.

office, such a display would perhaps be more mysterious, a bizarre bit of exotic paraphernalia, as only a few Frenchmen had then ever even encountered the Tuareg.

What, then, would be going on in the doctor's imagination, as he threatens the child with these African spears? What kind of emblems are the spears in Gide's imagination? What would it mean to threaten a young boy with castration by means of weapons from those people who would prove themselves for a short while so successful at resisting and killing Frenchmen? When Gide as a young man first goes to Algeria in 1893, Frenchmen venturing south from Algeria into Tuareg territory are still being killed. Even in 1903–4, when Gide writes the section of *Amyntas* (one of his early texts about North Africa) entitled "Le Renoncement au voyage," he tells of hearing an Arab from Touggourt speak of the Tuareg:

> He also said: "Out there, the Tuaregs know a country, in the mountains, big, so big, that you can walk straight ahead for ten days; to get there, only one way leads in, and only one man at a time can take it. After all the men have gone in there, the last one rolls a big stone over the way . . . a stone big as this table here, and then no one can see where the road goes. That is why they're not afraid of the French.—A Tuareg told me this in In-Salah." (132)[10]

The Tuareg spears seem to make a proliferation of fantasies possible. For the doctor they would be ideally suited for emasculation—they will prove or have proven their success at emasculating French colonial ambitions and thus represent the need for strong-willed Frenchmen willing to put their names to new territories. Autoeroticism will not do in the training of such men. Simultaneously, within Brouardel's Parisian office, such trophies are the perfect emblem of the extent to which Frenchmen are conquering the globe, signs of the expanding empire. But for Gide, the spears might come to carry the aura of relics from a Shangri-La, a place that could shut French out, an absolute non-France, where the authority of a Brouardel would make no sense and where the bourgeois sexual imbroglios of Parisian families such as his would be inconsequential, a place of perfect escape.

Gide's description of himself trying to avoid insertion into an oedipal structure thus contains, and will continue to contain throughout his life, a hint of an effort to escape from an oedipal *place* as well. The encounter with the Tuareg spears *on the walls of a Parisian doctor's office* of course reveals the extent to which it should have been impossible for someone like Gide to imagine in sustained fashion any absolute separation between such fantasmatically overburdened places. What I would like to examine here is the extent to which Gide can continue (as he becomes more and more aware of the sexual and political economy in which he lives) to conceive of his autoeroticism and of his relation to his mother as resistant

10. Il dit encore : — Là-bas, les Touaregs, ils connaissent un pays, dans la montagne, grand, grand, qu'on peut y marcher droit devant soi pendant dix jours; pour y entrer, il n'y a qu'un chemin, qu'un seul homme à la fois peut y passer. Après que tous sont rentrés là, le dernier roule sur le chemin une pierre . . . tiens, comme cette table-là; et plus personne ne peut voir la route. C'est pour ça qu'ils n'ont pas peur des Français. — Un Touareg m'a dit cela à In-Salah (186).

to oedipalizing narratives, the extent to which he can perpetuate the idealization of the mother–child bond as a way of resisting responding to the oedipal call of someone like Brouardel. I would also like to examine how his relation to colonial spaces will figure in this effort. Perhaps one way of characterizing what Gide is up to is to imagine him refusing exclusive oedipalization by imagining a space that endures *in spite of* oedipal impositions, refusing the assumption that we live our sexual lives within one and only one forward-moving temporal current, and looking for a place in which different currents might retain an integrity some would deny them.

Juliette and Anna

Gide's battle with Brouardel, then, is one skirmish in a larger battle against a normative univocity of fantasy. Gide cultivates the proliferating possibilities of fantasy, writes so as to make them obvious, highlights the struggle, even as he becomes more and more conscious of his own place in the social circles he shares with Brouardel, to resist the insistent call to normalize his fantasies. His struggle to go on imagining his mother within this split fantasmatic scene forms a major part of that larger struggle.

　　Gide's task will be made all the more difficult on the many occasions when his mother refuses to participate in his games, trying to ensure that the paternal function be given voice through her. As she writes to her son on March 18, 1895:

> Ah yes! your father would have known what [in you] was legitimate personality, true individuality, and what, being merely suckers growing off the main plant, would threaten to absorb the sap to no profitable end. And I assure you, your father would have been an expert gardener, and strict about cutting off the suckers. Further, given that your father would have wanted you to have a career to *ensure your independence* until your writings could give it to you, all this would have done you the immense favor of forcing you to discipline your nerves and your flights of fancy, to sober your imaginings, keeping them as dreams instead of trying to live them. Because, my poor child, I am asking myself this question: at the rate you are going, *what will you use* to put the chicken in the pot, since one cannot live off of the wind? (*Correspondance*, 644)[11]

Gide's nerves and his fantasy, his narcissism, his effeminacy and his lack of discipline, his lack of a sense of responsibility to his family name and to his money, all these things his *mother* will have to call to his attention. After his father's early death, Gide's mother feels obliged to take up the paternal pruning shears, to echo

---

11. Ah! oui, ton père aurait su ce qui était personnalité légitime, individualité propre, et ce qui, n'étant que gourmands, menaçait d'absorber le sève sans profit, et je te réponds qu'il eût été un jardinier expert et ferme pour enlever les gourmands. Puis, comme ton père aurait voulu que tu eusses une carrière pour *assurer ton indépendance* jusqu'à ce que tes œuvres te la donnassent, cela t'aurait rendu l'immense service de te forcer à discipliner tes nerfs et ta fantaisie, et d'assagir tes imaginations en les laissant à l'état de *rêves* sans vouloir *les vivre*. Car, mon pauvre enfant, je me pose cette question : au train dont tu vas, *avec quoi* mettras-tu la poule au pot, car l'on ne vit pas de l'air du temps?

and re-echo Brouardel's warning. How else will Gide ever be shaped into a responsible husband and father, how else will he perpetuate the Gide *foyer?*

As the letter just cited suggests, Gide's mother's relationship to *money* will be one of Gide's major problems, as will be her own sexuality, as he paints for us his continuing efforts to resist the oedipal solicitation. All of these problems come together in Gide's most extravagant confrontation with his mother, during which she wrote him that letter. The confrontation is provoked by Gide's fantastic efforts to alter the configuration of his mother's Parisian household, as if to explode the oedipal place by bringing the outside in, by bringing home his young servant from Biskra, Athman. Before arriving at that confrontation, I would like to spend some time examining how Gide writes of his growing consciousness of the relationship of women such as his mother to money and to sex.

Gide's mother would never have had any serious financial worries, but the same cannot be said for her friend Anna Shackleton. Though only nine years older than Juliette Gide, Shackleton first met Juliette when she was hired to be her tutor. Shackleton was never to marry, and it appears that Juliette Rondeaux was hesitant to marry ahead of her governess and friend. Jean Delay rather ruthlessly paints the situation this way: "If, in the social world, Juliette seemed to want to be self-effacing, as if better to show off Anna's natural ease, doubtless this was due to her sense of delicacy, but perhaps also because, next to this prettier, more talented and more cultivated young woman, this young woman unquestionably more seductive than she, Juliette experienced vividly that sense of inferiority that played so large a part in her psychology" (Delay, 1:52). In *Si le grain ne meurt,* Gide gives way to rhapsody in describing Shackleton, a maternal figure who never married: "Anna Shackleton! Once more I see your calm face and pure brow, the slight severity of your mouth, your smiling eyes that showered such loving-kindness on my child-hood. I wish I could invent fresh words in which to speak of you—more vivid, more respectful, more tender words" (25/28–29). Yet, even toward this seemingly perfectly unambivalent maternal figure the young Gide apparently entertained ambivalent and guilty aggressive feelings. At the end of the first chapter of *Si le grain ne meurt,* he wishes that he could think of "one gracious act, one look or word of childish affection" (31/36), as testimony to his devotion to her. Instead, he can only remember an embarrassing remark he made to her as a young child invited to lunch one day:

> As I was eating that morning with an excellent appetite and it was clear that Anna, with her small means, had done her best:
> "Oh, Nana!" I cried, "I shall eat you out of house and home!" (the words are still ringing in my ears). . . . At any rate, I had no sooner pronounced them than I felt that no one of any delicacy of heart could have said such a thing, that Anna was hurt by them, that I had a little wounded her. (32)[12]

12. Comme je mangeais ce matin-là de fort bon appétit et qu'Anna, avec ses modiques ressources, avait visiblement fait de son mieux :

Aggression in relationship to maternal figures is a well-known constant across Gide's writings, and as he writes of its occurences during his childhood, he is careful to indicate its way of fitting into his growing awareness of social networks and his way of drawing on his growing social awareness in producing his aggressive moments. Thus, as he writes, casting an eye backward, he claims certain encounters as worthy of being woven into his web of oedipal evasions, even as he shows the potential of those encounters to serve oedipal ends. His attitude toward Anna would be a case in point.

Predictably, the line of attack that the young Gide follows in his perverse effort to subvert his own idealization of Anna relies on the weak position of "independent" women within the prevailing economy. Anna Shackleton may be more cultivated, more talented, more seductive than Juliette Gide. Nonetheless, her failure to marry, for whatever reason, means that her talents do not turn a profit and her economic resources remain "modiques." The young Gide learns this point of weakness early on and uses it to bite the hand that feeds him, so to speak. Certain similarities with the scene where he bites his cousin should not, I think, be ignored. By juxtaposing another woman with his mother, Gide creates a wider field over which to distribute his feelings of tenderness or aggression, a wider field in which to assign attributes such as purity or desire. Such distributions and assignations form a pattern of essays, efforts to find the proper field for a sexuality that is itself continually inchoate.

Gide chastises himself in *Si le grain ne meurt* for his cruelty to Anna, upset that he has not paid enough respect to her purity. Could we read this purity, this spinsterly "independence" as an interesting refusal on Anna's part of certain social forms, a refusal Gide might learn to respect? And could the cruelty of the young Gide reside precisely in his ability to mouth a social condemnation he has learned elsewhere? From his mother, for instance, so intimidated in her allegiance to the bourgeois social realm? This possibility is clearly raised in a scene Gide describes in "Ma mère," where *Juliette's* aggressive impulses toward Anna are emphasized.

"Everything that was natural in my mother I loved," declares Gide in that text. "But it happened that her impulses were checked by convention and the bent that a bourgeois education too often leaves behind it." In this particular case, the trait that her bourgeois education had inculcated in Juliette Gide, the trait that prevented her from being herself, was parsimony:

> My mother announced to me her intention of giving Anna, our poor friend, whom I loved filially, a Littré dictionary as a present. I was bursting with joy, when she added:
> "The one I gave your father is bound in morocco. But I thought that for Anna shagreen would do."

— Mais Nana, je vais te ruiner! m'écriai-je (la phrase sonne encore à mon oreille) . . . Du moins sentis-je, aussitôt ces mots prononcés, qu'ils n'étaient pas de ceux qu'un cœur un peu délicat pouvait inventer, qu'Anna s'en affectait, que je l'avais un peu blessée (36).

I immediately figured out that shagreen was much less expensive than morocco, something I hadn't known before. My heart became suddenly joyless. My mother must have perceived this, since she quickly added:

"She won't notice the difference." ("Ma mère," 35)[13]

The contrasting expense of the bindings apparently marks the importance Gide's mother was trying to give to conjugal relations over ones between women friends. Perhaps it marks a bit of continuing unease in her relationship to her old companion. It marks, in a painfully clear way, Juliette Gide's awareness of social status. What troubles André Gide is the anger he feels against his mother and the rationale he feels compelled to provide for the anger. In his mother's parsimony, this trait that he insists is not natural to her, he sees a reflection of himself:

Why did those few sentences of my mother's engrave themselves so deeply in my heart? Perhaps because, despite the violent reprobation they woke within me, I felt so eminently capable of thinking and saying them myself. Perhaps because at that moment I became conscious of that bent I would have to struggle against, and I was sadly astonished at finding it in my mother. (36)[14]

He finds in his mother not just parsimony, we should insist, but also a subtle lack of tolerance for those who remain (by choice?) socially marginal. For the more or less unspoken insult and condescension toward Anna are indeed the expression of a certain reprobation.

Reprobation and sympathy or desire can, of course, coexist—indeed, often coexist—producing in the swirl of their discordance various kinds of phobia. Jacques Lacan, for example, commenting on a somewhat concealed current of lesbianism in the relationship between these two women (a relationship so close that Juliette would, against her family's wishes, willingly put off marriage for so long), writes of

this young woman as much discouraging to suitors as lacking in graces, who filled the space left by a marriage late in coming with a passion for her governess, whose letters Jean Delay impassively allows to speak: jealousy and despotism, perhaps not obviously exhibited, should nonetheless not be ruled out, nor should the embraces of a joyful innocence, however much a routine part of maiden existence they may have been. Surely, beyond all these unarguable manifestations, we must imagine for this attachment another kind of depth in order to explain its resistance—to the point of

13. Ma mère m'annonça son intention de faire cadeau d'un Littré à Anna Shackleton, notre amie pauvre, que j'aimais comme filialement. Je laissais éclater ma joie, lorsqu'elle ajouta:

— Celui que j'ai donné à ton père est relié en maroquin. J'ai pensé que, pour Anna, une reliure en chagrin suffirait.

Je compris aussitôt, ce que je ne savais pas encore, que le chagrin coûtait beaucoup moins cher. La joie s'en alla soudain de mon coeur. Et sans doute ma mère s'en aperçut-elle, car elle reprit bien vite :

— Elle ne verra pas la différence (1100–1101).

14. Pourquoi ces quelques phrases de ma mère se gravèrent-elles si profondément en mon cœur? C'est peut-être que je me sentais capable de les penser et dire moi-même, en dépit de la réprobation violente qu'elles soulevèrent en moi. C'est peut-être que je pris alors conscience de ce pli contre lequel j'aurais à lutter, et que je m'étonnais tristement de découvrir en ma mère (1011).

waging a successful rebellion—to the prejudices of those in its entourage who objected to the attachment on the grounds of rank. (Lacan, "Jeunesse de Gide," 749)[15]

By the time of the Littré episode, such rebelliousness had mostly disappeared, although it is tempting to imagine André Gide as revivifying this part of his mother's inheritance in his own rebellions. Gide never gives any strong hints about any speculations he may have had about his mother's feelings for Anna, but it is clear that he senses—if only through the odd form of his mother's hostility—the complexity of their relationship and senses in that relationship a potential form of desire outside normative expectations, a desire to which he might pay some antioedipal allegiance. Such allegiances are acknowledged more fully in another scene from *Si le grain ne meurt*, where Gide almost admits of some form of sexual expression in his mother.

Juliette and Marie/Anna

In his article "Jeunesse de Gide," Lacan compares the rapport between Anna Shackleton and Juliette Rondeaux to that between two servants in the Gide household, the faithful Marie (whose name, Delay informs us, was really *Anna* Leuenberger, but who was called Marie to avoid "une confusion de prénom" with Anna Shackleton [Delay, 1:84]) and Delphine, the cook. Lacan plays up the class differences between the two pairs of women by saying that the expressions of attachment between the two servants are "like, in Marivaux, the games of the maidservants alongside the pathos of the loftiest characters" (749). Gide writes such comedy as he describes the night he overhears the sounds of the two servants' sorrowful leavetaking.

Now Gide's mother, he insists, would not have appreciated overhearing what he overheard:

> My mother, who was disposed to think she had a moral responsibility for the people she took an interest in, would never have tolerated an intrigue that was not to be eventually consecrated by the ties of Hymen. This was no doubt why I never knew Marie with any other passion than the one which I accidentally discovered she had for Delphine, our cook, and which my mother would certainly never have dared to suspect. . . . Some obscure instinct kept me from speaking of this to my mother. (49–50)[16]

15. cette jeune fille aussi peu avenante aux prétendants qu'aux grâces, et qui, des noces tard à venir, comble le vide par une passion pour sa gouvernante, dont Jean Delay fait impassiblement parler les lettres: jalousies, despotisme n'y sont pas à reléguer, pour n'être pas affichés, ni les étreintes d'une joie innocente, pour ancrées qu'elles soient dans des routines de vestales. Assurément, faut-il bien concevoir, par delà ces manifestations inattaquables, une autre profondeur à cet attachement pour qu'il résiste, d'une rébellion à les vaincre, aux préjugés de l'entourage qui y objecte au nom du rang.

16. Ma mère, qui se croyait volontiers une responsabilité morale sur ceux à qui elle s'intéressait, n'aurait souffert aucune intrigue qu'un hymen ne vînt consacrer. C'est sans doute pourquoi je n'ai jamais connu à Marie d'autre passion que celle que je surpris pour Delphine, notre cuisinière, et que ma mère, certes, n'eût jamais osé soupçonner . . . je ne sais quel obscur instinct me retint d'en parler à ma mère (58).

Gide discovers this passion that his mother would never *dare* suspect on the night Delphine is leaving the Gides' service to get married. He is able to discover the passion because as a child, his room is closer to the servants' quarters than is anyone else's. The queer noises the two women make wake him up:

> The noises . . . were more peculiar and mysterious than alarming—like a kind of dirge for two voices, which I can compare now-a-days to the *keening* of Arab women, but which seemed to me then like nothing on earth: a melancholy chant, interrupted spasmodically by sobs and cluckings and cries; I listened for a long time, sitting up in the dark and feeling in some inexplicable fashion that this was the expression of something more powerful than decency or sleep or the darkness of the night. (50).[17]

In the phrase "plus puisssant que la décence" and in the comparison of the noises the women are making to those of "des pleureuses arabes," in his subsequent condescension about the "uncontrolled behaviour of servants in general" (59/50–51), in his precise description of an arrangement of an apartment such that the child's bedroom is separate from the rest of the apartment and therefore closer to the servants' quarters, we can once again observe Gide marking the boundaries of bourgeois sexuality in a sufficiently precise way so as to create a space outside to which he has access.[18] He sees his mother as policing those boundaries, even as she cannot but fail to observe them in her own case.

When Gide does portray his mother engaged in some form of sexual expression, it is in large part unconscious, linked to a female servant, linked to aggression, and decidedly queer. It is a scene that happens every morning, when Marie spends half an hour brushing Madame Gide's hair:

> My mother sat with the *Temps* newspaper in her hand, alternately reading three lines and looking at herself in the glass, in which she could see the top of her head and Marie's hand brandishing the brush or comb; whatever Marie did, she did it as if in a fury.
>
> "Oh, Marie! You're hurting me," my mother would moan. . . .
>
> I raised my eyes now and then to look at my mother's handsome profile; her features were naturally grave and gentle, but on such occasions a little hardened by the dead white of her dressing gown and by her resistance to Marie tugging her hair back.
>
> "Marie, you don't brush, you bang!"
>
> Marie stopped a moment and then started again with renewed vigour. Then mamma would let the paper slip off her knees and fold her hands in a way she had to mark her resignation. . . .

17. Les bruits . . . étaient bien plus bizarres et mystérieux qu'effrayants. On eût dit une sorte de lamentation à deux voix, que je peux comparer aujourd'hui à celle des pleureuses arabes, mais qui, dans ce temps, ne me parut pareille à rien; une mélopée pathétique, coupée spasmodiquement de sanglots, de gloussements, d'élans, que longtemps j'écoutai, à demi dressé dans le noir. Je sentais inexplicablement que quelque chose s'exprimait là, de plus puissant que la décence, que le sommeil et que la nuit . . . (58–9).

18. In *The History of Sexuality*, vol. 1 Foucault writes of "the attention focused on infantile sexuality, the supposed dangers of masturbation, the importance attached to puberty, the methods of surveillance suggested to parents, the exhortations, secrets, and fears, the presence—both valued and feared—of servants: all this made the family, even when brought down to its smallest dimensions, a complicated network, saturated with multiple, fragmentary, and mobile sexualities" (46).

"Madame had better do her hair herself; then she won't complain." (128–29)[19]

The repetitive nature of the scene, its ritualistic elements, the rhythmic nature of the action involved and the contractions the young boy sees in his mother's face, her moaning, her submission to her servant, all of these mark this scene as one where a sexual imagination is at work. As Marie continues to do her best to make Gide's mother beautiful, Gide's imagination performs a rather startlingly shameless displacement downward:

> But mamma's hairdressing needed some little artifice and she would have had great difficulty in doing without Marie's assistance. Her hair was parted in the middle and smoothly brushed down on either side of her face, below a low crown of plaits, and it was only with the help of certain extraneous adjuncts that it could be made to puff out becomingly above her temples. In those days such things were stuffed into all sorts of places; it was the hideous period of "bustles." (129)[20]

Of course, one can notice the fascination with the artifice going into his mother's appearance and the assertion that Marie is better at supplying the artifice than Juliette Gide would be on her own. One also notices the strange and strangely detailed sentence describing the *coiffure* itself. But what most startles is Gide's own sudden turn into the "tournures," the bustles of the period, as if thinking of the props Marie adds to his mother's hairdo to make it fall gracefully naturally draws his imagination down to a woman's buttocks, and to the devices one would insert into dresses in order to transform that region, to make it, in Gide's words, "hideous." The sudden phobic appearance of that word confirms the uncomfortable nature of the sexuality of this scene, a problematic relationship to genitality and anality, a precarious lack of ease on the borders of the oedipal. There is a sense in this scene, but not an assured one, that female–female sexual expression could serve as a model for the writing of Gide's own sexuality. There is an equal fear that a full acknowledgment of that sexual expression would compromise the limits of the sexuality Gide was striving to inhabit and to express.

---

19. Ma mère, alternativement, lisait trois lignes du *Temps* de la veille au soir, qu'elle tenait en main, puis regardait dans le miroir. Elle y voyait le dessus de sa tête et la main de Marie armée du peigne ou de la brosse, qui sévissait; quoi que fît Marie, c'était avec l'apparence de la fureur.

— Oh! Marie, que vous me faites mal! geignait maman.

. . . Je levais un instant les yeux vers le beau profil de ma mère; ses traits étaient naturellement graves et doux, un peu durcis occasionnellement par la blancheur crue du peignoir et par la résistance qu'elle opposait, quand Marie lui tirait les cheveux en arrière.

— Marie, vous ne brossez pas, vous tapez!

Marie s'arrêtait un instant; puis repartait de plus belle. Maman laissait alors glisser de dessus ses genoux le journal et mettait ses mains l'une dans l'autre en signe de résignation . . .

— Madame ferait bien mieux de se coiffer elle-même; comme ça elle ne se plaindrait plus (154–55).

20. Mais la coiffure de maman comportait un peu d'artifice et se fût malaisément passé de l'assistance de Marie. Séparés par le milieu, de dessous un couronnement de tresses formant chignon plat, deux bandeaux lisses, au dessus des tempes ne bombaient de manière séante qu'à l'aide de quelques adjonctions. En ce temps on en fourrait partout : c'était l'époque hideuse des « tournures » (155).

Sex and Money—Athman and North Africa

Our understanding of the subtle conflicts underpinning Gide's description of his mother's sexuality can now help us to comprehend Gide's own somewhat futile effort to express his sexuality to his mother by concocting a plan to bring home with him to Paris *his* servant Athman, from Biskra.[21] The context necessary to understand this plan includes Gide's own bafflement as to his mother's role in enforcing social normativity even as he imagines both her sexuality and his relationship to her as somehow circumventing aspects of bourgeois sociality; it includes issues of class and money in sexuality and a seeming belief that an escape from Europe or a transgression of class boundaries might enable an escape into a new sexual economy or keep such an economy alive even as social forces seem to work to assign it to oblivion.

Before turning to Gide and Athman, let me quickly sketch a few more scenes to complete the context, scenes in which class, money, and non-European sexual economies assume increasingly obvious importance. When Gide was 15, he tells us, his ever-vigilant mother noticed an article in *Le Temps* that indicated that a certain passage du Havre, a street near the Lycée Condorcet, was a place frequented by prostitutes. One of Gide's companions at the time, named Bernard Tissaudier, happened to attend the Lycée Condorcet. Gide's mother, spreading her concern even to her son's friends, queries: "I hope at least that your friend Tissaudier doesn't use the passage Du Havre as he leaves school? . . . You should tell him to avoid it." Thereby passing the maternal mantel to Gide, she nonetheless withholds the actual details about the situation in the street in question, telling her son only that it is "frequented by a bad crowd." Gide's imagination, he tells us, did not quite know what to do with this information: "I had a vision of poor Tissaudier being orgiastically torn to pieces by hetaerae." The extravagance of the imagination finds itself matched by the queer histrionics of the moment when young Gide begs his friend not to take that way home from school:

> Shaken by sobs, I flung myself down before my schoolfellow.
> "Bernard!" I cried; "oh, I implore you, don't go that way."
> My voice, my vehemence, my tears were those of a madman. . . . But Bernard, who had been brought up in a Puritan family like myself, did not for a moment misunderstand the nature of my emotion.
> "Do you suppose then," he said very naturally and in the tone of voice best fitted to calm me, "that I don't know all about the profession?" (159–60)[22]

21. The relationship between Marie and her mistress will be much in Gide's mind as he concocts this plan (opposed by both his mother and Marie) to bring Athman, his own domestic, back to his mother's apartment. It will hardly be accidental that the reason he will give in *Si le grain ne meurt* for giving up his plan is "a distracted letter from our old Marie . . . She swore she would leave the house on the day my "negro" came into it. What would become of mamma without Marie? I gave in; I had to" (294/354).

22. Tout secoué de sanglots, me précipitant aux genoux de mon camarade :
    — Bernard! Oh! je t'en supplie : n'y va pas.

Gide is here having a lesson in economics. But as in the scene concerning the Littré, in which Gide realizes what he claims never to have known—that shagreen is cheaper than moroccan—so here it seems that knowledge of economic relations is to be not so much learned as brought from the unconscious into the conscious part of his mind. As soon as Bernard says "métier," Gide becomes conscious of the fact that women are paid by men for sex:

> The word *profession* sounded painfully in my ears; it introduced a practical and vulgar element into what I had hitherto only seen as a dramatic mixture of the hideous and the poetical; *I really believe* it had never occurred to me that the question of money had anything to do with debauchery, or that pleasure could be financed; *or perhaps* (for all the same, I had read a certain amount and don't want to make myself out more of a simpleton than I was) it was seeing someone younger and, so to say, tenderer than myself, aware of it, that upset me so. (161; final two emphases added)[23]

With the contrast between his "I really believe" and his "or perhaps" Gide intentionally confuses himself and us as to what he could have known, could have absorbed from his readings, about the status of prostitutes in Paris. He seems to find a way to play the parent's and the child's role almost simultaneously, on the one hand shocked to find that a young boy such as Bernard could be so well informed about the world even as on the other he remains the young boy who is surprised to find out what he seems always to have known: that sexual relations between men and women are often (if not always) economic relations as well. Knowing the future, he liminally cultivates an ignorance of it, an ignorance that depends for its forcefulness on an intentional stepping back from the knowledge. "The word *profession* ["métier"] that Tissaudier had used resonated in my memory," says Gide a few pages later, when he describes himself walking past a group of prostitutes on the street in Paris.

"Métier" will come up again in the second half of *Si le grain ne meurt* as Gide tries to describe the sexual habits of the 'Uled-Nayl women he meets in Biskra. They are not really prostitutes, Gide will want to insist, even though they practice a "profession," even though he and his friend Paul Laurens pay them in order to have sex with them:

> A troop of women live [at Biskra] who make a trade of their bodies; the French government treats them, it is true, like the prostitutes of vulgar brothels; registration

---

L'accent de mes paroles, ma véhémence, mes larmes étaient d'un fou . . . Mais Bernard Tissaudier, d'éducation puritaine ainsi que moi, ne se méprit pas un instant sur la nature de mon angoisse; du ton le plus naturel et le plus propre à me calmer :

— Tu crois donc que je ne connais pas le métier? me dit-il (191–93).

23. Le mot « métier » sonnait péniblement à mon oreille, apportant une signification pratique et vulgaire où je n'avais vu jusqu'alors qu'un pathétique mélange de hideur et de poésie; *je crois bien que* je ne m'étais encore jamais avisé que la question d'argent entrât en rien dans la débauche, ni que la volupté se finançât; *ou peut-être* (car pourtant j'avais quelque lecture et ne voudrais pas me peindre par trop niais) était-ce de voir quelqu'un de plus jeune, et j'allais dire : de plus tendre que moi, le savoir, qui me désarçonnait ainsi (194, final two emphases added).

is enforced on them for purposes of supervision (thanks to which Dr. D. was able to give us the necessary information about each of them), but their manners and habits are different from those of ordinary licensed prostitutes. (252)[24]

In his book on the colonial postcard, postcards of Algerian women sent back to Europe by French tourists, Malek Alloula speaks of a "triple agency," a tripartite signifying system for such postcards: the most that they could *avow* explicitly was that they were part of an ethnographic exploration, photographs taken out of innocent scientific interest; they would leave *unsaid* their participation in a colonial ideology, a participation nonetheless perfectly obvious in the fact that they were taken in the colonial situation at the instigation of a colonial photographer; they would (in the name of scientific objectivity or photographic innocence) *repress* the fantasm about Algerian women the postcard was constructing for its Western audience (Alloula, 28). Gide's description of the 'Uled-Nayl participates in all three of these activities. He is ostensibly clarifying ethnographically for his French audience the "true" meaning of the exercise of a certain "métier" by these women:

> By an ancient tradition, the tribe of the 'Uled-Nayl exports its daughters every year when they are barely nubile, and a few years later they return with a dowry that enables them to purchase a husband, who accepts, without considering it dishonorable, what in our countries would cover him with ridicule or shame. The real 'Uled-Nayl have a great reputation for beauty, so that all the women who practise the profession in those parts call themselves by that name. (252)[25]

Gide moreover manages to make more than obvious what he does not say explicitly, that this ancient tradition has been somewhat changed by the advent of the French colonial administration. As Gide and his friend know the French doctor in town, and as the French administration treats these women as "real" prostitutes, the two young Frenchmen know more or less which ones they can sleep with without catching any unwanted diseases. The confluence of tribal tradition, the French colonial administration, and young, wealthy French tourists thus makes the act of naming these women and what they do rather complicated. This problem of naming is one of the main supports of the repressed fantasmatic content of this scene for a European who would like to be convinced that sex paid for with money in North Africa might be called something different than it would be called in Europe. Thus, the very name "Oulad Naïl" takes on an aura that any woman in North Africa can use in order to attract the curious European—and that any

24. Un troupeau de femmes y habite (à biskra), qui font commerce de leur corps; si le gouvernement français les assimile aux prostituées des vulgaires maisons de débauche, et les contraint, pour les pouvoir surveiller, de s'inscrire (grâce à quoi le docteur D. pouvait nous donner sur chacune d'elles tous les renseignements souhaités), leurs allures et leurs mœurs ne sont point celles des filles en carte (303).

25. Une antique tradition veut que la tribu des Oulad Naïl exporte, à peine nubiles, ses filles, qui, quelques années plus tard, reviennent au pays avec la dot qui leur permette d'acheter un époux. Celui-ci ne tient point pour déshonorant ce qui couvrirait un mari de chez nous ou de honte, ou de ridicule. Les Oulad Naïl authentiques ont une grande réputation de beauté; de sorte que se font appeler communément Oulad Naïl toutes les filles qui pratiquent là-bas ce métier (303-4).

European male can use to assuage any guilt he might feel for this act he is trying to rename.

Confused by the many economies (monetary and sexual) that haunt this description—the economy of the 'Uled-Nayl women and their tribe, the different economic relation of European men to European women, the economy of tourism in one's nation's colony—Gide may write partly as if he wished to believe he were somehow escaping the patriarchal sexual and economic structures he has been shunning. Colonialist ethnography and colonial tourism in a certain way use the same threshold structure as does Gide to keep the oedipal at bay. One steps back from one's knowledge of the colonial apparatus in order to participate in autochthonic rituals as if seized by a purity, a good faith that would perpetually postpone the knowledge being disowned.

There is necessarily, then, a certain, even a high, degree of failure in any attempt to escape from dominant ideology to a colonial space. If, in the hints of oppressed forms of female sexuality Gide encountered at home, he sensed some form of marginality to which he could pay allegiance, then certainly he could hope to find in North Africa other, differing forms of sexual expression on which he could draw to understand the resistances of his own sexuality. But the difficulty he finds himself in, a difficulty apparent in the writing of *Si le grain ne meurt,* is that he represents, to an extent he finds difficult to determine, the economic power that distorts and transforms the very culture he visits. To what extent does he participate in colonial fantasies, to what extent do his visits to North Africa aid him in establishing the grounds of his own resistance to and alienation from his own culture? The frustration of these questions leaves its mark on the writing of *Si le grain ne meurt.* As we will see in chapter 5, it is a frustration central to Gide's *Voyage au Congo* as well.

The fantasy in which Gide indulges, of an Africa to which a European can escape in order to find forms of sexuality that break the rigid boundaries of a bourgeois European *foyer,* was far from original with him. His mother, Juliette Gide, for instance, was familiar with it. In February 1894 she had traveled to Biskra to care for André, who was seriously ill. *Si le grain ne meurt* recounts how one morning she observed Mériem, one of the 'Uled-Nayl, leaving Paul Laurens' bedroom and how Gide insisted on telling her that Mériem visited him as well. One can thus easily imagine her chagrin a few months later, when her son, still recuperating, writes her from Switzerland to tell her that he is already planning his next trip to Biskra for January 1895. She responds:

> If only I could have the peace of mind of seeing you in an interior in accord with your heart and the time left to enjoy that, what a great joy, a great happiness, a great sweetness, it would be for me, dear child!
> Also, this morning, receiving your letter full to the brim of travel plans (Biskra, Ravenna, Brindisi) *I'm not enthused, I assure you;* it really made me lose heart to see that anxious, agitated, restless mood begin to seize hold of you again, to master you,

to make you lose touch with all feelings except this need for change, for novelty. As for returning to Biskra, at least for this year, *I would be most preoccupied* if I saw that happen; I can only repeat what I said to you already last year: I saw so well that that climate was not suitable for your nervous state. (*Correspondance,* 529)[26]

Gide *was,* in fact, trying to imagine an interior in which he could be happy but seemed unable to decide whether that interior would have to be in a non-European climate or whether, somehow, a European interior could be rearranged so as to accommodate the demands of his fantasmatic constructions. In any case, Gide was not to be swayed from his traveling plans and spent from late January to mid-April of 1895 in Algeria, a good deal of the time in Biskra. During that period he used some money he had inherited from his grandmother to buy a plot of land in Biskra; he also put together and then abandoned the plan to bring his servant Athman back to Paris with him. His correspondence with his mother during these months (almost the last of her life, in fact) is fast and furious. Juliette Gide reaches one of her most belligerent moments on April 15, 1895, writing to a son who, having finally been persuaded to give up his plans about Athman, is dawdling in Algiers, unwilling to return to Europe:

> So, the sea was in such a bad state that it kept you eight days longer in Algiers? Do you know that having once detected a smile both incredulous and full of innuendo, I no longer dared offer that reason for your delay? Do you know that all at once I feel a painful sadness in my heart? And in a flash I understood all the talk your land purchase in Biskra would give rise to! Really, suppose that it was Albert Saussine, Edouard Rondeaux, Pierre Louÿs or anyone else we know of that ilk who told us such a story, what would we think? And how often would we be right? And if it was the mother who told such a story, what would we think of her, letting herself be taken in by such baseness? (*Correspondence,* 656)[27]

The implication is clear. Men buy land in Africa in order to house women with whom they are illicitly involved. African women drain away French capital from French households. It may well be that they serve one French economic interest—bringing capital to the colonies—even as they disserve another—lessening the ability of a given household to sustain itself. Gide, for example, apparently sells off

---

26. Si je pouvais avoir le repos d'esprit de te voir un intérieur suivant ton cœur et le temps encore d'en jouir, ce serait une grande joie, un grand bonheur, une grande douceur pour moi, cher enfant!

Aussi, ce matin en recevant ta lettre toute pleine de projets de voyage (Biskra, Ravenne, Brindisi), j'en prends et *j'en laisse, je t'assure,* cela m'a assez démoralisée de voir cette humeur inquiète, agitée, remuante, recommencer à s'emparer de toi et à te maîtriser, et à te faire perdre tout sentiment des choses autres que ce besoin de changement, de nouveauté. Quant à retourner Biskra, cette année-ci du moins, je le verrais avec *la plus grande préoccupation;* je ne puis que te répéter ce que je t'ai dit déjà, l'année dernière : je voyais tellement bien que ce climat ne convenait pas à ton état nerveux.

27. Donc, l'état de mer a été assez mauvais pour te retenir huit jours à Alger? Sais-tu qu'ayant surpris un sourire incrédule et plein de sous-entendus, je n'osais plus donner ce motif de ton retard, et que j'en ai tout d'un coup une émotion douloureuse au cœur? Et en une seconde j'ai compris les commentaires qui accueilleraient ton acquisition à Biskra! Car enfin, mettons que ce soit Albert Saussine, Edouard Rondeaux, Pierre Louÿs ou telle autre de nos connaissances, qui nous raconte cela, qu'en penserons-nous? Et combien de fois sera-ce la vérité? Et si c'est la mère qui le dit, que penserons-nous d'elle, de se laisser prendre à d'aussi grossières histoires?

some of the bonds he has inherited from his grandmother to finance his purchase of land in Biskra. His mother, doing her best to hinder the purchase, to keep the foyer intact and in Europe, even tries to call in a few debts André owes her. In a letter listing how much he owes her, she reminds him:

> Since 1890 and the inheritance from your aunt Briançon, your expenditures have always exceeded your income by *several thousand* francs. . . . I wonder how you can afford to use up part of your income to pay for your land purchase . . . for which you will, without a doubt, be obliged to *sell* some of your investments and *deprive yourself of their income*. (*Correspondance*, 630)[28]

The danger, of course, is that if Gide spends too much of the principal of his fortune, he will cut down his revenue (having no "métier" of his own) and thereby lessen his chances of being able to afford to get married and run a household. Gide's mother would prefer Gide's bonds (obligations) to remain intact and in France—better he pay off a debt to his mother than that he become financially tied to Biskra. But Gide himself imagines buying this land as a way of setting up a different kind of household and even turning a profit. About the house he dreams of building in Biskra, Gide tells us, "My dream was to arrange the ground floor . . . as a Moorish café and make Athman the manager; in imagination, I had already invited all my friends. I did not mention this last scheme to my mother, the rest was quite enough already to make her think me mad" (293–94/354). The project of buying land in Algeria is thus linked as much or more to Gide's desire to live with Athman as it is to his passing fascination with the women of North Africa.[29] It is also a further effort to resist the call to adult behavior. With that call

28. Depuis 1890 et l'héritage de ta tante Briançon, ta dépense a *toujours* dépassé de *plusieurs milliers* de francs tes revenus . . . je me demande comment tu pourras prélever sur ton revenu de quoi payer ton acquisition . . . et pour laquelle tu vas sans aucun doute être obligé de *vendre* de tes titres et *te priver de leur revenu*.

⋮

See also her letter of June 16, 1894, for another example of her efforts as financial adviser to her prodigal son (402–4).

29. More details on Athman Ben Salah (Gide refers to him always as Athman) can be found in Guy Dugas, "André Gide et Athman: Le roman d'une amitié vraie." Dugas is careful to point out (as was Gide, apparently) that the relationship was a nonsexual friendship (Dugas 265, 266). But for a relationship to be relevant to a given sexuality or to constitute a resistance to a particular sexual economy, it is not necessary to "have sex." See also a letter by Alan Sheridan to the (London) *Times Literary Supplement* of March 5, 1993, where, defending Gide against an attack by Ernest Gellner, Sheridan leadenly writes, "Gide probably never had sex with Athman, his first Arab friend/guide/servant, yet he showed constant concern for him over many years." Gellner, in the *TLS* of February 19, 1993, reviews Edward Said's *Culture and Imperialism*, a book containing a brief and intelligent discussion of Gide, and somehow turns obsessively to an attack on Gide as a way of attacking Said: "No doubt it was easier to find attractive homosexual partners in Biskra than among the *haute bourgeoisie protestante*, but this does not mean that the Algerian oasis was a residue of ancient Mediterranean sensuous harmony, liberty and fulfillment. Said here fails to pursue his quarry as it deserves to be pursued, and misses out on how terribly wrong Gide was, how shamelessly he used Algeria for a projection based on his own need. Said fails to show up Gide fully because, like Gide, he also is more interested in his own theme than in the Algerians." The best that can be said of such thoughtless writing is that it indicates the extent to which Gide continues to function as a lightning-rod for certain phobic flashes.

Jonathan Dollimore, on the other hand, comments carefully in *Sexual Dissidence* on the complexity of Gide's relationship to Athman: "Epitomized in this struggle over Athman, and especially in Gide's correspondence with his mother, is a hesitant yet certain knowledge of how sexual discrimination relates inextricably to other kinds of discrimination. . . . Discrimination works through the asymmetry of subject positioning, and the plurality of hierarchies, as well as the brute fact of inequality institutionalized in hierarchy itself" (336–37). See also 342–43.

now being emitted so forcefully by his mother, Gide has to face the question, How could he ever invite her to Athman's cafe, a cafe set up in some ways, it has to be admitted, in her honor?

Gide's simultaneous decisions to bring Athman to Paris *and* to buy land in Biskra where he could build a house in which to keep Athman show him working at two solutions to the same problem: the establishment of an antioedipal space in the presence of a mother who seems, in the end, almost fully oedipalized. The letters to his mother during the Athman affair are surely the most ferociously aggressive ones in the correspondence. Even though Gide never tells his mother of his dreams of establishing Athman in his projected home in Biskra, he does try to force himself and Athman on her attention by imagining the changed living arrangements that will be necessitated in his mother's apartment by his return to Paris with his servant. He suggests that there is room for Athman with other servants on the top floor of the building. His mother insists she has no extra space, and, in any case: "this life on the top floor, this promiscuity of men and of women, can you see Athman in the middle of all that!" (*Correspondance*, 616). What would it mean for Gide to throw his young friend into the midst of Parisian promiscuity? Athman has, of course, already served as the go-between in many of the sexual encounters of Gide and his friends with both male and female North Africans, yet Gide and his mother both keep up the rhetoric of the need to protect Athman from bad influences, thus in a certain way making Athman himself the emblem of a threshold, the place of a denial: threshold and denial of an object choice that would spit out and yet retain loyalty to different versions of the feminine; a threshold opening onto a world of ostensibly pure and nonoedipal sexuality even as it defines itself over against the oedipal.

Athman is also an example of how the fantasmatic struggle in which Gide and his mother are engaged (a struggle about normalization, regression, and deviation) can make use of whatever material life presents. Certainly the specificities of the politics of homosexuality explicitly structure this scene, even as other aspects of Athman's cultural specificity fade in and out of focus—a fact Gide glancingly acknowledges in describing his failed farewell to the boy as he returns to his mother:

> When, on the third morning I looked for Athman to say good-bye to him, he was nowhere to be found and I had to leave without seeing him again. I could not understand his absence; but suddenly, as I sat in the speeding train, a long way already from El Kantara, I caught sight of his white burnous on the banks of the oued. He was sitting there with his head in his hands; he did not rise when the train passed; he made no movement; he did not give a glance at the signs I made him; and for a long time as the train was carrying me away, I watched his little motionless grief-stricken figure, lost in the desert, an image of my own despair. (296)[30]

---

30. Lorsque le troisième jour, au matin, je cherchai dans sa chambre Athman pour lui dire adieu, je ne le trouvai point et dus partir sans l'avoir revu. Je ne pouvais m'expliquer son absence; mais tout à coup, du train qui fuyait, très loin déjà d'El Kantara, j'aperçus au bord de l'oued son burnous blanc. Il était assis là, la tête dans les mains; il ne se

True, Gide registers his discomfort at Athman's silent refusal to acknowledge Gide's grief on leaving. Yet, it is the embarrassment of that last phrase (one that seemingly denies Athman even his own despair at being abandoned) to claim a reciprocity between the two figures we know to be illusory. (Gide claims he finally brought Athman to Paris four years later, doubtless four years too late.[31]) In the years following the publication of *Si le grain ne meurt* a longer trip to Africa began to take shape in Gide's mind. That later trip, too, would be haunted by the ghost of his mother (supplemented by the figure of his wife Madeleine, left behind in France). Yet, henceforth any haunting by a figure of the maternal would also be a haunting by Athman, also left behind, whose imaginary edifice—"Poor Athman! I had not the heart to bring down at one blow the imaginary edifice which every day some fresh hope had come to strengthen" (294/354–55)—was indeed torn down, just as his café was never built, all out of respect for the structure of a Parisian apartment. In the later *Voyage au Congo* (see chapter 5), it will be to these fantasmatic ruins, ruins in which no place was to be found for Athman, that Gide will return, ever hopeful of finding a new building from which to write home.[32]

"You will have to find room for Athman," Gide had written to his mother from Biskra,

> and not at a hotel, in our house. . . . I would like, no matter how ridiculous it seems to you, to have him sleep on the small iron bed in the guest room. And when Madeleine visits (as I hope she will) and stays in my room, only then will he go up to the servants' floor, where you know perfectly well that there's a room we are only using for storage—O terrible bad faith of Madame Gide!—unless, of course, we don't both sleep in the guest room, to which, personally, I would be completely indifferent. (*Correspondance*, 623)[33]

When his cousin, Madeleine, the woman he hopes to marry, comes to visit, she will sleep in his room. "Indifferent," he will at that moment move in with his servant in the guest room. His fiancée will be safely sleeping in his bed. Athman and Gide, together in the guest room, will both be safe from all dangerous Parisian promiscuity. His mother's response: "I will tell you straight out . . . that Athman will *never* sleep in the apartment, and there is no space on the sixth floor. Would you then want to create the spectacle of a widowed mother, with an only son who lives apart from her because of an Arab?" (*Correspondance*, 635). Gide's effort was

---

leva pas lorsque le train passa; il ne fit pas un geste; il ne regarda même pas les signaux que je lui adressais; et longtemps, tandis que le train m'emportait, je pus voir cette petite figure immobile, perdue dans le désert, accablée, image de mon désespoir (357).

31. See Guy Dugas, 262, on Athman's trip to France.

32. My thanks to Sarah Banks, whose comments on Athman's absence helped me write these paragraphs.

33. Il faut trouver à loger Athman, et pas à l'hôtel, chez nous . . . et je voudrais, quelque ridicule que cela puisse te paraître, le faire coucher sur le petit lit de fer dans la chambre d'ami. Et quand Madeleine viendra (comme je le souhaite) prendre ma chambre, alors seulement il irait au sixième, où tu sais parfaitement qu'il y a une chambre qui n'est qu'une resserre à malles — ô terrible mauvaise foi de Madame Gide! — à moins que nous ne couchions tous deux dans cette chambre d'ami, ce qui, personnellement, me serait complètement indifférent.

a failure. His mother's apartment would never be transformed into a new kind of household, where he, his mother, his fiancée, his man-servant, and faithful Marie could all live together with rather complicated sleeping arrangements.

His mother in any case put an end to the experiment by dying a few months later. Such an end, of course, could not resolve his dilemma as to where his sexual allegiances lay, conditioned and complicated as that dilemma was by the social and political world in which he and his mother lived. Whatever tentative allegiances Gide would feel to various forms of female sexuality, allegiances experienced complexly around his mother, he would be hard-pressed to imagine any acknowledgeable support for his sexual bent coming from her quarters.[34] Gide remained as a result resolutely antimaternal throughout the rest of his life, in a form of repetitively unsuccessful spitting, subject to constant renewal. This antimaternal (yet also loving) pulsation, never to be stilled, is the surest sign that Gide, no matter how far he traveled, in fact remained forever haunted by his mother and her simultaneously normative and queer sexual potential, a fact he found simultaneously satisfying and unbearable.

In chapter 3 I return to the question of Gide's understanding of the oppression of female sexuality and the complicated ways this understanding both finds expression in Gide's writing and influences the expression of his own sexuality. I relate this question to his phobic flashes around not only women but also the question of anal sexuality, flashes we have had occasion to observe several times in these first two chapters. In chapter 4 I return more specifically to Gide's ways of both participating in and resisting the narrativization of the onset of sexuality and adumbrate a bit further what Gide counterposes to *narratives* of sexuality: the concept of a pulsation that disrupts any one temporality, emphasizing that sexuality insists in repeated moments that are never reducible to any one temporal line.

34. In a paroxysm of homophobic invention, Jean Delay suggests that the realization of Gide's homosexuality might have caused his mother's fatal stroke. According to Delay's fantasy, Gide's mother would have read in the newspaper on May 5, 1895, of Oscar Wilde being sentenced to two years of hard labor, would have spent a few days rereading her son's letters from the time spent in North Africa with Wilde and Douglas a year or so earlier, would have perhaps spent some time thinking over the recent tussle concerning Athman, and then would have promptly keeled over, unable, in her puritanism, to bear the force of the unpleasant truth of her son's sexuality (Delay, 2:553–54). Gide understood his mother's complexity better than Delay. This is not to say that Delay's perverse, sadistic, ideologically offensive melodrama might not, in its tabloid sensibility, have had some appeal for Gide, who was always slightly fascinated by the macabre.

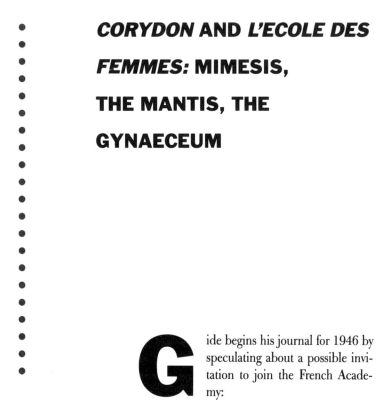

CHAPTER 3

CORYDON AND *L'ECOLE DES FEMMES:* MIMESIS, THE MANTIS, THE GYNAECEUM

Gide begins his journal for 1946 by speculating about a possible invitation to join the French Academy:

The Academy? . . . Yes, perhaps, accept becoming a member if I can do it without making solicitations, groveling, paying visits, etc. And immediately afterward, as my first act as an Immortal, a preface to *Corydon,* declaring that I consider that book to be the most important and the most *serviceable* of my writings (French doesn't really have the word I want, and I don't even know if this English word expresses exactly what I mean: of greater usefulness, of greater service for the progress of humanity). I believe this and it would not be difficult to prove it. (*Journals,* 4:256)[1]

It seems that both *Corydon* and *Retour de l'U.R.S.S.* occupied a special place in Gide's heart (he links the two in a journal entry from November 1947),[2] as

1. Académie? . . . Oui, peut-être, accepter d'y entrer, si sans sollicitations, courbettes, visites, etc. Et sitôt après, comme premier acte d'Immortel, une préface à *Corydon,* déclarant que je considère ce livre comme le plus important et le plus *serviceable* (nous n'avons pas de mot, et je ne sais même si ce mot anglais exprime exactement ce que je veux dire : de plus grande utilité, de plus grand service pour le progrès de l'humanité) de mes écrits. Ce que je crois et qu'il n'est pas malaisé de démontrer (*Journal, 1939–1949,* 287).

2. "A Swedish interviewer asked me if I did not regret having written any particular one of my books (I do not know whether he was thinking of *Le Retour de l'U.R.S.S.* or of *Corydon*). I replied that not only did I not disown any of my writings, but that I should certainly have bade farewell to the Nobel Prize if, in order to obtain it, I had had to disown anything" (*Journals,* 4:275; *Journal, 1939–1949,* 308).

somehow his two riskiest books, the two books most successful at giving offence. And Gide seems to view as one of *Corydon*'s major ongoing successes precisely its continuing power to shock. The first part of the journal passage just quoted is thus a delightful fantasy of *Corydon* in 1946 providing the grounds for a disruption of one of French culture's most vulnerable ceremonial institutions, by insisting on Gide's sexuality, insisting on the publicity of what many in the public or the Academy knew or could have known if they hadn't imagined ignorance to be more comfortable.

But as for *Corydon* (a set of four dialogues about homosexuality published partially in a tiny 1911 private edition, fully in a 1920 private edition, and finally publicly in 1924) being Gide's most important and socially useful book, a claim he made several times late in his life, such a claim seems a little hard to swallow. How could a declared homosexual writer who had, while still somewhat closeted, written as apparently homophobic and misogynistic a book as *Corydon*, later in life claim that book as his most important for the good it might do for gay men? That question has been the burden carried by most of the scarce recent writing on the book; it is a question I try here to acknowledge without answering it. Instead, I offer a reading of *Corydon* aimed at illustrating how this question comes to be posed so acutely by this particular text.

It might conceivably be tempting somehow to invoke the concept of irony to rescue Gide, salvage him personally from responsibility for the homophobia that pervades the comments made by the two interlocutors in the set of four imaginary interviews that make up *Corydon*. Gide himself remarks regretfully the presence of irony in *Corydon*, in another of his late reflections on the book:

> In my eyes, *Corydon* remains my most important book; but it is also the one with which I find the most fault. The least well done is the one it was most important to do well. Doubtless I was ill advised to treat ironically such serious questions, ones normally viewed as matter for reprobation or for jesting. If I went back to them, people would not fail to think I am obsessed by them. People prefer to keep silent about these things, as if they played but a negligible role in society, and as if negligible was the number of people tormented by such questions. (*Journals*, 4:130)[3]

Caught between the desire to testify accurately and the apparent embarrassment of being labeled as obsessed with sex and homosexuality, Gide regrets not having managed to say exactly what *he* meant in *Corydon*. Who meant what actually gets said in the imaginary dialogues, then? By constructing a treatise or tract on, an apology for homosexuality in dialogue form, did Gide render the content of the

---

3. *Corydon* reste à mes yeux le plus important de mes livres; mais c'est aussi celui auquel je trouve le plus à redire. Le moins réussi est celui qu'il importait le plus de réussir. Je fus sans doute mal avisé de traiter ironiquement des questions si graves, où l'on ne reconnaît d'ordinaire que matière à réprobation ou à plaisanterie. Si j'y revenais, on ne manquerait pas de penser que je suis obsédé par elles. On préfère les passer sous silence, comme si elles ne jouaient dans la société qu'un rôle négligeable et comme si négligeable était dans la société le nombre des individus que ces questions tourmentent (*Journal, 1939–1949*, 142).

speeches unassignable? Do the form of the dialogue and the concept of irony together create in *Corydon* a rift between form and content, thereby problematizing the act of testifying on a sexual question?

I do not claim that my goal in this chapter is to restore to *Corydon* some ideologically redemptive importance I am unable to perceive it as having. Still, I must insist that it should not be read phobically but rather in a way that watches the relation between homosexuality and homophobia at work in the text and recognizes and resists the possibility of their continuing to work together. Too often the dismissive gestures of critics toward *Corydon* arise out of a failure to consider the complex interplay of form and content within the text and the issues this interplay raises. Indeed, *Corydon*'s volatile mixture of form and content seems frequently to reproduce in the gestures of its critics the very homophobia it embodies in its two characters: the "I" of the text ("a frequently boorish, utterly un-Gidean bigot," as Richard Howard describes him),[4] and the eponymous Corydon, virile enough to imagine writing a defense of pederasty that would necessarily exclude "inverts, sick men" (18/30), a defense that would concurrently involve the protective sequestration of adolescent women. Unlike other Gidean texts, where sexuality seems to achieve its own expressivity through the work of the writing, the effort in *Corydon* seems instead to be to channel and control sexuality, rigidly to legislate its expression. (Of course, *Corydon* may not be entirely successful in its effort, and the reasons for its less than entire success merit scrutiny.) This phobic air of sexual policing, an air in which the two critics we will look at in a moment choose to thrive, contributes to the difficulty of reading the text.

The effort of learning to read phobic texts without reproducing phobia can teach us a great deal about the potential presence of homophobia (and misogyny) within even the queerest of subjectivities. Moreover, in the course of this effort, we may find areas of resistance to phobia within the phobic response itself: as we become familiar with a phobic arrangement of the set of variables that make up the Gidean discourse of sexuality in *Corydon*, other less odious permutations of those variables may present themselves as somehow emergent from the phobic construct in which they are embedded.

Mimesis lies at the heart of both *Corydon* and its reception. *Corydon* raises questions about the relationship of mimicry to the discovery of a homosexual preference; it touches on examples of mimicry in insects; the dialogue form itself is traditionally linked to the philosophical problem of mimesis.[5] Moreover, *Corydon* causes critics to mimic its exclusionary ideological gestures. Mimesis as a concept might serve a radical approach to sexuality well, if used as a tool to demonstrate the learned nature of all sexual practices, if used to open to question any assumptions

4. In "1911: From Exoticism to Homosexuality," 838. See also his preface to his translation of *Corydon*. Howard is the only commentator I know successfully to have bucked the homophobic current and who thereby has something interesting to say about *Corydon*.

5. See, on this subject, David M. Halperin, "Plato and the Erotics of Narrativity."

of pre-scripted sexual scenarios—assumptions that tend, in fact, to ignore the role of scripts and memory in the ways we produce ourselves and are produced as sexual beings. *Corydon* fails to use mimesis in this radical way. Indeed, *Corydon* denies (as best it can) sexuality "properly" construed any radicalness at all, preferring to find in sexuality confirmation of conservative ideologies. In fact, *Corydon* erects phobic barriers against the concept of mimesis to the extent that that very concept might appear to challenge certain conceptions of sexual difference and certain orthodox ways of understanding kinds of sexual object choice. In turn, it is often by mimicking *Corydon*'s production of such barriers that critics reproduce the text's phobia.

How might one negotiate with, participate in, perhaps challenge this interlacing set of formal and conceptual concerns, inflected by the various voices of *Corydon:* by the "I" of the dialogue, by Corydon, and by the "I" (Gide?) who speaks in prefaces and footnotes to the text? Why do readers almost inevitably associate Gide with Corydon, not with the text's "I" (who is, perhaps, not all that "un-Gidean")? And why does this association, too easily made, so easily reproduce the phobic structures the text itself sets forth?

"N'écrivez plus jamais JE," Wilde had told Gide, speaking with all the authority of his carceral experience: "Never again write I." For better or for worse, Gide sought out places and methods in which and with which to resist this advice. But *Corydon* is not obviously one of those places. Indeed, he is conceivably following such Wildean advice in this awkward text. The result is that the relationship of the problematic "I" of *Corydon* to its homophobia and to the closet must be scrupulously analyzed if the text is to be "serviceable" in any meaningful way. *Corydon* plays a game of power and knowledge around issues of openness, a game that explicitly attaches shame to certain forms of desire in order to free others from that same shame, thereby suggesting a redefinition of the borders what we call a closet might have.[6] This game of shame is essential to the phobic maintenance of the closet, to the policing of sexual communication. I would like to observe in what follows the centrality of a process of mimicry or mimetic identification to the playing of this game. I begin by watching two of the game's players, two recent critics who find themselves caught in *Corydon*'s mimetic spin.

The Mimetic Spin

One example of how the complementary pair of homophobes who dialogue in *Corydon* produce in their audience the mimesis of their own ideology of exclusion is a problematic 1990 review of a series of books on homosexuality by G. S. Rousseau. Any review that begins with an excursus on how AIDS has forced a new

6. See, on this subject, Eve Kosofsky Sedgwick, *Epistemology of the Closet,* 67–90.

generation of gay men to take one further step on the path to a healthier sexual attitude has, of course, already forfeited its claim on a sympathetic hearing from many gay men:[7]

> There is a new generation of homosexual men and women under the age of twenty-five. They grew up in a world in which AIDS was a given, and for reasons that still require articulation they appear to have a healthier attitude toward their fellow homosexuals than their forebears. They treat each other, in general, as peers rather than as objects to be used and discarded and their intimate relations already give indications of being healthier than those of the previous generations'. These generational differences remain inchoate, but there are strong clues that the new generation will be a healthier group than the last was. (Rousseau, 225)

That last sentence is particularly distressing because it can be read as meaning perhaps more than it intends. Does "healthier" mean that fewer people in this "new generation" will contract HIV? Unfortunately, current statistics on HIV infection rates are a bit too ambiguous to bear out any such uniform assumption. Perhaps we could choose to have "healthier" here mean simply less homophobic: in this case it would need to have fewer policing implications for the sexual practices of this "new generation." Indeed, one might hope they would be less censorious and orthopaedically inclined than Rousseau, who actually sounds a bit like Corydon.

Small wonder, then, that, so resembling Corydon, Rousseau would dislike Gide. (Corydon is a gay man with a distaste for many other classes of gay men.) In commenting on a chapter on Gide in one of the books he is reviewing, Rousseau's scorn comes out in full force:

> Gide advocated reason and resignation rather than rebellion. His entire life—his heterosexual marriage, inveterate pederasty in North Africa, sexual promiscuity at home, and the *apologias pro vita sua* he constructed to neutralize and nullify these contraventions in the face of his other so-called normal life in order to win the respectability he so desperately craved—all these converged on his belief about rational passivity. Never did he face a *crise de conscience* about this position or attempt to veer from it. In the continuum of the historical libertarian struggle, Gide was the *persona non grata* who did little to further its cause, as Jean Cocteau, Edward Carpenter, and others acidly pointed out. (Rousseau, 237)[8]

As Rousseau would have it, Gide is no member of the wiser, more humane "new generation"; he represents no step forward on the path to healthy homosexuality, a straightforward path Rousseau, like Corydon, feels capable of foreseeing. Rousseau thus easily considers Gide, his pederasty, his promiscuity, and his passivity craven and unhealthy, something to be discarded as the homosexual community

---

7. See, on this subject, Douglas Crimp, "Mourning and Militancy," esp. 12–14.

8. Rousseau is discussing Antony Copley, *Sexual Moralities in France, 1780–1980: New Ideas on the Family, Divorce, and Homosexuality*. Even Copley, in a response following Rousseau's review, comments in bemused fashion: "I thought I was being hard enough on André Gide, so I'm puzzled by the harshness of the reviewer's judgment" (241).

advances. In analogous fashion, Corydon insists that he is defending *only* pederasty as a healthy institution; his aspersions will be cast at the *invertis*. The "I" of
Corydon confronts him with the putative unhealthiness of certain types of homosexuals:

> "But will you deny that homosexuality is often accompanied by certain intellec-
> tual defects, as is claimed by more than one of your colleagues (I'm speaking to you
> in your role as a doctor)?"
> "If you please, we'll drop the inverts by the wayside for now. The trouble is that
> ill-informed people confuse them with normal homosexuals. And you understand, I
> hope, what I mean by 'inverts.' After all, heterosexuality too includes certain degen-
> erates, people who are sick and obsessed." (119–20)[9]

One might then note, without surprise, how the structure of phobic mimicry
exemplified by Rousseau's article associates him with writers of a less appealing
bent. Rousseau sounds, for instance, a bit like John Weightman, the author of an
unfortunate article in *The American Scholar* entitled "André Gide and the Homosexual Debate." From a magisterial position somewhere in the British Isles,
Weightman happily responds to a bizarre query by an American editor. The editor
writes to him: "André Gide . . . seems from here [in America], rather small and
beside the point. Is that how it looks from where you are? . . . Odd, with homosexuality now something like a small political movement, one would have thought
much more would have been made of Gide, who very early uncloseted himself"
(Weightman, 591). Weightman seems quite content to answer authoritatively, as if
well positioned in a safely uncontaminated viewing place from which gay men are
seen to form a small enough movement that one can know for sure all they think
about, all they read. "Gide does seem by now, some forty years after his death, a
relatively forgotten figure, although there is still, of course, a Gidian academic
industry." (Should I consider myself a worker in that abstruse factory?) With Gide
safely long dead, Weightman proceeds to survey his career for us. (But why bother,
if there's no interest? Where is the interest? Why would *The American Scholar* be
interested? Why would the space for a flash of phobia be opened again here?) The
"I" of *Corydon* is Weightman's model, in fact, someone constantly looking phobically for that *cordon sanitaire* that allows one to differentiate normal men from
the gay boys, even as it allows those normal folk to write curiously about the gay
ones. If Rousseau mimics the salutary, purifying discriminations of Corydon, by
contrast, it is with contamination that Weightman, like the "I" voice, is obsessed.
And in the process of coming to believe himself not to be anything like Gide,
Weightman easily manages to assume that Gide is, in fact, Corydon:

9. — Nierez-vous donc que l'homosexualité s'accompagne souvent de certaines tares intellectuelles, ainsi que le
prétend plus d'un de vos confrères? (c'est au médecin que je m'adresse).
— Si vous le voulez bien, nous laisserons de côté les invertis. Je leur tiens à grief ceci, que les gens mal
renseignés confondent les homosexuels normaux avec eux. Et vous comprenez, je l'espère, ce que par « inverti » je
veux dire. L'hétérosexualité tout de même compte aussi des dégénérés, des maniaques, des malades (131–32).

> From the start, Corydon is naively presented as a distinguished figure, greatly superi-
> or to his interlocutor in manner, intelligence, and knowledge. . . . Corydon . . .
> decided to devote himself to proving to other homosexuals . . . that what they may
> feel ashamed of as an anomaly is, in fact, an innocent, natural appetite that has
> always existed. . . . I am not sure that Corydon, or Gide, ever sees clearly that Nature
> is useless as a moral criterion, since a homicidal maniac could equally well invoke it
> to justify his undoubtedly inherent impulses. (593)

Anyone familiar with the banalities of the homophobic discourse about the unnaturalness of gay practices (of which this is only a slightly more sophisticated version)
knows that lurking around the corner is the image of an "inherently" degenerate
gay man as the dangerous psychopath (the near homonym status of "homicidal"
and "homosexual" would appear to make them almost irresistibly synonymous in
this context) capable of single-handedly destroying the moral fiber of entire na-
tions. Weightman does not disappoint:

> But if Nature is as indefinite as Gide [Corydon?] says, pederasty may be infectious or
> habit-forming, with debatable consequences for the good of society or the happiness
> of the individual. Contemporary European society has, on the whole, moved to the
> position of recognizing homosexual relations between consenting adults as an inno-
> cent fulfillment of their nature, but there is still a question mark against pederasty, as
> against pedophilia. How is Corydon [Gide?] going to deal with this? (594)

A rhetoric of corruption and addiction appears more intellectually appealing to
Weightman than a rhetoric of nature. Indeed, the AIDS-and-drugs subtext contributes greatly to the unpleasantness of this passage that insinuates that Gide/
Corydon is, through his sexual proclivities, perhaps the perfect AIDS victim, and
worse, carrier. (Rousseau's prose is not innocent of this same insinuation when he
speaks of Gide's "inveterate pederasty," his promiscuity and his "craving" for
respectability.)[10] Thus, Gide's participation in unsafe and unsavory sex ruins him
for any contemporary gay reader: "Certainly, in the sexual area, neither his theories
nor his personal conduct were coherently exemplary, and this no doubt helps to
explain why he has not become an international hero of homosexuality" (597).
Thank goodness no one reads him, he's such a bad example. This last bit of
condescension to the apparently desperate international search of gay men for
heroes (as if that would be the only reason gay men ever read, all of them craven,
hungry for heroes; none of them capable of any other form of curiosity), could, in
fact, be from either the article by Rousseau or the one by Weightman. That
similarity and the whole rigged exclusionary rhetoric of bad examples so willingly
participated in by both parties might lead us to conclude that both the "I" of
Corydon and Corydon himself (both Rousseau and Weightman) are, in fact, in
their various phobias, somehow importantly the same.[11]

10. Eve Kosofsky Sedgwick has valuably and eloquently analyzed many of these aspects of homophobia. See
Epistemology of the Closet, esp. 18–22, 40–43, 57–58, and 171–78.
11. See Eve Kosofsky Sedgwick's readings of homophobic/homosexual pairs such as Claggart/Billy Budd or
Wilde/Vidal in *Epistemology of the Closet*, 100, 153.

Mimesis

Sameness, mimicry, phobia, and homosexuality—the first time a clear set of links between these terms can be seen in *Corydon* is during the narration, in the first dialogue, of Corydon's discovery of the nature of his object choice. That first dialogue is presented as a space in which Corydon, through a moving personal confession, is to win the sympathy, to win back the friendship, of his hostile interlocutor. The two were high school friends, the first-person pronoun tells us: "After leaving the lycée where we had been students together, we remained fairly close friends for a long time. Then several years of travel separated us, and when I returned to Paris to live, the deplorable reputation his behavior was acquiring held me back from associating with him" (3–4).[12] But the occasion of *Corydon* is precisely a visit of this moralist to his wayward former friend. Why this sudden turnabout? What hidden motivations would there be for suddenly picking up the loose ends of this broken friendship? From the outset, we are given the material that might make us suspicious of the motives and agendas of this "I," motives and agendas of which even he, we are led to believe, is conceivably unaware.

Corydon's interlocutor has apparently decided to catch up with his old school friend because "l'uranisme" has recently been a hot topic in all the Parisian cafes. The cause of this recent topicality is a "scandalous" recent court case that once again concerned allegations of homosexuality.[13] Rather than listen to all the loose talk in the cafes, Corydon's friend decides to go to the source itself:

> Impatient with theories and exclamations offered on all sides by the ignorant, the bigoted, and the stupid, I wanted to know my own mind; realizing that reason rather than mere temperament was alone qualified to condemn or condone, I decided to go and discuss the subject with Corydon. He, I had been told, made no objection to certain unnatural tendencies attributed to him; my conscience would not be clear until I had learned what he had to say in their behalf. (3)[14]

Convenient pretense, one might scoff, and use the implication of the chafing together of his desire and his repression to account for all the suspect energy this fellow then uses to distance himself from Corydon, even as he returns for talk after talk. ("I nearly decided not to come back," he says to Corydon the first time he

---

12. Au sortir du lycée où nous avions été condisciples, longtemps une assez étroite amitié nous unit. Puis des années de voyage nous séparèrent, et lorsque je revins m'installer à Paris, la déplorable réputation que ses mœurs commençaient de lui valoir me retint de le fréquenter (15–16).

13. For information about the events being referred to, see James D. Steakley, "Iconography of a Scandal: Political Cartoons and the Eulenburg Affair in Wilhelmin Germany." See also Patrick Pollard, *André Gide: Homosexual Moralist*, 126–37, for an extensive list of homosexual scandals large and small from the time and for a discussion of Gide's interest in them.

14. Las d'entendre à ce sujet s'exclamer ou théoriser au hasard les ignorants, les butés et les sots, je souhaitai éclairer mon jugement et, ne reconnaissant qu'à la raison, non point au seul tempérament, le droit de condamner ou d'absoudre, je résolus d'aller interviewer Corydon. Il ne protestait point, m'avait-on dit, contre certains penchants dénaturés dont on l'accuse; j'en voulus avoir le cœur net et savoir ce qu'il trouvait à dire pour les excuser (15).

returns, and Corydon knowingly, archly, responds, "I knew you would say that . . . and that you would come all the same" [25/37].) The same energy could be used to explain the eagerness with which this man waits to drink up Corydon's melodramatic confession of his coming to terms with his sexual bent—as if, somehow, an explanation of the origins of Corydon's sexuality would both vicariously satisfy and yet also clear the first person once and for all, whereas, in fact, Corydon's narration is one of mimetic contamination, a narration hardly meant to calm the energies of repression.

Corydon narrates his near seduction at the hands of a younger man, the brother, in fact, of his fiancée. Engaged to the perfect woman, but worried at his lack of desire for her, the young Corydon is all the more disconcerted to find that her brother desires him and that this desire somehow echoes within his own body: "But Alexis was no longer a child; he was a charming and perceptive adolescent. The avowals he made to me then were all the more upsetting because in every revelation he made, all drawn from his precocious and singularly exact self-observation, I seemed to be hearing my own confession" (14).[15] One could think here of the mature Gide reflecting back on his games as a toddler with the son of the concierge: "Which of the two of us had taught them to the other? And who had this first one learned them from? I don't know. You just may have to admit that a child sometimes invents them all from scratch." Or one could think of him writing the confused encounter with Ali in the dunes, where the perfect sexual encounter is one in which two identical desires seem to meet and begin an act that neither person clearly initiates or takes responsibility for and in which both actually perform the same roles, a desire that strangely would come to belong to the self only because it is so clearly imitated not only *from* but also *by* the other (see chapter 1). One might also observe the chain of mimicry at work outside Corydon's story, its next link gradually forming, as Corydon confesses himself for himself, but also perhaps the other for the other: "When we used to see each other, you were still a student. Did you already have such a clear notion of yourself back then? Speak—I'm looking for a confession" (11). (Howard translates this as, "Tell me—I want to know the truth," which seems wrong. He precisely doesn't want the truth, he wants the mirroring cathexis of a confessional.)[16] The similarities between Corydon listening to his fiancée's brother and the narrator/interlocutor listening to Corydon seem harder and harder to ignore ("il me semblait me confesser moi-même"/"C'est une confession que j'attends"), especially as Corydon initially responds to Alexis in typical homophobic fashion, provoking the younger man to

15. Mais Alexis n'était plus un enfant; c'était un adolescent plein de grâce et de conscience; les aveux qu'il me fit entre temps, me déconcertèrent d'autant plus que, dans tout ce qu'il me révélait, qu'il observait en lui précocement avec une perspicacité singulière, il me semblait me confesser moi-même (26–27).

16. Lorsque nous nous fréquentions, vous étiez encore étudiant. A ce moment, aviez-vous déjà vu clair en vous-même? Parlez! C'est une confession que j'attends (23).

suicide through another mimetic process. Alexis writes to Corydon in his suicide note: "You haven't understood me—or, what is worse, you have, and you feel contempt for me; I see that I am becoming an object of disgust to you—as I am for myself for that very reason. If I can't change my awful nature, at least I can get rid of it" (16).[17] Once Alexis has absorbed Corydon's homophobia, Corydon is then "freed" of it: "in memory of this victim, I want to cure other victims" (17/29). Thus, Corydon becomes a doctor of souls, champion of the pederast, and *Corydon* becomes an elaborate game of transference, with homophobia and homosexual desire passed around through some odd circuitry, the one replacing the other as if they shared some deep congruency. The narrator/interlocutor seems then almost inevitably to be only a shuffle away from becoming a container of that homosexual desire from elsewhere, as the flow of mimesis moves his phobia on to someone else.

Is not this transference game as narrated, this rhetoric of desire as contamination, inherently homophobic? We remember, for instance, Weightman's phobic chatter: "But if Nature is as indefinite as Gide says, pederasty may be infectious or habit-forming with debatable consequences for the good of society or the happiness of the individual," doing his best, one can only assume, to participate in this game of shame that, in all its melodrama, does indeed produce suicides like Alexis'.

There could be a temptation, faced with such homophobia, to respond to the "I" of *Corydon* and others such as him: "Admit it, you're nothing but a fag yourself. However you try to disguise your prurient interest, it gives you away." To do so would be to a certain extent to join in *Corydon*'s game, to play the game of contamination in order to turn it back on itself. As a strategic response to certain instances of homophobia, giving way to such a temptation is doubtless useful and gratifying. It's not clear that such a strategy would be useful here, where no obvious benefits are to be gained from outing (or at least annoying) the "I" of the text. Rather, we might scrutinize *Corydon* as a text that plays with rhetorics of contamination (*Les Faux-Monnayeurs,* as we will see in the next chapter, is another) and that in that playing reveals limits to those rhetorics. In that revelation, perhaps alternatives to these rhetorics can begin to come into view. This seems to me to be more obviously the case in *Les Faux-Monnayeurs* than in *Corydon,* but reading a text as noteworthy as *Corydon* against its grain seems nonetheless a necessary response to its provocation.

At a certain point a bit later in the text Corydon becomes sufficiently outraged by the discussion he is having that he comes out against contamination and tries to replace it with invention:

17. Tu ne m'as pas compris; ou ce qui est bien pis, tu m'as compris et tu me méprises; je vois que je deviens pour toi un objet d'horreur; je le deviens du même coup pour moi-même. Si je ne puis rien changer à ma monstreuse nature, je puis du moins la supprimer (28).

> But if, in spite of advice, invitations, incitements of all kinds, [the adolescent] should manifest a homosexual tendency, you immediately blame his reading or some other influence . . . it has to be an acquired taste, you insist; he must have been taught it; you refuse to admit that he might have invented it all by himself. (29)[18]

Corydon's own narration, like other Gidean narrations we have seen, complicates this possibility, as if such narration, in its way of blurring unidirectional, straight-forward temporalities, makes impossible the clear assertion of an invention—or even the clear assertion of an imitation. We recall again the claim of *Si le grain ne meurt* as to the origins of Gide's "nasty habits": "You just may have to admit that a child sometimes invents them from scratch. As for me, I can't say if someone taught me or how I discovered pleasure, but no matter how far back my memory pushes, it is there." Through memory one tries to decide between invention or imitation, but that process of rememoration itself undermines the assuredness of any particular assessment one would make.

What are the methods *Corydon* might use to keep in abeyance any decision between invention and imitation? The passage from *Corydon* just cited uses the word *penchant* to describe an inflection of the general category of *plaisir,* that something that has always been present for Gide, no matter how far back his memory searches. What is the relation between *penchant* and *plaisir?* This is a necessary corollary question to the question of whether sexual practices are in-vented or imitated, and it turns out to be in many ways the central question discussed in *Corydon.* What path is taken, how is that path constructed, how chosen, how does it compare to other paths, how are deviations recognized, how, by noting those deviations, will one work to establish and justify, or else to under-mine, the concept of perversion? In the analytical separation of pleasure from practice, a practice frequently becomes something learned, internalized, imitated. Analyses of sexuality that separate an abstract notion of pleasure from a particular practice often find themselves at some point timorously retracing their steps, hesitant about the furthest pursuit of this claim: that, however one imagines learning taking place, *all* practices might be *equally* learned. All practices may be learned, backpedallers find themselves claiming, but some are more learned than others, and the more learning involved, the more questionable the practice. Or they might even baldly assert, against their previous analysis, that all practices are learned except for one innate one, their favorite. Let us watch how this works in *Corydon.*

Startled by Corydon's vehement defense of the possibility of invention in a gay adolescent, his interlocutor concedes the point (not entirely gracefully): "Calm down! Calm down! Your uranist is a great inventor." To which Corydon responds, correcting his own vehemence, "I'm not saying he always invents—I'm saying that

---

18. Mais si, malgré conseils, invitations, provocations de toutes sortes, c'est un penchant homosexuel {que l'adolescent} manifeste, aussitôt vous incriminez telle lecture, telle influence . . . c'est un goût acquis, affirmez-vous; on le lui a appris, c'est sûr; vous n'admettez pas qu'il ait pu l'inventer tout seul (41).

when he imitates it's because he wants to imitate; I'm saying that the example corresponded to his secret preference" (29–30).[19] Corydon here tries sneakily to move *plaisir* and *penchant* a bit closer by introducing a set of intermediary terms. *Plaisir* is now linked to a "goût secret" that would limit the paths it would naturally follow to fulfillment. This *goût*, this disposition, thus prejudices the *envie d'imiter*, the desire to imitate; it is in fact the first sign of a slope, just waiting for the right example to imitate in order to become a full-fledged inclination, a *penchant*.

A bit later on in *Corydon*, the effort to move *invention* further and further away from imitation takes its next predictable step backward, moving invention closer to innateness, thereby running the risk of losing the radical potential of separating all sexual practices in their constructedness from *plaisir*. The homosexual penchant, Corydon asserts, with its particular "envie d'imiter" is, in fact, closer to nature than heterosexuality:

> I believe—forgive my temerity—that homosexuality in either sex is more spontaneous, more naïve than heterosexuality. . . . This is what Barrès realized so clearly when, wanting to portray in his *Bérénice* a creature very close to nature, and obeying instinct alone, he made her a lesbian. . . . It is only by means of *education* that he raises her to heterosexual love. (90)[20]

Such an observation is surprising for a number of reasons. Given the misogynistic tenor of most of the comments of both the narrator and Corydon, it seems strange that at the moment when Corydon is being most audacious in his claims about homosexuality, he should use a lesbian as his example; all the more so, since, as we will see, it has been the burden of much of *Corydon* to insist that male and female sexualities are not parallel cases, that there is in male sexuality, and in male sexuality only, a possible diversion from a precise *instinctive* object choice, a *liberation from instinct* that makes object choice "imprecise" and thus opens the door to homosexual possibilities.

Instinct thereby becomes another critical term in *Corydon*, a term whose usage slips in ways that reveal important inconsistencies in the text. Would it be better to be closer to instincts that apparently represent nature's voice, or liberated from instincts understood as constraints worth overcoming? The difference between gay male sexuality and lesbianism propounded in *Corydon* turns precisely on this question. Indeed, the text does not miss the chance every now and then to ridicule lesbianism, thereby showing its own confusion, its inability to control the swirl of meanings it is itself putting into play around the words *instinct, inclination,* and *mimesis, mimesis* hesitating in meaning ambiguously between instinc-

19. — Calmez-vous! calmez-vous! Votre uraniste est un grand inventeur.

— Je ne dis pas qu'il invente toujours; mais je dis que, lorsqu'il imite, c'est qu'il avait envie d'imiter; que l'exemple flattait son goût secret (41–42).

20. Je crois, excusez mon audace, l'homosexualité dans l'un et l'autre sexe, plus spontanée, plus naïve que l'hétérosexualité . . . C'est ce que Barrès a si bien compris lorsque, souhaitant peindre dans sa *Bérénice* une créature toute proche de la nature et n'obéissant qu'à l'instinct, il en fit une lesbienne . . . Ce n'est que par *éducation* qu'il l'élève jusqu'à l'amour hétérosexuel (102–3).

tually constrained behavior (*Corydon*'s lesbians) and a liberating exercise of volition (*Corydon*'s pederasts).

At a certain point, for example, the two men are discussing the odor given off
by certain female animals in heat. Insisting that this odor cannot be interpreted as
somehow showing nature's heterosexual intentions, Corydon points out that male
animals are not attracted to females *except* when they are in heat (instinctually
constrained behavior) and then adds that even female animals are sometimes
attracted to another female in heat:

> This odor is so powerful and so disturbing to the animal's senses that it exceeds the
> role which sexuality assigns it (if I may use such an expression) and like a simple
> aphrodisiac intoxicates not only the male but also other females that approach the
> female in heat and even make clumsy attempts to mount her. Farmers separate a cow
> in season from the rest of the herd when she is being molested by other cows.
> (57–58)[21]

At this point the text refers to a footnote. (There is often a first-person pronoun in
the footnotes to *Corydon,* and as the tone of these footnotes is in general supportive
of Corydon's arguments, it is sometimes taken for granted that it must be Gide
saying "I" in the footnotes, and not the "I" of the main text. One would thereby be
safe in assuming Gide and Corydon to be the same, or at least to think the same.
But then perhaps Corydon manages to take over the first person for the space of
the footnotes, somehow to include footnotes in his speeches. How would one
decide, and what would it mean to decide?) The footnote in question has to do
with precisely these cows too much given to mimesis:

> "One even sees cows in season trying to mount each other, *either because they have the*
> *notion of thereby provoking the male, or because their visual representation of the desired*
> *act compels them to attempt a simulation of it,*" M. de Gourmont writes, after saying a
> few lines earlier that "in general, animal aberrations require only the simplest of
> explanations." He then adds: "A marvelous example, because so absurd, of the
> motive force of images" (*The Physiology of Love*). I am afraid it is more absurd than
> marvelous. (58)[22]

Why would this example be more absurd than marvelous? Surely it is a good
example of much of what the text is out to demonstrate: the mimeticism of desire,
the fact that libido exists in order to be inflected, and that in a pinch, any image
will do. Why would this inflection not suit the argument? Perhaps because the

---

21. Ce parfum, pour les sens de l'animal, est si fort, si troublant, qu'il déborde le rôle que la sexualité lui assigne
(si j'ose m'exprimer ainsi) et grise comme un simple aphrodisiaque non seulement le mâle, mais aussi d'autres
femelles qui viennent contre la femelle en rut, essayer de maladroits rapprochements. Les fermiers écartent du
troupeau la vache en chaleur qu'importunent les autres vaches (70).

22. « On voit même des vaches en chaleur monter les unes sur les autres, *soit qu'elles aient l'idée de provoquer*
ainsi le mâle, soit que la représentation visuelle qu'elles se font de l'acte désiré les force à en essayer la simulation » écrit M.
de Gourmont, après avoir dit quelques lignes plus haut : « En général, les aberrations animales demandent des
explications toutes simples. » — Puis il ajoute : « C'est un exemple merveilleux, parce qu'il est absurde, de la force
motrice des images. » Je crains qu'il ne soit encore plus absurde que merveilleux (70).

cows are doomed to failure in their imitation of heterosexual intercourse, because their homosexuality does not define itself sufficiently over against heterosexuality? Or perhaps because the text is uncomfortable with spectacles of unbridled female sexuality, a sexuality it tends to associate with mimesis as automatism, not mimesis as the sign of an intelligent liberation/deviation from instinct.

These cows, and, by aspersion, lesbians in general, thus could be seen as *Corydon*'s mimetic scapegoats: examples of that pure mimeticism that would undercut, challenge the coherence of our notions of selfhood and volition. Philippe Lacoue-Labarthe has carefully discussed this problem, the perception of "the danger of an originary absence of subjective 'property,'" in other contexts:

> For it is necessary, in the rejection of the "bearer of mimesis," that the victim incarnate in one way or another this impropriety. . . . That is to say, not only the undifferentiation and endless doubling which threatens the social body as a whole, but, on an underlying level and actually provoking them, *mimetism* itself, that pure and disquieting *plasticity* which potentially authorizes the varying appropriation of all characters and all functions (all the roles), that kind of "typical virtuosity" which doubtless requires a "subjective" base . . . but without any other property than an infinite malleability: *instability* "itself." (Lacoue-Labarthe, "Typography," 115)[23]

In choosing to reject this particular "bearer of mimesis," *Corydon* falls short of the full analytic complexity necessary to understand the concept of mimesis in a way that would circumvent a combined homophobia and misogyny. As a way of pursuing the troubled relation of female sexuality to gay male sexuality that *Corydon* seems to present, I would like to investigate a bit further *Corydon*'s preoccupation with the contagious mimetic malleability it seems to frown on. *Corydon* fails to allow for, or it strives to contain, the disruptive politics of sexuality, just as it seems to want to repress the kinds of hesitant allegiances between potentially gay sons and potentially lesbian mothers and maidservants that we saw so glancingly presented in the preceding chapter. But it does nonetheless trace some kind of link we might profitably analyze between male and female sexualities.

The Mantis

If one were looking for a central obsession in *Corydon*, one might choose to find it not in the various apologies for pederasty but in its subliminal fascination with the misogynistic control of female sexuality, that same fascination of which we also found traces in *Si le grain ne meurt*, in the fantasmatic construction of Mme Gide's sexuality and the effort to negotiate the question of whether or not the son's

23. Several other essays in this volume of Lacoue-Labarthe's have been helpful to me in working on this chapter, especially "Diderot: Paradox and Mimesis." It occurs to me that if one is looking to place *Corydon* generically, one would do well to situate it in a series of texts presenting themselves as dialogues, texts that would include Diderot's "Paradoxe sur le comédien" that Lacoue-Labarthe analyzes so carefully in that essay. One might also think of Wilde's "The Decay of Lying," or "The Critic as Artist."

homosexuality begins in the mother's. For example, at a certain point in the discussions making up *Corydon*, Corydon is developing the theme that males in general are given to sexual expenditure and genetic variation (catagenesis) whereas females are given to sexual conservation, genetic protection (anagenesis).[24] As evidence of this trait, he observes, "But usually the female, immediately after fertilization, remains at rest."[25] Females are not naturally given to excessive dissemination; they are not constantly on the prowl. His listener takes the opportunity for a typically snide interjection: "I see you are speaking of animals" (43/55). No such seeming modesty is to be found, according to him, in the modern-day woman, whose sexual behavior apparently exceeds natural bounds. ("Le saphisme jouit parmi nous d'une indéniable faveur," he has already commented in another of his snotty asides, "Sapphism actually enjoys a certain favor among us nowadays" [18/31].)

Now what makes these banal interjections interesting is the way in which they form a context for what is perhaps the most astonishing footnote in *Corydon*, a footnote concerned with the unseemly and unbounded sexual appetite of the female praying mantis, an insect that might actually seem somehow to contradict the whole trend of Corydon's argument. I cite this bizarre note in its entirety:

> It is remarkable that precisely in this species (*Mantis religiosa*) and despite the small number of males, each female is prepared to consume an inordinate number of them; she continues to offer herself for coitus and remains attractive to the male even after fertilization; Fabre tells of how he saw one female welcome and then devour seven males in succession. The sexual instinct, which we see here to be imperious and precise, immediately exceeds its purpose. I was naturally led to wonder whether, in these species where the number of males is proportionately inferior, where consequently the instinct is more precise and hence no unemployed substance remains on which the catagenetic force can operate, no "material for variation"—whether under such circumstances dimorphism does not operate in favor of the female sex—or to put it differently: whether the males of these species are not *less* showy in appearance than the females. And this is precisely what we can establish in the case of the praying mantis, the male of which is "dwarf, frail, drab, and shabby" (to borrow Fabre's adjectives) and cannot aspire to that "many-colored posture" in which the female exhibits the strange beauty of her broad, diaphanous, green-edged wings. Moreover, Fabre takes no notice whatever of this singular reversal of attributes, which here corroborates my theory. These considerations, which I relegate to a footnote—since they depart from my main line of reasoning—where I fear that they will pass

24. For the crassest possible presentation of this kind of late-nineteenth century "scientific" discourse, which still, it should be added, crops up frequently in various contemporary moral disquisitions, see Alfred Fouillée, "La Psychologie des sexes et ses fondemens physiologiques." For instance: "The reservoir of feminine energies having as its principal object the life of the race, it is understandable that everything serving for muscular or cerebral expenditure, supports of individual life, would be less developed in women. . . . Man's role and his social occupations, even if they don't demand genius, demand an intellectual energy, a scientific vigor of mind, that are not necessary for women, and that could even be harmful to her in the performance of her real functions. . . . In the realm of material things, the unquiet and ambitious will of man pleases itself through acquisition, that of the woman through conservation" (415, 421, 422). For a helpful article tracing the background to this kind of thought, see Karen Offen, "Depopulation, Nationalism, and Feminism in Fin-de-Siècle France."

25. Mais la femelle, d'ordinaire, aussitôt après la fécondation se tient coite.

unnoticed, seem to me of the greatest interest. Having taken this new and admittedly speculative theory to its conclusion, the joy I experienced on discovering a confirming example coming, so to speak, to meet me, is comparable only to that of Poe's treasure hunter who unearthed the casket full of jewels at the exact spot where his deductions had convinced him it must be. —Perhaps I shall someday publish further observations on this subject. (69–70)[26]

Obsessive and manic in tone, the writing in this footnote resembles the character of William Legrand, the strange treasure-hunting protagonist of Poe's story "The Gold-Bug," to which the footnote so incongruously refers. Manic, and even hysterical, one might be tempted to say, in its roundabout way of displaying and hiding things at the same time: here, buried, but I hope you will all see it, is the confirming piece of evidence for my outlandishly daring theory, but it's really too much an unnecessary distraction from my main line of argument, and besides perhaps it even contradicts everything else I've said. For the voracious female praying mantis exhibits a sexual appetite that, in terms of the theory Corydon has been expounding, could only be described as male. It is excessive, not exhibited in well-defined temporal periods, committed to luxury in the total lack of attention it pays to what reproduction in its most efficiently organized state might actually require.[27] Compare in this regard a passage from a little later on in *Corydon:*

> The male has much more to expend than is required in order to answer to the reproductive function of the opposite sex and to ensure the reproduction of the species. The expenditure to which nature prompts him is quite difficult to regulate and risks becoming prejudicial to law and order as Western peoples understand them. (104)[28]

26. Il est remarquable que, précisément chez cette espèce (*mantis religiosa*) et malgré le petit nombre de mâles, chaque femelle est prête à en faire une consommation déréglée; elle continue à s'offrir au coït et reste appétissante au mâle même après la fécondation; Fabre raconte avoir vu l'une d'elles accueillir puis dévorer successivement sept époux. L'instinct sexuel, que nous voyons ici impérieux et précis, aussitôt dépasse le but. Je fus tout naturellement amené à me demander si, chez ces espèces où le nombre des mâles est proportionnellement inférieur, où, partant, l'instinct est plus précis, et où par conséquent il ne reste plus de matière inemployée, dont puisse jouer la force catagénétique, de « matière à variation » — si ce n'est pas, dès lors, en faveur du sexe féminin que se manifeste le dimorphisme — autrement dit : si les mâles de ces espèces ne sont pas d'aspect *moins* brillant que les femelles? — Or c'est précisément ce que nous pouvons constater chez la *mantis religiosa*, dont le mâle « nain, fluet, sobre et mesquin » (j'emprunte à Fabre ces épithètes) ne peut prétendre à cette « pose spectrale » durant laquelle la femelle déploie l'étrange beauté de ses larges ailes diaphanes et lisérées de vert. Fabre ne fait du reste pas la moindre remarque sur ce singulier renversement des attributs, qui corrobore ici ma théorie. Ces considérations que je relève en note, — parce qu'elles s'écartent quelque peu de la ligne de cet écrit — où je crains bien qu'elles ne passent inaperçues, me paraissent présenter le plus grand intérêt. La joie que j'éprouvai lorsque, ayant poussé jusqu'au bout une théorie si neuve et, je l'avoue, si hasardée, je vis l'exemple la confirmant venir, pour ainsi dire, à ma rencontre — cette joie n'est comparable qu'à celle du chercheur de trésors d'Edgar Poe lorsqu'en creusant le sol il découvre la cassette pleine de joyaux exactement à cette place où ses déductions l'avaient persuadé qu'elle devait être. — Je publierai peut-être quelque jour d'autres remarques à ce sujet (81–82).

27. Cf. this passage, which Corydon quotes from one of his scientific allies, Lester Ward: "[The masculine sex] too has its characteristic. This showy finery, these glamorous means of seduction are in fact no more than a vain display of dead parts, the sign of a senseless expenditure, of an inordinate prodigality of the organism, the mark of a temperament which externalizes but knows no economy" (46/58).

28. Le mâle a beaucoup plus à dépenser qu'il ne convient pour répondre à la fonction reproductive de l'autre sexe et assurer la reproduction de l'espèce. La dépense à laquelle l'invite la Nature est assez incommode à régler et risque de devenir préjudiciable au bon ordre de la société telle que les peuples occidentaux la comprennent (116).

In the case of the mantis, those excessive, luxurious, catagenetic signs of display usually accorded in Nature to the male, the true repository of that beauty that is excess, here fall to the female. The praying mantis, it would appear, is a true *inverti(e)* within nature, the females arrogating the male privilege of beautiful bodies, excessive display, even size, as if in drag, while the males become effeminate drones.[29] They are not only effeminate—in fact they do the female's work. The footnote is not entirely clear on this point, but the argument would probably go something like this: the female praying mantis is so taken by luxurious display that it has no time to accumulate within its body the nutrients necessary to allow for gestation of the young, therefore it eats the male which impregnates it and thereby ingests the necessary nutrients for successful reproduction of the species.[30]

Other stories are possible. Perhaps this odd behavior is instinctual nymphomania. The female praying mantis is so carefully "hard wired" for pleasure, some assert, that she carefully eats those parts of the male's nervous system that inhibit maximal sexual performance:

> Much of insect behavior is "hard wired," so unlike the flexibility of our own actions (and a primary reason why sociobiological models for ants work so poorly for humans). Copulatory movements are controlled by nerves in the last abdominal ganglion (near the back end). Since it would be inconsistent with normal function (and unseemly as well) for males to perform these copulatory motions continually, they are suppressed by inhibitory centers located in the subesophageal ganglion (near the head). When a female eats her mate's head, she ingests the subesophageal ganglion, and nothing remains to inhibit copulatory movement. What remains of the male now operates as a non-stop mating machine. (Gould, 48)

Pseudoscientific speculation on and sociological extrapolation from the behavior of the praying mantis have a long history.[31] Every story needs to be read as ideological fiction, and the problem here is to understand what motivates the particular combination of fictions that occurs in *Corydon*. Two elements of the combination that need to be highlighted here are the desire in *Corydon* successfully to fence in female sexuality, and the desire, in so doing, somehow to justify an association of the male sex with an unbounded liberational sexuality. The mantis example would appear to show an instinctual basis for an aggressive, devouring female sexuality, and so would hardly seem suitable material for the argument in question. It also shows these male insects as enslaved to a strictly heterosexual

29. On some of these questions of gender, drag, and inversion, see Judith Butler, "Lana's 'Imitation': Melodramatic Repetition and the Gender Performative," and also her *Gender Trouble*, esp. 50–57. For a modern-day liberal American rewriting of the praying mantis story, see Stephen Jay Gould, "Only His Wings Remained."

30. Theories such as this one are discussed by Roger Caillois, in his essay "La Mante religieuse," 53–55.

31. The history includes Gide and Caillois, of course. Caillois' essay "La Mante religieuse" includes an extensive bibliography. Gould updates it slightly in his article. Gide and Caillois both cite J.-H. Fabre, *Souvenirs entomologiques. Etudes sur l'instinct et les mœurs des insectes,* as does Remy de Gourmont, who participates heartily in the tradition in *Physique de l'amour* (1903). And, finally, there's Corydon's favorite Lester F. Ward, whose *Pure Sociology: A Treatise on the Origin and Spontaneous Development of Society* (1903) advocates, as does Corydon, the "gynæcocentric" theory of development, whereby the females came first, but the males ended up with heavier brains. According to this "theory," the male praying mantis was not far enough along the evolutionary scale so that the hungry females were still more than capable of outwitting him.

desire that imperiously propels them forward to death. Thus, the subsequent history of sexual development within the chain of life can be written as the male's enfranchisement from *this* instinctual phase, best left to the insects. Many of these texts betray their ideological interests when they choose to imagine female sexuality as somehow remaining on this early instinctual/insect level whereas the males, in their sexuality, pursue a forward-moving, liberatory path. Indeed, the ideological biases of such texts are often most apparent in those moments where they specify precisely what aspects of sexual behavior are (to continue Gould's metaphor) hard-wired and what are merely programmed; what is instinctual and what is chosen, what is predisposition and what is learned behavior, and where, if anywhere, choice enters the picture.

Caillois' Virile Distinctions

I would like at this point to work my way back to the question of mimesis by taking a slight detour through a set of two essays by Roger Caillois that share many of the preoccupations of *Corydon:* "La Mante religieuse" and "Mimétisme et psychasthénie légendaire," printed back to back in Caillois' 1938 book *Le Mythe et l'homme.* This detour will, I think, allow us some insight into these different gender scripts, into the temptation of these texts ideologically to ascribe sexuality to men and women differently. Mimesis is often a crucial aspect in the difference in these ascriptions, and often the one aspect that fosters homophobia and misogyny.

I begin by asking how these two Caillois essays are related: the first on the praying mantis, an essay that spends a great deal of time ruminating on male fantasies of castration of men by women; the second on mimesis in the insect world and its relation to a human personality disorder that Caillois follows Pierre Janet in labeling "psychasthénie" ("a drop in the level of psychic energy, a kind of subjective detumescence, a loss of ego substance, a depressive exhaustion close to what a monk would call *acedia*"[32]). Denis Hollier suggests that the two essays are linked by their shared preoccupation with a question much discussed by Caillois and others of his fellow members of the Collège de Sociologie:

> When the Munich crisis broke out in September 1938, the Collège circulated job offers in which it described itself as an "energy center" dedicated to the struggle against what it called "man's de-virilization." There is no reference here to the praying mantis, but it is clear that both mimesis and castration were equal threats to difference. ("Mimesis and Castration," 12)[33]

32. The definition is Denis Hollier's, in "Mimesis and Castration 1937," 11. Hollier's article has helped me to formulate my ideas, as will be clear in what follows. See also another essay of his that discusses Caillois: "On Equivocation (between Literature and Politics)." "Mimesis and Castration 1937" was published in *October* as a prelude to an English translation of Caillois' "Mimétisme et psychasthénie légendaire." I will be citing that translation in what follows. Translations from Callois' other essay, "La Mante religieuse," will be my own.

33. *Corydon* also contains disquisitions on virility and on the fear that Germany might be more virile than France. We will see this thematic in other Gidean contexts later in this chapter.

If castration threatens an anatomical distinction between the sexes, then mimesis, the imitation of something in your surroundings, threatens a distinction between subject and milieu. Difference or distinction: "between waking and sleeping, between ignorance and knowledge. . . . Among distinctions, there is assuredly none more clear-cut than that between the organism and its surroundings." So writes Caillois in "Mimicry and Legendary Psychasthenia" (17). Hollier calls Caillois a man of distinction: "He makes the difference between those who make the difference and those who do not. The lure of the void may be universal, but some do not succumb to it" ("Mimesis and Castration," 11). But how, precisely, one must still wonder, does the concept of difference or distinction unite mimesis and castration? How could mimesis and castration be *equal* threats to difference, as for Caillois one is marked by the effacement of difference between organism and milieu and the other depends on an economy of sexual difference? How can "de-virilization" come to be the name for the threat embodied by both of these effacements? How can this association be anything but a willful disregard of the difference between castration and mimesis?

The impulse to imitate the milieu in which an organism exists is, for Caillois, an impulse to evade life:

> Alongside the instinct of self-preservation, which in some way orients the creature toward life, there is generally speaking a sort of *instinct of surrender* [instinct de l'abandon] that orients it toward a mode of reduced existence, which in the end would no longer know either consciousness or feeling. . . . It is on this level that it can be gratifying to give a common root to phenomena of mimicry . . . and to psychasthenic experience, since the facts seem so well to impose one on them: this *attraction by space* [sollicitation de l'espace], something as elementary and mechanical as are tropisms, and by whose effect life seems to lose ground, blurring in its retreat the frontier between the organism and the milieu. ("Mimicry," 32)

The boundary transgressed by castration, on the other hand, seems perhaps more straightforward, and not obviously parallel to the boundary transgressed by mimesis of the milieu. First of all, as Hollier carefully points out, mimetic behavior (among insects, for instance) is shared by male and female of the same species. Castration, on the other hand, seems to involve the different sexes of the same species. As Hollier puts it:

> [In the case of the praying mantis] the assimilated creature and the assimilating one belong to the same species . . . while both male and female of the mimetic species assimilate themselves to their surroundings. Caillois' discarding of sexual difference should not itself be discarded as insignificant. But one might wonder if the very disappearance of sexual difference in the shift from castration to mimicry might not itself be counted as one of the many tricks of mimicry: just another sham.[34]

How precisely might that sham work? Late in the essay on the praying mantis, Caillois introduces the subject of his following essay on mimesis:

---

34. This crucial difference, which Hollier chooses "not to dwell on here," is mentioned by him, appropriately enough, in a footnote ("Mimesis and Castration," 13–14, n. 31).

> One shouldn't fail to mention the mimetism of the mantis, which *illustrates* in a sometimes stupefying fashion the *human desire* for reintegration into an original insensibility, something one necessarily compares to the pantheistic conception of fusion with nature, a frequent philosophical and literary translation of the return to a pre-natal state of unconsciousness. ("La Mante religieuse," 75; my emphasis)

The slip from castration to mimesis depends for its occurrence on the slippery analogizing Caillois performs so frequently from insect world to human world: such moves often permit a sly rhetorical slippage by which the human world becomes the world of men, and women remain more than analogically linked to the insects. In the passage just quoted one sees the shadow of this analogizing maneuver in the verb *illustrates*. What is the force of an illustration in linking man to mantis? And why does one have the suspicion that what the supposed desire for a return to nature is being compared to is mainly the desire of the *male* child to return to the maternal body? The most obvious example of the sexist tendency of this analogizing occurs a bit earlier in the praying mantis essay:

> In any case, normal behavior itself reveals at least one characteristic which represents the connection between nutrition and sexuality: the love-bite at the moment of intercourse, already noted by ancient poets and codified by oriental erotologues. It is, to my eye, extremely significant that this behavior is principally exhibited by women, who thereby *sketch out [esquissent]* the behavior of the praying mantis, and especially by idiot girls or by women from savage races, that is to say, wherever instinct for whatever reason is less controlled. . . . That it is in this practice, which can become the source of the most violent sexual aberrations, a question of instinctive, *automatic* behavior, without any sadistic complications, cannot be doubted, because the woman simply seeks to clutch and to bite anything, completely *unconscious* of the effects produced on the victim, effects by which she is subsequently the first to be astonished. ("La Mante religieuse," 59)

Here it is not the insect that illustrates a human desire, but women who illustrate (*esquisser*) insectlike instincts. Automatism, the unreflective imitation of archaic behavior, is the quality that links women to insects; this automatism constitutes the threat they represent to virile independence. "Instinct, and consequently automatism, dominate the existence of the insect; intelligence, the possibility to examine, to judge, to refuse, in general, everything that loosens the relation between representation and action, characterizes that of man." ("La Mante religieuse," 71). It would appear that for women there is less play available than there is for men in the wiring of action to representation. Women and mantises are analogous to automatons, constrained in their behavior by the emphasis on hard wiring, no reflection on action, mimesis out of control.[35] Caillois emphasizes this final point in the following passage:

> Literature too knows, in its chapter about the *femme fatale,* the idea of a woman-machine, artificial, mechanical, nothing in common with living creatures, and above

---

35. Lacoue-Labarthe has helpful things to say about different conceptions of mimesis and ways of mapping them on to gender. See, for example, "Diderot: Paradox and Mimesis," 264.

> all, murderous. . . . This fantasm is more or less explicitly evoked by the mantis. In effect, besides its articulated rigidity, which itself might make us think of the rigidity of armor or of an automaton, there are in fact few reactions the mantis is incapable of performing while decapitated, that is to say, in the absence of any center of representation or of voluntary activity: thus it can . . . and this is truly disconcerting, faced with danger or following some peripheral stimulus, fall into a false and cadaverous immobility: I intentionally use this roundabout way of expressing myself since it seems to me that language has a great deal of difficulty expressing and thereby understanding that, dead, the mantis can play dead. ("La Mante religieuse," 73–74)

This passage in its first sentence or two also seems to make clear the equation woman = mantis, even though the decapitated mantis a few lines later might in fact be that somewhat forgotten male mantis, unwittingly turned into a sex robot in the service of the insatiable female. The mantis is an emblem of a dangerous mimesis in that males and females seem to imitate roles normally assigned to the other sex in such a dizzying fashion that both sexes collapse into one, and the nonvirile males, in their inversion, exhibit that feminizing loss of *voluntary* representation and activity. "What makes mimesis strange," Hollier says, paraphrasing Caillois, "is precisely the fact that an organism gives up that distinction, abdicates that fundamentally vital difference between life and matter, between the organism and the inorganic" ("Mimesis and Castration," 11). The sacrifice of vitality, as it shades into a sacrifice of volition, becomes a sacrifice of masculine gender traits as well. The combined discourses of homophobia and misogyny of *Corydon* seem close at hand. We might, in fact, begin to edge our way back to *Corydon* by underlining again the extent to which it seems to share Caillois' disapproval of entropic mimesis, of an unbounded and devirilizing female sexual appetite, and of its links, through drag, to "inversion."

The Gynaeceum and the Fear of Devirilization

The Cailloisesque, culturally omnipresent scenario by which a Corydon/Gide could inextricably interweave his misogyny with the homophobia he directs against the "invertis" he claims to detest has been analyzed by Leo Bersani in another context in his article "Is the Rectum a Grave?":

> Promiscuity is the social correlative of a sexuality physiologically grounded in the menacing phenomenon of the nonclimactic climax. Prostitutes publicize (indeed, sell) the inherent aptitude [*sic*] of women for uninterrupted sex. Conversely, the similarities between representations of female prostitutes and male homosexuals should help us to specify the exact form of sexual behavior being targeted, in representations of AIDS, as the criminal, fatal, and irresistibly repeated act. This is of course anal sex. (211)

Anal sex is thus understood as the devirilizing mimesis of female sexuality: inhuman in its failure to embody a selfhood understood through ideas of volition;

feminine—and therefore inhuman, mantic—in its limitless capacity for pleasure. Later in his article, Bersani refers to "the heterosexual association of anal sex with a self-annihilation originally and primarily identified with the fantasmatic mystery of an insatiable, unstoppable female sexuality." This is clearly the Caillois, Corydon/Gide tradition. Bersani goes on to suggest: "It may, finally, be in the gay man's rectum that he demolishes his own perhaps otherwise uncontrollable identification with a murderous judgment against him" (222). The suggestion is intriguing: that through a bodily act one could eliminate, or at least erase for a moment the ideological programming Gide's *Corydon* and Caillois' two essays not only argue is essential, prescripted, ineradicable but also reinforce in their writing. But is the eradication of this programming, the eradication of "masculinist" identifications through mimetic allegiances to "feminine" sexual practices the surest way of undercutting or undoing the phobic prescriptions of heterosexist binaries? Does it give us access to as wide an array of queer allegiances as we might hope for? Should we imagine there to be any temporally coherent (first women, later the fags who imitate them),[36] stable, unified kind of mimesis anal intercourse could be said to perform? One might wonder whether fantasms and their ideological content could be so unequivocally erased—whether, by assuming the abject position the gender binary has constructed, the reactivation and perpetuation of that structure could be so definitively resisted—just as one might wonder if one particular way of having sex (and one particular way of imagining what is going on in that act) would be the most analytically evident route to such an end.

With such questions in mind, we could return to the central question of this chapter: are there ways of reading *Corydon* queerly so that it does not perform its reinforcing work, so that, even as we watch it try to shore up certain ideological scaffoldings, we notice its own potential to demolish what it attempts to build? What analytic relation to mimesis does this require us to assume?

Corydon echoes the Caillois theme of devirilization in the final pages of his last conversation with his interlocutor. Out of the blue, he asks his old school-friend if he has any idea why the Napoleonic Code included no laws against homosexuality. The listener replies, surprised, that probably Napoleon never thought of it or saw no reason to legislate what people would instinctively condemn. Corydon has a different theory:

> Perhaps it was also because such laws would have embarrassed some of his best generals. Reprehensible or not, such habits are so far from being enervating, are so close to being military, that I must admit to you I've trembled for us during those sensational trials in Germany, which even the Kaiser's vigilance could not succeed in suppressing; and even earlier, at the time of Krupp's suicide. Some people in France were naïve enough to see such episodes as signs of decadence! while I was thinking

---

36. Judith Butler's work contains thorough and brilliant analyses of questions of logical priority in relation to imitation as regards gender and sexuality. See her *Gender Trouble* and "Critically Queer."

to myself: Beware of a people whose very debauchery is warlike and who keep their women for the exclusive purpose of providing fine children. (118)[37]

One doubts such an invocation of the utility of same-sex eroticism to a state's military prowess would have achieved much success in pre– or post–World War I France.[38] This model is occasionally appealed to today[39] and is as worthy of being rejected now as it would have been then, not on homophobic grounds ("we don't want *them* in the military"), but because of what Corydon's way of describing this imagined relationship between homosexuality and the military makes clear: its homophobic and misogynistic potential, its interest in reinforcing repressive stereotypes of sexual roles. The too easy appeal to the gay man of certain construals of masculinity can lead, *Corydon* shows us, to odious participation in statist, militaristic, misogynistic construals of sexuality in general. Bersani states this point clearly:

> The dead seriousness of the gay commitment to machismo (by which I of course don't mean that all gays share, or share unambivalently, this commitment) means that gay men run the risk of idealizing and feeling inferior to certain representations of masculinity on the basis of which they are in fact judged and condemned. The logic of homosexual desire includes the potential for a loving identification with the gay man's enemies. And that is a fantasy-luxury that is at once inevitable and no longer permissible. Inevitable because a sexual desire for men can't be merely a kind of culturally neutral attraction to a Platonic idea of the male body; the object of that desire necessarily includes a socially determined and socially pervasive definition of what it means to be a man. ("Is the Rectum a Grave?" 208–9)

Corydon is intriguing in that it displays this mechanism, this "logic" of homosexual desire, in its very dialogic structure, in the alter ego relationship of the two characters, in the way they express or repress their desire for each other precisely through an ongoing game of macho one-upmanship. The victims of their particular virile mimetic game, in this military-state version are thus those they construe as *differently* mimetic, women and men who "imitate" them.

Thus after Corydon suggests the military usefulness of pederasty, his listener responds that this might have a negative effect on another military problem, "the disturbing decrease in the French birth rate." One should encourage heterosexual activity as much as possible to improve the situation. Corydon responds:

37. C'est peut-être aussi que ces lois eussent d'abord gêné certains de ses généraux les meilleurs. Répréhensible ou non, ces mœurs sont si loin d'être amollissantes, sont si près d'être militaires, que je vous avoue que j'ai tremblé pour nous, lors de ces retentissants procès d'outre-Rhin, que n'a pu parvenir à étouffer la vigilance de l'empereur; et, déjà peu avant, lors du suicide de Krupp. Certains, en France, ont eu la naïveté de voir là des indices de décadence! tandis que je pensais tout bas : défions-nous d'un peuple dont la débauche même est guerrière et qui réserve la femme au soin de lui donner de beaux enfants (130).

38. Corydon is trying to draw on the appeal of the cultural model provided by ancient Greece. For a good introduction to recent criticism of that model, see David M. Halperin, "Two Views of Greek Love: Harald Patzer and Michel Foucault." See also John J. Winkler's "Laying Down the Law: The Oversight of Men's Sexual Behavior in Classical Athens."

39. By John Boswell, for instance, in a shoddily argued article entitled "Battle-Worn": "The most counterintuitive aspect of ancient same-sex eroticism is not its frequency, which is well known, but its long and hallowed relationship to democracy and military valor. . . . As is widely recognized even by opponents of admitting homosexuals openly to the U.S. military, gay and lesbian soldiers have served faithfully and courageously in every conflict since

> Don't tell me you really believe that all these inducements to love will result in the birth of a great many children? Do you imagine that all these women who offer themselves to love will consent to getting themselves knocked up into the bargain? You're joking!
>
> I tell you, the shameless stimulation of our popular imagery, theaters, music halls, and a host of publications serves only to lure woman away from her duties; to make her into a perpetual mistress [*une amante perpétuelle*], who no longer consents to maternity. I tell you that this is quite as dangerous for the state as the very excess of the other kind of debauchery. (118–19)[40]

A nice touch that the "mante" would be so close to the "amante perpétuelle." The phrase "les excitation éhontées des images" (the shameless stimulation of our popular imagery) might recall for us those unfortunate cows Gourmont was so amused to find humping each other: "their visual representation of the desired act compels them to attempt a simulation of it." Not wired to handle the conjunction of image and desire, these females deviate into sexual aberrance and thereby menace the state.

It would at this point be hard to believe that the author of *Corydon* would ever set to work writing a set of feminist narratives, yet this Gide would do in his trilogy: *L'Ecole des femmes* (1929), *Robert* (1929), and *Geneviève* (1936). The very title of the first of these could be seen as a complicated reference to *Corydon,* since *Corydon*'s reflections on the problem of unbounded female sexuality include a suggested solution to that problem, the creation of a space where that sexuality will learn ("naturally") to direct itself toward maternity. That space is precisely a gynaeceum: a school for wives. "The Greek girl was raised not so much with a view to love as to maternity. Man's desire, as we have seen, was directed elsewhere; for nothing seemed more necessary to the State, nor to deserve more respect, than the tranquil purity of the gynaeceum" (110).[41] The gynaeceum is given as a counter-

---

World War II. There is, in other words, an ancient correlation not only of military service and homosexuality, but of democracy in particular with military service on the part of all citizens, which extends from ancient history to the present day. It is perhaps time that one of the leading modern democracies in the world recognized it" (15, 18).

   Boswell is not terribly convincing on the essential links between military service and democracy, nor on how to slip in homosexuality in the modern context. Have armies *ever* really had as a function to equalize, normalize, or overcome, say, class difference, racial discrimination, gender discrimination, discrimination based on sexuality, thereby furthering some democratic program? A military's relation to democracy and its relation to homosexuality seem considerably more troubled and troubling. Is it not in fact more usual that the military as an institution enforces these various discriminations? *Corydon*'s rhetoric at least admits this. Boswell's covers it over.

   40. Quoi? Vous croyez vraiment qu'il va naître beaucoup d'enfants de toutes ces provocations à l'amour? Vous croyez que toutes ces femmes, qui se proposent en amoureuses, vont consentir à se laisser charger! Vous plaisantez!

   Je dis que les excitations éhontées des images, des théâtres, des music-halls et de maints journaux, ne travaillent qu'à détourner la femme de ses devoirs; à faire de la femme *une amante perpétuelle,* qui ne consente plus à la maternité. Je dis que cela est autrement dangereux pour l'Etat que l'excès même de l'autre débauche . . . (130–31, my emphasis).

   41. La jeune fille grecque était élevée non point tant en vue de l'amour, que de la maternité. Le désir de l'homme, nous l'avons vu, s'adressait ailleurs; car rien ne paraissait plus nécessaire à l'Etat, ni mériter plus le respect, que la tranquille pureté du gynécée (122).

example to two seemingly less distant institutions that could count as more modern perversions of it: the brothel and the harem. The brothel and the harem come up in the context of an antisemitic discussion of a book by Léon Blum, *Du mariage*.[42] Corydon here describes the problem he sees Blum as setting out to solve in his book:

> "The male has much more to expend than is required in order to answer to the reproductive function of the opposite sex and to ensure the reproduction of the species. The expenditure to which nature prompts him is quite difficult to regulate and risks becoming prejudicial to law and order as Western peoples understand them."
>
> "Hence that nostalgia for the harem in Blum's book, which as I say is repugnant to our morals and to our Western institutions, which are essentially monogamous."
>
> "We prefer brothels."
>
> "How dare you!"
>
> "Let's say: prostitution. Or adultery." (104)[43]

The straight man erects an absolute opposition (one not notable for its historical accuracy) between Jewish and Western ways of structuring sexuality—monogamy falling on the Western side. Corydon undercuts this opposition by claiming some degree of parentage between the supposedly Jewish/oriental (a conflation demonstrating a similar disregard for accuracy on the part of Corydon) structure of the harem and the Western institution of prostitution. In no way offering a feminist critique of prostitution, Corydon sees heterosexual hypocrisy in the pretense that *male* sexuality easily finds satisfaction within marriage. That there might be links to be drawn between the constraints placed on female sexual expression and the opprobrium attached to homosexuality seems not even vaguely implied in such passages.

42. See *Corydon*, 103–5/115–17. This passage has been discussed by Jeffrey Mehlman in his article, "'Jewish Literature' and the Art of André Gide." See, for example, p. 79: "The fourth dialogue of *Corydon*, his apology for and celebration of pederasty, in fact, offers itself as a refutation of *Du mariage*. Corydon's interlocutor, admittedly a foil for Gide's protagonist, waxes vehemently anti-Jewish. Corydon, though never quite rallying to the anti-Semitic line he is offered, is intent on finding a solution other than Blum's to the specific problem of prostitution. His answer is self-consciously *un-* (if not *anti-*) Jewish: recourse to the Greek institution of pederasty as an outlet for the surplus of male sexual energy in nature. As for female sexual pleasure, we are told that it is irrelevant: 'Girls in Greece were raised with an eye not so much to love as to maternity.' Whereupon the antipathy to the Jewish feminist, Sara, in *Geneviève*, its role as a figure of Gide's own inability to complete that work, again reveals its coherence."

Mehlman helpfully precedes me in linking *Corydon* and the *Ecole des femmes* trilogy. Emily Apter is also helpful not only in her linkage of certain texts but also specifically in her way of dealing with the *Ecole* trilogy. See her fifth chapter entitled "The Etiology of the Unspoken: Negation and Gender in the *Récits*," in *André Gide and the Codes of Homotextuality,* esp. 108–10 and the section entitled "Female Impersonations," 134–50.

43. Le mâle a beaucoup plus à dépenser qu'il ne convient pour répondre à la fonction reproductive de l'autre sexe et assurer la reproduction de l'espèce. La dépense à laquelle l'invite la Nature est assez incommode à régler et risque de devenir préjudiciable au bon ordre de la société telle que les peuples occidentaux la comprennent.

— D'où cette nostalgie du sérail, dans le livre de Blum, qui répugne ai-je dit à nos mœurs, à nos institutions occidentales, essentiellement monogames.

— Nous préférons le bordel.

— Taisez-vous.

— Disons : la prostitution. Ou l'adultère (116).

But in this connection there is an important scene from *Si le grain ne meurt* that might remind us that the links *Corydon* is notably failing to make are made elsewhere. We might first of all usefully remember here Gide's division faced with his mother's sexuality (examined in chapter 2), particularly in the scene where Marie is brushing his mother's hair. In that scene there was a complex interaction of allegiance to and revulsion from his mother's and Marie's shadowy forms of sexual expression. There was allegiance to whatever in that expression remained socially marginal and thus somehow exemplary for Gide's own sexual marginality, yet there was also a forcefully intervening revulsion, when Gide abruptly associated the supplements Marie would add to his mother's hairdo with the supplements, the horrifying bustles, that women used to alter the form of their buttocks—a sign of a female sexuality Gide was compelled to write about in order to be unable to countenance it.

Similar complexities are evoked on an evening, also described in *Si le grain ne meurt,* when Gide reads aloud to his mother. The young Gide has up to a certain point in his life been denied access by his mother to his father's library. As a compromise, at a certain age Gide is to be given access to the library, but he will read the books he chooses aloud to his mother. He defiantly chooses Gautier: "Gautier, for me and for numbers of schoolboys in those days, stood for scorn of conventionality, for emancipation, for licence. . . . Maman wanted to read with me! Very well! We would see which of the two would cry for mercy first." (We might here usefully remember Gautier as the author of *Mademoiselle de Maupin,* a text one of whose many importances would be the place it occupies in the history of French representations of lesbianism.) On the night described in *Si le grain ne meurt,* the Gautier text chosen is "Albertus ou l'âme et le péché," a poem about a mean old witch with an insatiable sexual appetite who falls in love with the handsome young Albertus and turns herself into a beautiful young woman in order to seduce him into a night of extravagant love-making. "I had started off gaily enough, but as the text became more ribald my voice became less confident. . . . Mamma plied her needle with an ever more nervous hand; as I read, I caught the flash of its moving point out of the corner of my eye" (166–67).[44] Much to his relief, Gide says, his mother interrupts him in stanza 101, takes the book from him, reads ahead, decides how many stanzas he should skip, gives him the book back showing him where to start again, and then summarizes what he will have missed in the stanzas where Albertus makes love to the beautiful young Véronique, as yet unaware that she will soon be revealed as a horrendous old hag, and that he is, in fact, to end the night like a male mantis, dead, the life sucked out of him. "'Yes . . . Here: *She was worth a whole seraglio in herself,*' said she, quoting the

---

44. J'avais commencé très allégrement, mais à mesure que j'avancais, ma voix se glaçait, tandis que le texte devenait plus gaillard . . . Maman tirait l'aiguille d'une main toujours plus nerveuse; tout en lisant j'accrochais du coin de l'œil l'extrémité de son mouvement (201).

line which she thought would best sum up the verses she had censored—and which I became acquainted with long after, to my considerable disappointment" (168).[45] "Me voici donc, un soir, dans la chambre de ma mère, assis près d'elle," Gide had said at the beginning of this description. "There I was one night, in my mother's chamber, seated near her." In the gynaeceum itself, the sewing mother's voice pronounces to the beloved gay son the very word that names the negative correlative of the space they occupy: this one single woman, this disguised old witch, is so well disguised that she could take the place of a whole harem.[46] The actual verse from Gautier reads: "Seule elle valait un sérail." On her own she was the equivalent of a harem: so sexually ravenous that she was more than a match for the most emancipated and available male desire. How might the reading of this text threaten or enhance the silent complicity of mother and son in their shared social privilege and sexual marginality? What forms of comfort might be lost were that silent complicity to acknowledge itself? Who or what is actually being protected in this scene of claustration always about to explode, this mother's chamber into which licentious books find their way, bits of antimatter that by their very combination with this new space seem to begin a structural critique? For that silent complicity between mother and son, which *Si le grain ne meurt* seems to want to break down, helps energize that kind of sexual policing in which homophobia and misogyny unite themselves.

    Corydon also seems to share a bit of this unrealized potential to dynamite itself, constructing and displaying the very homophobia it criticizes; displaying its fascination with female sexuality and its desire to be imbricated in it even as it argues for shutting it away; on the one hand, arguing for an essential distinction between the sexes and disapproving of those forms of homosexuality it imagines as constructed through abjectly mimetic relations between them; on the other hand, displaying (in its confused understanding of the mantis, in its muddled effort to free male sexuality from any instinctual constraint) a half-conscious knowledge of the analytic inevitability of travesty and mimeticism—of inversion even, apparently its greatest horror—a half-conscious knowledge that pushes toward a realization that gender systems never really allow for clean distinctions and that there is no nonideological, no "natural" way to read back to sex or to "instinct" after having been trained in gender. This exploding potential in *Corydon* is not embodied in either of the characters, and it is clearly not assignable to any presence in the text we might label "Gide." However it exists in *Corydon*'s writing, it is probably the thing in the text most worth reading.

45. —Oui . . . Enfin :
Elle valait tout un sérail.
dit-elle, citant le vers qui pouvait le mieux résumer, d'après elle, les strophes censurées — et dont je ne pris connaissance que beaucoup plus tard, pour ma parfaite déception (202).
46. For a discussion of the relationship between gynaeceum and harem in the context of French colonial literature, see Emily Apter, "Female Trouble in the Colonial Harem," esp. 215–20.

L'Ecole des femmes

It seems to me that Gide's feminist trilogy needs to be read in similar fashion to the way I have tried to read *Corydon*, a reading that challenges the text's "logic" (which is not one) in order to bring out what that "logic" is a defense against. I suggested that Gide's *L'Ecole des femmes* could be read as a new attempt to construe the space of the gynaeceum. What one might hope for in a new construal of that space would be some effort to write more explicitly about the kinds of allegiances between marginal sexualities that might be traced across genders. In particular, one might hope for a new account of lesbianism, more respectful of that sexuality's complexities.

In 1930, the year after publishing *L'Ecole des femmes* and *Robert*, Gide published *La Séquestrée de Poitiers* (*The Sequestered Woman of Poitiers*), a retelling of the bizarre story of Mélanie Bastian, who was discovered by the Poitiers police in 1901, having been locked up in a tiny bedroom, for roughly a quarter-century, by her mother and brother. The two of them were apparently punishing her for having given birth to an illegitimate child that was somehow done away with upon its birth. Such a sequestration takes the policing potential of the gynaeceum imagined in *Corydon* to an obscene extreme, and Gide's piecing together of the documents making up this case represents a clear step away from the ideological position given voice in *Corydon*.

Geneviève, the final narrative in his feminist trilogy, tries to imagine a further step. It tells of a young woman whose bond with her mother is formed through her own efforts to escape the ideology of the gynaeceum and through her growing awareness of how that ideology has distorted her mother's life, of how much her mother has sacrificed in order to help her daughter escape that ideology. The signs of Geneviève's liberation will include lesbian attachments, ardent feminist sentiments, and the decision to have a child as a single mother.

Gide wrote two parts to *Geneviève* and projected a third that he never finished. The second part ends with the death of Eveline, Geneviève's mother. Geneviève was meant to achieve some personal and ideological breakthrough after this point, but Gide claims to have found himself unable to imagine it. In May of 1936 he writes in his *Journal* that he has torn up all he had written of the third part, and plans to give up trying to write it.

> I should have liked to make Geneviève catch hold of herself after her mother's death, say to herself: "The way I take hardly matters, but only where I am heading." This was to be the beginning of the third chapter, and I strove in vain to slip this sentence into the very end of the second; it would have ruined everything. I preferred to give up. (*Journals*, 3:343)[47]

47. J'aurais voulu faire Geneviève se ressaisir après la mort de sa mère; se dire : « Par où je passe n'importe guère, mais seulement vers où je vais. » Ce devait être le début du IIIᵉ chapitre, et j'ai cherché en vain à glisser tout à la fin du IIᵉ cette phrase; elle eût tout abîmé. J'ai préféré lâcher prise (*Journal, 1889–1939*, 1252).

That he had some resistance to the work he had to do in order to imagine this heroine of what was to be his most feminist text, Gide freely admits, in his inimitably sexist way:

> But I feel no satisfaction in writing, femininely, with rapid ease, and I dislike everything I write this way. I begin to doubt that this style lacking in density can have any value and sometimes fear I am hazarding a desperate undertaking, unworthy of all the other projects which I then reproach myself with having forsaken for this one. I must admit to myself that this book does not touch me very deeply and does not reply to any profound exigency. (*Journals,* 3:100–01)[48]

Now everything we have read should convince us of the dishonesty of that last remark. The confrontation with the space of the gynaeceum is unquestionably central to Gide's project of writing out his sexuality. It may well be a confrontation that ultimately, despite repeated approaches, he was never able to bring about. I would like to look at one more of those approaches here, that of *L'Ecole des femmes,* and some of its limitations, to establish some of the reasons why this confrontation never fully happened. I will myself approach *L'Ecole des femmes* by looking at a number of Gide's comments on women and grammar, as grammar is a subject of some consequence within that narrative.

Imperfect Subjunctives

We therefore first turn to one of the oddest parts of the Gidean corpus, a short piece he wrote toward the end of World War I, provoked by the many mistakes in the use of the subjunctive he was seeing in the French press. Even though the mistakes he cites are mostly from the newspapers, Gide imagines them as beginning in the mouth of a working woman, who often doesn't realize she is using the subjunctive because it frequently has the same spelling and sound as the indicative:

> For example, the working-class woman who writes to her lover: "Don't be surprised that I give you the shove (or: that I let you go)" could employ the subjunctive without knowing it. [In French, here, one would use the subjunctive, but its first-person singular form is identical to that of the indicative (*plaque/plaque*).] Saying: "I don't want you to think" perhaps she imagines she is using the subjunctive, or perhaps not. [Here, too, the subjunctive is necessary, and *sounds* the same as the indicative, but is *spelled* differently (*croies/crois*).] And because of the confusion that has been created, now she will find it pretentious to use the subjunctive to say "I don't want you to

48. Mais je n'éprouve aucune satisfaction à écrire, fémininement, au courant de la plume, et tout ce que j'écris ainsi me déplaît. Je doute que ce style sans densité puisse avoir quelque valeur et crains parfois de m'aventurer dans une entreprise désespérante, indigne de tous les autres projets, que je me reproche dès lors de délaisser pour elle. Ce livre, il faut que je me l'avoue, ne me tient pas directement à cœur et ne répond à aucune profonde exigence . . . (*Journal, 1889–1939,* 977–78).

leave." [In this final case, the necessary subjunctive differs from the indicative both in spelling and in pronunciation (*ailles/vas*), the woman's error, in this worst-case scenario, thus being both legible and audible.] ("Crise du Français," 162)[49]

There is perhaps little coherent interest in linguistic transformation here; instead, there is a certain amount of hostility toward women, especially when, after managing to explain in a grammatically correct way to their partners that they are *leaving* them, they no longer have a sufficient command of the language to ask the men later, in proper French, to *stay* with them. The situation becomes even more puzzling when, reading through a list Gide provides of examples of fairly mundane errors in the use of the subjunctive, we suddenly come across this one: "« . . . Me laissant pour que je profitasse de l'air de la mer » (Proust, *Sodome et Gomorrhe*, II, 3, p. 212)."

From working women and typesetters to Proust is a bit of a shift, and one Gide has to work to account for. We might think of looking for the source of the rub in "profitasse" not so much in the grammar of the passage as in its content. Where there is *mer* (sea), of course, there is *mère* (mother); and if we trace this passage back to its context in *A la recherche du temps perdu*, we do encounter Marcel's mother and also Marcel trying to act the man's role, this time dealing with Albertine:

> And, one evening, as *Maman* was setting out next day for Combray, where she was to attend the deathbed of one of her *mother*'s sisters, leaving me behind so that I might continue to benefit, as my grand*mother* would have wished, from the *sea* air, I had announced to her that I had irrevocably decided not to marry Albertine and would soon stop seeing her. I was glad to be able, by these words, to gratify my *mother*'s wishes on the eve of her departure. (*Remembrance*, 2:1150)[50]

Of the many reasons this passage would have caught Gide's eye, grammatical ones seem far from the most likely, even though it is through them that he expresses his displeasure. We could perhaps instead imagine Gide's discomfort as he watches Marcel having to choose between giving satisfaction to his mother or to his own desires, and choosing temporarily the, for Gide, less virile option of giving in to his mother. But it has to be admitted that *there is no mistake* in the use of the subjunctive. Gide, in fact, acknowledges this: "This is in no way a mistake, but my firm opinion is that one should reserve the past of the subjunctive for more distant

49. Par exemple, l'ouvrière qui écrit à son amant : « Ne t'étonne pas que je te plaque (ou : que je te lâche) » peut employer le subjonctif sans le savoir. En disant : « Je ne veux pas que tu croies » elle s'imagine peut-être dire : « Je ne veux pas que tu crois » — ou réciproquement. Et la confusion qui s'établit fait qu'il lui paraîtra bientôt prétentieux de dire : « Je ne veux pas que tu t'en ailles »; elle dira : « Je ne veux pas que tu t'en vas ».

50. Et, un soir, comme *maman* partait le lendemain pour Combray, où elle allait assister dans sa dernière maladie une sœur de sa *mère*, me laissant pour que je profitasse, comme grand'*mère* aurait voulu, de l'air de la *mer*, je lui avais annoncé qu'irrévocablement j'étais décidé à ne pas épouser Albertine et allais cesser prochainement de la voir. J'étais content d'avoir pu, par ces mots, donner satisfaction à ma *mère* la veille de son départ (Proust, *A la recherche*, 2:1112, emphasis added).

relationships. Otherwise, what tense would one use with 'Having left me be-hind . . .'?" ("Crise du Français," 165).[51] Having indicted the proletarian woman for not using the present subjunctive because she found it too pretentious, Gide is about to indict Proust for being pretentious in that he uses the *imperfect* subjunctive too readily.

> The important thing is the subjunctive, not its imperfect. . . . And really, would you call someone wrong who found it a little pretentious to say: he wanted me to write [*écrivisse*, imperfect subjunctive] to him. . . . As long as there is still time to write . . . I believe that the present subjunctive suffices, and it is fitting to reserve the imperfect to express something which can no longer be done. (166)[52]

Gide is clearly a hard man to please.[53] As we will see in a moment, he does not necessarily live up to his own grammatical prescriptions; the imperfect subjunctive is a favorite tense of his. Jean Cocteau, another of Gide's literary rivals, found *Gide*'s use of the tense extremely annoying. Cocteau was once taken to task by Gide shortly after World War I in an open letter, for being too clever, and not a serious enough artist. Cocteau, in his responding open letter, gave examples of some of Gide's annoying stylistic quirks: "You have, Gide, a complete system of mysteries, reserves, *imperfect subjunctives*, alibis and entanglements" (in Peters, 61, 66; my emphasis). Consider a passage where Gide is at his most egregious, so ridiculous as to require us to laugh him off at the same time as we must take him quite seriously. Notice, too, the final imperfect subjunctive, exquisitely correct following a conditional, a place where some might have thought a present subjunctive would have done just as well.

> Je souhaite d'être contredit; mais il me paraît, hélas, que les principaux ouvriers de la désagrégation d'une langue, ce sont les femmes. Les femmes: parce que leur esprit est capable d'une moindre logique; parce que leur susceptibilité toujours vive ne supporte pas qu'on les reprenne et que, du reste, la bienséance, à défaut de la galanterie empêcherait qu'on le *fît*. (169; my emphasis)
>
> [I hope to be contradicted, but, alas, it appears to me that those whose work is principally at fault in the deterioration of a language are women. Women: because their mind is capable of a lesser logic, because their acute sensitivity cannot with-stand correction; and, when it comes down to it, decorum, if not gallantry would stop one from correcting them.]

Now, the ideology of this passage and the preceding ones should be familiar to us as readers of *Corydon*. Proust is cast in the role of the *inverti*, trapped by his *tares intellectuelles* into effeminately pretentious, overly luxurious imperfect sub-

---

51. Ceci n'est nullement une faute; mais mon avis très net est qu'il faut réserver le passé du subjonctif pour des relations plus reculées. Qu'employer, sinon, avec « M'ayant laissé » . . . ?

52. L'important c'est le subjonctif, non l'imparfait de celui-ci . . . Et vraiment donnerez-vous tort à celui qui trouve un peu prétentieux : il voulait que je lui *écrivisse?* . . . Tant qu'il est encore temps d'écrire . . . j'estime que le présent suffit et qu'il sied de réserver l'imparfait pour exprimer ce qui n'est plus à faire.

53. For more evidence of his regulatory obsession as to the use of the subjunctive, see his journal entry for October 23, 1927.

junctives. Gide is more restrained, he would have us believe, in his use of that tense, less spendthrift. As for his elegant *fît,* such a usage apparently indicates a "relation plus reculée," a "more distant relationship." It is thus too late for women, too late to correct them, just as it is too late for fags such as Proust. Too late, perhaps, because they are instinctually bound. The *ouvrière* is the woman who has not only escaped the gynaeceum's beneficent education, she could never have made use of it. As confused as the poor cows of that ludicrous *Corydon* footnote, she can no longer, and never could, sustain her conservative linguistic role, no longer preserve the *bien parler,* the *bien écrire.*[54] "Ehontée," she now unwittingly contributes to the crumbling of the nation through the crumbling of her language, repeating whatever she hears, exerting no will to shape her language into elegance.

Grammar and the Nation

The rhetoric of the crumbling of the family and of the nation is escalated in similar writings by Gide from the World War II period. When the war was finally over, he went on the offensive in a series of occasional articles for *Le Figaro* and *Le Figaro littéraire* entitled "Défense de la langue française." My favorite passage from these articles, one relevant to the discussion going on here, occurs in the first of them, on the front page of the *Figaro* for December 10, 1946:

> I have saved for last a mistake that seems important to me, but particularly difficult to inveigh against, for it doesn't usually find its way into print, at least not yet. One doesn't read it, one hears it, more and more often, and in the best conversations—I mean in cultivated society, or society that imagines itself as such. It is unbecoming to protest when one hears a woman (and it seems, I don't know why, that this is a particular specialty of women), a lady, even, say: *"pour ne pas que."* It should be her husband's task to correct her, but he would first have to notice the error, and even then. . . . Unhappy marriages can often be recognized by the speech errors of the wife. Sometimes, ignoring propriety and the husband's silence, I allow myself to express some astonishment when I hear someone say: "I reprimanded that child so as not to have him start up again [*pour ne pas qu'il recommence*]", or "I had him wear his heavy coat so as not to have him catch cold [*pour ne pas qu'il s'enrhume*]" (notice this faulty construction is usually only used in the third person). Then, in immediate response to my comment: "Well, how should one say this, according to you?" And my proposal: "so that he doesn't start up again [*pour qu'il ne recommence pas*]," or my "so that he doesn't catch cold [*pour qu'il ne s'enrhume pas*]," is judged flat, pretentious and weak. I retreat, unsure that I should ever have protested at all.[55]

54. See these comments by Sarah Banks on *L'Ecole des femmes:* "Robert embodies the principle of 'le bien écrire' in its driest, most stifling aspect; his corrections of Eveline's grammar aim at making women the preservers of the language so that men will be able to stray on experimental journeys." In "Pris au Jeu (ou au *je*): The Impossible Game of 'I' in Gide's Journals."

55. J'ai gardé pour la fin une faute qui me paraît importante, mais particulièrement difficile à dénoncer, car ce n'est pas dans les imprimés qu'elle se trouve; du moins pas encore. On ne la lit point; on l'entend, et de plus en plus, et dans les conversations du meilleur monde, je veux dire dans la société des gens cultivés ou prétendus tels. Il est

In a more serious vein, in 1940 and 1941, Gide was living in the south of France, the *zone libre*, trying in his journal to come to terms with his feelings about the German occupation and the Pétain government. He would end up detesting both before he left France in May of 1942 to spend the rest of the war living in northern Africa, but the pages in which he works out his thoughts make disturbing reading. On January 12, 1941, he pleads: "Oh, I should like to be left alone, to be forgotten! Free to think in my own way without it costing anyone anything and to express without constraint or fear of censure the oscillation of my thought" (*Journals*, 4:55).[56] It is this *balancement* that can make reading these pages so painful. On the one hand, at about this time he breaks with Drieu la Rochelle and the people now running his old journal, *La Nouvelle Revue Française,* in disapproval at their collaboration. On the other hand, he speculates, for example, about the possibility that the French, given the disarray of their culture, perhaps merited their defeat at the hands of the Germans (speculations that might recall Corydon's similar musings from much earlier).[57] The following passage, Gide's entry for May 10, 1941, is perhaps not the most disturbing, but, on balance, far from pleasant:

> If the English succeed in driving the Germans out of France, a party will form in our country to balk at that deliverance, to discover that the preceding domination had something to be said for it, since it at least imposed an order, and to prefer it to the disorder of freedom. A freedom for which we are not yet ready and that we don't deserve. Freedom is beautiful only because it permits the exercise of virtues that it is first essential to have acquired. How much time will be left to me to suffer from this period of turbulence? Shall I live long enough to see the dawn breaking beyond the confusion and not to die in despair? (*Journals*, 4:67)[58]

The tone of the entry is a bit difficult to pin down. It is hard to tell precisely to what degree these sentiments are being entertained. In any case, Gide seems concerned about the moral fiber of the French and about the social disorder that

---

malséant de protester lorsque l'on entend une femme (car il semble, et je ne sais pourquoi, que ce soit une spécialité presque uniquement féminine), une dame, dire : « Pour ne pas que. » Ce serait l'affaire du mari de la reprendre; mais il importerait d'abord qu'il y fût sensible lui-même; et puis . . . Les ménages désunis se reconnaissent souvent aux « cuirs » de l'épouse. Il m'est parfois arrivé, passant outre la bienséance et le silence de l'époux, de marquer quelque étonnement lorsque j'entendais dire : « J'ai réprimandé cet enfant pour ne pas qu'il recommence », ou « Je lui ai mis son gros manteau pour ne pas qu'il s'enrhume » (à remarquer que cette fautive expression ne s'emploie guère qu'à la troisième personne). Et tout aussitôt, en riposte à ma remarque : « Mais comment, selon vous, doit-on dire? » Et le « pour qu'il ne recommence pas », « pour qu'il ne s'enrhume pas », que je proposais à la place, était jugé plat, prétentieux et sans vigueur. J'en venais à battre en retraite, à douter si j'avais raison de protester.

56. Ah! je voudrais qu'on me laissât tranquille, être oublié; libre de penser à mon gré sans qu'il en coûtât rien à personne et d'exprimer sans contrainte ou crainte des censures le balancement de ma pensée (*Journal, 1939–1949,* 64–65).

57. A good account of Gide's oscillations at this time can be found in Pierre Hebey, *La "Nouvelle Revue Française" des années sombres, 1940–1941,* 153–79.

58. Si les Anglais parviennent à bouter les Allemands hors de France un parti se formera dans notre pays pour regimber contre cette délivrance, pour trouver que la domination précédente avait du bon, qui du moins imposait un ordre, et la préférer au désordre de la liberté. Une liberté pour laquelle nous ne sommes pas mûrs et que nous ne méritons pas. La liberté n'est belle que pour permettre l'exercice de vertus qu'il importerait d'abord d'acquérir. Que me sera-t-il laissé de temps pour souffrir de cette époque de turbulence? Vivrai-je encore assez pour voir, au delà de la confusion, poindre l'aube et pour ne pas mourir désespéré? (*Journal, 1939–1949,* 78).

has weakened this fiber. Throughout his life his relation to discipline and disciplines, to order and morality, was, as we have seen, complex. Sometimes he is ironic and rebellious, sometimes intensely conservative.

On June 14, 1941, about a month after the journal entry just quoted, Gide notes the occurrence of a new feature in the *Figaro:* "The *Figaro* has started a feature called 'Anti-Littré,' in which to point out the grammatical mistakes that can be found even in the best writers. It's enough to stop you writing" (*Journals,* 4:68).[59] The feature called "L'Anti-Littré ou les mauvais exemples" appeared for the first time in the *Figaro littéraire* on May 17, 1941. Here is its self-definition:

> Everyone makes mistakes in their French. Truly everyone, even those writing for the *Figaro*. In starting up this feature, we thus do not have the intention of setting ourselves up as arbiters of correct usage: that is neither to our taste nor within our competence. Our only ambition is, using examples from modern texts, to contribute to the restoration of the prestige of grammar, something deeply compromised, as are many other things in France. The Littré cites examples to use as models, drawing them from earlier authors. We will cite examples to be avoided, that, alas, are frequently used, even by worthy writers of today. We hope those writers will not take badly the use to which we put their prose and their name! Let them think instead of the interest in serving the cause to which we are devoted!

The palpable displacement of a discussion of France's defeat and occupation on to the subject of grammar is a displacement in which Gide also participates. Indeed, he renders the *Figaro*'s implicit connection quite explicit. From November 1941 to April 1942 Gide contributes a series of articles to the *Figaro*. Published in the form of dialogues between Gide and an invented interlocutor, they were later collected and published under the title *Interviews imaginaires*. At the end of the second interview the "interviewer" remarks on two dubious grammatical usages Gide had planted earlier in the interview. The two grammatical questions form the subject of the third interview, and, as one might expect, one of those dubious usages involved the subjunctive. Here is part of the exchange, the Gide voice speaking first:

> In every period in the life of a people, their language is discreetly revealing. Even in questions like the decay of the subjunctive, something I began to complain about during the other war. The subjunctive is a mood that indicates a certain type of connection between two statements, a dependence of one on the other, a subordination for which people of today must no longer recognize the need.
> —In England the subjunctive disappeared a long time age, leaving hardly more than traces.
> —Precisely! Independence. . . . (20)[60]

59. *Le Figaro* a institué rubrique « anti Littré », où dénoncer les fautes de français que l'on peut relever même dans les meilleurs auteurs. C'est à ne plus oser écrire (*Journal, 1939–1949,* 79).

60. Le langage, à chaque époque de la vie d'un peuple, est discrètement révélateur. Jusque dans la défaillance du subjonctif que déjà je déplorais au temps de l'autre guerre; de ce mode qui marque, entre deux propositions et de l'une à l'autre, une dépendance, une subordination dont les esprits ne reconnaissent donc plus le besoin.

— En Angleterre, le subjonctif a presque totalement disparu depuis longtemps.

— Précisément! L'indépendance . . . (39).

The resonances between this passage and the journal entry we have seen about a possible liberation at English hands are startling. Gide's ellipsis after his final "indépendance" leaves us hanging as to the value of that apparently English virtue. A few pages later, Gide seems to remove some of the doubt. The interviewer gives Gide his opening by commenting, "Basically, the subjunctive is a useless mood." Gide responds: "Only if anything be useless which we manage, for better or worse, to do without. It is, it was, a sort of test, an invitation to discriminate, and its disappearance is simultaneously an indication of and an encouragement to a certain mental confusion." (This passage is left out of the English translation.)[61] The rhetoric of disapproval toward disappearing distinctions might well make us recall Caillois. Yet, Gide's vocabulary itself, we must note, is working toward a certain confusion of its own. Dependent, or subjoined, clauses seem somehow to be linked not only to dependent populations (the French under the Germans), they seem also to be linked to what Gide viewed to be important social and political hierarchies within a country. We can see this again in the very sentence that apparently provoked the whole discussion, one in which Gide exhibits his grammatical daring by in fact extending the use of the subjunctive, employing it against custom in a clause beginning with "si":

> And when we hear that "our country is in danger," the important thing is that we rise up and unite to defend it; what does it matter if that which we defend be [*si ce soit*] specifically, for the farmer, our crops; for the intellectual, our Culture; for the manufacturer and the worker, our industry; and even, for the man with a private income, his dividends. (11–12)[62]

In the environs of this marked subjunctive, all the diverse levels of French society find their place and can suddenly put up a united front against the enemy.

The power of the grammatical subjunctive to draw politics and ideology into the discussion is not something we find only in Gide's work. The observation that the subjunctive has almost entirely disappeared from English need not be disputed, but suppose we go back to a grammar written while it was disappearing. William Cobbett, for example, in his 1818 *Grammar of the English Language*, warns against the dangers of using this mood without truly understanding it:

> There is a great necessity for care as to this matter; for, the meaning of what we write is very much affected, when we make use of the modes indiscriminately. Let us take an instance. "*Though* her chastity *be* right and becoming, it gives her no claim to praise; because she would be criminal, *if* she *were* not chaste." Now, by employing the subjunctive in the first member of the sentence, we leave it *uncertain* whether it

---

61. Si tant est que soit inutile tout ce dont on arrive, tant bien que mal, à se passer. C'est, c'était, une sorte d'épreuve, une invite à discriminer, et sa disparition est à la fois le témoignage et l'encouragement de certaine confusion des esprits (43).

62. Et lorsque nous entendons que « la Patrie est en danger », l'important c'est que nous nous levions et unissions pour la défendre; et qu'importe si ce que nous défendons, ce *soit* particulièrement, pour le paysan, nos cultures; pour l'intellectuel, notre Culture; pour l'industriel et l'ouvrier, notre industrie; et même, pour le rentier, ses revenus (27–28, emphasis added).

be *right* or *not* for her to be chaste; and, by employing it, in the second, we express *doubt as to the fact* of her chastity. We mean neither of these; and, therefore, notwithstanding here a *though* and an *if*, both the verbs ought to be in the indicative. "Though her chastity *is* right and becoming, it gives her no claim to praise; because, she would be criminal, *if* she *was* not chaste." (Cobbett, 135–36)

One and a quarter centuries before Gide, on the other side of the Channel, the subjunctive, improperly used, causes confusion not necessarily about social status but about proper sexual behavior. A person who moves too quickly in grammar, it seems, who aims for the sophistication of the subjunctive before having learned the proper morality, runs the risk of being led astray.[63] In fact, in Gide's trilogy of narratives, *L'Ecole des femmes, Robert,* and *Geneviève,* the excuses Robert provides for his wife Eveline's revolt against his rule follow precisely this paradigm. She ventured out into realms of thought headier than her hastily and improperly educated mind could handle. Robert is clearly not a sympathetic character, and his suggested narrative explanations are hardly credible, but we will find in his mouth concerns about grammar similar to those Gide expresses, concerns about feminine nature close to those of *Corydon.* This, I think, should force us into a serious examination of what, if anything, constitutes the feminism of *L'Ecole des femmes,* Eveline's telling of her gradual growth away from her pompous husband and revulsion from her stifling marriage.

The Gynaeceum Revisited: *L'Ecole des femmes*

In the *Interviews imaginaires* Gide and his interviewer discuss two different kinds of grammatical difficulties. Not only questionable uses of the subjunctive but also questionable uses of the comparative, it seems, annoyed Gide. The following sentences provoke this grammatical discussion:

> I was pleased to learn that other French departments are somewhat better supplied than ours. On the other hand, I also know that many regions are more impoverished, and that even in the most favored districts many people are in worse straits than I am [*plus courts que moi*]. (10)[64]

The topic of this grammatical interlude is the seemingly clumsy "plus courts que moi." The expression "être à court," to be short on something, seems more usual, but Gide pedantically informs us that Littré labels "être à court" as a faulty usage.

---

63. Cobbett's political project in his *Grammar* is complicated. In fact, his *Grammar* is meant to be a liberating tool, at least for working-class *men.* He was fighting a battle against decadent, "corrupt," artificially complicated linguistic usage, meant to exclude the uneducated, and thus he wrote a grammar advocating a more simple and accessible, enfranchising kind of language instruction. For a discussion of Cobbett and the grammatical and political struggles of his time, see Olivia Smith, *The Politics of Language, 1791–1819,* esp. 239–48.

64. J'apprends avec sympathie que les autres départements sont mieux approvisionnés que le nôtre. Je sais aussi, par contre, que quantité de pays le sont moins; et que, même dans les contrées les plus favorisées, quantité de gens sont plus courts que moi (24–25).

"Etre court" is the legitimate (older) usage. Unfortunately, the former has become so popular that the correct form "runs the risk today of sounding archaic and affected." Not only that, but the two expressions have begun to diverge in meaning:

> "*Etre court de tabac* now means to have very little tobacco: *à court de* . . . to have none at all."
>
> "With the result," my interviewer said, "that the latter expression, if I understand you correctly, cannot be used in the comparative."
>
> "That is another reason why I said 'plus court que moi.' Since the French Academy and Littré too regard the word 'court' as an adjective, shouldn't it be treated accordingly?" (18)[65]

The point of laboring through this discussion on the importance of making refined distinctions between parts of speech is that it comes up in *L'Ecole des femmes.* Aided by the context provided by the *Interviews imaginaires,* we can better problematize that moment within *L'Ecole des femmes* where we begin to realize the full extent of the mistake Eveline is making in deciding to marry Robert. It is a grammatical moment. Robert is greatly concerned with Eveline's ability to make grammatical distinctions, an area where she has some difficulties, as she confides to her journal early on:

> Nothing irritates [Robert] so much as the use of "very" in front of words which he quite correctly points out have no comparative (or superlative, I can't quite remember). Before he pointed it out to me, I quite readily said "j'ai très faim" or "j'ai très sommeil" or "j'ai très peur."
>
> "Why not go straight ahead and say 'j'ai très courage' or 'j'ai très migraine?'" he asked me.
>
> I think I grasp the shade of difference, which I confess I never dreamed of before, but now I hardly dare use the word "very" for fear of making a mistake. (36–37)[66]

How pedantic is Robert on this point? How close or far from Gide? What effect might the proximity of Robert's pronouncements to Gide's have on the sincerity of the feminist message the book seems to put forth? We read a few lines later that Eveline wants to be able to understand all these grammatical points and "to get

---

65. *Etre court de tabac* se dirait, je crois, lorsqu'on n'en a plus que très peu; *à court de* . . . , lorsqu'on n'en a plus du tout.

— De sorte que cette dernière locution, si je vous entends bien, ne supporterait pas le comparatif.

— C'est bien aussi pourquoi j'ai dit : « plus courts que moi ». Considéré, ici, en adjectif par l'Académie (v. Littré) ce mot ne doit-il pas être traité comme tel? (36).

66. Rien ne l'irrite (Robert) autant que l'emploi de « très » devant les mots qui, comme il dit très justement, ne comportent pas le comparatif (ou le superlatif, je ne sais plus bien). Avant qu'il ne me l'ait fait remarquer je disais couramment : « J'ai très faim », ou « J'ai très sommeil », ou « J'ai très peur ».

— Pourquoi pas tout de suite : « J'ai très courage », ou : « J'ai très migraine »? — m'a-t-il dit.

Je crois comprendre la nuance, à laquelle j'avoue que je n'avais jamais songé; mais maintenant, par crainte de me tromper, je n'ose presque plus employer le mot « très » (43).

into the habit of applying them; for Robert considers it ought to be women's special business to maintain the purity of the language, because they are in general more conservative than men" (37/43–44). How much irony shall we choose to read in these words? (We find ourselves faced with the same kind of question posed in *Corydon* by the difficult separation between Gide and Corydon.) *L'Ecole des femmes* acts out the gender ideology developed by the speakers of *Corydon*. In watching that acting out, could we again hope to find a way to watch the writing work against the ideology it expresses?

At the outset of the narrative, Eveline is taken in by Robert and marries him, but across the narrative she gradually comes to believe that his love is artificial, that his culture, his patriotism, and his religious faith are only a display, not the real thing. In the course of her story, *she* apparently becomes *authentically* cultured, retains or gains a *true* patriotism, and loses any desire to participate in displays of organized religion. In the first half of the narrative she is positioned in an alliance with Robert against her father. The triad reveals itself neatly in a scene where Robert and "papa" are sitting in the smoking room of an Italian *pension* reading newspapers. Robert offers to lend Eveline's father the copy of *La Libre Parole* (Edouard Drumont's antisemitic newspaper) that he had been reading. Her father is so outraged that he spills his cup of coffee in his lap. Eveline comments:

> Robert made a great many apologies, but it really wasn't his fault. And while Papa was wiping himself with his handkerchief, Robert, who had caught sight of me in the drawing-room, expressed his regrets by a very discreet little dumb show that he performed for my benefit, which was so comic that I couldn't help laughing; but I turned away quickly, because it looked as if I were laughing at Papa. (16)[67]

This triangle transforms itself in the second half in a way that provides some ideological relief. No longer a question of a reactionary young man-about-town and an ignorant young woman teasing her liberal father, now it is Eveline and her stridently independent daughter Geneviève united against the ever-pompous Robert. While Robert moves to the seat of ridicule, his daughter takes his place as instigator; Eveline remains the timid one, not wanting to push Geneviève too far in her revolt against her father.

> I have just had a terrible conversation with her; I see now that she is the one person with whom I might come to an understanding, but at the same time I see why I do not wish to come to an understanding with her. It is because I am afraid of coming face to face in her with my own thoughts, but my own thoughts grown so bold that they terrify me. . . . I begged her to lower her voice, fearing that her father might hear her, but she went on:

---

67. Robert s'est beaucoup excusé, mais il n'y avait vraiment pas de sa faute. Et, tandis que papa s'épongeait avec son mouchoir, Robert, qui m'avait aperçue dans le salon, a dirigé vers moi une petite mimique très discrète mais très expressive où il exprimait ses regrets, si comiquement que je n'ai pu me retenir de rire et me suis vite détournée, car j'avais l'air de me moquer de papa (22).

"Oh, well, let him hear us! I am quite ready to repeat to him everything I have been saying to you. . . ."

She seemed to have lost all control of herself. (70–71)[68]

Perhaps to her misfortune, self-control and self-possession remain Eveline's chief virtues, and the surest sign of such self-possession might well be the classically correct French prose she has carefully learned. Nothing daring is allowed; precision and clarity rule. In both of the two triangulations I have just sketched out, the characteristics of Eveline's position do not change. If, in the first, she is aligned with Robert by way of her infatuation, in the second she remains so aligned by way of the very style she has learned, the linguistic practice she has absorbed. The subjunctive in the phrase from the second scene, "craignant que son père pût l'entendre," thus takes on a certain special poignancy as the mark of her own masochistic insistence on her subordinate, timid, conservative position. The freedom to err remains beyond her grasp, belonging first to Robert, later to Geneviève whose errant lesbianism will be as conflicted, as ideologically confused, as one might expect after reading *Corydon*.[69]

When she first began to feel annoyed at Robert, to be able to see through her infatuation, Eveline was pleased to find her feelings shared by Doctor Marchant: "And that evening I felt a kind of relief at feeling I was not the only one to be exasperated by the habit Robert has fallen into of always saying 'he thinks he ought' to do what he simply does because he wants to do it" (46).[70] The distinction *avoir envie/devoir* (want to/ought to) lies at the root of Eveline's problem. Her aggressive concern for linguistic accuracy demands that this distinction remain clear. The first time she met Dr. Marchant was over dinner at the exclusive Tour d'Argent, a dinner arranged by Robert as a favor to Eveline, who wanted to ask Marchant to offer a job to a friend of hers. "Is it true," Marchant asks gruffly, "that she wants so badly to enter my service?" Eveline's response, where she fails in her duty (*devoir*) as grammatical guardian, could conceivably count as the primal scene of her marriage: "'I know that she would really like to [qu'elle en a *très* envie],' I began rashly; and then I felt Robert's glance fixed upon me and realized my grammatical mistake, so that I no longer dared to add anything" (39).[71] The terror of grammatical error closes off the possibility of expressing desire (*envie*),

---

68. Je viens d'avoir avec elle une conversation terrible, où tout à la fois j'ai compris que c'était avec elle que je pourrais le mieux m'entendre, compris également pourquoi je ne veux pas m'entendre avec elle : c'est que je crains de retrouver en elle ma propre pensée, plus hardie, si hardie qu'elle m'épouvante . . . Je l'ai priée de baisser la voix, craignant que son père pût l'entendre, mais elle alors :

— Eh bien! quand il nous entendrait . . . Tout ce que je te dis, je suis prête à le lui redire . . .

Il me parut qu'elle ne se possédait plus . . . (78–79).

69. On *Geneviève*, see both Jeffrey Mehlman, 77–80, and Emily Apter, *André Gide and the Codes of Homotextuality*, chapter 5. See also Apter's "La Nouvelle *Nouvelle Héloïse* d'André Gide: *Geneviève* et le féminisme anglais."

70. Et ce soir-là j'ai été comme soulagée de comprendre que je n'étais pas seule à être exaspérée par cette habitude qu'a prise Robert de toujours dire qu'il a « cru devoir faire » tout ce que, simplement, il a fait parce qu'il en avait envie . . . (55–56).

71. — Je sais qu'elle en a *très* envie — ai-je dit imprudemment; et tout aussitôt j'ai senti se fixer sur moi le regard de Robert et me suis aperçue de ma faute de français, de sorte que je n'ai plus osé rien ajouter . . . (46).

except in the inadequate form of a masochistic effort to do her duty (*devoir*) as a conserver of grammar.

"C'est à ne plus oser écrire," grumbled Gide, faced with the possibility of finding his own style criticized in the columns of *Le Figaro*'s "Anti-Littré." "De sorte que je n'ai plus osé rien ajouter," are Eveline's words under Robert's severely grammatical gaze, and thus a certain silence marks one of the moments at which she begins to form the project of writing her own story of failed liberation. Yet, conceivably, what one desires but dares not write can nonetheless be found in the interstices of the writing so dutifully performed.

When Robert, at the outset of the narrative that carries his name, responds to his wife's text, he snottily brings up her writing:

> I was indeed far from suspecting that Eveline wrote so well. I had no means of judging, for, as we always lived together, she had no occasion to write me letters. People have even gone so far as to suppose—superlative praise indeed!—that the diary was written by you, M. Gide, who. . . . Certainly the pages that follow can aspire to no such distinction. (101)[72]

Gide provides a footnote to that ellipsis after "who," which slyly mentions that at that point three lines (that would have commented on Gide's relation to Eveline) have been suppressed. What I've been trying to show is that Eveline's failure to write her way out of her situation could well lie in that suppression, where Gide's allegiances hesitate between Robert and Eveline, and where Eveline's successful Gidean style seems as much entrapment as liberation. The "superlative praise," the "suprême éloge" of the critics thus in some ways would be a sinisterly funereal one, as the volume of their critical discourse threatens to drown out the silence in which a certain liberation nonetheless struggles to find expression. Such liberation could perhaps have found expression, had the potentially queer allegiance between Gide and Eveline worked precisely to *demolish* stylistic and ideological complicities between the two in order that they no longer run the risk of dutifully furthering that repression under whose burden they both occasionally labored.

72. Et j'étais loin de me douter qu'Eveline pût si bien écrire. Je n'en pouvais guère juger, car, comme nous vivions toujours ensemble, je n'avais point à recevoir de lettres d'elle. Suprême éloge : on a même été supposer que ce journal avait été écrit par vous, M. Gide, qui . . . Certes, les pages que voici ne peuvent point aspirer à donner le change (109).

CHAPTER 4

WITHOUT DELAY: *LES FAUX-MONNAYEURS*, LACAN, AND THE ONSET OF SEXUALITY

Dans l'intervalle, la sexualité.

—Jacques Lacan

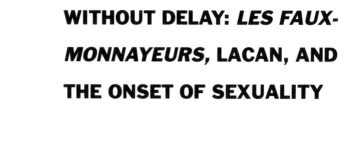

L es Faux-Monnayeurs (*The Counter-feiters*) is, along with *Corydon* and *Si le grain ne meurt,* one of the trio of texts Gide published between 1924 and 1926 that insisted on the publicness of his homosexuality. Now if all that Gide was doing was letting people know about his sexuality, there would, of course, be no real reason to concern oneself overlong (or at all) with the homosexuality present in his novel. Indeed, one of the more startling things about the bulk of the criticism since written on *Les Faux-Monnayeurs* is its consistently demonstrated ability to avoid mentioning homosexuality, or, if it should mention it, to avoid including it within the frame of the critical discussion of the novel, as if the subject had a relation only to the author, had only an inessential relation to the novel's project. But finally the presence of homosexuality in *Les Faux-Monnayeurs* needs to be understood as more than an oblique and glancing form of personal confession. Like *Si le grain ne meurt* and *Corydon, Les Faux-Monnayeurs* is a text in which sexuality comes to be theorized. That the criticism demonstrates an insistent inability or unwillingness to come to terms with this, as if it wanted to thwart at least the theoretical import of Gide's effort at publicness, need not, though it often could, be understood as a conscious intention of an individual critic. It is more a product of the categories in which critical discussions of the novel tend to run, categories that function to marginalize any consideration of the novel's theorization

108

of sexuality, and that therefore need to be examined in their own right in order to understand how they allow or encourage a phobic distanciation from questions of sexuality in this novel.

Sincerity and Phobia

Take, for example, Alain Goulet's *André Gide, "Les Faux-Monnayeurs," mode d'emploi* (1991). In his opening biographical overview, Goulet positions *Les Faux-Monnayeurs* quite clearly next to *Corydon* and *Si le grain ne meurt:*

> In many ways *Les Faux-Monnayeurs,* the third wing of the triptych, constitutes the novel which, in an experimental and critical fashion, puts diverse facets of homosexuality into play at the very heart of human relations. Alongside the pure love that unites Edouard and Olivier, the dangerous detour that delivers the latter into the hands of Passavant reveals the dangers of perversion that arise as soon as inauthenticity and a lack of respect for the other sneak in. And in the background of this central mixup of partners, a latent or unacknowledged homosexuality spreads its shadows and mysteries with the figures of Armand, La Pérouse, Strouvilhou, Sarah. (Goulet, *André Gide,* 33)[1]

This passage is typical in many ways. First of all, by being included in Goulet's opening biographical overview, and constituting in all its brevity one of the most substantial discussions of homosexuality in this "user's manual," this passage licenses the near complete exclusion of any discussion of homosexuality from those sections of Goulet's book devoted to analysis or criticism.[2] Moreover, this passage demonstrates the two most common critical gestures through which homosexuality usually receives mention in discussions of *Les Faux-Monnayeurs.* The first conceives the novel entirely in terms of an opposition between sincerity and inauthenticity. It is good to be sincere, bad not to be. Sincerity is the sign of firm character, inauthenticity the sign of weakness and depravation of the soul. To the extent that

---

1. Goulet has, I should add, written an article in which he speculates about a possible homosexual overture made to the adolescent Gide by a friend of his. Goulet imagines that Gide refused this overture and later, when his friend committed suicide, was overcome with a guilt so deep that it eventually necessitated the production of *Si le grain ne meurt, Corydon,* and *Les Faux-Monnayeurs.* See Alain Goulet, "Sur une figure obsédante — Vers une origine de la création littéraire." Whatever one thinks of this kind of speculation, it unfortunately adds little to an effort to understand what the novel itself might be saying about sexuality.

Another recent book on Gide, Patrick Pollard's *André Gide: Homosexual Moralist,* might seem an exception to this critical trend. And indeed it is, in its frank confrontation of sexual issues and its detailed study of the reading Gide did on sexuality. However, it, too, indulges in all the traditional categories of criticism of Gide and *Les Faux-Monnayeurs* (sincerity/inauthenticity, good fag/bad fag) that have rendered so difficult any investigation of the place of sexuality in the novel. See, for example, the conclusion of Pollard's discussion of *Les Faux-Monnayeurs:* "Is Edouard really innocent and chaste? Gide is discreet, for he only tells us that Edouard and Olivier 'stayed together until the next morning.' Nobody doubts that he is good. His honesty and openness are in total contrast with Passavant's (and other people's) double-dealing and falseness. . . . Because he is a homosexual he provides a touchstone when love is discussed. By studying his attitudes the reader may arrive at a satisfactory moral conclusion" (395). In Gide the links between sexuality and morality are much more complicated than this. Indeed, it might be best to hold off permanently on considering Gide a moralist, so preoccupied is he with the ideological violence of importing moral concepts into the sexual realm his works spend so much time trying to delineate.

2. There is a brief discussion later in Goulet's book of the way *Les Faux-Monnayeurs* incorporates in the relationship between Olivier and Edouard some of the theorizations of pederasty found in *Corydon.* See Goulet, 152–54.

certain phobic cultural discourses paint homosexuality as a depravity given to masquerade, mimicry, deception, a reliance on the opposition between sincerity and inauthenticity seems ill-conceived as a way of resisting, from a queer perspective, the work of homophobia. This fact becomes all the more clear when one notices the second common critical gesture as regards homosexuality evinced in the passage from Goulet.

This second gesture, constituting a subset of the sincerity game, is the "find the good fag" game, where Edouard usually wins and Passavant usually loses: "Olivier, pledged to an evil master, alienated and denatured by Passavant, allows all the false values of the world to echo within himself, thereby becoming a fake [*un truqueur*, a word also meaning a prostitute who blackmails his clients]" (114). As a subset of the "find the good fag" game, one might also mention the "find all the fags" game. There's not only Edouard, Passavant, and Olivier, but also Armand, La Pérouse, Strouvilhou, and Sarah. And even that list leaves out perhaps a few equally obvious candidates such as Georges, Gontran, and, most crucially, Boris. All of these typical critical gestures seem to me inadequate to understanding the position and theorization of sexuality within this novel.

It is important initially to understand the full extent of the links between the "find the good fag" game and the sincerity game. We could do this by looking at one of the more theoretically sophisticated recent readings of *Les Faux-Monnayeurs* that, for all its sophistication, does not successfully extricate itself from these incapacitating critical maneuvers. Jean-Joseph Goux's *Les Monnayeurs du langage* plays on all the various possible meanings of the novel's title as it attempts to establish perhaps too absolute a homology between the loss of a gold standard, the loss of a faith in realistic language, and the loss of faith in a patriarchally organized family: "Gide's novel . . . *has as its radical subject the historical crisis of the universal equivalent form*" (48).[3] "*Language, currency,* the *father* have ceased to be the nodal center guaranteeing meaning and values. No more transcendental signified, no more eternal standard. Henceforth a generalized counterfeiting: in linguistic, monetary, and intersubjective circulation" (64). This discussion of a suspiciously sudden disappearance of a universal equivalent (would not its putative presence already have opened up a field of possibilities around its imagined absence, or would not its imagined absence depend on positing its presence?) recasts the sincerity game into economic terms, which Goux then applies homologically to diverse realms. In these applications we can begin to sense how easily the sincerity game (aka the universal equivalent game) leads into both misogynistic

3. The concept of a universal equivalent is from Marx's *Capital:* "The universal equivalent form is a form of value in general. It can, therefore, be assumed by any commodity. On the other hand, if a commodity be found to have assumed the universal equivalent form, this is only because and in so far as it has been excluded from the rest of all other commodities as their equivalent, and that by their own act. And from the moment that this exclusion becomes finally restricted to one particular commodity, from that moment only, the general form of relative value of the world of commodities obtains real consistence and general social validity.

The particular commodity, with whose bodily form the equivalent form is thus socially identified, now becomes the money commodity, or serves as money" (79–80).

and homophobic assertions of the valued stability of what is nonetheless a clearly imaginary prerequisite normativity against which free-floating and spuriously subsequent perversions will be measured and found wanting. Goux, for example, will rate the heterosexual Bernard as superior to his gay friend Olivier, the "truqueur," to use Goulet's word, and will assign the responsibility for Bernard's higher level of authenticity to the normalizing intervention of a true woman:

> It is not without importance, of course, that it is in relation to a woman that Bernard overcomes, or believes himself to overcome, the effect of falseness which is attached to any element entering into the monetary logic of the universal equivalent. It is not without importance that it is a woman who allows him to resolve what had seemed impossible oppositions, between nature and the law, truth and convention, desire and reason, the heart and understanding. In the extremely rigorous structural system Gide's novel puts into place, two women characters (Laura and Sophroniska) occupy a very precise location that opposes everything pertaining to the logic of monetary abstraction—whereas a third (Lilian), by way of her insatiable double desire for *money* and for the *phallus*, stirs up the libidinously driven basis of the system. (73)

My impulse would, in fact, be to count Sophroniska as one of the central villains of the novel, precisely because her treatment of Boris is a form of orthopedics meant to force him body and soul into the phobic game of sincerity Bernard is apparently learning to play at Laura's knee. The relation of Sophroniska to Boris is one I will discuss in more detail a bit later. Here I will merely suggest that the apparently "rigorous" system Goux uncovers in *Les Faux-Monnayeurs* need not be seen as such, unless one has a stake in inauthenticity versus sincerity, in standards versus an unanchored system of desires. Should one have such a stake, one will perhaps follow out certain suggestions clearly offered in the novel and pound that stake through the vampiric hearts of the nymphomaniac Lilian and her friend, the all too inverted Passavant. But then one might wonder if an analytic acceptance of the first set of categories a novel seems to offer is the surest way of understanding what it's up to. For no doubt one could insist that the novel *encourages* phobic responses to Lilian and Passavant, just as perhaps it encourages condescending acceptance of the good fag Edouard, and that it fails to offer its readers any alternatives to the phobic violence it directs against a Lilian or a Passavant or against the orthopedic violence Sophroniska directs against Boris. I am advocating, in parallel fashion to what I suggested about critics of *Corydon* at the beginning of the previous chapter, a useful form of critical rigor that consists in not reproducing the phobic gestures the novel puts on display and perhaps invites its readers to reproduce.

Goux makes another linkage that can further pinpoint for us an association between the game of sincerity and a particular criticism of homosexuality that has become a commonplace of Gide criticism: linking homosexuality to a certain kind of deficit that typically (so the association goes) leads to an attenuation of a "sense of reality," an attenuation that, indeed, Gide often ascribed to himself.[4] Pierre

---

4. For a discussion of some relevant passages, see Catharine Savage Brosman, "« Le Peu de réalité » — Gide et le moi."

Janet had as one of the central concepts of his psychological theory *la fonction du réel,* an ability to cope with the events of the real world. One of the characteristics of the condition he called psychasthenia was a weakness in this function. As one commentator puts it:

> Janet points out that those suffering from psychasthenia behave normally while they keep themselves in the world of fantasy and to abstract thinking, but that their weaknesses appear as soon as they have to perform some action in real life. One example of this is a sick person who found it easy to add together fictitious numbers, but who found it extremely difficult to go through the household accounts and check the accounts rendered by suppliers. (Sjövall, 121)[5]

Jean Delay, a psychobiographer of Gide working in Janet's tradition, will note Gide's weak nerves, his tendency to illusory, abstract thinking, and argue that this made him especially susceptible to being influenced as regards his sexual preferences. Not born gay, but turned gay by Oscar Wilde, aided and abetted by Gide's congenitally weak nervous constitution—such is Delay's verdict, to which we will return. Delay's link between weak nerves, abstract thinking, and homosexuality is picked up in a slightly different register by Goux, who ascribes it to Edouard, the novelist busy writing a novel called *Les Faux-Monnayeurs* within the world of Gide's own *Faux-Monnayeurs.*

> What Gide understood is that in a society whose mediations are entirely mercantile, that is to say, where the relations described in political economy end up becoming the only relations existing and the structural model of all relations, there comes about a "depersonalization" of the subject (Edouard expresses this depersonalization) that has as its literary correlative the disappearance of characters. (80)

Edouard's theorizations about depersonalization, his attempt to work his theories into the novel he is trying to write and to cope with his own experience of the phenomenon, all turn on the notions of sincerity and firm character, things apparently disappearing as fast as Goux's gold standard. The imbrication of sincerity and depersonalization has been discussed by David H. Walker:

> The difficulty in being sincere stems from the essential instability of the self, so that it is impossible to know what one is to be sincere *about,* particularly since the self may

---

5. On this general topic, see also John H. Smith, "Abulia: Sexuality and Diseases of the Will in the Late Nineteenth Century." Here is an example of Gide ascribing a mild case of this condition to himself:

> The feeling of the unreality of everything surrounding us, or, if you prefer, the loss of the feeling of *reality,* is not so rare that some of us cannot observe it or experience it momentarily ourselves. I admit that I am somewhat subject to this odd illusion, just enough so that I can very well imagine what it could develop into if one gave in to it self-indulgently, or when the ability to react is weakened. . . . (*Journal of "The Counterfeiters,"* 460n)

> [Le sentiment de l'irréalité de ce qui nous entoure, ou si l'on préfère, la perte du sentiment de la *réalité,* n'est pas si rare que certains n'aient pu l'observer, ou l'éprouver momentanément par eux-mêmes. J'avoue que je suis assez sujet à cette singulière illusion, juste assez pour pouvoir imaginer fort bien ce qu'elle peut devenir, si l'on y cède avec complaisance, ou lorsque les facultés de redressement s'affaiblissent . . . (*Journal des Faux-Monnayeurs,* 100–101n).]

be only a projection of the imagination—"what I think myself." This is compounded by the split within the self which is the very condition of conscious existence:

> I am constantly getting outside myself, and as I watch myself act I cannot understand how *the person I see acting can be* the same as the person who is watching him act, and who *is struck with astonishment, and doubts whether* he can be actor and watcher at the same moment.

(Walker, 138–39, citing a passage from Edouard's journal in chapter 8 of the first part of *Les Faux-Monnayeurs;* emphasis Walker's)

What fascinates in the citation Walker gives of Edouard's journal is the similarity of the terms of Edouard's self-analysis to statements Janet ascribes to his most severely psychasthenic patients. The similarities are especially striking if one adds a few other sentences from the same page of *Les Faux-Monnayeurs:* "This anti-egoistical force of decentralization is so great in me, that it disintegrates my sense of property—and, as a consequence, of responsibility" and a bit later: "It seems to me sometimes that I do not really exist, but that I merely imagine I exist. The thing that I have the greatest difficulty in believing in, is my own reality" (71).[6] Compare those statements to the following extract from an article by Pierre Janet:

> Laetitia is a patient I have often called "the Sleeper, or Sleeping Beauty"; she is above all, and for years, a psychological asthenic and has nothing about her of a persecution complex. Nonetheless, she often says: "Pay no attention to what I say, someone else is acting and speaking in my place; I listen to myself speak and am amazed if what I say actually matches what I think. . . . My legs walk like those of a well-adjusted automaton; I am a mechanical woman. I give you my hand, but it is not I who give it to you; it seems to me I would give it to you differently; I would have felt something else. I am not responsible for anything I do, someone else is responsible." Are we dealing here with a feeling of depersonalization or with one of imposition? I might recall numerous other citations I've already given: "Everything about me is a dead letter; I am no longer a woman with a heart. I'm nothing but a poor mannequin pulled by strings in every direction. My thoughts are being stolen, my soul; I've been loaned someone else's soul. Every second I change proprietors. Behind the wall there is someone to whom I belong, since my actions and thoughts are at his disposition." (Janet, 152)

We will have occasion to return to the discourse of this psychasthenic woman and to the importance both to her and to Edouard—and indeed to Boris, Armand, and La Pérouse—of concepts of self-division and of automatic behavior, of dispossession, of loss of property in oneself. But if we leave behind Janet's Sleeping Beauty to return briefly to Goux's psychasthenically gay Edouard, we find a cure ready and waiting. The same cure that Bernard found in fact, although it apparently fails in Edouard's case.

---

6. Cette force anti-égoïste de décentralisation est telle qu'elle volatilise en moi le sens de la propriété — et, partant, de la responsabilité . . . Il me semble parfois que je n'existe pas vraiment, mais simplement que j'imagine que je suis. Ce à quoi je parviens le plus difficilement à croire c'est ma propre réalité (73).

Goux points to a passage in the opening pages of the novel where Dhurmer, another schoolmate of Olivier and Bernard's, is discoursing loudly about a novel he apparently dislikes, his reason being that he read as far as page thirty without finding a color mentioned. Even when the author mentions a *woman*, Dhurmer complains, he doesn't know if her dress is blue or red. Why bother to continue reading the novel? Why bother to take Dhurmer seriously?[7] Goux seems to. Immediately after citing Dhurmer's complaint, Goux continues (in his own voice? in what he imagines to be Gide's?): "A woman, that we can imagine. It's imagination itself. And it would be only too easy to show how what is at stake in the botched relations between Edouard and Laura is a lack [*carence*] both in regard to the *feminine* and to the *image*" (120; Goux's emphasis). Laura works out for Bernard; he doesn't share Edouard's lack, his *carence*. Should Bernard ever write novels, there would be no lack of character due to a psychasthenic tendency toward abstraction and purely formal relations. Bernard's books would be balanced; he'd keep his characters straight; he'd keep them from disappearing; his women would be dressed in red or blue.[8]

As a footnote to the sentence just cited (continuing the tradition of keeping homosexuality in the margins), Goux adds:

> Thus one might read Edouard's homosexuality as a symbol of this image deficit. What a strange setting chosen by Gide: it is in the temple itself, while reflecting on the white, colorless, rigid, abstract architecture before him, and while meditating simultaneously on Laura (whom he no longer loves) and on this "early starvation of the senses which drives the soul so perilously far beyond appearances" that Edouard sets out to seduce his young nephew Olivier. (120)

Is Goux suggesting that in the novel homosexuality is nothing more than a symbol for an aesthetic (and personal and ethical) failure? Or is he imagining a necessary poverty of the homosexual? And in what would this poverty consist—in a lack of appreciation for color, the feminine, the concrete? In a lack of a sense of place?

---

7. How to take Dhurmer is an interesting question. He could, for instance, be added to the list of potential gays in the novel. For if Bernard, as we shall see, usurps Olivier's place at his uncle Edouard's side for a good portion of the novel, Olivier usurps Dhurmer's as chief editor of Passavant's new review and as assistant to Passavant. Thus, when, in an atmosphere of generalized phobia later in the novel, Dhurmer calls Olivier a sissy and provokes a rather violent response, the mixings of sexuality might indeed make us curious about what is going on when Dhurmer says he resents an author because that author does not help him imagine women concretely enough.

8. We might notice, at this point, that Edouard, in one of the novel's many sleepy passages, speculates precisely about the issue Dhurmer is raising (although he comes to a diametrically opposite conclusion) when he muses about the relation of his own imagination to Laura's image:

> Edouard dozes; insensibly his thoughts take another direction. He wonders whether he would have guessed merely by reading Laura's letter that her hair was black. He says to himself that novelists, by a too exact description of their characters, hinder the reader's imagination rather than help it, and that they ought to allow each individual to picture their personages to himself according to his own fancy. (73)

> [Edouard somnole; ses pensées insensiblement prennent un autre cours. Il se demande s'il aurait deviné, à la seule lecture de la lettre de Laura, qu'elle a les cheveux noirs? Il se dit que les romanciers, par la description trop exacte de leurs personnages, gênent plutôt l'imagination qu'ils ne la servent et qu'ils devraient laisser chaque lecteur se représenter chacun de ceux-ci comme il lui plaît. (75)]

Once the universal equivalent is gone, Goux's train of thought implies, once abstract thinking governs all relations, the new world seems as a result better suited to the psychasthenic and narcissistic gay man, the abstract man who doesn't know how to reach out to the concrete world around him, the man who likes boys only insofar as they are an earlier image of himself. (Postmodernism gone awry welcomes the fag; postmodernism within bounds produces good citizens such as Bernard.) Like Goux, Gide's biographer Delay will be doomed to homophobia by his similar failure to question the ideological functioning of the commonplace categories that have governed both ways of viewing gay men and ways of reading *Les Faux-Monnayeurs*. For Goux "the Phallus is the universal equivalent of *objects*" (48). Thus those of us who, unlike Bernard, are for some reason unable to resist the excesses of the postmodern, postuniversal-equivalent world are, in our bad object choices, likely to have a perverted relation to the phallus: the nymphomaniacal Lilian, for example, who, "by way of her insatiable double desire for *money* and for the *phallus,* stirs up the libidinously driven base of the system" (73), or the weary invert Passavant, or Edouard, libidinous without a sense of place. This way of conceiving perversion is entirely compatible with a traditional understanding of the male homosexual (current long before postmodernism) as trapped in a narcissistic object choice, his relationship to other men merely a slightly elaborated form of autoeroticism. Such is the viewpoint of Jean Delay in his *Jeunesse d'André Gide:*

> When the organism has become exclusively habituated to its solitary vice, as to a kind of drug addiction, sexual instincts begin to concentrate themselves exclusively on the organ from which this habitual pleasure is drawn, and desire is then only capable of being transferred to a human object possessing this same advantage. Thus the finality of the instinct—the meeting of two opposite sexes for a complementary union—finds itself frustrated; the homosexual is no longer attracted by difference but by that homology that recalls for him his own sex, object of all his indulgences. (Delay, 2:536–37)

The passages from Delay and Goux make clear the strength of the tendency to ascribe a deficit to the gay man, dooming him to fail at being sincere, concrete, self-possessed, mature. Yet discourses like Delay's and Goux's clearly do not *discover* this doom; they *produce* it, leaving others to carry its burden. As Armand says in *Les Faux-Monnayeurs,* "Others . . . have the feeling of what they possess; I have only the feeling of what I lack. Lack of money, lack of strength, lack of intelligence, lack of love—an everlasting deficit. I shall never be anything but below the mark" (286).[9] Yet Goux and Delay do hold out a cruel hope that some deficits of this kind could be paid back. If only Armand would find the right girl or the right doctor, perhaps the origin of the deficit could be found, some repayment schedule worked out. Delay imagines one such schedule for Gide:

---

9. D'autres ont le sentiment de ce qu'ils ont . . . je n'ai le sentiment que de mes manques. Manque d'argent, manque de forces, manque d'esprit, manque d'amour. Toujours du déficit; je resterai toujours en deça (278).

Setting aside the possibility of a constitutional predisposition for which there was no evidence in his case, Gide's homosexuality was not innate, and therefore inevitable [*fatale*], but acquired, and therefore subject to modification. It was not inscribed in his nature, but produced by a diversity of factors truly so closely intricated that their unravelling would have represented a difficult but not impossible task. It was a case of neurotic homosexuality, in other words, a sexual neurosis that is not inaccessible to the resources of medicine, at least in our day. (2:555)

Gide, as a result of a neurotic deficiency, it would seem, acquired homosexuality as an unnecessary supplement. Homosexuality is merely symptomatic in a medical regime that views such symptoms as erasable once the underlying deficit is identified, isolated, and paid back. A removal of the symptom will reveal the true and fulfilling script of a person's nature. If Armand's discourse and Delay's go hand in hand, if *Les Faux-Monnayeurs* has indeed provided its critics with the very terms of the sincerity game they happily replay, then perhaps *Les Faux-Monnayeurs* really *is* about the deficit of the homosexual. Perhaps the novel is out to pinpoint the onset or origin of this deficit, in order to enact some sublimating form of repayment, some masochistic and supremely moral and sincere compensation. The text could in this case even be read as a bizarre version of a prospective, longitudinal sociological study.[10] One might draw curves and find standards to deviate from. Will it be at Boris' age that sexual patterns are fixed? Is Georges' criminal behavior the sign of a nascent transgressive homosexual impulse? Or is it in late adolescence that homosexuality might set in, perhaps originating in the influence of an older man? Could Olivier or Bernard still be turned gay or straight? Is the père Védel a future version of Boris? How did La Pérouse arrive at his state?

But this cross section of the sexually troubled need not be understood as a developmental series begging for normative interventions. Such an understanding—and such a belief in the potential success of intervention in redirecting the inauthentic symptoms of sexuality toward a script more faithful to a person's inherent truth—underlie the critical tradition playing the sincerity game. Finding a new way of looking at the series might be the best way of putting the sincerity game to sleep. Many critics comment on the novel's refusal of *consequence* in its portrayal of characters,[11] and its understanding of sexuality might be investigated in this light as well. There might be, the novel could suggest, no onset and no true path of sexuality to be found. I would like to give up the typical critical gestures of the sincerity game in favor of a way of reading that respects the novel's hesitancy about fixing sexuality's defining moments. In this reading, as in readings from earlier chapters, sexuality will need to be understood through concepts such as repetition and return; we will need to be attentive to how it stages itself in an intervallic space,

10. An example would be something like Richard Green, *The "Sissy Boy Syndrome" and the Development of Homosexuality*, an unfortunate text, worthy of being scrutinized and criticized for its own problematic temporalizing gestures. Such a critique can be found in Eve Kosofsky Sedgwick, "How to Bring Your Kids Up Gay," an article that touches in a helpful manner on many of the central issues of this chapter.

11. For example, Walker, *Modern Novelists: André Gide*, 140–41.

whose structure *problematizes* notions of before and after, too early and too late, deficit and surplus, sincerity and inauthenticity, self-possession and dispossession.

Sexuality or Consequentiality

> On every point you have advanced with such penetration, so pertinently exposed to the light of day the most secret psychological workings—and with such a sense of measure, logic and clarity, such progression in the reasoning, such convincing power in the fit of the argumentation, and so little *parti pris*, so exclusive a search for truth—that your conclusions impose themselves with the tranquil force of the *obvious*.[12]
> —Roger Martin du Gard to Jean Delay

"When thwarted, I seldom give up; at most I delay" (294).[13] With these words Gide, in *Si le grain ne meurt,* explains his failure to bring Athman back to Paris when he first intended to, his postponement of the realization of that project for four years. The words caught the eye of Jacques Lacan, who quotes them in the middle of his essay, "Jeunesse de Gide," an essay that is in large part a review of the two-volume psychobiography of Gide by Jean Delay. Though Lacan's tone is in general laudatory, it seems also that his article brings out the serious theoretical shortcomings of Delay's detailed (and useful despite its shortcomings) reconstruction of Gide's childhood and mental and artistic development. The shortcomings Lacan brings out have precisely to do with this notion of delay.

Delay's book, as we will see in more detail shortly, elaborates on a rigid developmental structure. Delay believes that it is possible to say when and where many of Gide's character traits began, whether they could have been avoided, what part of their onset was due to Gide's nature, what part to his environment. Nothing would seem further from a Lacanian project, or indeed from a Gidean one, where questions of beginnings, onsets, nature and nurture are always considered slippery enough to be answered only provisionally, with the understanding that the very way in which the provisional answer is put, its framing, its discourse, somehow affect its reliability, its proximity to immediate accuracy.

Lacan, for example, is at pains in his article to show the theoretical sophistication with which Gide's discourse presents the gap between a subject and its own self-representation, the very gap Delay, following Janet, would isolate as the beginning of psychasthenia:

> This *Spaltung,* or splitting of the ego . . . seems to be the specific phenomenon here. Here we might once again be astonished that the common sense of psycho-

---

12. See Delay, *Discours de réception de M. Jean Delay à l'Académie Française et réponse de M. Pasteur Vallery-Radot,* 103.

13. Il ne m'est pas arrivé souvent de renoncer : un délai, c'est tout ce qu'obtient de moi la traverse (355).

analysts excludes the phenomenon from any careful reflexion, instead sealing itself off in abstractions like the notion of a weakness of the ego, whose pertinence for the subject Gide can once again be measured by the assertion he is capable of producing, without his behavior ever belying it: "Il ne m'est pas arrivé souvent de renoncer : un délai, c'est tout ce qu'obtient de moi la traverse." ("Jeunesse de Gide," 752)[14]

Certain psychiatrists (including Delay) find a fascination with self-representation and questions of splitting and doubling to be signs of a certain weakness of the ego. Lacan suggests instead that we use Gide as a case study for understanding doubling and self-representation as concepts more importantly and inevitably linked to a concept of a temporal delay that inhabits *every* subject:

> When Gide . . . declares himself: "We must all play our parts," and when in his ironic *Paludes,* he interrogates himself as to being and appearance, there are those who, in order to possess the mask they are renting, persuade themselves that they have a face underneath it, and think: "literature!" without suspecting that he is there expressing so personal a problem that it is in fact exactly the problem of the person. (752)[15]

Gide's constant questioning of relations between self, self-representation, and some external reality need not be read as signs of some deficit in his ego. Instead, that very theorization of the notion of a deficit can be seen as symptomatic of a certain will to ignorance in which Gide does not participate. Thus, Lacan's point in citing Gide's "un délai, c'est tout ce qu'obtient de moi la traverse" is that Gide was not misspeaking, that he was sufficiently nonpsychasthenic eventually to bring Athman to Paris (however ambivalent a gesture we have seen that to be), to fulfill a desire we might call homosexual even in the face of the opposition put up by all those surrounding him. Furthermore, the very terms Gide uses suggest his insistent understanding that sexuality always manifests itself in *après coup* structures of experience, always within delay and always indirectly—lying obliquely (*en travers de, la traverse*) across the apparent path of our life. Gide's understanding of the distance between perception and reality that becomes so acutely rendered in the case of sexual experience has nothing to do with constitutionally weak nerves. Lacan makes this quite clear by stating that any psychasthenic paradigm drawn from Janet and applied to Gide will necessarily be inadequate, Gide's discourse being more theoretically sophisticated about the concepts than is Janet's:

> For if Jean Delay in passing finds confirmation of Janet's description of psychasthenia, it is in order to draw out Gide's description of his own states, a description

---

14. Cette *Spaltung* ou refente du moi . . . nous semble bien être ici le phénomène spécifique. Occasion de s'étonner encore que le sens commun des psychanalystes le bannisse de toute réflexion méditée, pour s'abstraire dans une notion comme la faiblesse du moi, dont la pertinence se mesure une fois de plus pour le sujet Gide par l'assertion qu'il peut produire sans que la démente sa conduite. « Il ne m'est pas arrivé souvent de renoncer : un délai, c'est tout ce qu'obtient de moi la traverse. »

15. Quand Gide . . . se déclare : « Nous devons tous représenter », et quand dans son ironique *Paludes,* il s'interroge sur l'être et le paraître, ceux, qui, d'avoir un masque de louage, se persuadent qu'ils ont par dessous un visage, pensent: « littérature! » sans soupçonner qu'il exprime là un problème si personnel, qu'il est le problème tout court de la personne.

that matches Janet's in all details, except that Gide's is more strict. It is easy to see how one might ask if those scientific functions articulated by the theory, *fonction du réel, tension psychologique,* aren't really just metaphors of the symptom, and if a symptom so poetically fecund is not in itself constructed like a metaphor, which would in any case not reduce it to a *flatus vocis,* as the subject is here covering the expenses of the signifying operation with the elements of his person. (747)[16]

This passage is complicated and worth unpacking a bit because we can find here helpful information about an understanding of the way in which sexuality functions that resists the rigid temporalizations of a theoretician such as Delay. Metaphor, as Lacan uses it, is the key concept in this resistance.

The relation between metaphor and symptom is important throughout Lacan's work from this period, and this complicated passage from the Gide essay resonates with several passages from the roughly contemporaneous essay "L'Instance de la lettre dans l'inconscient" ("The Agency of the Letter in the Unconscious"), with this passage in particular: "Between the enigmatic signifier of the sexual trauma and the term that is substituted for it in an actual signifying chain there passes the spark that fixes in a symptom the signification inaccessible to the conscious subject in which that symptom may be resolved—a symptom being a metaphor in which flesh or function is taken as a signifying element" (166).[17] The noun *étincelle* (spark) occurs in this essay conjoined with adjectives such as "poétique" and "créatrice." For example, "The creative spark ["L'étincelle créatrice"] of the metaphor does not spring from the presentation of two images, that is, of two signifiers equally actualized. It flashes between two signifiers one of which has taken the place of the other in the signifying chain, the occulted signifier remaining present through its (metonymic) connexion with the rest of the chain" (157/264–65). A symptom is poetic, fecund in that it translates the (occulted) sexual trauma, which a subject cannot allow itself to know or speak, into a series of terms it can know, speak, or at least act out with its body. A symptom is a possibility for expression that makes something of the subject, of its body, of its person, even if the subject doesn't comprehend what undergirds the making. What Janet or Delay understand as pathology, Lacan implies, Gide understands as a mix of psychic structure and poetic process. Metaphor/symptom as a founding, but necessarily unknowing poesis, an act that opens the possibility for the interpretation of its own enigmatic substitutions; metaphor/symptom as a spark that is perhaps "logically" prior to its interpretations but "chronologically" more complicated, because it can only be approached through *après coup/Nachträglich* temporal structurings (such

16. Car si Jean Delay trouve au passage à confirmer la description faite par Janet de la psychasthénie, c'est pour relever que celle que Gide fait de ses propres états, la recouvre, à ceci près qu'elle est d'une langue plus stricte. On voit comment on peut se demander si les savantes fonctions dont s'articule la théorie, fonction du réel, tension psychologique, ne sont pas de simples métaphores du symptôme, et si un symptôme poétiquement si fécond, n'est pas lui-même fait comme une métaphore, ce qui ne le réduirait pas pour autant à un *flatus vocis,* le sujet faisant ici avec les éléments de sa personne les frais de l'opération signifiante.

17. Entre le signifiant énigmatique du trauma sexuel et le terme à quoi il vient se substituer dans une chaîne signifiante actuelle, passe l'étincelle, qui fixe dans un symptôme — métaphore où la chair ou bien la fonction sont prises comme élément signifiant, — la signification inaccessible au sujet conscient où il peut se résoudre (277).

as those analyzed in chapter 1);[18] metaphor/symptom as an extratemporal introduction to the temporality of interpretation; metaphor/symptom as the onset of a
possible before and after: the complexity of this perception seems more likely to
account for what Gide is up to when he deals with sexuality. Thus, the vaguely
Lacanian ring to certain of Gide's familiar formulations: "The secret motive of our
acts—I mean the most decisive ones—escapes us, and not only in memory but
even at the moment they are happening."[19] Or, from another passage in *Si le grain
ne meurt* on which Lacan comments in "The Agency of the Letter in the Unconscious": "I realized as she was speaking that it was now and forever impossible to
make her understand the secret motives of my conduct; and to tell the truth, they
were no longer very clear to myself."[20] These "motifs" and "mobiles secrets,"
unknowable "à tout jamais," could well be understood as what Slavoj Žižek, in one
of the most interesting discussions of the Lacanian concept of the symptom, has
called the "foreclosure proper to the order of the signifier as such." Žižek continues, "the symbolic structuring of sexuality implies the lack of a signifier of the
sexual relationship" and suggests a bit further on that the continual production of
the symptom out of this founding foreclosure (Lacan's unfixable moment of the
poetic spark) might be precisely what "gives consistency to the subject."[21] The
structure of sexuality, the way sexuality gives consistency to the subject, would then
not be temporal or narrative but, rather, irruptive, interruptive, intervallic, pulsative.

Delay would not give Gide consistency but rather consequence. His becoming homosexual has no consistency: "Gide's childhood does not foretell any allo-
eroticism, but it reveals an auto-eroticism full of ambivalence. . . . And it is much
more this abnormally prolonged narcissism that will play a role in the genesis of
the pedophilic mores of the author of *Corydon*" (1:252). The strange incomplete-
ness of Delay's hypothesis here is striking. "C'est bien plutôt ce narcissisme"—
this youthful narcissism is much more responsible for his turning queer, but more
responsible *than what*? Any little boys with whom he might have masturbated
under the table? Some biological predisposition? Gide's homosexuality is for

18. The chronological/logical distinction is Lacan's. See, for example, his seminar on psychosis: "Prior to any
symbolization—an anteriority which is *not chronological, but logical*—there is a stage, the psychoses make clear, at
which one part of symbolization may not take effect" (*Le Séminaire*, vol. 3: *Les Psychoses*, 94. Quoted and translated in
Michael Walsh, "Reading the Real in the Seminar on the Psychoses," 75).

19. Le motif secret de nos actes, et j'entends : des plus décisifs, nous échappe; et non seulement dans le souvenir
que nous en gardons, mais bien au moment même.

20. Je me rendais compte, à mesure qu'elle parlait, qu'il me serait à tout jamais impossible d'éclairer pour elle
les mobiles secrets de ma conduite; et, à dire vrai, ces mobiles, je ne les distinguais plus bien moi-même.

⚫ ⚫ ⚫

The two Gide quotations are from *Si le grain ne meurt*, 299 and 145, respectively (*If It Die*, 248 and 121). Lacan
comments on the latter in "L'Instance de la lettre," 286 ("The Agency of the Letter," 173).

21. See Slavoj Žižek, *The Sublime Object of Ideology*, 71–75. He is also interesting on the ideas of *après coup* and
delay. See pp. 55–62. See also his article "Rossellini: Woman as Symptom of Man," 21: "[the symptom is] a
particular signifying formation which confers on the subject its very ontological consistency, enabling it to structure its
basic, constitutive relationship towards enjoyment." (One might choose to see in some of Žižek's formulations on
those pages a rush toward *hetero*sexuality rather more resolute or hasty than Lacan's, who seems to have taken his time
over his reading of Gide.)

Delay the consequence of three things: too much masturbation; weak nerves ("However one looks at it, the sole notable anomaly in Gide's constitution was not of a sexual nature, but of a nervous one. His temperament was that of someone given to nervous weakness" [2:526]); and a meeting with Oscar Wilde.

Let's not exaggerate. "We are certainly not claiming that if he had never met Wilde, Gide would not have become homosexual, but it is likely that he would not have so quickly adopted and interiorized the attitude of an arrogant pederast, insistent on claiming his anomaly as his norm" (2:547).[22] (Allow Delay here his own inconsistencies. Wilde apparently both is and is not responsible for turning Gide gay.) It is unfortunate the extent to which this model of moral influence has been taken as crucial to *Les Faux-Monnayeurs,* as if the mature Edouard and Passavant, and the adolescent Olivier and Bernard were playing a game of elective affinities according to the rules Delay sees as governing Gide's encounter with Wilde:

> Certainly the influence of a homosexual only works on those who possess analogous latent tendencies, but if one admits that these tendencies are more or less latent in many adolescents whose tastes are not yet definitively fixed, then we will agree that a famous example can in part be responsible for numerous deviations. (2:548)

The question is, what can be done with *Les Faux-Monnayeurs* to show that it can defy Delay's consequences, that it has a different consistency that shows more subtlety and less *parti pris* in dealing with what we might call *le coup de la sexualité,* the onset of sexuality?

Among all the semantic complexities of the word *coup,* we should, in what follows, be attentive to at least four: the *coup* of *après coup,* the retrospective revision of our tellings of our sexuality; the insistent blows (*ces coups pressés*) knocking on Lacan's door to wake him out of a dream we are about to look at, the repetitive call to the waking state; the *coup* in another expression from the telling of that same dream—*sous le coup du réveil*—under the influence of, caught by awakening, just as one might be *sous le coup de la sexualité,* acting under the influence of sexuality, as if not really awake—a state of great importance in *Les Faux-Monnayeurs;* and finally, *coup* as gunshot, in particular the gunshot that kills Boris at the end of the novel, a *coup* in which these other three uses of the word are crucial: Boris, who can no longer stand to be awake; Boris, who acts in excruciating pain under the influence of a sexuality he cannot comprehend; Boris, whose sexuality has been too easily patterned by others as a symptom to be cured without delay, a symptom that can be erased with no after effects.

22. Jonathan Dollimore has commented on Delay's ascription of Gide's sexuality to Wilde. See *Sexual Dissidence: Augustine to Wilde, Freud to Foucault,* 43. Dollimore has interesting things to say about Gide throughout his book. Unfortunately, he, too, misses the complexities of the structure of Gide's discourse on sexuality and accepts the terms of the sincerity game (although I find him to be one of its few sympathetic players): "For Gide transgression is in the name of a desire and identity rooted in the natural, the sincere, and the authentic" (14). Or: "Whereas for Wilde transgressive desire leads to a relinquishing of the essential self, for Gide it leads to its discovery, to the real self, a new self created from liberated desire" (13).

"To die, to sleep—
To sleep, perchance to dream"

People are always either dozing off or waking up in *Les Faux-Monnayeurs*. Falling asleep *punctuates* the novel consistently and thereby consistently raises questions about the consequentiality of our waking life, about the imaging of ourselves and our sexuality that we indulge in while awake. The space of falling asleep or of returning to a waking state is thus the space the novel provides in which we can find a discourse of discontinuous repetition, a discourse that insistently questions the work being done by that other discourse heretofore given critical predominance: that of sincerity, authenticity, self-possession. Consider the opening of chapter 6 in part 1:

> Bernard has had an absurd dream. He doesn't remember his dream. He doesn't try to remember his dream, but to get out of it. He returns to the world of reality to feel Olivier's body pressing heavily against him. While they were asleep (or at any rate while Bernard was asleep) his friend had come close up to him—and, for that matter, the bed was too narrow to allow for much distance; he had turned over; he is sleeping on his side now and Bernard feels Olivier's warm breath tickling his neck. Bernard has nothing on but his short day-shirt; one of Olivier's arms is flung across him, weighing oppressively and indiscreetly on his flesh. For a moment Bernard is not sure that Olivier is really asleep. (56)[23]

At the opening of the novel Bernard discovers that he is the product of an extramarital affair of his mother's and that his father is not his real father. This precipitates his decision to quit the paternal home, and he depends on his best friend Olivier's hospitality for the first night following his impetuous decision. The next day, he will hook up with Olivier's uncle, the homosexual novelist Edouard, on whom Olivier has a crush. He will convince Edouard to hire him as his secretary, usurping Olivier's hoped-for place. Edouard, Bernard, and Laura—an old flame of Edouard's who is trying to hide from her husband and family while she decides what to do about her recent illicit pregnancy—will go off to Switzerland together, where Bernard will claim to fall in love with Laura. Olivier, feeling betrayed by his best friend and by his uncle, will go off for the summer vacation with the insalubrious Passavant. This crisscrossing will untangle itself slightly at the end of the summer, once everyone is back in Paris. On the same night that Olivier and Edouard finally sleep together, Bernard will sleep with Sarah, Laura's younger sister. (While in Switzerland, Bernard's unacknowledged desire to meet Sarah is

23. Bernard a fait un rêve absurde. Il ne se souvient pas de ce qu'il a rêvé. Il ne cherche pas à se souvenir de son rêve, mais à en sortir. Il rentre dans le monde réel pour sentir le corps d'Olivier peser lourdement contre lui. Son ami, pendant leur sommeil, ou du moins pendant le sommeil de Bernard, s'était rapproché, et du reste l'étroitesse du lit ne permet pas beaucoup de distance; il s'était retourné; à présent, il dort sur le flanc et Bernard sent son souffle chaud chatouiller son cou. Bernard n'a qu'une courte chemise de jour; en travers de son corps, un bras d'Olivier opprime indiscrètement sa chair. Bernard doute un instant si son ami dort vraiment (58).

revealed to us by the narrator: "He wanted . . . to know Sarah, the younger sister; but his curiosity remained a secret one; out of consideration for Laura, he did not even own it to himself" [218/213].) This splitting up of the initial couple of Bernard and Olivier, their progress through various pairings, finally will not mean that the two have successfully extricated their desire from its complicity with the other. In the end, neither of them comes to possess in integrity their desire or their sexuality.

The details of Bernard waking up already indicate the dispossessing effects of sexuality—and our waking attempts to compensate for that dispossession—by placing sexuality in a problematic space between waking and sleeping. What kind of a dream, one might ask, would Bernard have had in bed with Olivier, Olivier's breath warm on his neck, Olivier's arm in a near embrace—"en travers de son corps," holding him down, holding him back, an obstacle to the sequence of his life? The dream is dismissed into the realm of the absurd, and Bernard takes no responsibility for it, running from the dream and from sleep back to reality, only to find reality marked by the gravity and indiscretion of Olivier's body. Twice over there is a hint that Olivier knows what he is up to in ways Bernard does not. First, the narrator hints that perhaps only Bernard was asleep when Olivier decided to roll over ("pendant leur sommeil, ou du moins pendant la sommeil de Bernard"). Bernard takes the hint a few sentences later: "Bernard doute un instant si son ami dort vraiment." Who is responsible for what happens during sleep, and why is only Olivier's sleep in question here? How does desire speak in sleep, and how do we represent ourselves in relation to that desire and to our sleep?

Gide wrote a preface to Stendhal's novel *Armance* for a new 1925 edition. In that preface he talks at length about the impotence of Octave, Armance's suitor. Stendhal, Gide explains, never mentions that impotence in the novel itself, only in a letter to Mérimée. Gide is fascinated by the condition, precisely because it represents another manifestation of a split between consciousness and the expression of desire. He says that he has interviewed a number of impotent men himself:

> Of the few "*babylans*" (to use Stendhal's word) who have confided in me, the saddest case . . . seems to be that of a young man, perfectly normal in appearance and physiologically whole, but incapable of sensual pleasure. The only release allowed him came during his sleep, but he did not feel it and became conscious of it only upon awakening. For him, pleasure was a *terra ignota* of which he dreamed constantly, which he tried in vain to attain, and toward which the smug tales of travelers to that land attracted him. ("Preface to *Armance*," 269)[24]

---

24. Des quelques « Babylans » (pour reprendre le mot de Stendhal) dont j'ai reçu les confidences, le cas le plus douloureux . . . me paraît être celui d'un jeune homme parfaitement normal d'apparence et physiologiquement complet; mais incapable de volupté. Le seul échappement qui lui restât permis, c'était durant le sommeil, insensible, et dont il ne devenait conscient qu'au réveil. Le plaisir demeurait pour lui la *terra ignota* à laquelle il rêvait sans cesse, qu'il s'efforçait en vain d'atteindre, et vers quoi l'attiraient les récits complaisants des voyageurs ("Préface à *Armance*," 78–91).

Like Bernard, this person doesn't remember his dreams; nonetheless, he "dreams" of someday achieving a waking orgasm—as if to suggest that only in dreaming (one way or the other) can one represent oneself as in possession of one's sexuality. *Les Faux-Monnayeurs,* insofar as it succeeds in imagining the onset of sexuality and its dispossession, does so in an intervallic space between sleeping and waking. Insofar as it manages to respect and protect this impossible space of necessary dispossession, it necessarily critiques its own production of the phobic discourse of sincerity and counterfeiting.

Delay was interested in Gide's relationship to sleep as well. In fact, another way of seeing the difference between Delay and Lacan would be to look at the differences in their treatments of the state half-way between sleeping and waking, a state Delay calls *prædormitio* and to which he suggests Gide was too attached:

> He mostly experienced this feeling of a second reality, neither the true reality of the waking state nor the dream of the sleeping state, in that intermediary state between waking and sleeping. "During the day, my suspicions remained uncertain, but I felt them become precise and firm at night, just before falling asleep." *Prædormitio,* the hypnagogic instant when those mental syntheses that ensure an adaptation to reality and an attention to life loosen, is in effect an eminently favorable instant for this obscure perception—of which we all share more or less the experience, but—and precisely this is important—more or less. (1:147)

Too much given to this apparently luxurious experience, Gide is thus likely less able to assemble his capacities in order to deal with day-to-day life. The experience of *prædormitio* is a universal one, yet one dangerous to dwell on.

Sophroniska (the analyst of *Les Faux-Monnayeurs* encountered by Edouard in Switzerland) agrees with Delay on this point.[25] The moment just before sleep is often a masturbatory moment, and this Sophroniska knows to be one of her charge Boris' problems. Boris has been taught to masturbate by a friend. In Edouard's words: "They believed in all good faith that they had discovered a secret that made up for real absence by illusory presence, and they freely put themselves in a state of hallucination and ecstasy, gloating over an empty void, which their heated imagination, stimulated by their desire for pleasure, filled to overflowing with marvels" (206).[26] Boris' cure would thus consist in getting him to wake up and smell the coffee, to work toward self-possession. As Sophroniska puts it, "I talked the whole thing over with him, and made him ashamed of having preferred the possession of

25. The character Sophroniska is drawn in part from a Polish psychoanalyst who came to Paris in 1921 with whom Gide had some contact. Some of the details of Boris' case are drawn from one of her published case histories and are also obviously related to episodes from Gide's own childhood, as recounted in *Si le grain ne meurt.* For more information, see Michel Gourévitch, "Eugénie Sokolnicka: Pionnier de la psychanalyse et inspiratrice d'André Gide." For more information on Gide's knowledge of Freud and his writings, see David Steel, "Gide et Freud." For an idea of what is at stake in naming this character Sophroniska, see Michel Foucault's discussion of the word *sōphrosunē* (temperance) in *Histoire de la sexualité,* vol. 2: *L'Usage des plaisirs,* esp. 74–90 (*The Use of Pleasure,* 63–77).

26. Ils croyaient de bonne foi avoir découvert un secret qui consolât de l'absence réelle par la présence illusoire, et s'hallucinaient à plaisir et s'extasiaient sur un vide que leur imagination surmenée bondait de merveilles, à grand renfort de volupté (202).

imaginary goods to the real goods which are, I told him, the reward of effort"
(208)[27]—coffee and some real activity, to make sure Boris stays firmly in the realm
of the waking.

Lacan's Interval

For Lacan, unlike for Delay and Sophroniska, dwelling on this experience of being
between waking and sleeping seems essential to arriving at an analytic understanding of a subject's own self-representation, and so this moment is subject to
extended analysis in his seminar *The Four Fundamental Concepts of Psycho-
Analysis:*

> Just the other day, was I not awoken from a short sleep in which I was looking for
> repose by something that was knocking at my door just before I awoke? For already,
> with these hurried knocks, I had formed a dream, one which manifested for me
> something other than these knocks. When I do wake up, these knocks—this per-
> ception—if I become conscious of them, it's to the extent that around them I
> reconstitute my entire representation. I know that I'm there, when I fell asleep, and
> what I was looking for in that sleep. When the noise of the knocking attains, not my
> perception, but my consciousness, it's because my consciousness reconstitutes itself
> around this representation—it's that I know that I am caught up by awakening, that
> I am *knocked*.
>
> But here I must question myself as to what I am at that precise moment—at
> that instant, so immediately before and so separate, which is that in which I began to
> dream caught up in the knock which apparently wakes me up. I am, as far as I know,
> *before even I awake*. (56)[28]

Here Lacan is reflecting on the necessity of a certain delay structuring the space
between an event, a perception, and a conscious representation of the perception.
In the interval of that delay lies an experience of dispossession—or perhaps better
put, the effort to hide from the experience of that dispossession often governs our
waking life, and one lapse in that effort lies in that precise moment between
sleeping and waking when we almost are, but not quite yet, caught up by awakening. Once we are awake, our self-representation attaches itself to and forms itself

---

27. Je lui ai fait honte d'avoir pu préférer la possession de biens imaginaires à celle des biens véritables, qui sont,
lui ai-je dit, la récompense d'un effort (204).

28. L'autre jour, n'ai-je point été éveillé d'un court sommeil où je cherchais le repos par quelque chose qui
frappait à ma porte dès avant que je ne me réveille. C'est qu'avec ces coups pressés, j'avais déjà formé un rêve, un rêve
qui me manifestait autre chose que ces coups. Et quand je me réveille, ces coups — cette perception — si j'en prends
conscience, c'est pour autant qu'autour d'eux, je reconstitue toute ma représentation. Je sais que je suis là, à quelle
heure je me suis endormi, et ce que je cherchais par ce sommeil. Quand le bruit du coup parvient, non point à ma
perception mais à ma conscience, c'est que ma conscience se reconstitue autour de cette représentation — que je sais
que je suis sous le coup du réveil, que je suis *knocked*.

   Mais là, il me faut bien m'interroger sur ce que je suis à ce moment-là — à l'instant, si immédiatement avant
et si séparé, qui est celui où j'ai commencé à rêver sous ce coup qui est, en apparence, ce qui me réveille. Je suis, que
je sache, *avant que je ne me réveille* (55–56).

around our consciousness of a perception; but the temporal quirk of that intermediate dream (the knocking we perceive causes us to wake, but first we have time to construct a dream around it) opens the possibility of a space between that perception and the coming to consciousness around it:

> The primary process—which is simply what I have tried to define for you in my last few lectures in the form of the unconscious—must, once again, be apprehended in its experience of rupture, between perception and consciousness, in that nontemporal locus, I said, which forces us to posit what Freud calls, in homage to Fechner, *die Idee einer anderer Lokalität,* the idea of another locality, another space, another scene, *the between perception and consciousness.* (56)[29]

Lacan delimits this intervallic space in this and the next several sessions of his seminar by way of commentaries on a series of dreams. It might seem initially that the crucial aspect of the moment of falling asleep or waking up lies in the revelation it embodies that our conscious representations of ourselves are insufficient to account for who we are—that is, such a moment reveals for us that we have an unconscious to which dreams might give access. But Lacan seems more interested in the question of repose, repose precisely from the trauma of representation, a representation sufficiently anchored in the social world that it inevitably also represents a dispossession of the subject—dispossession from a "logically" prior atraumatic state that is not subject to representation. Thus the following description of an infant falling asleep:

> I, too, have seen with my own eyes, opened by maternal divination, the child, traumatized by the fact that I was going away despite the appeal, precociously adumbrated in his voice, and henceforth more renewed for months at a time—I have seen him, even much later, when I would take him, this child, in my arms—I have seen him let his head droop onto my shoulder and fall into slumber, that slumber alone being capable of giving him access to the living signifier that I had become since the date of the trauma. (63)[30]

The child escapes the trauma of the social, but into what? Into the repose offered by the contact of two bodies, one slumbering, harmoniously given over to gravity, perhaps.[31] Perhaps the child dreams. There remains some question as to whether

---

29. Le processus primaire — qui n'est autre que ce que j'ai essayé pour vous de définir dans les dernières leçons sous la forme de l'inconscient — il nous faut bien, une fois de plus, le saisir dans son expérience de rupture, entre perception et conscience, dans ce lieu, vous ai-je dit, intemporel, qui contraint à poser ce que Freud appelle, en en faisant l'hommage à Fechner, *die Idee einer anderer Lokalität* — une autre localité, un autre espace, une autre scène, *l'entre perception et conscience* (55).

30. J'ai vu moi aussi, vu de mes yeux, dessillés par la divination maternelle, l'enfant, traumatisé de ce que je parte en dépit de son appel précocement ébauché de la voix, et désormais plus renouvelé pour des mois entiers — je l'ai vu, bien longtemps après encore, quand je le prenais, cet enfant, dans les bras — je l'ai vu laisser aller sa tête sur mon épaule pour tomber dans le sommeil, le sommeil seul capable de lui rendre l'accès au signifiant vivant que j'étais depuis la date du trauma (61).

31. See this passage from *Les Faux-Monnayeurs,* a conversation between La Pérouse and Edouard:

> "Have you observed that the whole effect of modern music is to make bearable, and even agreeable, certain harmonies which we used to consider discords?"

dreams could offer a complete escape from the trauma of the social—this is one of the important complications of Lacan's argument. For instance, one both does and does not find self-possession in dreams. Dreams can be an experience of dispossession, as well. Lacan's example for discussing this problem of the *lack* of repose in dreams is the famous dream of the burning child from the beginning of Chapter 7 of Freud's *Interpretation of Dreams*. Freud recounts that a father had been keeping watch at the bedside of his son who had just died of a fever. He goes into the next room to sleep for awhile, leaving an old man who was being paid to watch over the dead child. The old man falls asleep; a candle accidentally tips over and starts a fire, burning the cloth covering the corpse, and one of its arms. The father incorporates the light from that fire, perceived through his eyelids and the open door, into a dream out of which he wakes: "After a few hours' sleep, the father had a dream that *his child was standing beside his bed, caught him by the arm and whispered to him reproachfully: 'Father, don't you see I'm burning?'* He woke up, noticed a bright glare of light from the next room, hurried into it . . ." (Freud, *The Interpretation of Dreams*, 547–48). The father constructs a dream similar to Lacan's, a dream that takes an external stimulus and builds a dream around it in order that the sleeper need not waken. Lacan even speaks as if it is a knocking noise that wakes the father, even though Freud speaks of the "glare of light" from the accidental fire. But Lacan also points out that it is probable that, unlike in Lacan's own knocking dream, the bit of reality that forces the father into a waking state is not that insistent perception attaining the subject's consciousness, but the actual reproach spoken by the dead child in the dream.

> There is, don't you think, more reality in this message than in the noise by which the father also identifies the strange reality of what is happening in the room next door. Is not the missed reality that caused the death of the child expressed in these words? . . . And is not the action, apparently so urgent, of preventing what is

---

"Exactly," I rejoined. "Everything must finally resolve into—be reduced to harmony."

"Harmony!" he repeated, shrugging his shoulders. "All that I can see in it is familiarization with evil—with sin. Sensibility is blunted; purity is tarnished; reactions are less vivid; one tolerates; one accepts. . . ."

"To listen to you, one would never dare to wean a child. . . . But you don't pretend to restrict music to the mere expression of serenity, do you? In that case, a single chord would suffice—a perfect and continuous chord."

He took both my hands in his, and in a burst of ecstasy, his eyes rapt in adoration, he repeated several times over:

"A perfect and continuous chord; yes, yes; a perfect and continuous chord. . . ." (165)

[« "Avez-vous remarqué, que tout l'effort de la musique moderne est de rendre supportables, agréables même, certains accords que nous tenions d'abord pour discordants?

« — Précisément, ripostai-je; tout doit enfin se rendre et se réduire à l'harmonie.

« — A l'harmonie! répéta-t-il en haussant les épaules. Je ne vois là qu'une accoutumance au mal, au péché. La sensibilité s'émousse; la pureté se ternit; les réactions se font moins vives; on tolère, on accepte . . .

« — A vous entendre, on n'oserait même plus sevrer les enfants . . . Vous ne prétendez pourtant pas restreindre la musique à la seule expression de la sérénité? Dans ce cas, un seul accord suffirait : un accord parfait continu.

« Il me prit les deux mains, et comme en extase, le regard perdu dans une adoration, répéta plusieurs fois :

« " Un accord parfait continu; oui, c'est cela : un accord parfait continu . . . " » (162–63)]

happening in the next room also perhaps felt as being in any case too late now, in relation to what is at issue, in the psychical reality manifested in the words spoken? Is not the dream essentially, one might say, an act of homage to the missed reality—the reality that can no longer produce itself except by repeating itself endlessly, in some never attained awakening? (58)[32]

The dream world does not offer repose. The father dreams to escape the waking world, yet is forced to run from the dream back to it. In the waking world it is too late to take any meaningful action. Only in a moment impossible to prolong or even control, of almost attaining to awakening, can there be the hint of a possible solace, tainted though it be here by the terrifying return of the dead.[33] It is more *the gap* between dreaming and waking that holds out the *hope* of repose, a repose that is achieved, if it ever is, out of a recognition of how the self-possession game plays itself out, over and over.

Within a dream world, a subject cannot imagine itself controlling the creation of representations whose coherence may offer a sense of self-possession. As Lacan puts it, a subject may say to itself within a dream, "I am dreaming," but the dreamscape is outside of his possession:

> He may even on occasion detach himself, tell himself that it is a dream, but in no case will he be able to apprehend himself in the dream in the way in which, in the Cartesian *cogito,* he apprehends himself as thought. He may say to himself, *It's only a dream.* But he does not apprehend himself as someone who says to himself—*After all, I am the consciousness of this dream.* (75–76)[34]

It is the experience of a *difference* between one's way of apprehending oneself in a dream and while awake, a difference vaguely glimpsed in the half-awake state, that offers a strange form of consistency and a measure of solace and repose. In that difference lies consistency.

To make this point, Lacan brings in Choang-tsu, who dreamed he was a butterfly, and then woke to wonder whether, while waking, he might not be a butterfly dreaming he is Choang-tsu. In this protopsychasthenic Lacan finds much to admire. For Choang-tsu seems to recognize and respect the important difference between waking and dreaming acts of representation:

32. Il y a plus de réalité, n'est-ce pas, dans ce message, que dans le bruit, par quoi le père aussi bien identifie l'étrange réalité de ce qui se passe dans la pièce voisine. Est-ce que dans ces mots ne passe pas la réalité manquée qui a causé la mort de l'enfant? . . . L'action, si pressante soit-elle selon toute vraisemblance, de parer à ce qui se passe dans la pièce voisine — n'est-elle pas peut-être, aussi, sentie comme de toute façon, maintenant, trop tard — par rapport à ce dont il s'agit, à la réalité psychique qui se manifeste dans la phrase prononcée? Le rêve poursuivi n'est-il pas essentiellement, si je puis dire, l'hommage à la réalité manquée? — la réalité qui ne peut se faire qu'à se répéter indéfiniment, en un indéfiniment jamais atteint réveil (57).

33. Žižek has an interesting commentary on this dream and the dream of the butterfly we are about to look at. See *The Sublime Object of Ideology,* 45–47.

34. Il peut même à l'occasion se détacher, se dire que c'est un rêve, mais il ne saurait en aucun cas se saisir dans le rêve à la façon dont, dans le *cogito* cartésien, il se saisit comme pensée. Il peut se dire — *ce n'est qu'un rêve.* Mais il ne se saisit pas comme celui qui se dit — *Malgré tout, je suis conscience de ce rêve* (72).

When he is the butterfly, the idea does not occur to him to wonder whether, when he is Choang-tsu awake, he is not the butterfly that he is dreaming of being. This is because, when dreaming of being the butterfly, he will no doubt have to bear witness later that he represented himself as a butterfly. But this does not mean that he is captivated by the butterfly—he is a captive butterfly, but captured by nothing, for, in the dream, he is a butterfly for nobody. It is when he is awake that he is Choang-tsu for others, and is caught in their butterfly net. (76)[35]

Perhaps because he has no expectations of self-possession, Choang-tsu almost seems to achieve it, at least when he's dreaming he's a butterfly and is thus unconscious of the fact that he needs self-possession. It would seem that Lacan is suggesting that something in this dream represents an escape from the social, or at least a tentative *après coup* memory of such an escape, because while he is dreaming Choang-tsu is a butterfly *"for nobody."* Bearing witness to his representation, and thereby being alienated from it, comes "later." So even though he can only *recall* having been a butterfly, it was at that moment inaccesible to consciousness except through memory, that he was himself: "In fact, it is when he was the butterfly that he apprehended one of the roots of his identity—that he was, and is, in his essence, that butterfly who paints himself with his own colours—and it is because of this that, in the last resort, he is Choang-tsu" (76).[36]

Choang-tsu's consistency, the moment when he could paint himself with his own colors, reveals itself only in sleep and in the discrepancy between dreaming and waking. The phrase, "that butterfly who paints himself with his own colours," recalls a turn of phrase Lacan used when discussing the relation between metaphor and symptom in Gide: "the subject is here covering the expenses of the signifying operation with the elements of his person." Consistency is here imaginable only in the tension between that logically prior atraumatic space and its interpretation, a tension that the gap between dreaming and waking briefly reveals, the determinants of that gap—legible and illegible—being the individual colors, the elements of that person. The brief access can be repeated indefinitely, the solace of the access often being matched or overwhelmed by the simultaneous repetition of the trauma of dispossession. Choang-tsu does not seem particularly traumatized, but Lacan immediately points out that others will be. His example is the Wolf Man, who also dreamed about a butterfly.

It is when he is awake that he is Choang-tsu for others, and is caught in their butterfly net.

35. Quand il est le papillon, il ne lui vient pas à l'idée de se demander si, quand il est Tchoang-tseu éveillé, il n'est pas le papillon qu'il est en train de rêver d'être. C'est que, rêvant d'être le papillon, il aura sans doute à témoigner plus tard qu'il se représentait comme papillon, mais cela ne veut pas dire qu'il est captivé par le papillon — il est papillon capturé, mais capture de rien, car, dans le rêve, il n'est papillon pour personne. C'est quand il est éveillé qu'il est Tchoang-tseu pour les autres, et qu'il est pris dans leur filet à papillons (72–73).

36. Effectivement, c'est quand il était le papillon qu'il se saisissait à quelque racine de son identité — qu'il était, et qu'il est dans son essence, ce papillon qui se peint à ses propres couleurs — et c'est par là, en dernière racine, qu'il est Tchoang-tseu (72).

> This is why the butterfly may—if the subject is not Choang-tsu, but the Wolf
> Man—inspire in him the phobic terror of recognizing that the beating of little wings
> is not so very far from the beating of causation, of the primal stripe marking his being
> for the first time with the grid of desire. (76)[37]

The Wolf Man case history recurs throughout the *Four Fundamental Concepts,* and
much of its importance can be gleaned from this brief reference. The Wolf Man
case history is a locus from which to consider the relation between the initial
traumatic moment and the onset of sexuality, to reflect upon the place of repetition
in the understanding of sexuality, to ponder the ways in which the concept of
causation might be wrenched from its association with consequence and made to
relate to consistency.

   The Wolf Man's butterfly comes up in the final two sections of Freud's "From
the History of an Infantile Neurosis." The Wolf Man had a memory of once as a
child chasing a large butterfly with yellow stripes. "Suddenly, when the butterfly
had settled on a flower, he was seized with a dreadful fear of the creature, and ran
away screaming" ("From the History of an Infantile Neurosis," 281). Through a
complicated series of associations, Freud is able to show that the Wolf Man
associates the butterfly with a particular woman from his childhood. The Wolf
Man also tells Freud that "the opening and shutting of the butterfly's wings while it
was settled on the flower had given him an uncanny feeling. It had looked, so he
said, like a woman opening her legs" (282). Thus, the butterfly stands in for a
relation to sexual objects; the phobic energy it produces, says Freud, has its origins
in the defensive anxiety created by the Wolf Man's fear of castration and his
repression of certain homosexual impulses:

> It may truly be said that the anxiety that was concerned in the formation of these
> phobias was a fear of castration. This statement involves no contradiction of the view
> that the anxiety originated from the repression of homosexual libido. Both modes of
> expression refer to the same process: namely the withdrawal of libido by the ego from
> the homosexual conative tendency, the libido having then become converted into free
> anxiety and subsequently bound in phobias. The first method of statement merely
> mentions in addition the motive power by which the ego was actuated. (307)

One of the great tensions of the Wolf Man case history is, of course, between the
search for priority and sub- or consequence, on the one hand, and, on the other,
an awareness of the problematic role of repetition, rememoration, and reconstruction in the establishment of putative priority and sequence. At a certain, specific
moment, the anxiety was bound *this* way, and that moment was subsequent/
consequent to the onset of a homosexual object choice that came about at a certain

---

37. C'est quand il est éveillé qu'il est Tchoang-tseu pour les autres, et qu'il est pris dans leur filet à papillons.
      C'est pour cela que le papillon peut — si le sujet n'est pas Tchoang-tseu, mais l'homme aux loups — lui
inspirer la terreur phobique de reconnaître que le battement des petites ailes n'est pas tellement loin du battement de
la causation, de la rayure primitive marquant son être atteint pour la première fois par la grille du désir (72–73).

moment and was repressed at a certain later moment. Lacan seems fascinated by the way the Wolf Man's perpetually renewed, pulsative anxiety will be feverishly subjected to a regime of causality by both the Wolf Man and Freud.

> If you wish to understand what is Freud's true preoccupation as the function of phantasy is revealed to him, remember the development, which is so central for us, of the *Wolf Man*. He applies himself, in a way that can almost be described as anguished, to the question—what is the first encounter, the real, that lies behind the phantasy? We feel that throughout this analysis, this real drags the subject along with it, forcing it along, so directing the research that, after all, we can today ask ourselves whether this fever, this presence, this desire of Freud is not that which, in his patient, might have conditioned the belated accident of his psychosis. (54)[38]

If for Freud it is necessary to trace with accuracy the Wolf Man's passage through an oedipal stage and to demonstrate how that passage, under the influence of the memories of various traumatic moments from infancy, results in the binding of anxiety over object choice into specific phobias, for Lacan precisely those aspects of Freud's analysis that try insistently to turn this *passage* through sexuality into a *progress* fuel a fever that can never do away with the unsatisfying explanatory status of any progress. Thus, the experience of the Wolf Man and his analysis is, *on the one hand,* of a relentless analytic moving backward (in order to remove a symptom so that the patient's future progress will be unimpeded), a moving backward toward an originary traumatic scene that for Lacan—even though, or exactly because it is "fiercely tracked down"—remains in its own way relentlessly "factitious." *On the other hand,* it is an experience of the pulsative ongoing repetition of a traumatic encounter with the real, in a sequence of continual onset that only a misplaced analytic will would subject to causation. This subjection to causation, it would seem, *is precisely what continually re-energizes the phobic state.* Lacan's focus is thus less on a subjection to causation than on understanding that something is consistently missed in every repetition of the trauma's onset and that this very consistency works against causation:

> That is why, in the misunderstood concept of repetition, I stress the importance of the ever avoided encounter, of the missed opportunity. The function of missing lies at the centre of analytic repetition. The appointment is always missed. . . . Cause might be formulated on the basis of the classical formula of the *ablata causa tollitur effectus*—I would have only to stress the singular of the protasis, *ablata causa,* by putting the terms of the apodosis in the plural *tolluntur effectus*—which would mean that *the effects get along well only in the absence of cause.* All the effects are subjected to the pressure of a transfactual, causal order which demands to join in their dance,

---

38. Rappelez-vous le développement, si central pour nous, de l'*Homme aux loups,* pour comprendre quelle est la véritable préoccupation de Freud à mesure que se révèle pour lui la fonction du fantasme. Il s'attache, et sur un mode presque angoissé, à interroger quelle est la rencontre première, le réel, que nous pouvons affirmer derrière le fantasme. Ce réel, nous sentons qu'à travers toute cette analyse, il entraîne avec lui le sujet, et presque le force, dirigeant tellement la recherche qu'après tout, nous pouvons aujourd'hui nous demander si cette fièvre, cette présence, ce désir de Freud n'est pas ce qui, chez son malade, a pu conditionner l'accident tardif de sa psychose (54).

but, if they held their hands tightly, as in the song, they would prevent the cause intruding in their round. (128)[39]

Sexuality happens too early and too late; too early and too late for causation to break the dance of the effects. It happens between metaphor and metonymy, between symptom and interpretation, in an interval whose difficult access I have been tracing here. The effects of the onset of sexuality, constantly renewed and revised, evade the imposition of causality. Lacan summarizes the analytic problems this raises:

> In *Three Essays on the Theory of Sexuality,* Freud was able to posit sexuality as essentially polymorphous, aberrant. The spell of a supposed infantile innocence was broken. Because it was imposed so early, I would almost say too early, this sexuality made us pass too quickly over an examination of what it essentially represents. That is to say that, with regard to the agency of sexuality, all subjects are equal, from the child to the adult—that they deal only with that part of sexuality that passes into the networks of the constitution of the subject, into the networks of the signifier—that sexuality is realized only through the operation of the drives in so far as they are partial drives, partial with regard to the biological finality of sexuality. (176–77)[40]

In the repetitive onset of sexuality, child and adult are on equal footing, because whatever part of sexuality occupies them, it occupies them from that always logically prior moment of subjective constitution. And any imagined biological finality to the sexual act is a posterior ideological imposition, a causal reasoning meant to evade the impulse of sexuality. We might think here of the unanswerable question central to the first chapter of this study, Which came first, sex or politics? Here Lacan argues for the simultaneous institution of sexuality and the entry into the social, but that act of institution is unfixable; and through a repetition from whose discomfort the subject will perhaps never escape, the question of sexuality and the question of social positioning will be chasing each others' tails throughout that subject's foreseeable future.

Sexuality's pulsative nature might, in the way it challenges the feverish search for originary moments, challenge the notion of fixing that moment at which one

---

39. C'est pourquoi j'ai mis en relief dans le concept méconnu de la répétition ce ressort qui est celui de la rencontre toujours évitée, de la chance manquée. La fonction de ratage est au centre de la répétition analytique. Le rendez-vous est toujours manqué . . . {La cause} se formulerait à partir de la formule classique de l'*ablata causa tollitur effectus* — nous n'aurions qu'à souligner le singulier de la protase, *ablata causa*, en mettant au pluriel les termes de l'apodose, *tolluntur effectus* — ce qui voudrait dire que *les effets ne se portent bien qu'en l'absence de la cause.* Tous les effets sont soumis à la pression d'un ordre transfactuel, causal, qui demande à entrer dans leur danse, mais, s'ils se tenaient bien la main, comme dans la chanson, ils feraient obstacle à ce que la cause s'immisce dans leur ronde (117).

40. Dès les *Trois essais sur la théorie de la sexualité,* Freud a pu poser la sexualité comme essentiellement polymorphe, aberrante. Le charme d'une prétendue innocence infantile a été rompu. Cette sexualité, pour s'être imposée si tôt, je dirais presque trop tôt, nous a fait passer trop vite sur l'examen de ce qu'elle représente en son essence. C'est à savoir, qu'au regard de l'instance de la sexualité, tous les sujets sont à égalité, depuis l'enfant jusqu'à l'adulte — qu'ils n'ont affaire qu'à ce qui, de la sexualité, passe dans les réseaux de la constitution subjective, dans les réseaux du signifiant — que la sexualité ne se réalise que par l'opération des pulsions en tant qu'elles sont pulsions partielles, partielles au regard de la finalité biologique de la sexualité (161).

becomes, say, queer. Weak nerves, a difficult childhood, the early death of a father, a protective mother, a trip to North Africa, a chance encounter with Oscar Wilde. At which point is there no going back? Such is the genre of question Delay asks. And within *Les Faux-Monnayeurs* it is Armand who gives this question voice in his search for "l'instant extrême":

> "Six shipwrecked persons are picked up in a boat. They have been adrift for ten days in the storm. Three are dead; two are saved. The sixth is expiring. It was hoped he might be restored to life; but his organism had reached the extreme limit."
>
> "Yes, I understand," said Olivier. "An hour sooner and he might have been saved."
>
> "An hour! What are you saying? I want to calculate the extreme instant. Possible. . . . Still possible. No longer possible! My mind walks along that narrow ridge. That dividing line between existence and non-existence is the one I keep trying to trace everywhere. The limit of resistance to—well, for instance, to what my father would call temptation. One holds out; the cord on which the devil pulls is stretched to breaking. . . . A tiny bit more, the cord snaps—one is damned." (287)[41]

Armand and Boris are the two characters in the novel most disastrously affected by sexuality's troubles, and from this passage one can deduce why in Armand's case this is so. The fear of being gay and the belief that one might, by some action, manage to avoid some irrevocable turning point and not turn gay, or that almost by accident one might take that fatal step (the one from which there is no turning back) into homosexuality—this is one subtext to Armand's feverish imaginings and reveals how positivistic, developmental models of sexuality such as Delay's can reinforce homophobia in people confused about their sexuality, can divide them against themselves. *Les Faux-Monnayeurs* certainly gives this phobically inclined scripting space to express itself, but it also offers what I have been characterizing as an intervallic scripting, one according to which homosexuality's onset would never occupy any one moment (and certainly not any one *instant*, however extreme) or even any one *series* of moments. Its onset would need to be characterized in other terms, as nonnarrative, as disruptive, as ongoing.

It is worth insisting that the way I have been reading Lacan allows for a similar and valuable (and perhaps perpetual) postponement of questions as to the moment of sexual object choice. Lacan is not always read this way, which is hardly surprising, given that what is in question here is a disruptive consistency, a difficult

---

41. Six naufragés sont recueillis dans une barque. Depuis dix jours la tempête les égare. Trois sont morts; on en a sauvé deux. Un sixième était défaillant. On espérait encore le ramener à la vie. Son organisme avait atteint le point limite.

— Oui, je comprends, dit Olivier; une heure plut tôt, on aurait pu le sauver.

— Une heure, comme tu y vas! Je suppute l'instant extrême : On peut encore . . . On peut encore. On ne peut plus! C'est une arête étroite, sur laquelle mon esprit se promène. Cette ligne de démarcation entre l'être et le non-être, je m'applique à la tracer partout. La limite de résistance . . . tiens, par exemple, à ce que mon père appelerait : la tentation. L'on tient encore; la corde est tendue jusqu'à se rompre, sur laquelle le démon tire . . . Un tout petit peu plus, la corde claque : on est damné (279).

consistency that we might not expect either Lacan or his commentators to sustain. There is, for example, a frequent tendency to associate too quickly Lacan's understanding of the trauma of the introduction to the social with an engendering of the subject into the heterosexual order. One of Lacan's most interesting commentators, Kaja Silverman, perhaps symptomatically gives way to this consequential impulse in *The Subject of Semiotics:*

> The notion of an original androgynous whole, similar to that projected by Aristophanes, is absolutely central to Lacan's argument. The subject is defined as lacking because it is believed to be a fragment of something larger and more primordial.
>
> Lacan tells us that the only way the subject can compensate for its fragmentary condition is by fulfilling its biological destiny—by living out in the most complete sense its own "maleness" or "femaleness," and by forming new sexual unions with members of the opposite sex. It is by means of such unions that the subject comes closest to recovering its lost wholeness. (152–53)

In its baldness, this kind of statement seems incorrect, especially as in *Four Fundamental Concepts* Lacan explicitly distances himself from the myth of androgyny found in Plato's *Symposium.*[42] Silverman is more given to the notion of consistency and (consequently?), in my view, more interesting in the final pages of her recent essay, "The Lacanian Phallus":

> *Four Fundamental Concepts* . . . facilitates a very different reading of the Freudian castration complex than the one advanced in [Lacan's] "The Signification of the Phallus." It permits us to understand that event as the metaphoric reinscription and containment of a loss which happens much earlier, at the point of linguistic entry. . . . *Séminaire XI* implies that the drama which comes into play around the question of who has or does not have the phallus functions to rewrite the much more primordial sacrifice extracted from the male subject by primal repression. . . . In opening up a temporal and psychic space between primal repression and paternal metaphor, *Four Fundamental Concepts* also makes it possible for us to see not only that the phallus does not represent the agent of primary repression, but that it may not always be the primary, or even the earliest, signifier of desire. (113)

---

42. "The real lack is what the living being loses, that part of himself *qua* living being, in reproducing himself through the way of sex. This lack is real because it relates to something real, namely, that the living being, by being subject to sex, has fallen under the blow of individual death.

Aristophanes' myth pictures the pursuit of the complement for us in a pathetical and misleading way, by articulating that it is the other, one's sexual other half, that the living being seeks in love. To this mythical representation of the mystery of love, analytic experience substitutes the search by the subject, not of the sexual complement, but of the part of himself, lost forever, that is constituted by the fact that he is only a sexed living being, and that he is no longer immortal" (205/187).

· · ·

This passage could be put to good use in taking the notion of *deficit* adumbrated by Goux in such a potentially homophobic way and deflecting it toward more interesting possibilities. Thus, it is perhaps no accident that Lacan, on the same page as the passage on Aristophanes, short-circuits the usual notion of deficit as applied to the homosexual: "It is not because her father disappointed her that Freud's female patient (known as 'the homosexual') becomes homosexual—she could have taken a lover. Whenever we are in the dialectic of the drive, something else gives the orders" (206/187).

Such an analytic postponement of the consideration of castration anxiety, of the passage/progress to object choice, seems crucial to any understanding of Gide's writing on sexuality, and of wider strategic value in postponing the kind of analytic rush to assume the primacy of sexual difference in a heterosexist regime governed by castration. (This very rush is what I find troubling in critics such as Goux, and in the earlier passage from Silverman.[43] And even in the second passage from Silverman we might wonder if she hasn't jumped the gun slightly in imagining some "primordial" moment at which a particular sacrifice will be demanded of a *male* subject. In that imagining Silverman begins to write a unidirectional narrative of sexuality that gives "maleness" a strange [biological?] priority and thereby avoids considering the back-and-forth temporal problematics in the establishment of "male" subjectivity in any first place, however complexly that subjectivity relates to castration anxiety, however queer or straight.)

"—ay, there's the rub,
For in that sleep of death what dreams may come,
When we have shuffled off this mortal coil,
Must give us pause . . ."

When, in the passage that opens chapter 6 of part 1 of *Les Faux-Monnayeurs*, "Réveil de Bernard," Bernard runs both from the pressure of Olivier's arms and from sleep, we might wonder what chance he is missing. Bernard and the narrator, we noticed, both contribute to the vaguely phobic wake of that flight, trying to tip any and all responsibility for whatever has or hasn't happened back onto the dubiously somnolent Olivier. Bernard's responses to others and to himself remain consistently phobic. This is testified to by his effort, as he puts it, to be "a man of his word." Told by Edouard that this seems a bit prideful, he responds: "Call it by any name you please—pride, presumption, conceit . . . it's a feeling you won't succeed in cheapening in my eyes" (352).[44] If Armand is the novel's theorist of

43. One might well account for the shift in Silverman's two positions by certain ambivalences and variations in Lacan's own thought. Silverman discusses these interestingly in the rest of her article. See also Judith Butler's complex analysis in the same issue: "The Lesbian Phallus and the Morphological Imaginary." In Goux's article in that issue ("The Phallus: Masculine Identity and the 'Exchange of Women'") we can observe his same theoretical move of imagining an initial moment of stable phallic heterosexuality, and then imagining something more ambivalent coming after it: "Are we not entering an as yet unheard-of regime of the inconvertibility of the phallic token, detached from any natural anchoring (pure mediation, pure sign) just as the financial sign is nothing but the indefinite inscription and circulation of a debt by means of accounting, a writing game, without reference to any real goods? It is this incontestable phenomenon of denaturation which appears as the emergence of a neutral sex. The same 'dehumanization' of exchange relations by an indefinite fiduciary mediation, the same abolition of the direct teleology of trade is evident in both cases" (72). It would be better to consider that phallic heterosexuality has perhaps never had any (at least theoretical) *priority*.

44. Appelez cela du nom qu'il vous plaira : orgueil, présomption, suffisance . . . Le sentiment qui m'anime, vous ne le discréditerez pas à mes yeux (338).

"insuffisance" (286/278), Bernard is the corresponding theoretician of *suffisance*, a word meaning both sufficiency and conceit. For, indeed, Bernard's experiences of waking up should be teaching him a few of Armand's lessons, asking him to confront dispossession. His most notable experience of waking up besides the one in Olivier's bed is after that fateful night when Edouard and Olivier finally sleep together, the same night that Bernard sleeps with Laura's sister, Sarah:

> Bernard has not slept much. But that night he has tasted a forgetfulness more restful than sleep—the exaltation at once and the annihilation of self. Strange to himself, scattered, alleviated, novel, calm and tense as a god, he glides into another day. He has left Sarah still asleep—disengaged himself furtively from her arms. What! Without one more kiss? Without a last lover's look? Without a final embrace? Is it through insensibility that he leaves her in this way? I cannot tell. He cannot tell himself. He forces himself not to think, bothered that he has to incorporate this unprecedented night with the precedents of his history. No; it is an appendix, an annex, which can find no place in the body of the book—a book where the story of his life, as if nothing had happened, will continue—won't it?—will start up again. (307)[45]

The narrator's quiet hesitation in the final phrase, "va continuer, n'est-ce pas, va reprendre," suggests what is in question. As Bernard picks up the pieces of his self, scattered by sexual repose, will his life continue as if uninterrupted, or will it have to start up again ("reprendre"), having just been forced to a halt he is forcing himself not to think about? The very stutter of the repetition with a difference ("va continuer"/"va reprendre") and the subtle hint of negation in the intervening "n'est-ce pas" suggest what Bernard sees but will not see: his insufficiency, the inadequacy of his narrative in its attempts to imagine his sexuality as merely another easy chapter in his narrative self-portraiture. That he sees but will not see this is clear already in part 1, when he runs from his dream and Olivier's arm. Here the terms of his avoidance are more elaborate, as if a greater appreciation of what needs to be avoided makes its repression more work, makes the cracks in that repression, *n'est-ce pas*, more evident.

In any case, it's no longer entirely clear who is sleeping with whom on this particular evening. We know Bernard sees in Sarah a great resemblance to Laura. We know that Bernard has also read in Edouard's journal about the afternoon of Laura's wedding, when Edouard visited Armand, Olivier, Sarah, and Sarah's

---

45. Bernard n'a pas beaucoup dormi. Mais il a goûté, cette nuit, d'un oubli plus reposant que le sommeil; exaltation et anéantissement à la fois, de son être. Il glisse dans une nouvelle journée, étrange à lui-même, épars, léger, nouveau, calme et frémissant, comme un dieu. Il a laissé Sarah dormant encore; s'est dégagé furtivement d'entre ses bras. Eh quoi? sans un nouveau baiser, sans un dernier regard, sans une suprême étreinte amoureuse? Est-ce par insensibilité qu'il la quitte ainsi? Je ne sais. Il ne sait lui-même. Il s'efforce de ne point penser, gêné de devoir incorporer cette nuit sans précédents, aux précédents de son histoire. Non; c'est un appendice, une annexe, qui ne peut trouver place dans le corps du livre — livre où le récit de sa vie, comme si de rien n'était, va continuer, n'est-ce pas, va reprendre (296).

English girlfriend in a bedroom that used to be Laura's.[46] Edouard almost didn't recognize Sarah:

> Her neck and arms were bare. She seemed taller, bolder. She was sitting on one of the two beds beside Olivier and right up against him; he was lying down at full length and seemed to be asleep. He was certainly drunk; and as certainly I suffered at seeing him so, but I thought him more beautiful than ever. (108)[47]

Ever pretending to sleep, Olivier continues to do so throughout the scene, as it becomes more and more risqué, until finally Edouard finds it intolerable:

> [Sarah] had hitherto been sitting on the bed, but at that point she lay down at full length beside Olivier, so that their heads were touching. Upon which, Armand leapt up, seized a large screen . . . and with the antics of a clown spread it out so as to hide the couple; then, still clowning, he leant towards me and said without lowering his voice:
> "Perhaps you didn't know that my sister was a whore?"
> It was too much. I got up and pushed the screen roughly aside. Olivier and Sarah immediately sat up. Her hair had come down. Olivier rose, went to the washstand and bathed his face. (110)[48]

If the principals in this scene from the first half of the novel are Olivier, Sarah, Edouard, and Armand, with Bernard on the margins, eavesdropping by means of his reading of Edouard's journal, one might choose to see the novel as spending its time sorting out these lines of desire so that, finally, in the second half, Edouard will leave the banquet des Argonautes with Olivier, and Bernard with Sarah, with Armand playing his role as facilitator by locking Bernard in Sarah's room for the night. At last the novelistic dance ends; everyone finds what they are looking for, after a long intervening summer of misunderstandings. Alternatively, one might choose to see in these repetitions a continual dispossession, everyone's sexuality belonging endlessly to someone else, Bernard's heterosexuality belonging to Olivier as much as Olivier's homosexuality might belong to Bernard. Thus, when this

46. I'm sorry not to discuss Laura more fully in this treatment of the novel, governed by other obsessions. In many ways she is at the conflictual center of the configurations of sexuality—and not as the source of stability Goux imagines. Her bedroom, like that of Gide's mother in the passage from *Si le grain ne meurt* discussed in the preceding chapter, is another representation of the explosive combination of the gynaeceum and the seraglio. One could trace a line of such explosive scenes throughout Gide's work, certainly including various scenes with his mother in *Si le grain ne meurt*, scenes with Laura, Sarah, and Rachel in *Les Faux-Monnayeurs*, and on to *L'Ecole des femmes* and *Geneviève*. For the beginnings of a feminist reading of *Les Faux-Monnayeurs*, see Ann M. Moore, "Women, Socialization, and Language in *Les Faux-Monnayeurs*."

47. Sa robe découvrait ses bras et son cou. Elle paraissait grandie, enhardie. Elle était assise sur un des deux lits, à côté d'Olivier, contre lui, qui s'était étendu sans façons et qui semblait dormir. Certainement il était ivre; et certainement je souffrais de le voir ainsi; mais il me paraissait plus beau que jamais. (109)

48. Puis, sur ce lit où d'abord elle était assise, {Sarah} s'étendit tout de son long contre Olivier, de sorte que leurs deux têtes touchèrent. Armand tout aussitôt bondit, s'empara d'un grand paravent . . . et, comme un pitre, le déploya de manière à cacher le couple, puis, toujours bouffonnant, penché vers moi, mais à voix haute:
« Vous ne saviez peut-être pas que ma sœur était une putain? »
« C'en était trop. Je me levai; bousculai le paravent derrière lequel Olivier et Sarah se redressèrent aussitôt. Elle avait les cheveux défaits. Olivier se leva, alla vers la toilette et se passa de l'eau sur le visage (110–11).

sexual anxiety reaches one of its peaks, toward the end of the banquet scene, filled with verbal echoes of the earlier scene in Laura's former bedroom, and when, for an instant during a possibly violent altercation, the lights are turned off, and Bernard follows Sarah under the table, isn't he following in Olivier's footsteps? And when Olivier in turn follows the two of them under the table, is it Sarah he's following, or the pair, or just Bernard, who has spent most of the novel in the place marked out for Olivier at Edouard's side?

> Sarah . . . pressed up against Bernard, to pull him under the table with her. . . . Bernard had stayed only a second under the table, just long enough to feel Sarah's two burning lips crushed voluptuously against his. Olivier had followed them; out of friendship, out of jealousy. . . . That horrible feeling which he knew so well, of being left out, was exacerbated by his being drunk. When, in his turn, he came out from underneath the table, his head was swimming. He heard Dhurmer exclaim:
> "Look at Molinier! He's as sissy as a girl!"
> It was too much. Olivier, hardly knowing what he was doing, darted towards Dhurmer with his hand raised. He seemed to be moving in a dream. Dhurmer dodged the blow. As in a dream, Olivier's hand met nothing but empty air. . . .
> Edouard took him by the arm:
> "Come and splash a little water on your face. You look like a lunatic."
> (301–3)[49]

A feeling of being marginalized, a head that is spinning, a confusion of dream with reality—under the influence of sexuality, Olivier's experience is one of supreme dispossession, and even Edouard's timely rescue will not finally cover over that abyss through which Olivier's hand dreamily passes, finding nothing to hit against. When Olivier extricates himself from Edouard's bed ("I'm going to lie down a little on the sofa") later that night and then tries to asphyxiate himself in the bathroom, we might wonder whether this suicide attempt, and, indeed the whole fascination of the novel with suicide, shouldn't be understood precisely as a running away from sexuality's dispossession, a running—out of fear—from the difference between sleeping and waking. For even though Olivier might throughout the novel seem more content to experiment with the state of somnolence than, say, Bernard, that is no guarantee that an ecstatic experience of the insufficiency or consistent inconsistency of the moment of desire-being-acted-upon/being-acted-upon-by-desire would be for him any more endurable. A full acknowledgment that

---

49. {Sarah} se pressa contre Bernard pour l'entraîner sous la table avec elle . . . Bernard n'était resté sous la table qu'un instant; juste le temps de sentir les deux lèvres brûlantes de Sarah s'écraser voluptueusement sur les siennes. Olivier les avait suivis; par amitié, par jalousie . . . L'ivresse exaspérait en lui ce sentiment affreux, qu'il connaissait si bien, de demeurer en marge. Quand il sortit à son tour de dessous la table, la tête lui tournait un peu. Il entendit alors Dhurmer s'écrier:

    « Regardez donc Molinier! Il est poltron comme une femme. »

    C'en était trop. Olivier, sans trop savoir ce qu'il faisait, s'élança, la main levée, contre Dhurmer. Il lui semblait s'agiter dans un rêve. Dhurmer esquiva le coup. Comme dans un rêve, la main d'Olivier ne rencontra que le vide. . .

    Edouard le prit par le bras:

    « Viens te passer un peu d'eau sur le visage. Tu as l'air d'un fou. »

perhaps no one truly realizes when they are sleeping and that no one really knows whom they are sleeping with (even when sleeping alone) is more than anyone in the novel can put up with.

"Il faut vous dire que je dors très mal," La Pérouse tells Edouard at a point late in the novel. "I must tell you I'm sleeping quite badly." La Pérouse is both the novel's most careful analyst of sleep and the person whose discourse most closely resembles that of Janet's psychasthenic Laetitia.[50] (We can now appreciate the *à propos* of Janet's sobriquet for this patient: Sleeping Beauty, *La Belle au bois dormant*.) La Pérouse continues:

> A person who is properly asleep, doesn't feel that he is asleep. When he wakes up, he just knows that he has slept. . . . Sometimes I'm inclined to think that it's an illusion and that, all the same, I *am* properly asleep, when I think I'm not asleep. But the proof that I'm not properly asleep is that if I want to open my eyes, I open them. As a rule, I don't want to. You understand, don't you, that there's no object to it? What's the use of proving to myself that I'm not asleep? I always go on hoping that I shall go to sleep by persuading myself that I'm asleep already. (357–58)[51]

La Pérouse and Janet's Sleeping Beauty share at least two important features due to their ability to theorize the problems of sleep. They understand in almost excruciating detail the catastrophic confrontation of automatism and voluntarism represented by the moment of falling asleep, and as a consequence they understand how any use of the verb *vouloir* will fail to account for that consistency of dispossession that *Les Faux-Monnayeurs* understands as common to the experience of falling asleep and to the experience of sexuality.

Boris, La Pérouse's grandson, does not share an articulateness about this condition with his grandfather and Sleeping Beauty, but he lives in it and dies in it

---

50. Compare the following passage, where La Pérouse explains to Edouard why he has been unable to kill himself, to the passage about Janet's patient quoted earlier:

> Something completely foreign to my will held me back. As if God didn't want to let me go. Imagine a marionette who should want to leave the stage before the end of the play. . . . Halt! You're wanted for the *finale*. Ah! Ah! you thought you would be able to go off whenever you liked! . . . I understood that what we call our will is merely the threads which work the marionette, and which God pulls. (250)

> [Quelque chose de complètement étranger à ma volonté, de plus fort que ma volonté, me retenait . . . Comme si Dieu ne voulait pas me laisser partir. Imaginez une marionnette qui voudrait quitter la scène avant la fin de la pièce . . . Halte-là! On a encore besoin de vous pour le finale. Ah! vous croyiez que vous pouviez partir quand vous vouliez! . . . J'ai compris que ce que nous appelons notre volonté, ce sont les fils qui font marcher la marionnette, et que Dieu tire. (244)]

⋯

Gide comments in his *Journal des Faux-Monnayeurs* that the character La Pérouse is based on a former piano teacher of his, named Marc de Lanux, discussed at some length in *Si le grain ne meurt*. Gide even began referring to Lanux as La Pérouse in his journal entries. For helpful details on this matter, see Goulet, *André Gide, "Les Faux-Monnayeurs," mode d'emploi*, 218–30. Goulet also here provides the text of several intriguing passages about La Pérouse/Lanux that Gide did not include in his published journal but clearly used in the composition of *Les Faux-Monnayeurs*.

51. Celui qui dort vraiment ne sent pas qu'il dort simplement, à son réveil, il s'aperçoit qu'il a dormi . . . Parfois je suis tenté de croire que je me fais illusion et que, tout de même, je dors vraiment, alors que je ne crois pas dormir. Mais la preuve que je ne dors pas vraiment, c'est que, si je veux rouvrir les yeux, je les ouvre. D'ordinaire, je ne le veux pas. Vous comprenez, n'est-ce pas, que je n'ai aucun intérêt à le faire. A quoi bon me prouver à moi-même que je ne dors pas? Je garde toujours l'espoir de m'endormir en me persuadant que je dors déjà . . . (343–44).

in exemplary fashion. The first time we meet him is at a moment when his friend Bronja asks him if he wants to go for a walk:

> "Yes, I want to. No, I don't want to."
> The two contradictory sentences were uttered in the same breath. Bronja only answered the second:
> "Why not?"
> "Because it's too hot, it's too cold. . . . Vibroskomenopatof. Blaf blaf."
> "What does that mean to say?" [Qu'est-ce que ça veut dire?]
> "Nothing."
> "Then why do you say it?"
> "So that you shouldn't understand." . . .
> "When one talks it's in order to be understood." (174–75)[52]

Boris implicitly understands the problems with *vouloir*. It is too univocal a verb, a verb of consequence. Boris experiments with forms of speech that express his inconsequentiality—a consistent, symptomatic expressivity that neither Bronja nor her mother Sophroniska will have the ears to hear.

The other crucial example of this expressivity "qui ne veut rien dire" is Boris's fatal talisman, a piece of paper, on which are written the words "GAZ. TÉLÉPHONE. CENT MILLE ROUBLES." Five words, Sophroniska tells Edouard, whose meaning she had asked Boris for in vain:

> "But it means nothing—it's magic," he used always to answer whenever I pressed him. That was all I could get out of him. I know now that these enigmatic words are in young Baptistin's handwriting—the grand master and professor of magic—and that these five words were the boys' formula of incantation—the "Open Sesame" of the shameful Paradise, into which their pleasure plunged them. (207)[53]

Sophroniska finally convinces Boris to surrender the talisman to her, convinced this will have the consequence of curing him of his masturbatory tendencies. Then, in an act that could well serve to make her the most suspect character in the novel, Sophroniska gives this talisman to a certain Strouvilhou, a passing acquaintance "who took an interest in Boris" and had asked Sophroniska for a souvenir of him. Strouvilhou in turn gives the talisman to his cousin, the cruel Ghéridanisol,

---

52. — Oui, je veux bien. Non, je ne veux pas.
Les deux phrases contradictoires étaient dites d'une seule haleine. Bronja ne retint que la seconde et reprit:
— Pourquoi?
— Il fait trop chaud, il fait trop froid . . . Vibroskomenopatof. Blaf blaf.
— Qu'est-ce que ça veut dire?
— Rien.
— Alors pourquoi le dis-tu?
— Pour que tu ne comprennes pas. . .
— Quand on parle, c'est pour se faire comprendre (172–73).
53. « Mais ça ne veut rien dire. C'est de la magie », me répondait-il toujours quand je le pressais. C'est tout ce que je pouvais obtenir. Je sais à présent que ces mots énigmatiques sont de l'écriture du jeune Baptistin, grand maître et professeur de magie, et qu'ils étaient pour ces enfants, ces cinq mots, comme une formule incantatoire, le "Sésame ouvre-toi" du paradis honteux où la volupté les plongeait (202–3).

schoolmate of Boris, who secretly places it on Boris' desk one day, demoralizing him sufficiently, through its unexpectedness and its links to a past he had been taught to repress, to make him susceptible to the pressure to play a game of Russian roulette, a game ending in his suicide.

Sleeping Beauty had claimed, "my thoughts are being stolen, my soul; I've been loaned someone else's soul. Every second I change proprietors. . . ." What Sophroniska allows, by circulating the talisman, is for this dispossession to be taken to a new level. That is to say, she allows Boris to be dispossessed even of his symptom, of the consistency of his dispossession. If La Pérouse finally resists killing himself with his pistol because he is terrified, Hamlet fashion, that the noise of the shot would wake him up, instead of putting him to sleep ("and a detonation doesn't send one to sleep—it wakes one up. . . . I was afraid that instead of going to sleep I should suddenly wake up" [249–50/244]), Boris is left with no resistance, no consistency to go on expressing:

> So Boris stepped forward to the appointed place; he walked slowly, like an automaton—or rather like a somnambulist. . . . The shot went off. Boris did not collapse [ne s'affaissa pas] at once. For an instant the body stayed upright, as if caught in the corner of the recess; then the head, fallen onto the shoulder, carried it over; everything dissolved [tout s'effondra]. (391)[54]

The severity, the atrocity of this description lie in the insistence on the consequential nature of the body's relationship to gravity. For a moment, the inertia of the body keeps it standing, but grotesquely so, as if hooked to the wall. But then the head's weight and momentum carry the day, and the body gives in to its weight. The precision of the verbs is telling: *affaisser,* from *ad-* and *faix,* an intensification of a heavy weight, the submission to gravity, and the strangely synonymous *effondre,* from *ex-* and *fond,* the removal of the ground, the opening of an abyss. It's almost as if the verbs should exchange subjects: if we take the *tout* of "tout s'effondra" not in some metaphysical sense, but in the sense of the whole materiality at stake here, then surely that materiality is what gives way to gravity (*s'affaisser*), whereas *Boris* as a subjectivity dissolves into an emptiness without foundation (*s'effondre*), like the one Olivier encountered only so briefly: "Comme dans un rêve, la main d'Olivier ne rencontra que le vide." As the text actually has it, *Boris* falls down, and *tout* gives way. There is a certain respect in the excess of that "tout." For it is (only) the world in Boris' consciousness that disappears. Everyone else's is more or less intact. Yet, the writing's encouragement of our fleeting assumption of that experience might remind us of, remark for us, the violence of a narrative, consequential, progress-oriented view of sexuality, of which Boris is, within the world of *Les Faux-Monnayeurs,* the most notable victim.

54. Boris s'avança donc jusqu'à la place marquée. Il marchait à pas lents, comme un automate, le regard fixe; comme un somnambule plutôt . . . Le coup partit. Boris ne s'affaissa pas aussitôt. Un instant le corps se maintint, comme accroché dans l'encoignure; puis la tête, retombée sur l'épaule, l'emporta; tout s'effondra (374).

Les Faux-Monnayeurs is, after all, called *Les Faux-Monnayeurs*. What does it mean to claim it's not about what its title says it is about? One way of answering that question is to point out that, as *Les Faux-Monnayeurs* shows, the discourse of sexuality does not always produce itself with intention. It is Gide's ability to live with and write out of that fact, *sous le coup de la sexualité,* that gives his work its insistent presence. Gide's novel might well convey something other than the discourse mentioned in its title.

But one might try a different tack as well in order to challenge the title. People haven't been talking about authenticity in *Les Faux-Monnayeurs* for years without the discourse being there, in the mouths of the characters and in the mouth of the narrator as well. But if, as I have argued, the novel is punctuated by another discourse, if that sleepy discourse regularly disconcerts the characters, and if, rather than respecting the disconcerting effect, they run to notions such as Bernard's *suffisance,* to notions of self-possession and sincerity in order to protect themselves, then the dominance of the categories of authenticity, self-sufficiency, sincerity should, as categories to which one phobically flees, become suspect—the flight to them could even be seen as symptomatic. Recourse to those categories, in other words, should not be taken as a matter of course. Bernard, for instance, flees phobically from disconcertion into *suffisance;* he flees from a sense of himself as *épars, léger, nouveau* (scattered, alleviated, novel), from his life seen as punctuated by a series of discontinuous appendices. Analogously, Edouard would avert his novelistic gaze from Boris' suicide:

> Without exactly pretending to explain anything, I should not like to put forward any fact which was not accounted for by a *sufficiency of motive.* And for that reason I shall not make use of little Boris's suicide for my *Counterfeiters;* I have too much difficulty in understanding it. And then, I dislike bizarre little news items. There is something peremptory, irrefutable, brutal, outrageously real about them. . . . (394; my emphasis)[55]

Boris's suicide offers a peremptory challenge to consequence, just as the space of waking out of sleep does to *suffisance.* Edouard's novel may leave out the suicide, but the novel that includes him does not, and by including it, that larger novel offers a peremptory challenge to its own cult of sincerity, its own title, a challenge we should not fear taking up.

55. Sans prétendre précisément rien expliquer, je voudrais n'offrir aucun fait *sans une motivation suffisante.* C'est pourquoi je ne me servirai pas pour mes *Faux-Monnayeurs* du suicide du petit Boris; j'ai déjà trop de mal à le comprendre. Et puis je n'aime pas les « faits divers ». Ils ont quelque chose de péremptoire, d'indéniable, de brutal, d'outrageusement réel . . . (376; my emphasis).

CHAPTER 5

GRIBOUILLE EN AFRIQUE:
GIDE'S *VOYAGE AU CONGO*

In 1925, having finished *Les Faux-Monnayeurs*, in no way a novel of commitment [*un roman engagé*], he left for the Congo from whence he brought back the *Voyage au Congo*. When he had written *Le Voyage d'Urien*, Mallarmé had said to him, "You gave me quite a scare." The poet had feared from the title that Gide had written some kind of travel account, but was reassured upon perceiving that the ever so symbolic Urien had only voyaged among the fears and desires of his unconscious.

—Jean Delay, "Introduction" to *Correspondance André Gide–Roger Martin du Gard*

n July 8, 1925, Gide, nervous about his impending departure for Africa, writes to his friend Roger Martin du Gard about the arrangements he has made to put him in charge of the manuscript of *Les Faux-Monnayeurs*, finished during June. Martin du Gard is responsible for checking the proofs and takes care of most of the duties attendant on the novel's publication, which took place while Gide was away. The first time Martin du Gard sees Gide after his return from Africa roughly a year later, Gide seems changed and nervous. In his journal Martin du Gard remarks on Gide's "unhealthy and unaccustomed feverishness":

> And all at once, as if we had been apart since only last night, he begins to talk . . . —not of Africa, not of Coppet—not of the trip home—he talks only literary shop talk, accusations made against him, articles on *Les Faux-Monnayeurs* whose inaccuracies he wants to address . . . the current gossip at the N.R.F. . . . I am a little disappointed. I had thought that he would return from Africa as if he were coming back from Sirius, and that it would take him several months to shrink himself back

143

down to the level of these questions of critics and the press. (*Correspondance André Gide–Roger Martin du Gard,* 678)

But then Martin du Gard revises himself and decides that this behavior is merely some sort of frenzied cover, some overcompensation for the difficulties of readjusting to Parisian life, a symptom of the difficulties of the last exhausting stages of Gide's African voyage. This revision comes as Gide begins suddenly to talk of his current project, a report on the present situation in French colonial Africa. In the course of this oration, Gide calls Martin du Gard's attention to an official report from 1902 that he has been reading. The report tells of an African tribe oppressed by the French and of the taxation, forced labor, and other miseries imposed on them. At a certain point, reading from the report, Gide becomes so emotional that he can no longer continue:

> At this point he stops short, choked up, tries two or three times to swallow his saliva, to control his sobs, and then, unable to get himself under control, he holds the paper out to me, whispering "Here, you read it . . . I can't. . . ." He bursts noisily into sobs, gets shakily to his feet, and takes refuge in a neighboring room. On my own I read the end of the report: "decimated by an epidemic of recurrent fever." (679)

Martin du Gard is astonished by what he deems the excessive and atypical nature of Gide's response to the facts of the report (twenty-four years old after all). In order to explain the changes in his friend, the oddness of his behavior, his queer tears, Martin du Gard tells how he later learned the details of the final stages of Gide's voyage, details that might explain how Gide ended up in such a nervous state. Suffering from dysentery, with his traveling companion suffering from fever, Gide was obliged near the end of his voyage to backtrack to a medical post they had already passed. This three-week delay meant that Gide and his companion were forced to make their final trip back to the ocean during a period of intense heat. As Martin du Gard describes it:

> Gide, panic-stricken, sensing that he wouldn't hold out, that he would die before making it to the port, was feverishly forcing the daily stages, refusing the stops that should have been necessary every two or three days. And for a month it was a truly infernal route, death at their heels, breathing that burning air, covered in sweat, sweating anxiety as well, scarcely speaking any more, thinking only of the distance travelled and the distance still to go, calculating a hundred times an hour if their strength would hold out to the end.
>
> At the moment, Gide is paying for this month of morbid turmoil. (679)

No doubt. Gide's own description of this experience in his published travel journal does not quite achieve Martin du Gard's condensed drama, but even from Gide's description one imagines that recovering from such a voyage could reasonably be expected to take a good deal of time. What is jarring about Martin du Gard's story, however, is the way it is used to account for, almost to explain away, an emotion that might deservedly be strong. For even though the report that provoked Gide's strange outburst might be twenty-four years old, it's not too much of a stretch to imagine that Gide might be thinking of parallel instances to which he had recently been witness.

Martin du Gard's narrative and Delay's comment cited in the epigraph are both small examples of a tendency to mark a break in Gide's life at the time of his Congo trip. Delay, for instance, would insist that Gide's status as an *écrivain engagé*, a committed writer, can only be said to begin with this trip, thus excluding, for example, any possible political readings of texts such as *Corydon, Si le grain ne meurt,* or *Les Faux-Monnayeurs,* as if sexual questions had no political content. Martin du Gard, startled by Gide's agitation, his committed oratory, his sense of political purpose, and his uncontrollable emotions, looks for some immediate disturbance to account for something new in his friend's behavior.

In the several years following his trip to French Equatorial Africa, Gide would try to fulfill his political purpose of denouncing the French colonial enterprise first of all by publishing in two installments his journal from the trip: the *Voyage au Congo* first and, a bit later, the *Retour du Tchad;* he would talk up their political content and convince acquaintances such as Léon Blum to give them coverage in journals such as Blum's *Le Populaire;* he would consult with the leaders of such groups as the Ligue des Droits de l'Homme to see what pressure they could put on the French government;[1] he would write his own long article, "La Détresse de notre Afrique Equatoriale," which appeared in the *Revue de Paris* on October 15, 1927; he would publish, as an appendix to the *Retour du Tchad,* a collection of documents, including his long article from the *Revue de Paris* and a commentary on a mendacious letter responding to and complaining about Gide's book, a letter sent to Léon Blum from a director of one of the concessionary companies in Africa.[2]

Was there at this point in Gide's life a clear break that one needs to account for? It would seem that the answer should be both yes and no. Certainly, he began devoting a fair amount of time to political causes and organizations. What one should not do, I think, is to use the conceptualization of such a break as a way of refusing to make any connections between Gide's thinking and writing about his sexuality and his thinking and writing about other political subjects. One might try instead to conceive of ways in which to link the emotional force behind his decision to reflect openly on his sexuality with that behind his commitment to his writing about political issues.

In fact, one can find in *Les Faux-Monnayeurs* the material to begin thinking

1. See Gide's letters to Martin du Gard on January 11, 1928 and May 31, 1928. Catherine Coquery-Vidrovitch, in *Le Congo au temps des grandes compagnies concessionnaires, 1898–1930* (184–86), points out that passages from the *Voyage* were read aloud in debates in the Chambre des Députés. Gide writes of this in the appendix to *Retour du Tchad* (in *Voyage au Congo,* 485–88), where he also recounts some details of the government's debate and speaks of his conversations with government officials about the report he submitted to them after his trip.

2. For more details on Gide's efforts, see Daniel Moutote, *André Gide: L'Engagement, 1926–1939,* pp. 76–84, and also Gide's correspondence with Martin du Gard for the years 1926–28.

about such linkages. I have in mind two moments in the novel, where two different versions of an escape from Paris to Africa are imagined and carefully problematized. The first moment is early in the novel, when we read in Edouard's journal of his first encounter with his young nephew Georges. The encounter happens outside a bookstore, where Georges is looking through a display of used books. Edouard amuses himself by watching the boy, who pockets one of the books, and then, noticing that Edouard saw him do it, makes a big show of looking for some money with which to pay for the book. Finding he had none, he takes the book back out of his pocket and returns it. Edouard follows him and strikes up a conversation, asking what the book was. A guide to Algeria, he is told. He then gives Georges the money with which to buy the book, and when Georges returns with it, discovers that the guide is from 1871. Edouard comments that the book is too old to be of any use; Georges insists that the book will serve his needs.

Now this scene first of all recalls a scene from Gide's *L'Immoraliste*, where the protagonist Michel, during a stay in Biskra, watches in a mirror as the young North African Moktir steals a pair of scissors. In *L'Immoraliste*, that scene lets us watch Michel try to imagine that he has found a land in which he can, through the complicity he creates between himself and Moktir, learn and then internalize a form of transgression that separates himself from his past, from the European forms of sociality he so desires to escape. *L'Immoraliste* has its own ways of undermining the imagined ease of that complicity. The rewriting of this scene in *Les Faux-Monnayeurs* carries that undermining a step further. Through the presence of the "vieux guide Joanne," it problematizes for us any intent to use the French territories in North Africa as a place of imagined escape.[3] Georges, it is suggested, is too late for any such use. That such a mythology remains so available to him in fact indicates the extent to which the mythology is not transgressive but part of an established ideological program. French tourist guides are at his disposal to help him imagine his escape. The date of the guide, 1871, quietly reminds us of how long such encouragements had been available to the frustrated youths of France, how long it has been "too late": they were available before schoolboy Gide found himself in Dr. Brouardel's office being threatened with Tuareg spears—available, that is, a couple of decades before Gide's own first liberating trip to North Africa.

To say that the idea of Africa as a place of escape from France was an old one, that such imaginings and such trips of escape had already been commodified, carefully tied back into the economic structures of French life, is not to say that the alienation of people such as Georges would be any less real than that of their precursors. Nor is it to diminish the urgency of their need to find networks of alternative allegiances to help them resist the various interpellations of their culture that were busy simultaneously soliciting and alienating them. But the writing of

---

3. See, on this subject, Jonathan C. Lang, "Some Perversions of Pastoral: Or Tourism in Gide's *L'Immoraliste*."

this scene from *Les Faux-Monnayeurs* suggests that within Gide's writing there is an ongoing effort to come to terms precisely with the ways in which apparently transgressive desires for escape are structured into the social and economic fabric of French life, ways such "transgressive" desires might fail to be so.

The other mention of Africa in *Les Faux-Monnayeurs* continues this reflection. Lilian and Vincent, Olivier's older brother, have set off on an aristocrat's yacht for a naturalistic tour, and Lilian sends a letter to Passavant, saying that she and Vincent will be continuing their explorations on their own in French West Africa: "Perhaps on the banks of the Casamance, where Vincent wants to botanize, and I to shoot" (326/314). We learn that Armand also has an older brother, Alexandre, who has himself fled France. As Armand tells Olivier:

> "He began by coming to grief over his business and running through all the money Rachel sent him. He's settled now on the banks of the Casamance; and he has written to say that things are doing well and that he'll soon be able to pay everything back."
> "What kind of business?"
> "Who knows? Rubber, ivory, Negroes perhaps." (376)[4]

As one would expect in the novelistic world of *Les Faux-Monnayeurs,* Alexandre and Vincent cross paths, although Vincent has apparently by this point gone mad, killed Lilian, and lost his identity. Alexandre thus never finds out who he is, but nonetheless writes to Armand of his strange visitor: "A hideous Negro who came up the Casamance with him, and to whom I have talked a little, speaks of a woman who was with him, and who, I gather, must have been drowned in the river one day when their boat upset. I shouldn't be surprised to learn that my companion helped the accident along" (377).[5] Gide's *Voyage au Congo* is dedicated to Joseph Conrad. Conrad's *Heart of Darkness* lurks somewhere in the back of his mind as he travels and also seems to lurk in the background of this passage from *Les Faux-Monnayeurs.* (There are also interesting borrowings from *La Belle Saison,* the third volume of Roger Martin du Gard's *Les Thibault,* borrowings Gide acknowledges in his letter to Martin du Gard on July 8, 1925.) Perhaps even more to the point here would be to notice the way Lilian, Vincent, and Alexandre represent within *Les Faux-Monnayeurs* exemplary types of travelers to Africa: game hunters, wealthy naturalists, and sons who leave their families to make their fortune, later sending home dubious but much-needed money. Alexandre was clearly out to escape the

---

4. Il a commencé par faire de mauvaises affaires et bouffer tout l'argent que lui envoyait Rachel. Il est établi maintenant sur les bords de la Casamance. Il m'écrit que son commerce prospère et qu'il va bientôt être à même de tout rembourser.
    — Un commerce de quoi?
    — Est-ce qu'on sait? De caoutchouc, d'ivoire, de nègres peut-être . . . (361).
5. Un hideux nègre qui l'accompagnait, remontant avec lui la Casamance, et avec qui j'ai un peu causé, parle d'une femme qui l'accompagnait et qui, si j'ai bien compris, a dû se noyer dans le fleuve, certain jour que leur embarcation a chaviré. Je ne serais pas étonné que mon compagnon ait favorisé la noyade (362).

repressive Vedel family atmosphere. As he writes to Armand, if Armand ever wants to see him again, it will have to be in Africa. Alexandre doesn't plan to come home.

Now Gide's *Voyage au Congo* shows Gide wondering what kind of traveler he is. It allows us to watch him struggle with the questions, What am I doing in Africa? In what capacity am I here? The wealthy naturalist will be much in evidence in his pages, but so will the figure of the alienated young man who earlier fled to North Africa in order to try to imagine who he was. Although Gide doesn't set up a trading post, his economic position as a representative Frenchman will be very much on his mind as he travels. The barriers his economic position (along with his cultural status) sets up between him and the African people he meets will be a source of great frustration as those barriers hinder any escape from his own sociality, from the kinds of sexual or political alienations he might feel at home. He will not find it possible to escape through a magic identification with a different social order. Yet, perhaps the "excessive" emotionality observed by Martin du Gard in Gide's espousal of the anticolonialist cause could be understood as a sign that even though certain barriers could not be overcome during Gide's African voyage, certain emotional allegiances across diverse forms of alienation fell into place as best they could.

Frustration

> A trip to the Congo isn't something you do for fun.[6]
>
> —André Gide

> We set off again around 4:15. I'm absorbed in *The Master of Ballantrae*, which makes it a bit difficult for me to see the countryside. I tear myself away from my book. We are on a plateau covered with short green grass, about 30 cm. high, and with trees. It looks a bit like an orchard, but it's very different.[7]
>
> —Marc Allégret, *Carnets du Congo*

It was at the age of 55 that Gide in 1925 set out on a voyage of nearly a year through the French colonies in central Africa, with, as his traveling companion, the

---

6. "On ne voyage pas au Congo pour son plaisir." From Gide's article, "La Détresse de notre Afrique Equatoriale," reprinted as an appendix to the combined edition of his *Voyage au Congo* and *Retour du Tchad*. The English edition, *Travels in the Congo*, unfortunately does not include any of the material from the appendices to the French edition. It also, without mention, leaves out passages present in the French, sometimes including footnotes that had been attached to paragraphs left out of the translation. See the entry for August 24–25. I have often modified the translation and also silently filled in several of its omissions in the passages cited in this chapter.

7. Nous repartons vers les 4h15. Je suis plongé dans le *Master of Ballantrae*, ce qui me gêne un peu pour voir le paysage. Je m'arrache de mon livre. Nous sommes sur un plateau couvert d'une petite herbe verte, haute de 30 cm environ, et d'arbres. Cela ressemble un peu à un verger, mais c'est très différent.

twenty-five-year-old Marc Allégret.[8] Almost from the very first pages of his *Voyage au Congo,* the journal he kept while traveling, Gide seems to recognize that he will not be seeing Africa while he is there. What does this say about his profound desire to go on this trip? What consequences will this have for the political import of his apparently anticolonialist testimony?

Brazzaville was the first major stop on the trip, and after a few weeks there, on August 24, Gide is already commenting on the major problems of vision that become a central concern of the text:

> I am taking these notes too entirely for myself. I see now that I have said nothing about Brazzaville. At first I was delighted with everything; the novelty of the climate, of the light, of the vegetation, of the odors, of the bird-songs, and of my own self in the midst of all this was so great that I could find nothing to say from excess of astonishment. I did not know the name of anything. I admired without distinction. It is impossible to write well when one is drunk. I was in a state of intoxication.
>
> Now that the first surprise has worn off, I take no pleasure in describing a place I am already wanting to leave. The town, which is enormously distended, owes its whole charm to the climate and to its position along the river shore. . . . It is too vast for its small activities. Its charm consists in its indolence. And then I realize that it is impossible to get into contact with anything real; not that things here are factitious, but civilization interposes its film, so that everything is veiled and softened. (16)[9]

An admiration of and absorption in new sensory impressions leaves Gide intoxicated, ignorant, and almost mute. This experience of intoxication apparently threatens to displace description and leaves Gide with a problem as to whether what he is writing should be a journal of intoxication or a journal of description or something in between. The writing and the experience of the intoxication induce in Gide a familiar and yet contextually novel sensation of self-doubling: his vision of "moi-même aussi parmi cela" contributes to the astonishment that leaves him nothing to say, while the distance it provokes him to take from himself as a body undergoing experiences also marks the failure of the intoxication to endure and to be written.

Yet there is *something* to write. What Brazzaville looks like, for instance. But all Gide writes is that there would be no pleasure in writing this. Brazzaville has a

---

8. An excellent source for information about the trip is the informative introduction by Daniel Durosay to Allégret's *Carnets du Congo* (see 11–58). See also the *Bulletin des amis d'André Gide* 16 (October 1988), which includes a helpful selection of articles on the *Voyage*. I have also benefited from reading a seminar paper by Ann Gelder, "The 'Retour' of the Native: Film and Repetiton in Gide's African Travel Journals."

9. Je prend ces notes trop « pour moi », je m'aperçois que je n'ai pas décrit Brazzaville. Tout m'y charmait d'abord : la nouveauté du climat, de la lumière, des feuillages, des parfums, du chant des oiseaux, et de moi-même aussi parmi cela, de sorte que par excès d'étonnement, je ne trouvais plus rien à dire. Je ne savais le nom de rien. J'admirais indistinctement. On n'écrit pas bien dans l'ivresse. J'étais grisé.

Puis, passé la première surprise, je ne trouve plus aucun plaisir à parler de ce que déjà je voudrais quitter. Cette ville, énormément distendue, n'a de charmant que ce qu'elle doit au climat et à sa position allongée près du fleuve . . . Elle est trop vaste pour le peu d'activité qui s'y déploie. Son charme est dans son indolence. Surtout je m'aperçois qu'on ne peut y prendre contact réel avec rien; non point que tout y soit factice; mais l'écran de la civilisation s'interpose, et rien n'y entre que tamisé (28).

problem imposing its image on him. It is too distended, a typical problem in Africa, as we will see, making it radically incompatible with Gide's insistently classical prose. Typically African in its distension, it nonetheless also suffers from "civilization." That is, it is not "African" enough, not "purely" African, and thus uninteresting to contemplate with attention. How to break through this "écran de la civilisation"—produced *both* by Gide's eyes and by the French colonial presence, will be one of Gide's torments.[10]

In general, for Gide things in Africa will have a problem occupying space in a way that makes them seem real enough for him to write them down. A few days earlier, on a trip to an especially magnificent part of the rapids of the Congo, someone comments: "Imagine that a spectacle like this is still waiting for its painter." Gide thinks to himself: "This was an invitation to which I shall not respond. The quality of temperance is an essential one in art, and immensity is repugnant to it. A description is none the more moving because ten is put instead of one" (13).[11] And in general, Africa, like Brazzaville, like the rapids, will continue throughout his trip to be just too big for Gide to describe it, and even to see it. Africa continually fails to be subsumable by the classical prose in which Gide writes, a prose to which his vision has difficulty not conforming.

Further, Gide never stops worrying about seeing Europe while he's looking at Africa. Thus, Brazzaville is covered by a screen of "civilization" that hides Africa or, indeed, Gide implies, has chased it away.[12] And not only "Europe" but also "Africa as I imagined it" makes it seem impossible ever to see Africa while he's there. A few months after Brazzaville, on October 18, having traveled a ways up the Congo, branched on to the Oubangui, having arrived in Bangui and gone on a driving tour of the region, Gide confesses:

> My imaginary idea of this country was so lively (I mean that I had imagined it so vividly) that I wonder whether, in the future, this false image will not be stronger than my memory of the reality and whether I shall see Bangui, for instance, in my mind's eye as it is really, or as I first of all imagined it would be.
> However much the mind tries, it cannot recapture that emotion of surprise

---

10. And not just Gide's. This is a common topos in travel writing. Gide's writing in many ways follows the general patterns of this genre. One article I have found helpful in thinking about Gide in the Congo is by Vincent Kaufmann, on Michel Leiris' travel journal *L'Afrique fantôme:* "Michel Leiris: « On ne part pas »." Kaufmann points to a similar problem in Leiris: "The charms of exoticism run out so quickly that sometimes Leiris finds himself unsure of actually being in Africa: « I am obliged to look at the photos that have just been developed in order to imagine that I am in something like Africa »" (147). See also Mary Louise Pratt, *Imperial Eyes: Travel Writing and Transculturation,* for a helpful study of the genre.

11. C'est une invite à laquelle je ne répondrai point. L'art comporte une tempérance et répugne à l'énormité. Une description ne devient pas plus émouvante pour avoir mis dix au lieu d'un (25).

12. The evident racism of this particular civilized/uncivilized binary marks the whole of Gide's text and is analyzed in a helpful article by Anita Licari, "Lo Sguardo Coloniale: Per una analisi dei codici dell'esotismo a partire dal *Voyage au Congo* di Gide." See, for example, pp. 48–49: "[Gide's] discourse remains caught in cultural stereotypes we've already seen, in particular, that which contrasts warm and cold civilizations, where the first would be all heart, body and instinct, the second all intelligence, reasoning and perversions." My thanks to Natalie Melas for showing me this essay. For a sustained analysis of how this rhetoric works elsewhere in Gide, see Mary L. Pratt, "Mapping Ideology: Gide, Camus, and Algeria."

which adds to the charm of the object an enchanting strangeness. The beauty of the exterior world remains the same, but the eye's virginity is lost. (60)[13]

The vocabulary here echoes the Brazzaville passage, where "tout m'y charmait d'abord," but when, "passé la première surprise," Gide sits down to write, what marks the writing is interference with vision. Only in a state of surprise, almost, one might say, when you're not looking, could you actually catch a glimpse of something that might be Africa, and that charmed moment consistently proves evanescent, unsustainable. Gide's journal thus inevitably becomes punctuated with episodes of frustration. I will be trying to sketch that frustration and its effects in what follows.

Allégret's bland entry cited as an epigraph to this section also illustrates the failure of pleasure that structures the trip and its writing. The trip was long, and Gide and Allégret took a fairly extensive library of European literature along with them to while away the days. On November 30, 1925, Allégret was not simultaneously *walking* and reading R. L. Stevenson's *Master of Ballantrae;* he was being carried in a hammocklike contraption called a *tipoye.* Allégret's difficulty is to read as he is being jostled along by his porters; it's a further problem to decide between a novel and sightseeing; and when he finally tears himself away from the book, like Gide he doesn't so much see "Africa" as he sees "like Europe" and "not like Europe": "Cela ressemble un peu . . . mais c'est très différent." Most crucially, there is the difficulty of being carried. The displeasure at being carried and at the more general necessity of porters haunts the trip to an ever greater extent. The obsessive thought of it and the effort required to avoid the thought are observable everywhere.[14]

Indeed, one might say that this issue of porters, of *le portage,* of Allégret's and Gide's transportation, and the transportation of their supplies and belongings, becomes a sort of magnet that attracts all the most difficult social questions Gide and Allégret would face on their trip: questions of forced displacements of populations, of forced labor, of exploitation of all sorts for harvesting, for the building of roads and railroads, as well as for *le portage.* Gide and Allégret had their trip officially sanctioned by the French government. They would write a useful report about the state of the colonies on their return. It was a "mission officielle gratuite"; that is, they paid for the trip themselves, but this official recognition, Durosay tells us in his introduction to Allégret's *Carnets,*

13. Ma représentation imaginaire de ce pays était si vive (je veux dire que je me l'imaginais si fortement) que je doute si, plus tard, cette fausse image ne luttera pas contre le souvenir et si je reverrai Bangui, par exemple, comme il est vraiment, ou comme je me figurais d'abord qu'il était.

      Tout l'effort de l'esprit ne parvient pas à recréer cette émotion de la surprise qui ajoute au charme de l'objet une étrangeté ravissante. La beauté du monde extérieur reste la même, mais la virginité du regard s'est perdue (87).

14. About a similar passage in Allégret's notebooks, where he is reading *The Return of the Native,* Gelder comments, "Allégret . . . looks just like my mental image of Gide—riding through Africa on his tipoye with his nose in an English book, reading up on the natives who are carrying him, in order to deny the fact that they are doing so" ("The 'Retour' of the Native," 16). See also, on this topic, the cover illustration of Pratt's *Imperial Eyes* and also Pratt's comments on pp. 153–54.

assured the beneficiaries of the support of the [colonial] administration for the recruiting of porters, for replenishing provisions, and for lodging with administrators or in station-houses. As for free transport, more often than not the travellers settled with their porters out of their own funds. . . . But it is possible that they kept these accounts so carefully in order to allow for later reimbursement by the central administrators.[15]

The usual understanding of Gide's trip is that this idea of a socially useful investigatory mission was merely a pretext, that Gide's trip was undertaken out of his own need to travel and out of his own obsessions with Africa. Only *during* this trip, it is said, was Gide's social conscience awakened, and only slowly did his sense of a necessary political intervention on his return to France take shape. Thus Durosay, for instance, writes, "The departure for the 'Congo' had in effect progressively become, in the Gidean imaginary, a departure for a dreamed-up, Baudelairian land of natural liberty, of spontaneous erotism, of infinite sensuality" (13).[16] Durosay fills out the usual narrative by suggesting that the effect of Africa on Gide was to demystify it and to turn Gide into something of an *écrivain engagé:* "The political and economic calamities of French Equatorial Africa having, in a manner of speaking, belied, demythologized the fantasm, and having determined Gide to embark upon a polemical campaign, the direction of the voyage tends (more and more as the writer's political commitment becomes more pronounced) to turn from egotism to altruism" (13). It needs to be added that Gide's travel journal itself provides some support for this narrative. Thus, in a footnote to that same entry on the distension of Brazzaville, Gide muses retrospectively:

I could not foresee that these social questions of our dealings with the natives, which are so distressingly urgent and which I had then only caught a glimpse of, would soon engage my attention so much as to become the chief interest of my journey and that I should find in studying them the justification of my being in this land. At that moment, faced with them, what I mostly felt was my incompetence. But I learned as I went along. (16)[17]

In saying that his interests in and knowledge of social issues grew during the course of his trip, Gide doesn't actually say anything about a move from egotism to

---

15. Daniel Durosay, Introduction to Marc Allégret, *Carnets du Congo: Voyage avec Gide,* p. 25. Further references given parenthetically in text.

16. Other versions of this claim can be found in Licari, "Lo Sguardo Coloniale," 46–7. Or in Jacques Darras, "Le Voyage en Afrique." Durosay uses as evidence for this claim Gide's putatively anachronistic usage of the name "Congo" itself. "For from 1910 on, from the creation of French Equatorial Africa, the French Congo, former name of the colony, politically, administratively, no longer exists" (13). This seems to me a problematic argument—as if French administrative fiat should be able to abolish an African name with its own history, its own ongoing usage—a name, in fact, which, politically, administratively, is again in use even as Durosay writes. This is not to argue that Gide's use of the word Congo is a specifically anticolonialist reappropriation on his part, but clearly the motivation for and effects of his usage should be seen as more multivalent than Durosay allows for.

17. Je ne pouvais prévoir que ces questions sociales angoissantes, que je ne faisais qu'entrevoir, de nos rapports avec les indigènes, m'occuperaient bientôt jusqu'à devenir le principal intérêt de mon voyage, et que je trouverais dans leur étude ma raison d'être dans ce pays. Ce qu'en face d'elles je sentais alors, c'est surtout mon incompétence. Mais j'allais m'instruisant (29).

altruism. It's not a claim one would expect him to take to kindly, and in fact he does write strenuously against it a number of years later.

In a public exchange with Jean Schlumberger in 1935, Gide objects to Schlumberger's claim, in an article entitled "Gide, rue Visconti," that "it is during his trip to the Congo (1925) that Gide, for the first time, found himself face to face with social iniquity."[18] It would certainly seem that careful readings of texts such as *Si le grain ne meurt* and *Les Faux-Monnayeurs* could contradict this assertion. Gide the absolute aesthetic mandarin, Gide the pure egotist in search of self-liberating sensation: these are the premises of those arguments that insist on a new dawn of political awareness in the mid-1920s. Yet, simple narratives that feature something like "a late-blooming and slow-growing political awareness" combined with "a slow loss of selfishness and merely sentimental concern with others" seem insufficiently complicated, both to the *Voyage au Congo* and to prior writings by Gide.

Gide's defense in response to Schlumberger is typical in its slipperiness:

> Were I simply to have published my notes and my travel journal from the time of *Amyntas* (1893 to 1896) in their entirety, as I did for my Congo trip, or, more exactly, were I to have allowed all my preoccupations of the time to find their way into my notes, you would have seen, for example, the story of the beginnings of the phosphate industry at Gafsa and, above all, the story of the methodical, devious expropriation of small Arab farmers by the C . . . bank—and that these stories left me in no way indifferent. But what can I say? That wasn't my cup of tea. I would have felt that as an artist it was beneath me to turn my pen to such vulgar concerns. (*Littérature engagée,* 80)[19]

I have long been socially aware, and have the notes to prove it, Gide tells us; or rather, I would have had the notes had I allowed myself to write them down, had I not given way to such a strictly aesthetic self-censorship. Gide thus both denies a narrative model—I have been aesthetically selfish, but I'm learning to be otherwise—at the same time as he provides the evidence for it. The Congo journal poses the same problem: social concerns are necessarily present from the outset, yet apparently more obviously central at the end. Eric Marty, in his book *André Gide: Qui êtes-vous?* aptly expresses all sides of this tension:

> The journal he keeps throughout his trip progressively ceases to be solely a collection of impressions or of sensations sublimated by a literary sensibility, in order to turn

18. "Gide, rue Visconti" first appeared in *La Nouvelle Revue Française* (1 March 1935), 482–84. It is reprinted, along with Gide's letter in response, in *André Gide et notre temps,* 83–90. This book, which I discuss in my final chapter, is the record of a round-table discussion on the subject of Gide's communism, held at the *Union pour la Vérité* in January 1935. Gide's letter is also reprinted in his *Littérature engagée,* 79–82.

19. Eussé-je publié simplement et intégralement mes notes et mon journal de voyage de l'époque d'*Amyntas* (1893 à 1896), ainsi que je fis pour mon voyage au Congo, ou, plus exactement : eussé-je laissé libre accès dans mes notes à toutes mes préoccupations d'alors, on y eût vu que, par exemple, l'histoire des débuts de l'exploitation des phosphates de Gafsa et, surtout, celle de la surnoise et méthodique expropriation des petits cultivateurs arabes par la banque C . . . , ne me laissaient nullement indifférent. Mais quoi! ce n'était pas là *ma partie.* Je me serais cru déshonoré, en tant qu'artiste, si j'avais prêté ma plume à de si vulgaires soucis.

into an implacable account, a scrupulous and also revolted analysis of the economic exploitation and the poor treatment meted out to the blacks by the colonists. In fact, the quality of these two journals [*Voyage au Congo* and *Le Retour du Tchad*] is constituted precisely by the *alternation* of apparently insignificant notations on vegetation . . . fauna, climate, and human beings with remarks of an economic and social nature, but also with moments of compassion towards these mistreated peoples, or of disgust towards the French colonists. Gide discovers in himself a vulnerability, a wound caused by this spectacle, and which also becomes an obsession, an incandescent point that will subsequently mobilize his entire being. (117–18; my emphasis)

If I hesitate in what follows, as I have been hesitating throughout, to endorse developmental models (in favor of models that account for something like what Marty has called *alternation*), it is because a too quick recourse to developmental schemata often results in a moralizing abjection of the "undeveloped," "unconscious" early stage, whose political complexities then go unread in favor of a too celebratory identification with the virtues of a later moment, whose political complexities then go unread. Instead, by focusing on an ongoing model of frustration of pleasure as Gide travels, I hope to show how that constant frustration produces not only political discourse (some of it, as we will see, frankly unpleasant) but also a necessary politicization of the self's relation to pleasure, a politicization readable even when politics is not explicitly thematized.

Part of the unpleasantness of the political discourse of Gide's writings about his Congo travels is a result of his constant recourse to a dichotomy we have already observed him invoking—that between civilized and primitive cultures. It is, of course, a perfectly developmental model: Africans are "undeveloped" and "unconsciously natural" except when touched, tainted by the complexities of European civilization. Adoum, Gide's close personal attendant throughout much of the trip, comes to represent for Gide the true nature of Africans, and Gide, who improves Adoum's French and teaches him to read, inevitably, as he testifies to his growing tenderness for Adoum, attaches to that tenderness a racist tick:

> I am going on with Adoum's reading-lessons. His application is touching; he is getting on steadily, and every day I am becoming more attached to him. When the white man gets angry with the black's stupidity, he is usually showing up his own foolishness! Not that I think them capable of any but the slightest mental development; their brains as a rule are dull and stagnant—but how often the white man seems to make it his business to thrust them back into their darkness. (95–96)[20]

The tenacity of this rhetoric[21] explains, for instance, the position Gide took upon his return to France as he embarked on his campaign of polemics about the state of

20. Je continue mes leçons de lecture à Adoum, qui fait preuve d'une émouvante application et progresse de jour en jour; et je m'attache à lui chaque jour un peu plus. De quelle sottise, le plus souvent, le blanc fait preuve, quand il s'indigne de la stupidité des noirs! Je ne les crois pourtant capables que d'un très petit développement, le cerveau gourd et stagnant le plus souvent dans une nuit épaisse — mais combien de fois le blanc semble prendre à tâche de les y enfoncer! (130).

21. Compare an almost identical, but more extended and complicated passage from another moment of extreme tenderness near the end of the trip, when Gide is obliged to take leave of Adoum. As the tenderness is more deeply felt,

French Equatorial Africa. It was not, strictly speaking, an absolutely anticolonialist position. That much is clear from the title of the major article Gide wrote, setting out his position: "La Détresse de *notre* Afrique Equatoriale" ["The Distress of *Our* Equatorial Africa"]. As Licari puts it:

> Gide's denunciations show that for him too it is possible to think of a "good" colonization. In "La Détresse de notre Afrique Equatoriale" he defends himself against the charge of discouraging the colonialist initiative through his writings. He declares: "If the moral and material interests of two peoples, of two lands, I mean of the colonizing and the colonized lands, are not united, the colonization is bad." In sum, this is the idea that both good and bad colonialisms exist, and that to improve the situation of the colonized it will be enough that the colonizers become more generous, more equitable, less corrupt and less greedy. . . . In his opinion the question could be resolved through some bureaucratic intervention. (52)

Gide changes his mind about this later, to the point where, in the 1935 letter to Schlumberger he states: "It wasn't until much later that I was led, by an unavoidable progression, to see the connection between these particular abuses and a whole that was in itself deplorable, that I was led to understand that a system tolerating, protecting, favoring such abuses—for it profited from them itself—was bad from top to bottom" (*Littérature engagée,* 81).[22]

The system Gide encountered in Africa was complicated by the simultaneous existence in the colonies of both an administrative structure and a set of "concessionary companies," profit-making private organizations set up by the French government in 1899 and given thirty years to exploit their territories:

> The articles and conditions provided for full ownership of the conceded land if it was "developed"—a condition considered to be fulfilled if there was a harvest of rubber on twenty feet per hectare in five years, or if it provided one domestic elephant per 100 hectares, or cultivation or constructions covering one-tenth of the area.
>
> The companies were to pay into the colonial budget an annual rent, plus 15 per cent of their profits, give a surety bond and maintain navigational services on the rivers for their territories. In principle, they enjoyed no delegation of sovereignty, and their agents were to "avoid administrative or political interference." . . . In practice, however, the police forces (militia) were placed at the disposal of the company agents, and in the absence of the regular administrators, they assumed real political powers. (Suret-Canale, 20)[23]

the same racist tick seems more forcibly produced. Gide recounts intentionally giving Adoum 55 francs and telling him "Here are 50 francs," an experiment to see if Adoum would cheat on him. Adoum doesn't and then Gide comments: "I see nothing in him that is not childlike, noble, pure, and honest. The whites who manage to turn creatures like him into rogues are worse rogues themselves, or else miserable blunderers" (295/359). An unpleasantly awkward tale of a manipulative Gide, too closely resembling those whites he purports to criticize, before going on to say: "I do not want to make the black out more intelligent than he is; but his stupidity, if it exists, is only natural—like an animal's. Whereas the white man's as regards the black has something monstrous about it, by very reason of his superiority." The monstrosity being Gide's own, here presented if not acknowledged.

22. Oui, ce n'est que longtemps ensuite que j'en vins, par un enchaînement inéluctable, à rattacher ces abus particuliers à tout un déplorable ensemble, que je fus amené à comprendre qu'un système qui tolérait, qui protégeait, qui favorisait de tels abus, car il en profitait lui-même, était de fond en comble mauvais.

23. On the history of concessionary companies and their practices, see Suret-Canale, 17–42. See also Zoctizoum, *Histoire de la Centrafrique, Tome 1: 1879–1959,* 49–112. On the history leading up to the establishment of the concessionary companies, see Brunschwig, *Mythes et réalités de l'impérialisme colonial français, 1871–1914.*

Many abuses encountered by Gide and Allégret were carried out by the agents of concessionary companies, abuses the colonial administration could theoretically punish and prevent. As Durosay points out, Gide's trip was happening just a few years before the thirty-year leases were up for reconsideration and during a period when there was a high demand for rubber, a regional product, resulting in what Durosay calls "a veritable economy of pillaging, aiming to produce a maximum of profit in a minimum of time" (33). Gide seems throughout his travel journals to imagine himself as associated with the French colonial administrators and to differentiate himself from the economically interested agents of the concessionary companies.[24] This imagined separation of the colonial administration from economic interests, renounced by 1935, is also, as we will see, undercut throughout the text whenever questions of porterage or of the building of roads or railroads come up, for porters, roads, and railroads represent a colonial infrastructure that necessarily links economic interests with other construals of the colonial mission, even "disinterested" travel such as Gide's.

Butterflies and Termites

In a helpful study of travel writing, *Imperial Eyes,* Mary Louise Pratt investigates the complicated interrelations between "disinterested" travel through colonized spaces and the project of colonizing itself. The naturalist is one category of disinterested traveler with a long history that Pratt traces back to the figure of Carl Linné or Linnaeus, who in 1735 proposed a descriptive system that could in theory be used to classify any form of plant life on earth.

> As his taxonomy took hold throughout Europe in the second half of the [eighteenth] century, his "disciples" . . . fanned out by the dozens across the globe. . . . Arrangements with the overseas trading companies . . . gave free passage to Linnaeus' students, who began turning up everywhere collecting plants and insects. . . . Alongside the frontier figures of the seafarer, the conqueror, the captive, the diplomat, there began to appear everywhere the benign, decidedly literate figure of the "herborizer," armed with nothing more than a collector's bag, a notebook, and some specimen bottles, desiring nothing more than a few peaceful hours alone with the bugs and flowers. (25–27)

24. The famous Pacha affair, in which a local chief mistakes Gide for an Administrator and so brings to him a complaint against a particularly brutal agent of the Compagnie Forestière Sangha-Oubangui reflects the complexities of the situation. This case preoccupies Gide in late October and early November (63–93/91–127), and again on his return to France. See his annotations to the justificatory letter from M. Weber, Director of the Compagnie Forestière. Gide reprints the letter with his own annotations as an appendix to his *Voyage au Congo* (458–73). Zoctizoum in his *Histoire de la Centrafrique* points to the natural difficulty of Africans in understanding the different categories of Europeans with whom they were obliged to deal: "In central Africa and in particular in the Oubangui-Chari territory, it was difficult for the people of the country to differentiate between the civilian commander, the military commander, the economic agents of the concessionary societies, and even the priest—in spite of his cassock. . . . In this regard the people were right, since they were all in one way or another agents of the colonial society. Even the Europeans had trouble telling them apart" (93).

Gide had been since childhood an avid botanist and entomologist, and spends a fair amount of time in Africa on these pursuits. In doing so, he clearly longs for the innocence, the benign status of a quiet observer whose interest, being scientific, might somehow remain disinterested. He also imagines, in the same footnote to the Brazzaville passage considered earlier, that somehow the purity of those disinterested interests might solve the problems of vision he had already begun to encounter:

> A traveller who has just arrived in a country where everything is new to him is forced by indecision to come to a halt. Being interested equally in everything, the traveller simply isn't up to it, and at first, unable to take note of everything, notes nothing. Happy the sociologist who is interested only in manners and customs; the painter who cares only for the country's appearance; the naturalist who occupies himself with insects or plants! Happy the specialist! His whole time is not too much to devote to his limited domain. If I had a second life, I could be happy spending it merely in the study of termites. (16)[25]

Hesitating, stopped short by indecision, oppressed by excessive vision, Gide turns to Virgilian cadences—"happy the specialist"—in an effort to pastoralize the landscape so that his vision itself might be pastoralized, freed from colonial contradictions.[26] The plaintive desire for a second life constitutes an admission of the inevitable failure of the pastoralizing project, a failure that makes itself felt throughout Gide's prolonged hesitation in writing about what he sees in Africa.

Looking at termites and termitaries thus comes to represent for Gide a hope for a pleasurable freedom of vision, as if the social network undergirding the entire voyage could be effaced by the narrowing of a gaze to the point where it would be sufficiently purified so as to remain charmed into pleasure. Butterflies serve a similar function. In the entry to which the footnote just cited is attached, in the midst of the description of the trial of a French administrator for unspecified cruelties, there occurs the following happy intervention: "During the third and last session of this melancholy trial a very beautiful butterfly flew into the law-court, of which the windows were all open. After circling about for some time it settled most unexpectedly on the very desk at which I was sitting, and I managed to catch it without ruining it" (15).[27] As if a sign of his election, the butterfly distracts Gide from the sorry spectacle of a stupid, inexperienced administrator abusing his

25. Pour le voyageur nouveau venu dans un pays où pour lui tout est neuf, une indécision l'arrête. S'intéressant à tout également, il ne peut suffire et d'abord il ne note rien, faute de pouvoir tout noter. Heureux le sociologue qui ne s'intéresse qu'aux mœurs; le peintre qui ne consent à voir du pays que l'aspect; le naturaliste qui choisit de ne s'occuper que des insectes ou que des plantes; heureux le spécialiste! Il n'a pas trop de tout son temps pour son domaine limité. Vivrais-je une seconde vie, j'accepterais, pour mon bonheur, de n'étudier que les termites. (29)

26. For Virgilian examples of this figure of *makarismos,* see the conclusion to the botanical second book of the *Georgics:* "Felix qui potuit rerum cognoscere causas. . . ." [Happy he who has been able to know the causes of things. . . .].

27. Durant la troisième et dernière séance de ce triste procès, un très beau papillon est venu voler dans la salle d'audience, dont toutes les fenêtres sont ouvertes. Après de nombreux tours, il s'est inespérément posé sur le pupitre devant lequel j'étais assis, où je parviens à le saisir sans l'abîmer (27–28).

colonialist privileges and restores a moment of pleasure to a day of discomfort. Nature seems to hold out to Gide the possibility of an unfrustrated pleasure, a contrast to the continued alienations provided by the social world. The juxtaposition of the trial and the capture of the butterfly has its comic side as well: a bespectacled dignitary unable to pay attention to the matter at hand, squirming in his seat, his gaze entranced by a circling butterfly, his breath held in the childlike hopefulness that the butterfly will land close enough. . . . But the scene also works to trouble the hoped-for innocence, situating Gide's entomological excitement firmly within the arena of a French judicial encounter. The unavoidable context of a landscape traversed by colonial power relations is here condensed into a courtroom, a scene of juridical power. One might suspect that even outside any materially constructed courtroom, future butterfly hunts will nonetheless happen within these ghostly parameters.

Gide's election by, perhaps even identification with, this butterfly again represents some hope for a disinterested interest, a purely aesthetic vantage point, one that could be preserved even inside a courthouse, just as the butterfly could be seized "sans l'abîmer." Yet, the complications of that verb *saisir*—to grasp hold of, but also to take by force, to arrest—(not to mention the fact that many of Gide's preserved specimens rot later in the trip) come close to tainting Gide himself with a policing function at odds with the pure aestheticism of the (dead) butterfly.

Thus, a pastoral interlude within a policing action meant to punish abuses of colonial power, an entomological interlude, finds itself nonetheless inhabited by the very kinds of politics it had perhaps hoped to interrupt and ignore. Jonathan Dollimore, in the final chapter of his book, *Sexual Dissidence*, considers precisely what might be hiding behind an ecstatic or intoxicating drive toward the pastoral. Dollimore is writing about Gide's *Amyntas:*

> If ecstatic union with the other entails a liberating loss of inhibition and even loss of the self, by the very same token, it is then that desire may become most unaware of the plight of the other, especially when, as here, it is powerfully mediated through the pastoral genre. *Amyntas* is a pastoral narrative of self-redemption in relation to, in the desire for, *and* in the space of, the other. . . . The precondition for pastoral sublimity is the loss of history. (340)

Pratt suggests that this loss of history is typical of travel writing about Africa, which often goes so far as to construct for itself a landscape lacking people entirely:

> Where, one asks, is everybody? The landscape is written as uninhabited, unpossessed, unhistoricized, unoccupied even by the travelers themselves. The activity of describing geography and identifying flora and fauna structures an asocial narrative in which the human presence, European or African, is absolutely marginal, though it was, of course, a constant and essential aspect of the traveling itself. (*Imperial Eyes*, 51–52)[28]

28. See also her suggestive pages on Mary Kingsley's travels in West Africa (*Imperial Eyes*, 213–16). Of course, the landscapes Gide travels through are often underpopulated, many people having died of starvation or disease, fled to avoid conscription into work forces, or been conscripted and forcibly removed. See Suret-Canale, 36–37; Zoctizoum, 84–87.

Porters and modes of transport loom here as well, for the very *getting to* the place from which one could merely observe, merely describe, somehow continues to influence the ways in which one can simply *be* there. How does this problem play itself out in Gide's observations of the people he sees?

In his journal, Gide often expresses a desire to be *alone* with the landscape in order to experience the African sights more fully. Further, when he does put on a sociologist's hat for a moment and gazes at the people he encounters, he sometimes keeps the entomologist's hat on underneath, confusing, or at least comparing Africans with insects—so that sometimes it would seem as if Gide could almost be alone *in the presence* of Africans. Villages become landscape formations; human constructions are considered in the same manner as, say, the construction of a mason-fly.

> Native town. Rectangular enclosures, fenced round with palisades made of rushes (*seccos*). Behind these are the Saras' huts, where they live in families. The rush mats are just high enough so that a medium-sized man cannot see over them. Passing by on horseback, one looks down on them, and one's gaze falls upon strange intimacies. Quintessence of exoticism. Beauty of the huts with their lattice-work roofs, edged by a sort of mosaic made with straw. One might call it the work of insects. (158)[29]

The added height of being on horseback seems to raise the observer to a different plane of observation. The privacy the barriers are meant to provide seems not to be intended for him, privy to all interiors, and the quality of strangeness thus overseen is, as we would expect, a source of visual satisfaction. Yet, the dehumanizing quality of this "ethnographic" gaze seems clear even before the strange final assertion about the woven roofs: "on dirait un travail d'insectes." Doubtless this could be construed as a compliment—the work of these villagers *holds* Gide's attention, creates a focus in this unfocused land: "As usual, in this immeasurably vast country, there is no focus; the lines run incoherently in all directions; there is no limit to anything" (101/136). Illegible, impenetrable, and timeless—after experiencing the landscape in these terms, the attraction of "étranges intimités" into which one can plunge one's gaze, like the attraction of carefully, artistically constructed huts, seems clear. They seem to nourish and engage the gaze and also provide it with a satisfactory sense of mastery. At last something to be seen, something to be said.

Compare this with a passage about a mason-fly:

> When we got back to the station, we spent a long time watching a mason-fly at its extraordinary work. . . . In the space of a few minutes it completely walled up a spider in a mud cell, into which it began by forcing it. One stroke of my knife undid that work and brought to view several small spiders as well as the large one. . . . Each cell, when I cut it open, contained four or five spiders. . . . This arrangement is no

29. Ville indigène. Enceintes rectangulaires de claies de roseaux (seccos) formant enclos, où se groupent les huttes, où les Saras habitent par familles. Ces nattes sont juste assez hautes pour qu'un homme de taille moyenne ne puisse regarder par-dessus. En passant à cheval, on les domine et le regard plonge dans d'étranges intimités. Quintessence d'exotisme. Beauté des huttes au toit treillissé, liseré par une sorte de mosaïque de paille. On dirait un travail d'insectes (198).

doubt the grub's larder. . . . Unfortunately my eyesight is not so good as it was, and I did find it difficult to bring into focus things that are so minute. (102)[30]

The need to be able to focus obsesses Gide, just as does the need to have his attention held; to be able to gaze at something *for a long time,* and have that duration be pleasurable, is a constant aim.[31] Such an aim forces disruptions of intimacy, forces a cut of the knife through the admirable work of the fly. Later in the trip, in fact, the invasion of human intimacy and the cut of the knife combine to make the same point even more forcefully.

In February 1927 more than halfway into his trip, Gide will be fascinated by another set of dwellings, those of the Massa people.[32] Allégret will want to do some filming *inside* one of the huts, but to do so, needs light. The solution is to pay 50 francs so that the top of the hut can be cut off by several machete-wielding locals. "A flood of light entered it and after the dust had settled a little, Marc set his actors to rehearse" (279/341). Discovery rendered literal.

Gide's vision, in its need for pleasure and focus, in its need to be charmed, confuses sociology and entomology. In the midst of all its different kinds of trouble, in a discovery of some enchanting particularity, in the maddening failure to discover any particularity, what frequently seems to be effaced is the relation, often invasive and exploitative, of Gide to those Africans he does "see." We need to pursue in more detail the links between Gide's troubles seeing the landscape and his troubles seeing people.

As for the landscape, Gide's vision is troubled because there is nothing there, troubled because there is too much there, troubled because the very impression of something being the "quintessence d'exotisme" is frustratingly fleeting, soon to be overlaid by recognition. Thus, alongside the complaint already noted, that "there is no focus . . . there is no limit to anything," one should consider the following: "Whenever the landscape resolves itself, when it sets itself discrete boundaries and attempts to be a little better planned, it evokes in my mind some corner of France; but the French landscape is always better constructed, better drawn, and of more individual elegance" (136).[33] If social insects represent for Gide the quintessence

30. De retour au poste, nous observons longuement l'extraordinaire travail de la mouche-maçonne . . . En quelques minutes, elle a complètement muré une araignée dans l'alvéole de terre où elle l'avait forcée d'entrer. D'un coup de couteau, j'ai défait ce travail, découvrant, à côté de la grosse araignée, plusieurs petites . . . Chaque alvéole que j'ai crevée contenait quatre ou cinq araignées . . . Certainement, c'est là le garde-manger des larves . . . Malheureusement, ma vue baisse beaucoup, et je ne parviens plus à « mettre au point » les objets un peu délicats (137).

31. See Darras, "Le Voyage en Afrique": "For the desire to endure, to make desire itself endure, is more fundamental than anything for Gide, and takes pleasure in its own process—writing itself recharging pleasure [volupté]—which then becomes the pleasure of writing" (5). Also, on Gide's gaze, see Catherine Maubon, "Sguardo e scrittura in *Voyage au Congo,*" esp. 76–78.

32. See 217–20/274–77. Gide published a slightly different version of his pages on the Massa in *L'Illustration,* March 5, 1927. (See Alain Goulet, "Le Voyage en A.E.F. dans *L'Illustration.*") About these pages in *L'Illustration,* Durosay comments: "Guided, perhaps dazzled by his personal fantasy, Gide first of all sees a form responding to his need for natural harmony; the Massa hut, an exceptional success aesthetically, but qualified as showing an insect's perfection" (41). Gelder helpfully discusses filming inside the Massa hut in her "The 'Retour' of the Native."

33. Chaque fois que le paysage se forme, se limite et tente de s'organiser un peu, il évoque en mon esprit quelque coin de France; mais le paysage de France est toujours mieux construit, mieux dessiné et d'une plus particulière élégance (174).

of Africa, classicism itself seems the quintessence of France. Thus, any African landscape describable in Gidean language necessarily comes to seem French by way of its very describability. Termites and the termitaries that dot the African landscape offer a strange way out of Gide's hopeless vision—describable *and yet* African. Consider the following passage on those termitaries, a passage that further illustrates Gide's effort to escape the frustration his vision imposes on him—that he should be unable ever to find what he's looking for because as soon as he recognizes it, it is instantly not what he is looking for; and the rest of the time whatever he is looking for he cannot recognize:

> But what seems to me particularly curious is that in the whole country there is no sign of any recent termitary of the same monumental size; these, which are so immense, are in all likelihood several centuries old and must have been long ago abandoned. . . . It seems that another race of termites, whose buildings are on a small scale, now occupies the ground in place of the monumental ones. Some of these tumuli which I saw later had been cut straight through to make way for the road, and the mystery of their inside was displayed, with its passages, rooms, etc. I cursed the car for not letting me examine this matter more at leisure. (47)[34]

The initial surprise comes about here not through some successful vision; instead, Gide is overtaken by what he expects the landscape to reveal but finds it with-holding—*recent* monumental termitaries. This is one sign of passing time, a sign that Africa has at least a *natural* history that one might notice. We might wonder whether in the recognition of the disappearance of the monumental termites—in the admission of African natural history—there is some displaced recognition of the problem of human depopulation and some corresponding recognition of African social and political history, of the place the disruptive arrival of the colonial apparatus has in that history.

Late in the trip, Gide will talk about the ways brush fires and "displace-ments" keep the landscape looking new, ahistorical:

> On account of these perpetual fires, on account of the repeated displacements of races and villages, on account of the old forest's having been replaced by more recent vegetation, the constant and dominant impression—mine, at any rate—is of a new country, *without a past*, of immediate youth, of an inexhaustible spring of life, instead of the ancestral, prehistoric, prehuman feeling which travellers in this land prefer to talk of. (334–35)[35]

It is a complicated observation. All these displacements and replacements have social and historical causes that Gide chooses not to go into here. They form part

---

34. Mais ce qui me surprend, c'est de ne voir dans toute la contrée aucune termitière monumentale récente; celles {que je vois}, immenses . . . doivent, désertées depuis longtemps, vraisemblablement être vieilles de plusieurs siècles . . . Il semble qu'une autre race de termites à petites constructions soit ici venue occuper le sol à la place des termites monumentaux. Certains de ces tumulus, que je vois un peu plus tard tranchés net pour laisser passer la route montrent leur mystère intérieur: couloirs, salles, etc. Je peste contre l'auto qui ne me laisse pas le loisir d'examiner un peu mieux cela (65).

35. A cause de ces perpétuels incendies, à cause des déplacements de races, de villages, à cause du remplace-ment de la vieille forêt par des végétations plus récentes, l'impression constante de pays neuf, *sans passé*, d'immédiate jeunesse, d'inépuisable surgissement, domine encore, pour moi du moins, celle de l'ancestral, du préhistorique, du préhumain, dont parle de préférence ceux qui voyagent dans ce pays (403).

of the past of this land that appears to Gide to lack one. That past, that social history, he thus both notices and yet cannot find signs of in the landscape. Yet he also claims that this pastless atmosphere, this failure of history to leave any marks he can read, keeps his attention focused, stops him from wandering off into the fantasies of prehuman eras he finds so prominent and so problematic in other (asocial) writings of travelers to Africa.

At least in the case of the (perhaps prehuman) termites, the disappointment of their absence is slightly compensated for by the termitaries they did manage to leave behind. These termitaries, though, inevitably produce another frustration. Helpfully cut open, discovered by the passage of a road, the existence of that very road (a trace of the forced labor of Africans) means that Gide can here be transported at rapid speed by auto, thereby losing the leisure to focus on what interests him. Here, then, another uncomfortable reminder of Gide's impossible situation, his structurally necessary frustration: present because of his place in a colonializing culture, traveling its paths, he nonetheless only wants to see something different, some place those paths wouldn't yet have reached, some place inaccessible to his vision. Yet whatever traces of happy vision he does find, he finds only on those troubling paths.

The cut of the road itself removes the "necessity" of porterage, representing a new phase of colonial development. Gide's voyage traces the uneven developments of the colonial transportation network in French Equatorial Africa, and he even comments on this issue at one point: "Porterage exists, and will continue to exist for a long time in certain parts of Cameroon, where roads for automobiles are particularly difficult to establish. Here porterage remains necessary" (83 in the French edition. The passage is not included in English translation). The historical nature of this colonialist "necessity" and Gide's own implication in it, his own situation *at this particular moment* of uneven and enforced development, which determines *how* he travels through Africa, and even which parts he goes to, clearly structures his frustrated vision even as it implicitly haunts his writing.

To summarize: on the one hand, the landscape, the people, the flora and fauna sometimes seem to provide nothing but a uniform illegibility that Gide finds stupefying: "Everything is uniform; there can be no possible predilection for any particular site. I stayed the whole day yesterday without the least desire to stir. From one end of the horizon to the other, wherever my eye settles, there is not a single point to which I wish to go" (137).[36] On the other hand, Gide is occasionally surprised by an unsustainable ecstasy, the discovery of something exotic, a discovery immediately undercut, corroded—sometimes, as we have seen, and will see in more detail later, by the discomfitting pressures of his inevitably politicized presence, sometimes, as in the following passage, by the processes of memory, writing, representation:

36. Tout est uniforme — pas un site, pas une prédilection possible. Je suis resté tout le jour d'hier sans aucun désir de bouger. D'un bout à l'autre de l'horizon, et où que mon regard puisse porter, il n'est pas un point particulier, et où je me sente désir d'aller (175).

> Round the great trees, drowned in mists the sun was beginning to dissipate, floated strange perfumes. Soft, flexible vegetation, rich with hidden strength. Groups of trees, so fine, so great, so noble, that one said to oneself: "This is what I have come to see!" Songs of birds. Chirping of insects. My heart was flooded with a kind of obscure and complex adoration. But was it the exotic vegetation that filled me with admiration? . . . Was it not rather—above all—the spring itself? (370–71)[37]

This is the rhythm of ecstatic frustration the journal plays out over and over: a wealth of seemingly novel sensations, their description and naming, an evaluation of their exoticism, a fall into doubt as to its originality and uniqueness, a failure of its durability. "On se dit: c'est là ce que je suis venu voir." In little phrases such as this one Gide signals the discomfiture arising from his own place in the landscape: he generalizes himself as "on"; he notices the separation between himself and the object of his vision—"là"—a strange indeterminate deictic, pointing at something that, should it be seized, would prove frustratingly absent. More and more it seems that, rather than the search for any actual pleasure, it is the repetition of this frustration itself, and reflection on it, that sustains Gide's voyage.

There is one moment, just before the end of the *Voyage au Congo* and the beginning of the *Retour du Tchad,* when Gide does imagine putting an end to this rhythm. Such an end would have to be something like death. Gide imagines the transcendent moment as one of pure vision: a vision finally *free of all sociality,* all positioning; a vision *free of all memory,* of recognition,—a solitary, subjectless vision:[38]

> Ah! how I should have liked to stop, to sit down, there on the slope of that monumental termitary, in the dark shadows of that enormous acacia, and watch the gambols of the monkeys, and muse, and wonder! . . . Assuredly, I should not have had to stay motionless many minutes for the world of nature to close over me. Everything would have been as if I had not existed and I should myself have forgotten my own presence and turned all vision. Oh, what an ecstasy it would have been! There are few minutes of my life I would sooner live over again. And as I pressed on in the midst of this strange excitement, I forgot the shades that are already at my heels; this that you are doing you will doubtless never do again. (190–91)[39]

The temporal oddness of this passage in the French is perhaps most noticeable in the number of inaccuracies the translator felt obliged to introduce to render it into English. Every tense in the translation has been changed from the original, and, as

37. Près des grands arbres, noyés dans les brumes que le soleil va bientôt dissiper, des parfums inconnus flottent. Végétation flexueuse et molle, riche d'une force cachée. Groupes d'arbres si beaux, si grands, si nobles, qu'on se dit : c'est là ce que je suis venu voir. Chants d'oiseaux; bruissement d'insectes. Une sorte d'adoration confuse ruisselle de mon cœur. Mais est-ce la végétation exotique que j'admire? . . . N'est-ce pas surtout le printemps? (443).

38. Gelder has commented helpfully on the Emersonian resonance of this passage in "The 'Retour' of the Native."

39. Ah! que je voudrais m'arrêter, m'asseoir, ici, sur le flanc de cette termitière monumentale, dans l'ombre obscure de cet énorme acacia, à épier les ébats de ces singes, à m'émerveiller longuement . . . Assurément je ne serais pas immobile depuis quelques minutes, que se refermerait autour de moi la nature. Tout serait comme si je n'étais pas, et j'oublierais moi-même ma présence pour ne plus être que vision. Oh ravissement indicible! Il est peu d'instants que j'aurais plus grand désir de revivre. Et tandis que j'avance dans ce frémissement inconnu, j'oublie l'ombre qui déjà me presse : tout ceci, tu le fais encore, mais sans doute pour la dernière fois (239).

if to confess the problem, an extra past tense has been added by the translator to Gide's "Oh ravissement indicible!" [Oh inexpressible rapture!]: "Oh, what an ecstasy *it would have been!*"[40] Gide seems much less clear as to what tense he is in; he seems, in fact, to be in several present tenses simultaneously, to write prospectively and retrospectively at once, straining to express the frustration of a desire so tied to past and future it can never be present. The entry is written in the present, as if Gide were writing while walking, wanting to sit *here*, on the side of *this* termitary. The funereal possibilities of termitaries we have already noted: they represent the long-passed disappearance of what Gide had hoped to find. Vague worries about spying ("épier") on the intimacy of the monkeys make themselves felt, monkeys apparently being less accommodating of such invasions than some of the people Gide had overlooked while riding by. Then Gide seems to enter into this moment of marvel that he desires be prolonged. It is in this imaginary moment that all "would be as if [he] were not," that he would himself forget his own presence. Then, strangely, this imagined moment—one he has never, or not yet, lived—is the one Gide claims to want to live *again:* "Il est peu d'instants que j'aurais plus grand désir de revivre." Literally, "There aren't many instants that I would more wish to relive." Thanks to this special unlived, yet forcefully imagined moment he would come back to if he could, Gide walks on, forgetting what he is at the same time remembering, writing: "While I walk on . . . I am forgetting the shadow that is already weighing me down: you are doing all of this now, but doubtless for the last time." In the shadow he would sit down in and the parallel shadow already at his heels as he moves ahead we note the complex relation of this trip to fantasies of death, as if stopping long enough to see might involve disappearing. Gide hints constantly at these associations:

> At times one feels completely done up with fatigue—at the end of one's tether; one would like to give the whole thing up, like a child who calls out "Time out!" in order to get out of the game he is playing. But perhaps the finest thing about this journey is the necessity of going on, the impossibility, as a rule, of taking into account the state of the weather, of one's own fatigue. . . . (333)[41]

I would like to spend a few pages now trying to understand the significance of the knotting together in this passage of a subjectless vision, a frustratingly impossible temporality, an unspeakable pleasure, and the approach of death. To do so, I will return briefly to the way Gide, Lacan, and Delay have reflected on the frustrations of Gide's childhood (in particular on Gide's relation to a story by George Sand,

40. Dorothy Bussy found this text of Gide's the most difficult to translate. She mentions this in her letters to him of November 11, 1927, and June 25, 1928, commenting specifically that "l'emploi du présent est assez affolant" [the use of the present tense is fairly maddening] (*Correspondence André Gide–Dorothy Bussy, II: janvier 1925–novembre 1936*, 175).

41. Par instants on se sent recru de fatigue; on n'en peut plus; on voudrait lâcher la partie et, comme l'enfant pour sortir du jeu, crier « pouce ». Mais le plus admirable de ce voyage, peut-être, c'est cette obligation d'avancer, cette impossibilité, le plus souvent, de tenir compte de l'état du temps, de la fatigue . . . (401).

Gribouille), and on some of the ensuing particularities of Gide's experience of alienation from his social realm.

Gribouille: A Lacanian Interlude

L'Histoire du véritable Gribouille is the title of a fairy tale George Sand wrote in 1850. In *Si le grain ne meurt*, Gide tells us that this story provided him with one of his childhood "thèmes de jouissance":

> Gribouille throws himself into the water one day that it is raining very hard, not to avoid the rain, as his wicked brothers say, but to avoid his brothers, who are laughing at him. For some time, he struggles in the water and tries to swim; then he lets himself go and as soon as he lets himself go, he floats; then he feels himself becoming tiny, light, odd, vegetal; leaves sprout out of him all over his body; and soon Gribouille turns into a slender, graceful sprig of oak, which the water gently deposits on the bank of the stream . . . no schoolboy was ever troubled by any page of Aphrodite so much as I—ignorant little boy that I was—by the metamorphosis of Gribouille. (52)⁴²

Both Jean Delay and Jacques Lacan comment on this botanically ecstatic Gidean fantasy, and for both it becomes a knot in which one can see intertwined Gide's relation to the maternal and to a form of aggressivity directed inward in a self-destructive impulse. Delay views this fantasy as necessarily related to the repression of masturbation caused by the visit to Dr. Brouardel (discussed in chapter 2):

> The particular character of the fantasms that follow upon the repression of onanism seems to me to be the link between the images of failure, chastisement, destruction and sensual pleasure. This assuredly dangerous linkage, reactivated by the emotional shock from recent interdictions, was without a doubt an old one, contemporary with the first stages of childhood sexuality. We know what importance Freud placed on these initial stages in the genesis of sadistic and masochistic tendencies, the pleasure in punishing or destroying or in being punished or being destroyed. Now, precisely these tendencies subtend the sensual reveries of Gide's later childhood . . . the idea of abandoning oneself to, or losing or annihilating oneself in obscure forces, the impression of dissolving in a watery element. (1:248–49)

As he goes on, Delay's moralizing tone is once again in evidence: "no desire for the other, no search after contact, no need for caresses, embraces," he writes, claiming there is too much autoeroticism in Gide's fantasies of self-punishment (1:249). Yet

---

42. (Gribouille) se jette à l'eau, un jour qu'il pleut beaucoup, non point pour se garer de la pluie, ainsi que ses vilains frères ont tenté de le faire croire, mais pour se garer de ses frères qui se moquaient. Dans la rivière, il s'efforce et nage quelque temps, puis s'abandonne; et dès qu'il s'abandonne, il flotte; il se sent alors devenir tout petit, léger, bizarre, végétal; il lui pousse des feuilles par tout le corps; et bientôt l'eau de la rivière peut coucher sur la rive le délicat rameau de chêne que notre ami Gribouille est devenu . . . nulle page d'*Aphrodite* ne put troubler nul écolier autant que cette métamorphose de Gribouille en végétal le petit ignorant que j'étais (60–61).

Delay is simultaneously aware that these fantasies of self-punishment are not without relation to the outer world, for Delay clearly notices the *social* pressure behind the effort to interdict childhood erotic pleasures. He also assigns to Gide's mother a dominant role in the establishment of the fantasies he believes to be compensatory for that very interdiction. A few pages later, for instance, he cites a somewhat Lacanian (Gidean?) formula from Lamartine: "Le regard de notre mère est une partie de notre âme qui entre dans notre âme par nos propres yeux" ("Our mother's gaze is a part of our soul which enters there by way of our own eyes")—Lacanian in that it insists on the extent to which our own internal perception of ourselves is not wholly our own, that it is created in a social field of vision, a field in which we are seen, and, surreptitiously identifying with the position from which we are seen, see ourselves being seen. Delay continues: "Now the gaze of Juliette Gide was as severe as a minister's as far as moral purity— considered the most categorical of imperatives—was concerned" (1:254). That is to say, for Delay, and to a great extent for Gide, Juliette Gide occupies the place from which Gide would be able to see himself. Gide's fantasies of self-destruction are inflected by his mother's presence in that place of self-surveillance. We might be tempted to go so far as to say that when Gide watches himself disappear, he does so from behind what he imagines to be his mother's eyes.

Lacan comments on a similar point when discussing Gide's ensemble of childhood fantasies, including Gribouille. He notes a mistake often made in the delineation of a child's fantasies: ascribing them wholly to the child, ignoring that they might come to the child from somewhere, from some person or persons, from some household or social dynamic. In Gide's case, Lacan is curious about the influence of Gide's mother Juliette as Gide's fantasies form. But not only about Juliette. When Lacan explicates "what his mother was for that particular child, and what that voice was, by which love became identified with the dictates of duty," he finds significant not only Juliette Gide herself but also her loving relationship with Anna Shackleton; not only these two maternal figures lovingly linked but also Marie, the servant, and her loving relationship with yet another servant, Delphine. Lacan is clearly suggesting that the *figure* of the mother for Gide is not equivalent to just one woman but is more encompassing, conceivably including not only Juliette but also Anna, Marie, and their pasts, along with some of the women they might have loved. The maternal figure is thus not singular but social, and Lacan goes on to suggest that to understand a child's fantasies, one might do well to consider their possible transmission from this complicatedly *social* maternal space:

> We have classified these fantasms under the imagination of the child—with dark instincts—without having risen to the consideration that the mother too, as a child, had the same fantasms, and that by beginning to ask the question, by what paths do these fantasms travel to get from the mother to the child, we might put ourselves on

the very track from which they draw their real consequences. ("Jeunesse de Gide," 749–50)[43]

Fantasms pass from "mother" to child as if the two were somehow nonseparable. The frustrating sense of this nonseparability contains another frustration for the child, however obscurely felt—that of being divided: on the one hand, of watching yourself from a place that does not belong to you, and, on the other, of being watched by some stronger presence and being afraid of disappearing if things were otherwise. We are split between two forms of self-identification: identifying "ourselves" with the person being watched, yet also identifying with the alienating place from which that self-constituting watching happens. Slavoj Žižek helpfully characterizes this split, this gap, in the case of obsessional behavior:

> The gap is brought to its extreme with the obsessional neurotic: on the "constituted," imaginary, phenomenal level he is of course caught in the masochistic logic of his compulsive acts, he is humiliating himself . . . organizing his failure, and so on; but the crucial question is . . . how to locate the vicious, superego *gaze for which he is humiliating himself,* for which this obsessional organizing of failure procures pleasure. (*The Sublime Object of Ideology,* 106, my emphasis)

This dispossession of the subject by another gaze is a familiar Lacanian topos. Our signification is guaranteed by another's gaze, but clearly we are not there, or at least we are not entirely present at the place where that other gaze fixes our representation. As soon as the place of our representation is decided, our presence is divided, elsewhere.

> Where the subject sees himself . . . it is not from there that he looks at himself.
> But, certainly, it is in the space of the Other that he sees himself and the point from which he looks at himself is also in that space. (*The Four Fundamental Concepts,* 144)[44]

We are constituted within a landscape that is necessarily other. Both the image we imagine wanting to be and the place from which we see that image make up different facets of our alienation within *the space of another*—in the first instance, as Lacan has it, in *the mother's space,* with "mother" understood collectively. This alienation, this sense of a vacancy searching for a content in the desire of someone else, has a certain inevitability to it. Lacan tries to balance this *alienation* and allow us to approach our vacancy by another path, through a process he calls *separation.*

---

43. Nous avons rangé ces fantasmes dans le tiroir de l'imagination de l'enfant, aux noirs instincts, sans nous être encore élevés jusqu'à la remarque que la mère, elle aussi, enfant, eut les mêmes, et que rapprocher la question à se demander par quel chemin passent les fantasmes pour aller de la mère à l'enfant, nous mettrait peut-être sur la voie même dont ils empruntent leurs incidences effectives.

44. Là où le sujet se voit . . . ce n'est pas là d'où il se regarde.

Mais, certes, c'est dans l'espace de l'Autre qu'il se voit, et le point d'où il se regarde est lui aussi dans cet espace (*Les Quatre Concepts,* 132).

Here is how Žižek characterizes the back-and-forth motion between alienation and separation:

> Today, it is a commonplace that the Lacanian subject is divided. . . . However, the most radical dimension of Lacanian theory lies not in recognizing this fact but in realizing that the big Other, the symbolic order itself, is also *barré*, crossed-out, by a fundamental impossibility, structured around . . . a central lack. Without this lack in the Other, the Other would be a closed structure and the only possibility open to the subject would be his radical alienation in the Other. So it is precisely this lack in the Other which enables the subject to achieve a kind of "de-alienation" called by Lacan *separation:* not in the sense that the subject experiences that now he is separated for ever from the object by the barrier of language, but that *the object is separated from the Other itself,* that the Other itself "hasn't got it" . . . is in itself blocked, desiring. . . . This lack in the Other gives the subject—so to speak—a breathing space, it enables him to avoid the total alienation in the signifier not by filling out his lack but by allowing him to identify himself, his own lack, with the lack in the Other. (*The Sublime Object of Ideology,* 122)

Separation, as Lacan describes it, in fact does not *undo* alienation, does not fill up a sense of vacancy, of dependency on someone else's vision in order to desire; it does not satisfy one's longing to obtain or truly to be an object of some desire. But it does seem to allow one to guard against an annihilating absorption in the gaze of another, a Gribouillesque dissolution into a maternal element. It makes alienation bearable. In Lacan's words:

> *Separare,* to separate—I would point out at once the equivocation of the *se parare,* of the *se parer,* in all the fluctuating meanings it has in French. It means not only to dress oneself, but also to defend oneself, to provide oneself with what one needs to be on one's guard, and I will go further still, and Latinists will bear me out, to the *se parere,* the *s'engendrer,* the *to be engendered,* which is involved here. (214)[45]

A form of defense for that subject that has already experienced the alienating division of coming to representation in a gaze it does not possess, separation is a process by which the experience of lack is shared out—not to be lessened but to be generalized. The child, for instance, Lacan says, experiences separation in the asking of the question, "Il me dit ça, mais qu'est-ce qu'il veut?" ("That's what he says, but what does he want?"). For that question contains the realization that the Other's desire also frustratingly escapes representation, in fact, consistently disappears beneath it. In that question, the child realizes the Other's alienation, symmetrical to the child's own. Subject to representation, the adult also experiences the mortifying experience of not being able to be present within the representation that was to anchor the self. Lacan continues:

> The desire of the Other is apprehended by the subject in that which does not work, in the lacks of the discourse of the Other, and all the child's *whys* reveal not so much

---

45. *Separare,* séparer, j'irai tout de suite à l'équivoque du *se parare,* du *se parer* dans tous les sens fluctuants qu'il a en français, aussi bien s'habiller, que se défendre, se fournir de ce qu'il faut pour vous mettre en garde, et j'irai plus loin encore, ce à quoi m'autorisent les latinistes, au *se parere,* au *s'engendrer* dont il s'agit dans l'occasion (194).

an avidity for the reason of things, as a testing of the adult, a *Why are you telling me this?* ever-resuscitated from its base, which is the enigma of the adult's desire.

Now, to reply to this hold, the subject, like Gribouille, brings the answer of the previous lack, of his own disappearance, which he situates here at the point of lack perceived in the Other. The first object he proposes for this parental desire whose object is unknown is his own loss—*Does he want to lose me?* The phantasy of one's death, of one's disappearance, is the first object that the subject has to bring into play in this dialectic, and he does indeed bring it into play—as we know from innumerable cases, such as in anorexia nervosa. (214–15)[46]

Gribouille here becomes for Lacan exemplary of a child's initial convoluted efforts at separation. Spelling out this example, Lacan complicates the relation of alienation to separation. The one does not complete the other. Rather, the two seem repetitively or cyclically related. One is never finished with them. Further, even though it may seem in various descriptions that separation is a *remedy* for alienation, such an impression must be to some degree incorrect. Gribouille's initial separational steps, for example, are to take *his* perception of his own vacancy, *his* failure to be present in his own representation and then to blend that perception with his perception of the symmetrical suspicion of self-vacancy in his tormenting family members. The unfortunate result is that he *imagines them imagining him disappearing.* He comes up not with something liberating but with a self-destructive enactment of his own fantasy of lack, destruction as an imagined enactment of separation. (He thereby resembles Boris in *Les Faux-Monnayeurs.*)

How are we to understand Gide's pleasure at this self-destruction? In the Sand story, Gribouille of course survives his metamorphosis, floating downstream to a fairy island, where his human shape is restored. He eventually returns to his homeland, but only to repeat, in rather Lacanian and in rather more gruesome fashion, his first watery self-sacrifice—in the second instance throwing himself into a fire and burning to death in order to restore peace to his country. This repetition itself suggests the ongoing, never finished nature of this movement between alienation and separation. When he returns to his homeland after 100 years in the land of the fairies, his tormenting parents and siblings long gone, the resourcefulness of the fantasy of vacancy reveals itself in the way the story has *the social order itself* reissue the call to Gribouille's self-immolation:

> "Speak, dearest godmother," cried Gribouille; "to ensure your victory and to save this suffering land, there is nothing I would be incapable of suffering."

46. Le désir de l'Autre est appréhendé par le sujet dans ce qui ne colle pas, dans les manques du discours de l'Autre, et tous les *pourquoi?* de l'enfant témoignent moins d'une avidité de la raison des choses, qu'ils ne constituent une mise à l'épreuve de l'adulte, un *pourquoi est-ce que tu me dis ça?* toujours resuscité de son fonds, qui est l'énigme du désir de l'adulte.

Or, à répondre à cette prise, le sujet, tel Gribouille, apporte la réponse du manque antécédent, de sa propre disparition, qu'il vient ici situer au point de manque aperçu dans l'Autre. Le premier objet qu'il propose à ce désir parental dont l'objet est inconnu, c'est sa propre perte — *Veut-il me perdre?* Le fantasme de sa mort, de sa disparition, est le premier objet que le sujet a à mettre en jeu dans cette dialectique, et il le met en effet — nous le savons par mille faits, ne serait-ce que par l'anorexie mentale (194–95).

"Even death?" said the Queen of the Meadows, in a voice so sad that the bats, the lizards and the spiders sharing Gribouille's cell all woke in a cold sweat.

"Should it be death," Gribouille responded; "let the will of the celestial powers be done! So long as you, dearest godmother, remember me with affection, and so long as, on the Island of the Flowers, they sometimes sing a little couplet in memory of Gribouille, I will be content." (Sand, 74)[47]

The escalation of the Gribouille fantasy, beginning as dissolution in water to escape the eyes of the family, then becoming consumption by fire to quell social violence, suggestively recalls the piggybacking in Gide's African journals of a public, political quest on a personal, psychic one—a blending that regularly produces moments of crisis (for instance, as we will see again, in the word *transport:* simultaneously a lyrical, subjective ecstasy and a reference to the necessity of being carried and having one's goods carried, by people who would rather be doing something else, and who sometimes die in the course of this labor). What the Gribouille story evinces is a strange movement *from* the experience of alienation within and separation from the maternal or familial gaze, on the one hand, *to* the same cycle of alienation and separation in a wide sociopolitical field, on the other. The movement is not always most helpfully construed as a step forward, as a linear progress. It needs also to be understood as a reenactment. This reenactment of alienation/separation, a rhythmically repeated one, is productive of the frustration I have been arguing is to be found at the center of the writing of Gide's *Voyage au Congo* and *Retour du Tchad.* Every time that frustration is generated, one hears echoes on both a political and a personal plane, finally forcing us to consider that one of the characteristics of Gide's writing is to insist on a perception of these two planes as *having always been* inextricable.

Further, one of the major interests of these African journals lies in their explicit, almost exhaustive repetition of this fantastic confusion, as if through that repetition the fantasy and the frustration *could* be exhausted, entirely played out; as if an absolutely new political (and personal) relation could thereby be found; as if, remembering Lacan's almost apocalyptic promise toward the end of the *Four Fundamental Concepts* seminar, it would be possible to exist with the Other finally in a way that didn't insist on the aggressivity and alienation of identification:

> To break through the plane of identification is possible. Anyone who has lived through the analytic experience with me to the end of the training analysis knows that what I am saying is true. . . . It is in as much as the analyst's desire . . . tends in a direction that is the exact opposite of identification, that the breaking through of the identificatory plane is possible, through the mediation of the separation of the

47. — Parlez, ma chère marraine, s'écria Gribouille; pour vous assurer la victoire et pour sauver ce malheureux pays, il n'y a rien que je ne sois capable de souffrir.

— Et si c'était la mort? dit la reine des prés d'une voix si triste que les chauves-souris, les lézards et les araignées du cachot de Gribouille en furent réveillés tout en sueur.

— Si c'est la mort, répondit Gribouille, que la volonté des puissances célestes soit faite! Pourvu que vous vous souvenez de moi avec affection, ma chère marraine, et que, dans l'île des Fleurs, on chante quelquefois un petit couplet à la mémoire du pauvre Gribouille, je serai content.

subject in experience. The experience of the subject is thus brought back to the plane at which, from the reality of the unconscious, the drive may be made present. (273–74)[48]

One of the goals of the *Four Fundamental Concepts* seminar is to sketch an understanding of the unconscious as something that makes its appearance through a repetitive pulsation, a pulsation related to *la pulsion,* the drive, something that challenges the stability, the continuity of representations and identifications. In representations there is necessarily a failure to be present. The pain of division this failure provokes could lead, Lacan suggests, to an effort to grasp in experience the pulse itself. For the experience of that queer pulse is what allows the perception of *the continual movement between alienation and separation.* The perception of that movement is what gives some consistency to the subject, consistency not based on imaginary identifications, not occupying the locus of aggressivity.

In an interesting autobiographical moment in this seminar, a Gidean or Gribouillesque moment, one might say, Lacan provides an intriguing example of the effort to perceive the pulsation rather than to achieve stasis within an identification:

> It's a true story. I was in my early twenties or thereabouts—and at that time, of course, being a young intellectual, I wanted desperately to get away, see something different, throw myself into something practical, something physical, in the country say, or at the sea. One day, I was on a small boat, with a few people from a family of fishermen in a small port. . . . We were waiting for the moment to pull in the nets [when] an individual known as Petit Jean, that's what we called him—like all his family he disappeared quite promptly from tuberculosis, which at that time was a constant threat to the whole of that social class—this Petit-Jean pointed out to me something floating on the surface of the waves. It was a small can, a sardine can. It floated there in the sun, a witness to the canning industry, which we, in fact, were supposed to supply. It glittered in the sun. And Petit-Jean said to me—*You see that can? See it? Well, it doesn't see you!* . . .
>
> The point of this little story, as it had occurred to my partner, the fact that he found it so funny and I less so, derives from the fact that, if I am told a story like that one, it is because I, at that moment—as I appeared to those fellows who were earning their lives with great difficulty, in the struggle with what for them was a pitiless nature—I was a rather hilarious, unspeakable spectacle. In short, I was rather out of place in the picture. And it was because I felt this that I was not terribly amused at hearing myself addressed in this humorous, ironical way. (95–96)[49]

48. Ce franchissement du plan de l'identification est possible. Tout un chacun de ceux qui ont vécu jusqu'au bout avec moi, dans l'analyse didactique, l'expérience analytique sait que ce que je dis est vrai . . . C'est pour autant que le désir de l'analyste . . . tend dans le sens exactement contraire à l'identification, que le franchissement du plan de l'identification est possible, par l'intermédiaire de la séparation du sujet dans l'expérience. L'expérience du sujet est ainsi ramenée au plan où peut se présentifier, de la réalité de l'inconscient, la pulsion (245–46).

49. Cette historie est vraie. Elle date de quelque chose comme mes vingt ans — et dans ce temps, bien sûr, jeune intellectuel, je n'avais d'autre souci que d'aller ailleurs, de me baigner dans quelque pratique directe, rurale, chasseresse, voire marine. Un jour, j'étais sur un petit bateau, avec quelques personnes, membres d'une famille de pêcheurs dans un petit port . . . nous attendions le moment de retirer les filets {quand} le nommé Petit-Jean, nous l'appellerons ainsi — il est, comme toute sa famille, disparu très promptement du fait de la tuberculose, qui était à ce

Around the same time, then, that Gide is traveling in Africa, the young Lacan is indulging in his own complicated form of tourism. If, in the Gribouille story, the moment of psychic trauma (drowning to escape the family) and the moment of social trauma (burning to escape/cure the social) are spread out over time, in Lacan's story, as in Gide's travels, the two are carefully overlapped. The psychic splitting that produces alienation is clear. The young intellectual's image of himself as close to nature, close to the people, close to the food source, this ideal, imaginary and masterful image is brutally destroyed by Petit-Jean's Lacanian observation: "You see the can. The can couldn't be bothered to look at you." Petit-Jean leads Lacan's attention to a particular object, daring him to focus on it, as Gide focuses on the seized butterfly or the bisected termitary or the mason-fly's construction, and then having made Lacan focus in on this socially charged object—not a fish, but a discarded can of fish, not in a pure, aesthetic ocean, but in a polluted ocean, the ocean as social field—laughs at Lacan for focusing. "Si ça a un sens que Petit-Jean me dise que la boîte ne me voit pas, c'est parce que, en un certain sens, tout de même, elle me regarde," Lacan suggests rather untranslatably, playing on the difference between *voir* (to see) and *regarder* (to look at) and on the phrase *ça me regarde:* that matters to me, it concerns me. "If it made sense that Petit-Jean told me that the can wasn't seeing me, it's because, in a manner of speaking, the can concerned me/was looking at me." The can represents in a flash the evanescence of Lacan's self-representation, not only visually, but socially as well.

Visually, having imagined himself in control of his representation, the young Lacan is reminded that by the very fact that his representation takes its place within a *field* of vision, he is alienated from that representation. "Le tableau, certes, est dans mon oeil. Mais moi, je suis dans le tableau." ("Certainly, the tableau is in my eye. But I am also part of the tableau.") The field of vision in which I take up the place of representation encompasses me in a way that belies any pretense at mastery. The flash, the pulsing light reflected off the sardine can stands for this "depth of field" in which Lacan's image both comes into being and becomes "inénarrable," hilarious, incredible, untellable, insignificant.

Socially speaking, one might ask: Why is it a sardine can? Why, when, as the theory has it, the subject who is Lacan is the evanescent one, the one who is "fading," should it be Petit-Jean who, like Gribouille, actually "disappears"? What

---

moment-là la maladie vraiment ambiante dans laquelle toute cette couche sociale se déplaçait — me montre un quelque-chose qui flottait à la surface des vagues. C'était une petite boîte, et même, précisons, une boîte à sardines. Elle flottait là dans le soleil, témoignage de l'industrie de la conserve, que nous étions, par ailleurs, chargés d'alimenter. Elle miroitait dans le soleil. Et Petit-Jean me dit — *Tu vois, cette boîte? Tu la vois? Eh bien, elle, elle te voit pas!* . . .

    La portée de cette petite histoire, telle qu'elle venait de surgir dans l'invention de mon partenaire, le fait qu'il la trouvât si drôle, et moi, moins, tient à ce que, si on me raconte une histoire comme celle-là, c'est tout de même parce que moi, à ce moment-là — tel que je me suis dépeint, avec ces types qui gagnaient péniblement leur existence, dans l'étreinte avec ce qui était pour eux la rude nature — moi, je faisais tableau d'une façon assez inénarrable. Pour tout dire, je faisais tant soit peu tache dans le tableau. Et c'est bien de le sentir qui fait que rien qu'à m'entendre interpeller ainsi, dans cette humoristique, ironique, histoire, je ne la trouve pas si drôle que ça (88–89).

kind of an elegy for Petit-Jean is this? The sardine can question seems the easiest to answer. If Lacan had imagined this Breton interlude as an escape from his life (as Gide might have imagined his African trip), such an imagining—that there is an outside to the social realm in which one moves, that one does not carry the social with one as one travels—is convincingly belied. The Breton fishing industry keeps Lacan in sardines when he's back in Paris. Or to be as specific as the text is, the fishing industry capitalizes on Lacan's desire to be kept in sardines when he's in Paris. The sardine can, representing this point of view, sees nothing of *either* Lacan or Petit-Jean, who are both tokens within an economic game and thus both disappear, although only Lacan lives to tell the story. In fact, whatever elegiac, identificatory awkwardness remains in the telling could be construed as Lacan once again, repeatedly, like Gribouille, offering up the possibility of his own disappearance in the face of the unknown desire of the Other, "sa propre perte," the pulsation of incomplete alienation and incomplete separation, a pulsation reenergized by the unaccountable loss of Petit-Jean.

One of the parallels to be drawn between Gide and Lacan has to do with the elegiac burden we can observe them both carrying. I will concentrate on this parallel in a few pages, but first address here another. For the presence of this elegiac burden indicates the failure of a certain fantasy of tourism, a failure our two tourists share. The fantasy would be one of trading in one's habitual subjective landscape for another, thereby shrugging off the alienation that troubles one's social insertion. Yet, if one accepts, as both Gide and Lacan perhaps do, that a certain alienation is the necessary corollary of any social insertion, then such alienation is likely to travel along wherever one goes, though it may well shift shapes as it goes.

Such a shifting, however, could in certain circumstances be a great relief. Imagine trading the constant pressures of homophobia, for instance, for some new alienation. Such a hoped-for, if necessarily troubled, liberation perhaps energizes such passages as the one in which Gide imagines the ecstasy of disappearing into the African scenery and becomes explicit in his final text, *Ainsi soit-il,* when he expresses the wish that on his deathbed he remember the African boy Mala's face: "Sweet little Mala! On my deathbed it is your amused laugh and your joy that I should most like to see again" (126).[50] For among the many things Gide would remember about his experience with Mala would be the lack of any condemning social gaze surrounding it. Having noticed Mala, but not being sure how to approach him, Gide finally timorously asks Adoum for help:

> For, after all, I was never alone, and the least thing I did was seen by the whole troop of porters. . . . Adoum found my embarrassment hard to understand. He asserted that every one of the porters would consider it quite natural that some evening I should ask one of the two pages to "come and wield the punkah" under my mosquito

50. Gentil Mala! sur mon lit de mort, c'est ton rire amusé, c'est ta joie, que je voudrais revoir encore (1223).

✱ Proust: homosexual ≠ guilt

net. Let it be quickly added that it is impossible to see through the fabric of a mosquito net. It should also be added that the heat was stifling, so that the desire to have one's sleep fanned by a punkah could seem almost natural. And finally let it be added that what seemed most natural was what the expression "come and wield the punkah" signified in reality, so that no one in our group was struck by it. (125)[51]

Now all the caveats we observed in the analyses of sexual encounters in chapter 1 —in particular as to the hidden (or not so hidden) asymmetries of this particular liberatory encounter—clearly function here as well. The social meanings of the encounter for Gide and for Mala are not reconcilable; the politics of the encounter are not the same for each of them. As the encounter falls into the differing social webs through which it might achieve representation, part of the web that con- structs for Gide his feeling of relief—of dealienation as regards the prevailing social understanding of his sexuality—includes his social position as a gay travel- ing Frenchman, a position Mala hardly shares, a specific relief of which Mala himself may have no need and no comprehension. Just as the flash of a sardine can interrupts any chance Lacan imagined he had of truly leaving behind his bourgeois preoccupations, so the pulse of frustration Gide's writing so scru- pulously registers would somehow interrupt and render impermanent any moment of imagined liberation from his own sexual subjectivity and its accompanying social consequences—all forming a part of his identity he could hardly hope to separate off from the rest of the baggage he was carrying along with him.

Transport

> This question of porterage, and even of the *tipoye*-bearers is ruining the trip for me; nowhere along the way can I stop think- ing of it.[52]
>
> —Gide, *Voyage au Congo*

Gide's mother appears in the very first journal entry of the *Voyage au Congo*. On board the *Asie*, on the way to Africa, Gide is feeling a bit queasy, and in his discomfort his thoughts circle back to his childhood. "On ne bercera jamais assez les enfants," he writes. "Children will never be rocked enough."

> I even think it would be a good plan to calm them and send them to sleep by means of a special pitching- and tossing-apparatus. As for me, I was brought up according

---

51. Car enfin je n'étais jamais seul : le moindre de mes gestes avait pour témoin la pleine cohorte des porteurs . . . Adoum eut quelque peine à s'expliquer ma gêne : il m'affirma qu'il n'y aurait pas un de ces porteurs qui ne trouvât tout naturel que je demande, un soir, à l'un des deux pages de « venir faire pankas » sous ma moustiquaire. Ajoutons vite que le tulle d'une moustiquaire est complètement imperméable aux regards. Ajoutons aussi que la chaleur était étouffante, au point que le souhait d'éventer le sommeil par les battements d'un pankas pouvait paraître presque naturel. Ajoutons enfin que ce qui paraissait surtout naturel, c'était ce que l'expression : « venir faire pankas » signifiait en réalité; de sorte qu'il n'y eut personne de notre troupe pour s'en étonner (1222).

52. Cette question du portage, et même celle des tipoyeurs, me gâte le voyage; tout le long de la route je ne puis cesser d'y penser (123–24).

to rational methods and by my mother's orders never slept in beds that were not
fixed; thanks to which, I am particularly liable to seasickness. (3)[53]

The by now familiar pulse of aggression at maternal influence is clear here.
Presciently, Gide imagines an apparatus a bit like the *tipoye* he has not yet seen, in
which he will soon be carried: a contraption "profondément bousculatoire," seda-
tory in effect—a covered chair, suspended by two poles, carried by four Africans.[54]
Intermittently carried through Africa, rather as one might *porter un enfant,* Gide
will thus find his relation to the maternal almost kinesthetically resuscitated by the
ancillary movements of various modes of transport. That relation provides the
structure of frustration at a pleasure glimpsed, but never understood, or to the extent it is understood, understood to involve a dispersal impossible to confront,
impossible to enact. As this frustration, this pulse of aggression, even this pulse of
love, repeats itself during the Congo voyage, it seems to involve more and more a
never-articulated sense that the trip itself is structured around a necessary failure of
pleasure because of Gide's own limited positionality as a subject of colonial power,
a positionality he cannot shake off, no more than he can fully perceive its contours,
a positionality whose frustration gives added impetus to fantasies of dissolution as
escape.

When Gide stumbles across (more accurately, drives by) a group of women
repairing a road—apparently exclusively for his car—the maternal presence
comes to confront directly the question of how he gets through Africa:

> This miserable troop of cattle was streaming under the rain. A number of them were
> breastfeeding while working. Every twenty yards or so there were huge pits by the
> side of the road, generally about ten feet deep; it was out of these that the poor
> wretches had dug the sandy earth with which to bank the road, and this *without
> proper tools.* It has happened more than once that the loose earth has given way and
> buried the women and children who were working at the bottom of the pit. . . . We
> learned that the militiaman who is their overseer had made them work all night in
> order to repair the damage done by a recent storm and to enable us to pass. (67)[55]

Now the argument usually runs that yes, indeed, building roads and railroads costs
many lives and disrupts local cultures, but this is all necessary for the growth of
commerce, the future profit of the land. Thus, Gide comments in an early footnote
on the usefulness of the railroad between Matadi and Kinshasa in the Belgian
Congo, the construction of which he notes Conrad describing in *Heart of Darkness:* "There is no exaggeration in his picture; it is cruelly exact; but what lightens

53. Et même je serais d'avis qu'on usât, pour les calmer, les endormir, d'appareils profondément bousculatoires.
Pour moi, qui fus élevé selon des méthodes rationnelles, je ne connus jamais, de par ordre de ma mère, que des lits
fixes; grâce à quoi je suis aujourd'hui particulièrement sujet au mal de mer (15).

54. Gide describes the *tipoye* in a footnote to his entry of October 28 (96/68).

55. Ce pauvre bétail ruisselait sous l'averse. Nombre d'entre elles allaitaient tout en travaillant. Tous les vingt
mètres environ, aux côtés de la route, un vaste trou, profond de trois mètres le plus souvent; c'est de là que *sans outils
appropriés,* ces misérables travailleuses avaient extrait la terre sablonneuse pour les remblais. Il était arrivé plus d'une
fois que le sol sans consistance s'effondrât, ensevelissant les femmes et les enfants qui travaillaient au fond du trou . . .
Nous avons appris que le milicien qui les surveille les avait fait travailler toute la nuit pour réparer les dégâts d'un
récent orage et permettre notre passage (95).

its gloom is the success of the project which in his pages appears so vain. Costly as the establishment of this railroad may have been in money and human lives, it now exists to the immense profit of the Belgian colony—and of our own" (11).[56] At the very moment Gide was passing through the region, the French were building their own railroad, from Brazzaville to the ocean, on the other side of the river from the Belgian railroad that had been completed a quarter-century earlier. Durosay criticizes Gide and Allégret for not noticing and commenting sufficiently on the crisis provoked by this construction.[57] For this railroad, too, was costly in lives of Africans "recruited" for the labor. In the description of one historian:

> The announcement of a recruitment . . . caused "panicked terror" since it amounted, at least until 1928, to a probable "death sentence." In total, the official count was at least 10,200 deaths from 1921 to 1928, on the trip to the worksite as well as at it, plus 1,300 in 1929 and 2,600 from 1930 to 1932. Taking into account deaths masked as desertions, at least 20,000 men paid with their lives for the construction of the railroad. (Coquery-Vidrovitch, 195)

Gide's commentary on the issue comes long after he is out of the region, staying with his friend Marcel de Coppet, who is the French colonial administrator at Fort-Archembault.[58] One of Coppet's duties is to arrange to send groups of men off to work on the railroad. While Gide stays with him, the militia rounds up about 1500 recruits, 1000 of whom will eventually march south toward the worksite:

> The Brazzaville–Ocean railroad is a terrifying consumer of human lives. . . . The death rate has gone beyond even the most pessimistic predictions. To how many more deaths will the colony owe its future well-being? Of all the obligations incumbent upon the administration, that of recruiting "volontary enlistees" is certainly the most painful. But it is in this that the confidence that Marcel de Coppet has managed to inspire in this black people—who feel loved by him—manifests itself. (passage not included in published translation)[59]

The invocation of love here appears unseemly, a disguise, a cover for an unstatable discomfiture arising from one's inevitable participation in a social apparatus one would prefer to be outside. Gide's and Coppet's positions here are structurally

---

56. Aucune outrance dans ses peintures : elles sont cruellement exactes; mais ce qui les désassombrit, c'est la réussite de ce projet qui, dans son livre, paraît si vain. Si coûteux qu'ait pu être, en argent et en vies humaines, l'établissment de cette voie ferrée, à présent elle existe pour l'immense profit de la colonie belge — et de la nôtre (22).

57. See Durosay, Introduction to Allégret, *Carnets du Congo*, 28.

58. Even this commentary, Durosay points out, was present in neither Gide's manuscript nor its typescript. It appeared when the journal was first published in *La Nouvelle Revue Française* before appearing in book form. But there is also a brief mention of the question while Gide is in Brazzaville at the outset of his voyage: "La question de chemin de fer de Brazzaville à Pointe-Noire serait particulièrement intéressante à étudier" (29). The English translation skips this particular paragraph, but, strangely, includes the footnote attached to it, where Gide, overwhelmed by social issues such as the question of mortality rates among the railway workers wishes he had merely gone to study the termites.

59. Le chemin de fer Brazzaville-Océan est un effroyable consommateur de vies humaines . . . La mortalité a dépassé les prévisions les plus pessimistes. A combien de décès nouveaux la colonie devra-t-elle son bien-être futur? De toutes les obligations qui incombent à l'administration, celle du recrutement des « engagés volontaires » est assurément la plus pénible. Mais c'est ici que se manifeste la confiance que Marcel de Coppet a su inspirer à ce peuple noir, qui se sent aimé par lui (200–201).

similar to the one of Lacan, the sardine-eating city boy, who, no matter what self-representation he imagines, nonetheless plays an alienating, implicating part in the profitable, yet life-consuming, "industrie de la conserve."[60]

The haunting by Petit-Jean acted out in the sardine can passage finds its parallel here, too, in the patina of good will, confidence, love that attempts to camouflage the economic interests sending these Africans off to work and perhaps to die. In the passage about the road repair done by women, some of them nursing, the gravelike pits from which dirt is dug and in which women are sometimes buried alive, are similar haunting markers. "Cette route meurtrière," as Gide calls it, "this murderous road," seems even harder to assimilate to a discourse of necessary amelioration, as Gide clearly realizes that the road is traveled only by the representatives of the Compagnie Forestière, on their way to market once a month—by those representatives and by *Gide* of course, who, by traveling the road, underscores the links he would prefer to ignore between himself and private European economic interests. Indeed, to the extent that the road is repaired *only for Gide,* the very fact that he is there to see the sight and subsequently testify to it makes that testimony inculpatory—his very passage causing the event to whose horrors he testifies.

It was apparently a touchy point with the Compagnie Forestière to suggest that they exploited labor for unnecessary roadworks. M. Weber addresses this point at some length in his letter objecting to Gide's testimony:

> I'll pass rapidly over the story about the rebuilding of the Bambio road. The Compagnie Forestière does not itself make decisions about works of this kind. . . . It is ridiculous to say that this road serves only the Company's automobile. A road is the indispensable means of doing away with porterage—and porterage usually accomplished by women while their husbands dally in the charms of idleness is a greater evil than the effort to construct and maintain a suitable route. . . . One must have a singular imagination to reproach the Compagnie Forestière for having equipped its region with the means for modern transport, one of the most practically useful and salutary ameliorations in those lands where the only available beast of burden is man. (*Voyage au Congo,* appendix, 467–69)

Such a passage speaks all too well for itself, and Gide has no problem defending his assertions against its sophistries. But one understands the not terribly veiled discomfort of Gide in having to reassert: "Beyond the car we were in, I don't know that it [the road] had ever served, could ever have served any other car except that of the Company's representative." Only two cars have ever used the road, that of the Forestière's flunkey, and that of Gide's party—for whom women stayed up all

---

60. Coppet, friend of both Martin du Gard and Gide, apparently suffered a career setback as a result of the publication of Gide's *Voyage au Congo* and *Retour du Tchad*. Rumor had it that Coppet supplied Gide with the information he used to embarrass the concessionary companies and the government, that he manipulated Gide into expressing his own "disloyal" opinion, and that as a result he damaged his prospects, began being overlooked for advancement, for choice appointments, etc. See Martin du Gard's letters to Gide on February 9, 1928, February 14, 1928, and May 20, 1928.

night in the rain making repairs. What precisely distinguishes Gide's touristic exploitation of the colonial apparatus from that of the Forestière's representative? Clearly, his testimony does; but just as clearly, like Lacan in Brittany, he is aware of "faisant tache dans le tableau," and just as clearly, his fantasy of sitting on a termitary and disappearing into pure vision constitutes a displacement of other too numerous disappearances around him:

> Our boatmen are settling themselves on the sand-bank and preparing for the night, which threatens to be cold. There are nearly forty degrees' difference between the day and the night. And I am speaking of the *shade* temperature; but they toil in the full sun and with no clothes on. I cannot understand how they withstand it. (But some of them do not.) (212)[61]

In a complex moment of condensation, late in the text, a group of his African porters make Gide's discomfiture all too literal for him. Gide never portrays Africans speaking to him with Petit-Jean's intention to debunk and displace, but this group of porters manages the trick nevertheless. On and off throughout the trip, Gide and Allégret have porter problems: difficulty finding new ones, difficulty keeping those engaged content enough to continue; guilt at their very use, guilt at disrupting their lives, forcing them so far from home. Then there are the linguistic difficulties involved in simply communicating. A few smiles and kind words, Gide says, have calmed the present bunch down.

> Yesterday evening they refused to go any farther. And now, in their enthusiasm, they declare they are willing to go with us as far as Douala. One old man, who was carrying the heavy cinema packing-case, was seized with a fit of excitement [*crise de lyrisme*]. He began rushing wildly about in every direction, laughing and shouting; off into the bush and then back again; spinning round on his own axis; darting up to a tree he caught sight of and striking it three times with a javelin he had in his hand. Had he gone mad? Not at all; it was merely lyrical excitement. What we used to call "savage ecstasy" [*le transport sauvage*] when we were children. And at times the *tipoye*-bearers—to get a *matabiche*, no doubt—began thanking me, either separately or in chorus. They are no longer satisfied with calling me "Governor." They shout: "Thank you, Government, thank you!" (301–2)[62]

This happens during one of the most arduous sections of the trip, toward its end, in the Cameroon, where, as we have read, "roads for automobiles are particularly difficult to establish" and thus where porterage "remains necessary." It is ex-

---

61. Sur le banc de sable, nos rameurs s'organisent pour la nuit qui s'annonce froide. Vingt degrés de différence entre le jour et la nuit. Et je parle de la température à l'ombre; mais eux travaillent et peinent en plein soleil et toujours complètement nus. Je ne comprends pas comment ils résistent. (Mais certains ne résistent pas.) (269).

62. Hier soir, ils refusaient d'aller plus loin. A présent, par enthousiasme, ils se déclarent prêts à nous accompagner jusqu'à Douala. Un vieux, chargé de la lourde caisse du cinéma, est pris d'une crise de lyrisme. Il se met à courir dans tous les sens, à travers la brousse, en riant et criant; il tourne sur place, et, quand il voit un tronc d'arbre, court à lui, menaçant, et le frappe de trois coups de la javeline qu'il porte en main. Est-il devenu fou? Non. C'est du lyrisme, simplement. Ce que nous appelions, enfants : « le transport sauvage ». Et, par instants les tipoyeurs, sans doute pour appeler le matabiche, me remercient, soit séparément, soit en chœur. M'appeler « Gouverneur » ne leur suffit même plus. Ils crient « Merci, Gouvernement, merci. » (367).

tremely hot. An old man goes lyrical and runs around, in transport, with cameras and film equipment on his back. A chorus of people gather flatteringly around Gide and call him "Government," leading him in fact to reflect on how miserably low the government rates for porters are and to indicate that he and Marc work to remunerate their porters more richly than the government requires. An old man, while carrying a camera on his back, turns lyrically—*une scène à tourner,* one imagines, a scene worthy of being filmed. Transported, he is also the camera's transporter, doubtless creating a slight worry as to its safety, as it, too, turns lyrically on his back, unable to film his spontaneity precisely because he is still carrying it. Through his porterage any possibility of the camera being securely imagined as an innocent eye, outside the colonial apparatus, is carefully effaced. Alongside him, a chorus of other slightly importunate—but justifiably so—porters, hoping for tips, unwittingly, synechdochally confirm Government Gide's frustration at being unable to enjoy Africa because of who he is seen to be, who he sees himself to be.

Why would Gide choose to call the actions of this particular porter—perhaps somewhat enervated after a day of walking in remarkable heat carrying a load of probably around 40 pounds—a "crise de lyrisme?" Associating this behavior with some form of lyricism hints at a tentative, even fearful, identification with this older porter, who somehow ironically fulfills Gide's desire both to be the spectacle and to see/film it, to escape alienation by collapsing gaze and object into the same point. Such an ironic fulfillment of Gide's mission is possible because of the difficulty of establishing automobile transport uniformly throughout the colonies. A bit further on, porters are no longer necessary. Gide will finish the trip in a car—obviating for the last few days the "necessity" of porterage, and also leaving behind this strange, cruel lyricism as part of a colonial history whose transformation he is both witnessing and furthering.

On board the *Asie* again, about to leave for France, frustrated already to be back in the world of Europeans without having fully, lastingly taken in Africa, Gide worries about paying the boys who have accompanied him and about getting them home safely. He will buy them a ticket back down the coast to a place near his starting point and leave them plenty of cash, hoping they don't lose or misuse it as they make their way back to their homes:

> With four hundred francs and the ticket to Matadi as well, I hope they will not be held up for want of money. But I am terrified at the idea that they may be robbed of it, or gamble it away; and we agreed that they were to hand it over to M.M. until the day they leave (the 15th). But when we got on board the *Asie,* where they came to see us off, I caught them in the act of investing in an umbrella apiece, at the price of thirty-five francs. I arrived just in time to stop them. (374)[63]

63. Avec 400 francs, en plus du billet jusqu'à Matadi, j'espère qu'ils ne resteront pas en panne. Pourtant je tremble qu'ils ne se laissent voler, ou qu'ils ne jouent, et nous convenons qu'ils confieront à M. M. leur fortune jusqu'au jour du départ (le 15). Mais sur le pont de l'*Asie,* où nous allons nous embarquer et où ils nous accompagnent, je les surprends en train de se payer chacun un parapluie de 35 francs. J'arrive juste à temps pour les retenir (447).

One final reminder of economic disparity, one final "wise," paternal, economic intervention, a final attempt at love—frustrated. When Gide, on his return, weeps in Martin du Gard's presence, we might consider that it is this frustration that continues to do its work.

CHAPTER 6

SEXUALITY, POLITICS, AND CULTURE: GIDE'S TRIP TO THE SOVIET UNION

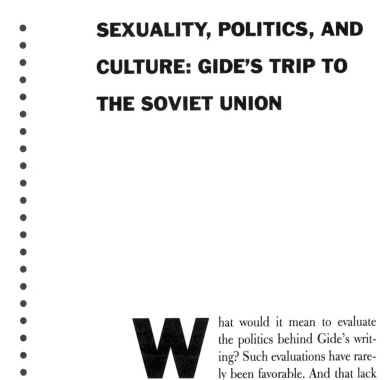

hat would it mean to evaluate the politics behind Gide's writing? Such evaluations have rarely been favorable. And that lack of favorable evaluation has often been due to an unspoken, or slyly, softly spoken critique of Gide's sexual relations. How might we discuss sexuality and politics in Gide differently, allowing ourselves to understand them as related, and yet not giving way to those plots that so easily see in most sexual relations between men merely a *reflection* (often an uncritical or craven one) of larger political structures? Adorno, for example, in "Freudian Theory and the Pattern of Fascist Propaganda" is willing to blend together fascism's "archaism" ("As a rebellion against civilization, fascism is not simply the reoccurrence of the archaic but its reproduction in and by civilization itself" [122]) with its exploitation of "unconscious homosexuality," thereby implying an archaic, atavistic, anticivil impulse within same-sex masculine desire. He comments that in German fascism, "the borderline between overt and repressed homosexuality, just as that between overt and repressed sadism, was much more fluent than in liberal middle-class society" (178n). Adorno's analysis here decontextualizes homosexuality and thereby essentializes its political content in a way that more extensive cultural analysis would not bear out. Indeed, later in this chapter we will be able to read a different account of the political potential of homosexuality out of one of Adorno's more autobiographical essays.

Alongside Adorno's decontextualizing abstractions, we might place another way of relating homosexuality and politics current at Gide's time. Consider the response given by the antiwar socialist novelist Henri Barbusse to an inquiry conducted in 1926 by the journal *Les Marges*. *Les Marges* solicited responses to three questions: Have you noticed that the literary preoccupation with homosexuality has increased since the war? Does this have an influence on morality, and is it bad for art? If this tendency should be combatted, by what means; or if tolerated, for what reasons? Barbusse replied:

> In my estimation, this perversion of a natural instinct, like many other perversions, is an indication of the profound decadence of a certain part of contemporary society. In every epoch, signs of decadence have manifested themselves in refinements and anomalies in sensations, impressions, and sentiments. The indulgence with which certain writers place their talents in the service of questions of this kind, at the same time as the old world—on the road to ruin or revolution—suffers intense economic and social crises, does little to honor this decadent phalanx of intellectuals. That indulgence can only reinforce the scorn that the healthy and youthful popular power feels for these representatives of sickly and artificial doctrines, and all this will only hasten, so I hope, the hour of anger and rebirth.[1]

Neither Adorno nor Barbusse leaves much room to maneuver for the writer who would try to link leftist politics and alternative sexualities. Suppose we add another voice to theirs, the voice of Daniel Guérin, from one of his autobiographical texts, *Le Feu du sang: Autobiographie politique et charnelle*. Guérin unabashedly asserts, in pleasing opposition to these other unnuanced positions:

> My transformation in the direction of socialism was not objective, of an intellectual order; rather it was much more subjective, physical, issuing from the senses and the heart. It is not from books, it's from myself, in the first instance, through years of sexual frustrations, it's from contact with oppressed young men that I learned to hate the established order. A carnal quest led me to overleap social barriers. Beyond the seduction of those bodies, hardened through effort, I looked for camaraderie. That camaraderie, multiplied a hundredfold, is what I was looking for in socialism. (13–14)[2]

Taking Adorno, Barbusse, and Guérin together, we can begin to see the complex discursive field in which Gide would be writing as a gay communist and as a member of that decadent phalanx to which Barbusse refers. Could Gide—would he want to?—affirm so direct a link as Guérin asserts between an initial sexual desire and a concomitant political position?

At the outset of this chapter on Gide's communist adventure, we might do

1. *Les Marges* published thirty or so replies to its queries in March and April 1926. This inquiry has been commented on by Barbedette and Carassou in *Paris Gay 1925*, 125–28.

2. On Guérin, see the article by Peter Sedgwick. See also the interview with him in Barbedette and Carassou, *Paris Gay 1925*, 43–55. See also the preface Guérin wrote to his edition of selections from the writings of Charles Fourier, *Vers la liberté en amour*, where he tries to theorize the relation between homosexuality and the abolition of class boundaries, esp. 25–35.

well to reassert some of the principles that have guided the analyses of the previous chapters; to wit, that there is no politics specific to, inherent in, sexuality "itself." Sexuality "itself" does not simply mirror certain preexistent, more centrally "political" forms. When we say that sexuality is necessarily political, we mean that on the one hand it is so *contextually* and on another hand that it is political *differently* from, say, the way class, race, or gender are political. Any sexual act, any representation of sexuality, any assumption of a sexual identity, takes on a political cast that has something in it that is *specific* to its sexuality. This specificity and its effects are never merely reflective of other political categories, even as they inflect and are inflected by them. The reception of Gide's communist commitment, along with the writing and reception of his book about his trip to the Stalinist Soviet Union make this clear.

What Ever Happened to André Gide?

In 1965 Paul de Man published an article, "Whatever Happened to André Gide?" in the *New York Review of Books* and spent several paragraphs of it discussing Gide's *Les Nourritures terrestres* in a slightly disapproving tone. "Bourgeois society is being rejected here not because it is morally wrong, but because it is restrictively moral" (135). A look at de Man's analysis can help us to review the traditional terms and tones within which Gide's politics has been understood. In his article de Man attempts to establish the relationship in Gide's work between politics, poetics, and sexuality. De Man's opening claim is that Gide, unlike many of his symbolist and modernist counterparts, was not interested in the "contemplation of his own consciousness"; instead, he was concerned with "the moment at which he reaches out for other people, in a gesture prompted by a combination of curiosity and interest" (132). A suitable moment to contemplate, no doubt, for someone trying to understand moral or political engagement, but the conjunction of curiosity and interest, de Man will reveal, is a dangerous one.

Speaking of Gide's *Paludes (Marshlands)*, a satire of aestheticism (and thereby an appropriate opening gambit for a young author such as Gide, out to be morally or politically engaged), de Man compliments Gide on the aptness of his technique: *paludisme*

> The hero, who bears the Virgilian name of Tityre, is a totally committed aesthete whose only purpose in life is the writing of a rather unpromising but rarefied literary text entitled "Marshlands." . . . The project itself is never undermined or ridiculed from the inside: the passages from the book that are being quoted are not in themselves ludicrous or inept. The satire is carried out in a different way, by showing how Tityre behaves in his natural social milieu. We see him being outdone by a more virile rival, watch him getting entangled in the amenities of literary parties and weekend escapades. . . . Transposed into a social setting, the aesthete reveals a

ludicrous aspect that remains hidden as long as he remains confined to his own self. . . . Gide transfers an inward experience to a social level and thus allows us to judge from a moral (and potentially political) point of view. (133–34)

To satirize aestheticism from the outside, rather than the inside, this passage seems ever so slightly to be hinting, is not *literarily* interesting. *Paludes* seems, poetically speaking, a perhaps somewhat inconsequential form of portraiture, however capably it performs a social critique of one person's failing manhood. The "we see him" and "we watch him" of de Man's passage, for example, suggest that in order to enjoy this satire, we must assume unquestioningly the kind of faith in mimeticism and referentiality that such an "outer" satire would necessarily require, even though mimeticism and referentiality were precisely two of the ideas aesthetic writers were most interested in putting into question. The suggestion overall seems to be that Gide is satirizing an effeminate, "aesthetic" form of behavior, perhaps more than he is successfully satirizing "aestheticism" as a literary school.

Passages of Tityre's writing, we are told, are not inept, which implies that Gide has a certain understanding of and a certain capability as regards the aesthetic practice of writing. What is that practice? De Man describes it here as:

a moment in which the writer moves away from others, toward a contemplation of his own consciousness as it confronts entities that are precisely not other human beings: the activity of the mind in relation to nature (sensation), in relation to time (memory), and to space (imagination). Even in realistic writers such as Flaubert, or Proust, or Thomas Mann, the deepening and generalizing power of the novels is always founded on the inwardness, the self-contemplation of the character; hence the importance of "poetic," i.e., metaphorical and symbolic modes of language more or less harmoniously combined with realistic detail. (132).

This passage complicates the status of de Man's seeming praise of Gide's "outward" writing in *Paludes*. De Man's compliment to Gide for his successful satire of aesthetic behavior might in fact be merely the obverse of a hidden dig at his literary profundity, putting into question whether a satire of behavior can in any way touch on the essential points about aesthetic writing. Consider once more another sentence from the superficially complimentary passage about *Paludes* quoted above, a sentence that sounds more and more sinister: "Gide transfers an inward experience to a social level and thus allows us to judge from a moral (and potentially political) point of view." Leave aside for the moment the problems of relating morality to politics, problems de Man represents by the parentheses. We have just read that inwardly and aesthetically oriented writers deal in metaphors and symbolic language. Now we read that Gide *transfers* (metaphorizes) those inward experiences outward. To state quickly the stakes here, Gide stands accused of too quick a transfer; he is the one who seems to use language with too easy an assumption of referentiality, and it is his detour around a consideration of inwardness, of self-contemplation, that permits his quick turn into outwardness.

The same turn, de Man tells us, "allows us to judge from a moral (and potentially political) point of view"—the implication being that a great many moral evaluations are judgments made too quickly, by a curiosity and interest that have been misdirected. De Man makes this same point in a different way in his much later essay "The Resistance to Theory":

> What we call ideology is precisely the confusion of linguistic with natural reality, of reference with phenomenalism. It follows that, more than any other mode of inquiry, including economics, the linguistics of literariness is a powerful and indispensable tool in the unmasking of ideological aberrations, as well as a determining factor in accounting for their occurrence. Those who reproach literary theory for being oblivious to social and historical (that is to say ideological) reality are merely stating their fear at having their own ideological mystifications exposed by the tool they are trying to discredit. (11)

The categories are slightly different, but analogous. Gide moves from "inward experience" to "moral (and political)" questions, failing to reflect on the rhetorical structures that allow him to do so. The resistance to theory de Man points to confuses linguistic reality and natural reality, or reference and phenomenalism.

That is an odd criticism, given that Gide's work, too, is haunted by the possibility that ideology lurks at a fundamental level of linguistic usage. Nowhere, it seems to me, is this clearer than in a text such as his *Retour de l'U.R.S.S.* (1936), the text that marks the end of his short period as an intellectual committed to communism. Although the text, a best-seller when published, is rarely discussed, or, when it is discussed, done so dismissively,[3] it is nonetheless filled with reflections on language's relation to politics. Indeed, the extent to which that text concerns itself with aberrations, ideological, linguistic, and erotic, astonishes the careful reader.

Aberration is a word around which a lot turns. It is a favorite word of de Man's, especially later in his career. (It is, for example, a central concept in, indeed the closing word of, *Allegories of Reading.*) In "Whatever Happened to André Gide?," de Man refers to Gide's homosexuality as "his personal aberrations," a complicated usage that doubtless carries its share of genteel homophobia along with it, no matter how valorized the term was to become in de Man's later lexicon. The force of the word itself remains strong enough to suggest that anyone aberrant in one category will be so in others. This is the burden of most unfavorable critiques of Gide. Purveyors of those critiques in fact always turn quickly from outside to inside, or vice versa. An aberrant style means an aberrant character, an aberrant sexual practice implies an aberrant political one. One of the things I will investigate in this chapter is the way in which Gide uses exactly this phobic habit of thought to generate critical tensions within his texts, in particular his *Retour de l'U.R.S.S.*, as if daring readers to focus too quickly on possible links between his

---

3. De Man is no exception here, commenting in "Whatever Happened to André Gide?" that "his *Return from the USSR* . . . certainly failed to show any striking insight into political realities." A notable exception to the trend would be Maurice Blanchot in his essay "Gide et la littérature d'expérience."

various forms of "aberration." Before we turn to that text, however, there remain a few further points in de Man's article on Gide that it will be helpful to keep in mind.

De Man's argument about Gide moves between the poles of *Paludes* and *Les Nourritures terrestres*, which we might quickly label as a satire and an erotic rapture, respectively. Although *Les Nourritures terrestres* was at one time viewed as a politically volatile text, calling on its reader to shake off the shackles of bourgeois morality, de Man correctly points out (in a citation quoted earlier in this chapter) that to complain about bourgeois morality and to reject bourgeois society are not the same thing. Gide's *Paludes* may have constituted an effective satire of an ineffectual aesthete, ridiculous in his parasitic dependence on a bourgeois society. Gide's *Nourritures* may have called for the reader to shake off some of that dependence. But when one bursts the shackles of a confining sexual morality, de Man suggests, one runs the risk of re-aestheticizing oneself in an equally unacceptable way. Sexual revolt is not he insists, inherently liberating:

> Sexuality can well be experienced as a bridge toward another, as a way to reenter the social world from which one has retreated in moral indignation. But this is not what happens in *Les Nourritures terrestres*. . . . The sexuality . . . is never oriented toward other human beings. It is a return toward the inwardness of the self, a way of using the outside world—including others—to explore and refine the awareness Gide has of his own selfhood.
>
> Gide's autoeroticism thus reintroduces, somewhat surreptitiously, the antisocial, inhumane element present in aestheticism, the negative side of a coin whose positive side is Mallarmé's self-reflection. (135)

It would thus appear that Gide was sexually inward, literarily outward—a double mistake, sex being meant as an arena for thinking outwardness, literature inwardness. Thus, we see here the dangers of the conjunction of curiosity and interest to which de Man is pointing. De Man claims that Gide (in spite of having satirized aesthetic behavior in *Paludes*) seems to have a nefariously aesthetic (literary?) self-interest at heart when he reaches out (sexually) to the other. A truly aesthetic writer "moves away from others, towards a contemplation of his own consciousness," as if fearful of the possibility of contaminating (literary) interest with (sexual) curiosity, fearful that there is no erotics not inclined to an aberrant and violently aesthetic autoeroticism.

We see emerging here a familiar lexical chain, consisting of words such as aberration, orientation, inclination, bent, autoeroticism, and self-interest. An (aberrant?) ability to hold together the (purely rhetorical, ideological) links in this chain constitutes one ground on which writing, *homo*sexuality, and politics converge. But there are many ways to construe this convergence. De Man's short but complicated essay has, in its own turns, exemplified many of the complexities of one such construal. The first half of the essay seemed mostly complimentary. Gide uses autobiography as a form of self-analysis "aimed at dispelling false constructs of the self." "It is perhaps not a very good sign for our own times," de Man suggests, "that he now receives so little attention." His "entire experience is an interpersonal one," and he has a "natural bent toward other human beings and society." De Man feels, notably, that Gide "did not have to contradict any fundamental part of himself when he moved into the political sphere, a move for which his particular bent of mind predestined him." But the major turn of de Man's essay indeed casts a different light on these compliments:

> Such a unified treatment of art, society, and morality would be an admirable achievement, even if it had to occur at the expense of a certain poetic inwardness. But unfortunately things are not that simple. . . . Gide's moral attack on aestheticism is most effective. . . . But, after this, Gide's evolution was much less clear: his later heroes, the Ménalque of *The Immoralist*, the Edouard of *The Counterfeiters*, the Thésée that appears in his last book, are a great deal more ambiguous.
>
> The ambiguity stems from a hidden confusion, in Gide's mind, between the other human being considered as a conscious, moral person and as an object for erotic gratification. (134)

Gide's attempt to turn outward, toward the social, turns out for de Man to be an erotic move, a queer move that constitutes an interested swerve inward, away from the social. For de Man, Gide's bent, then, is not, in the final instance, essentially social. Its essence is "the asserted priority of the self as Eros."

De Man's essay concludes, somewhat platitudinously: "Gide's work remains so important for us just because it reveals some of the difficulties involved in thus trying to reconcile the needs of the self with those of society" (136). Perhaps never acknowledged in the essay is the difficulty some have in placing *homo*sexuality *explicitly* within such a discussion. The "ambiguities" of Edouard, Ménalque, and Thésée, the "antisocial, inhumane" autoeroticism, Gide's "personal aberrations," not to mention any "particular *bent* of mind," all suggest a certain *implicit* and phobically colored image of a homosexual Gide as a social thinker *manqué*, his failure closely related to his sexuality. That image, never sufficiently acknowledged, is thus never subject to scrutiny and somewhat difficult to challenge. Any careful challenge to it would necessarily work to question the discussion's very terms, to question "aestheticism" the way de Man invokes it, to imagine a sexual politics within aestheticism whose effect disturbs a dominant understanding of Eros's relation to some "moral" self. To begin that questioning, I would like to turn to Gide's *Retour de l'U.R.S.S.* and its ways of being interested in situations that are erotically, linguistically, and politically complex.

Imagining the Future

In the summer of 1936, Gide, an indefatigable voyager then in his mid-sixties, spent nine weeks touring the Soviet Union. Mention of his growing interest in Soviet society had begun appearing in his journal in 1931. Those journal pages were published in *La Nouvelle Revue Française* in 1932, and from then until the publication of his *Retour de l'U.R.S.S.* in November of 1936 Gide's career as a fellow traveler was a great subject of discussion, at least within the intellectual circles of Paris.[4] Publication of his disillusioned *Retour* in 1936 lost him many of the left-wing friends his adherence to communism had won him and left his right-wing critics feeling superior, pointing out that *they* had not needed to visit the Soviet Union to know what it was like.

Gide, in fact, attempted to modulate his critique of the U.S.S.R., so that it would sound at least partly friendly. "The Soviet Union is 'in the making'," he writes in his Preface:

> one cannot say it too often. And to that is due the extraordinary interest of a stay in this immense country which is now in labour; one feels that one is contemplating the parturition of the future. . . .
>   To confine oneself exclusively to praise is a bad way of proving one's devotion, and I believe I am doing the Soviet Union itself and the cause that it represents in our eyes a greater service by speaking without dissimulation or indulgence. It is precisely because of my admiration for the Soviet Union and for the wonders it has already performed that I am going to criticize, because of what we still expect from it, above all because of what it would allow us to hope for. (xiii–xiv)[5]

In spite of the kind words of his Preface and of many cheerful scenes described along the way, in spite of ending the main body of his text with more praise for the Soviet Union for the aid it had begun to supply to the Spanish Republic, Gide's denunciations, scattered throughout the book, are harsh and direct. He writes:

> Now that the revolution has triumphed, now that it is stabilized and moderated, now that it is beginning to come to terms, and, some will say, to grow prudent, those that the revolutionary ferment still animates and who consider all these successive concessions to be compromises become troublesome, are reprobated and suppressed. . . .
>   And I doubt whether in any other country in the world, even Hitler's Germany, thought be less free, more bowed down, more fearful (terrorized), more vassalized. (41–42)[6]

Gide writes his *Retour de l'U.R.S.S.* in his usual limpid style, but most interesting for us here is that in spite of his superficial clarity and innocence,

---

4. The most comprehensive book on this subject is Rudolf Maurer, *André Gide et l'U.R.S.S.* Also helpful are: W. J. Marshall, "André Gide and the U.S.S.R.: A Re-appraisal"; Herbert R. Lottman, "Gide's Return," chapter 13 of *The Left Bank;* David Caute, *Communism and the French Intellectuals;* Emily Apter, "Homotextual Counter-Codes: André Gide and the Poetics of Engagement."

5. L'U.R.S.S. est « en construction », il importe de se le redire sans cesse. Et de là l'exceptionnel intérêt d'un séjour sur cette immense terre en gésine : il semble qu'on assiste à la parturition du futur . . .

C'est témoigner mal son amour que le borner à la louange et je pense rendre plus grand service à l'U.R.S.S. même et à la cause que pour nous elle représente, en parlant sans feinte et sans ménagement. C'est en raison même de mon admiration pour l'U.R.S.S. et pour les prodiges accomplis par elle déjà, que vont s'élever mes critiques; en raison aussi de ce que nous attendons encore d'elle; en raison surtout de ce qu'elle nous permettrait d'espérer (17–18).

6. Maintenant que la révolution a triomphé, maintenant qu'elle se stabilise, et s'apprivoise; qu'elle pactise, et certains diront : s'assagit, ceux que ce ferment révolutionnaire anime encore et qui considèrent comme compromissions toutes ces concessions successives, ceux-là gênent et sont honnis, supprimés . . . Et je doute qu'en aucun autre pays aujourd'hui, fût-ce dans l'Allemagne de Hitler, l'esprit soit moins libre, plus courbé, plus craintif (terrorisé), plus vassalisé (55).

he manages to encode his text with a complex set of references to his previous literary work, to the debates surrounding his "conversion" to communism, and to his own homosexuality and concerns about the fate of homosexuals in the Soviet Union. These subtexts, which sometimes take some work to decipher (and often overlap), seem to me, when taken together, to articulate some hesitant theory about the revolutionary hopes and possibilities for a writer such as Gide and the relation of those possibilities to his sexuality. One of the few critics to comment on this side of Gide was Walter Benjamin, who, in an article entitled "André Gide und sein neuer Gegner" (about the attacks on Gide by Thierry Maulnier, a Maurassian writing for the Catholic, rightist, nationalist, protofascist *Action Fran-çaise*), sketched a provocative theory about what a fascist aesthetics would be and gestured at the form of opposition to fascism Gide might represent. I would like first to tease out some of Gide's subtexts, to fill in some of the context to his trip, and then to develop Benjamin's comments. In the final section of this chapter, I would like to look at some of Benjamin's own observations about the Soviet Union and contrast his ideological position with that of Gide. In this final task, a different essay by Adorno, on the politics of using citations from foreign languages when one writes, will prove valuable not only in trying to understand some of the differences between Gide and Benjamin but also in helping to account for some of the interspersed foreign words we will be encountering in Gide's *Retour,* in particular to account for the part they play in expressing some of the specific frustrations of Gide's Soviet trip. I begin by concentrating on the beginning and ending of Gide's *Retour,* and on some of the early responses to Gide's proclamations of his communist sympathies.

Soviet Youth

> One day, he arrives at lunch handing me a moving article, a sort of call to pity for the Russian children abandoned after the revolutionary period. He says: "It's horrible," in a voice choked with emotion. Gide's emotion has something very singular about it; whether the emotion be of an aesthetic, sentimental or moral order, it translates into a sudden storm of tears. His own astonishment faced with his sensibility seems such that he has something like a desire or a need to make sure his tears are noticed, a preoccupation (for me visible) which distracts him immediately from his emotion; thus it always seems so brief, without continuation and must often appear without depth, or purely a nervous quirk.[7]
>
> —Maria Van Rysselberghe, *Les Cahiers de la Petite Dame, 1918–1929*

7. Un jour, il arrive au déjeuner en me tendant un article émouvant, sorte d'appel à la pitié pour les enfants russes, abandonnés après la période révolutionnaire. Il dit : « C'est abominable », d'une voix étranglée par l'émotion. L'émotion de Gide a quelque chose de très particulier; qu'elle soit d'ordre esthétique, sentimental ou moral, elle se

So writes Maria Van Rysselberghe in her notebook for 1923, hinting at one of the same concerns we saw de Man expressing earlier, that Gide's initial gesture toward another person immediately "translates" back into a preoccupation with himself. Is Gide's use of his emotions any different from journalistic exploitation? Are these children anything more than the necessary fuel for more literary self-reflection? Van Rysselberghe also presciently raises the question often posed by Gide's critics to dismiss his interest in communism: is it not based merely on emotional, unintellectual sympathy or the desire to be seen as sympathetic? The spark of interest in Russian children raises another specter: that the interest might not be merely emotional, but erotic.

This passage also calls to mind a moment that came up in the preceding chapter, the scene where Gide, newly returned from Africa, hands Martin du Gard a report on the distress of an African tribe and again bursts notably into tears. Neither of the observers seems interested in allowing such queer outbursts to have any "serious" content. Yet it would seem more than conceivable that the outbursts do indicate allegiances Gide imagines or experiences around a deeply felt, if always somewhat inarticulate, sense of shared alienation and oppression. The frustrations of the African trip were many. Africa could not be the escape from alienation Gide had since his youth tried to imagine it to be. It would instead be a place that, on the one hand, again suggested Gide's own alienation from his position in the French social and economic system, and yet, on the other hand, forced him to confront his own inescapable place within that system. These frustrations replay themselves during the trip to the Soviet Union. Could it be a place safe from the alienations, both sexual and political, that Gide had chosen to confront? Or would it again confirm Gide in his alienated position? Such questions bring themselves to the fore in Gide's treatment of the vagabond children that provoke his tears.

These *besprizornis*, abandoned Soviet children, become the subject of the final appendix to Gide's *Retour de l'U.R.S.S.* In the appendix we can observe the blending of Gide's social imagination and his erotic one. (We constantly find Gide marginalizing sexual moments in this text—including them in the final appendix, in the retelling of a Homeric hymn with which his account opens, in certain untranslated quotations from foreign languages, or in a footnote.) Here in the appendix he describes the *besprizornis* as follows:

> They are not quite the same type of child as in earlier times. Nowadays these children may have parents still living; they have left their native village, sometimes through love of adventure, more frequently because they could not conceive that anywhere else it was possible to be as wretched and as starved as they were at home.

---

traduit par un brusque jaillissement de larmes. Son propre étonnement devant cette sensibilité semble tel qu'il a comme le désir, le besoin de les faire constater; préoccupation (pour moi visible) qui le détourne aussitôt de son émotion; de là, qu'elle semble toujours si brève, sans prolongement et doit souvent paraître sans profondeur, ou purement nerveuse (185–86).

> Some of them are under ten. They are easily recognizable because they wear a great many more clothes (I do not say better clothes) than the other children. This is explained by the fact that they carry all their belongings about with them. The other children very often wear nothing but bathing-trunks. (91)[8]

An attentive and longtime reader of Gide might recognize here a retelling of his 1907 parable, *Le Retour de l'enfant prodigue,* where precisely those children who have the courage to leave home with only the clothes on their back, never to return, represent the hope for the future.

But the appendix takes a different turn from the earlier parable. Evasion from societal norms is no longer portrayed as so necessary for someone desiring independence. It does initially seem that the situation of these children parallels situations in Gide's earlier work. One day, the local police make a raid, rounding up the stray children. The next day the *besprizornis* are back: "'They wouldn't have us,' said the children. But it seems more likely that it was they themselves who refused to submit to what little discipline was demanded of them." (93) This is the encouragingly oppositional voice of *Les Nourritures terrestres* or of *Le Retour de l'enfant prodigue.* But Gide in fact chooses to end his final appendix on a strikingly conciliatory note. He comments that he sees two plainclothesmen dragging away one of the screaming children, but that, passing the same place an hour later,

> I saw the same child again. He had now calmed down and was sitting on the pavement. There was only one of the two policemen standing beside him, speaking to him. The child was no longer trying to run away. He was smiling at the policeman. A large truck drew up, and the policeman helped the child to get in. Where was he taking him? I do not know. And I only relate this little incident because few things in the Soviet Union moved me as much as the attitude of this man towards the child; the persuasive gentleness of his voice (ah, if I could only have understood what he was saying!), the kindness of his smile, and his caressing tenderness as he lifted him in his arms. (93–94)[9]

On one level this is clearly a utopian ending to the parable of the prodigal son as Gide told it—a society where the son rebelling against the crass materialism and restrictive morality of his family can nonetheless be received into the heart of a socialist community. It is also a picture of Gide, marginalized by his lack of

8. Ce ne sont plus tout à fait les mêmes que dans les premiers temps. Ceux d'aujourd'hui, leurs parents vivent encore, peut-être; ces enfants ont fui leur village natal, parfois par désir d'aventure; plus souvent parce qu'ils n'imaginaient pas qu'on pût être, nulle part ailleurs, aussi misérable et affamé que chez eux. Certains ont moins de dix ans. On les distingue à ceci qu'ils sont beaucoup plus vêtus (je n'ai pas dit mieux) que les autres enfants. Ceci s'explique : ils portent sur eux tout leur avoir. Les autres enfants, très souvent, ne portent qu'un simple caleçon de bain (89).

9. « On n'a pas voulu de nous », disent les gosses. Ne serait-ce pas plutôt eux qui ne veulent pas se soumettre au peu de discipline imposée? . . . J'ai revu le même enfant, calmé. Il était assis sur le trottoir. Un seul des deux agents restait debout près de lui et lui parlait. Le petit ne cherchait plus à fuir. Il souriait à l'agent. Un grand camion vint, s'arrêta; l'agent aida l'enfant à y monter, pour l'emmener où? Je ne sais. Et si je raconte ce menu fait, c'est que peu de choses en U.R.S.S. m'ont ému comme le comportement de cet homme envers cet enfant : la douceur persuasive de sa voix (ah! que j'aurais voulu comprendre ce qu'il lui disait), tout ce qu'il savait mettre d'affection dans son sourire, la caressante tendresse de son étreinte lorsqu'il le souleva dans ses bras . . . (90–91).

Russian, and apparently experiencing this linguistic marginalization in a more general way, even as a kind of erotic longing—a longing for a culture accepting of diverse forms of sexual expression, for a culture where transgression will be unnecessary, and where wayward subjects and police agents could be united in an embrace.

In 1935 Gide published *Les Nouvelles Nourritures,* an odd and provocative attempt to combine the rhapsodic style of the earlier *Nourritures terrestres* with his left-wing leanings. Because Gide was a renowned communist sympathizer, this volume was immediately translated and published in the Soviet Union, and Gide composed an additional "Adresse aux jeunes gens de l'U.R.S.S." to accompany its appearance.[10] The first two paragraphs of *Les Nouvelles Nourritures,* although probably actually composed in the 1920s,[11] nonetheless constitute a definite precursor text to the conclusion of the appendix on the *besprizornis:*

> You, dear one, who will come when I no longer hear the sounds of the earth and my lips no longer drink its dew—you who, later, perhaps, will read me—it is for you that I write these pages; because perhaps you are not astonished enough at being alive, you don't admire enough the astounding miracle of your life. It sometimes seems to me that you will drink with my thirst, and that which inclines you over this other being whom you caress, is already my own desire.
>
> (I admire how much desire, as soon as it is that of a lover, becomes imprecise. My love enveloped so diffusely and so all at once, the whole of the beloved's body, that, Jupiter, I would have transformed myself into a cloud without even being aware of it.) (169)[12]

These sentences are carefully constructed to confuse writing and sexuality, to confuse the desire to communicate with sexual desire. The homoerotic tones make them a remarkable introduction to the latest work of a prominent communist sympathizer. The voice and temporal sense of the passage are also dislocated in remarkable ways. The mixing of present and future tenses, the futuristic "already" of "that which inclines you over this other being whom you caress, is *already* my own desire," gives a bit of pause. The positioning of Jupiter in the middle of a sentence,[13] a parataxis with the hypothetical "if I were" noticeably absent, constitutes an equally odd usage, allowing the "I" to change into (in form, at least) his own enveloping desire. A few lines later we read:

---

10. See Maurer, *André Gide et l'U.R.S.S.,* 88.

11. See "Notice" on *Les Nouvelles Nourritures* in André Gide, *Romans, récits et soties, œuvres lyriques,* 1492–502.

12. Toi qui viendras lorsque je n'entendrai plus les bruits de la terre et que mes lèvres ne boiront plus sa rosée — toi qui, plus tard, peut-être me liras — c'est pour toi que j'écris ces pages; car tu ne t'étonnes peut-être pas assez de vivre; tu n'admires pas comme il faudrait ce miracle étourdissant qu'est ta vie. Il me semble parfois que c'est avec ma soif que tu vas boire, et que ce qui te penche sur cet autre être que tu caresses, c'est déjà mon propre désir.

(J'admire combien le désir, dès qu'il se fait amoureux, s'imprécise. Mon amour enveloppait si diffusément et si tout à la fois, tout son corps, que, Jupiter, je me serais mué en nuée, sans même m'en apercevoir.) (169).

13. These paragraphs might have as a subtext the story of Zeus' rape of Ganymede, where the (im)possibility of communion in an unproblematic relationship between lover/beloved (or author/reader) is figured by the barrier divine/human, the central theme of that Homeric hymn to Aphrodite that tells of the rape. (My thanks to Yopie Prins for helping my reading along here.)

Cède sans trop attendre
Au conseil le plus tendre
Et laisse l'avenir
Doucement t'envahir.

[Give in, without dallying too long, to this most tender counsel, and let the future quietly invade you.]

The tables are turned, and instead of his desire proleptically shaping and enveloping the future, the writer's plea is that the future come and inform the present. The language strains to figure a nontemporal, truly united erotic utopia. If the *Voyage au Congo* used tropes of the natural primitivism of Africa, tropes of an absolute past, to further Gide's efforts to reimagine himself, the *Retour de l'U.R.S.S.*, along with *Les Nouvelles Nourritures*, tries to imagine an absolute future into which one might leap as a form of transformation both personal and social:[14]

Ah, to be able to escape myself! I would overleap the barriers behind which self-respect has confined me. . . . I want now not to walk, but to leap; with a thrust of my legs to kick away, to deny my past; no longer to be obliged to keep promises: I have made too many! Oh future, how I would love you, unfaithful! (*Later Fruits*, 184)[15]

Les Nouvelles Nourritures and the appendix on the *besprizornis* both struggle to imagine de-alienated utopias where transgressive behavior ends in a vaguely erotic embrace—between policeman and youth, between older writer and a new generation. Yet, one might pause to wonder if Gide feels any slight identification with the policeman insofar as that policeman is understood as a remnant of an old order, insofar as the leap into this absolute future does not manage to happen cleanly, insofar as Gide's alienations somehow for him remain necessary to his vision of this magical, unfaithful, inaccessible future.

Further evidence of this complicated, frustrating interest in the future can be found in another startling confusion in the text of *Retour de l'U.R.S.S.* between sexual and political desire: the liminal retelling of the Homeric hymn to Demeter, which recounts how, while looking for Persephone, Demeter disguised herself for a few days as a nursemaid and took charge of Demophoon, infant son of the queen Metaneira. One night Demeter takes the child from his soft cradle and places him on a bed of hot ashes. Gide writes:

I imagine the mighty Demeter bending over the radiant nursling as over the future race of mankind. He endures the fiery charcoal; he gathers strength from the ordeal. Something superhuman is fostered in him, something robust, something glorious beyond all hope. Ah, had Demeter only been able to carry through her bold attempt, to bring her daring venture to a successful issue! But Metaneira becoming anxious,

---

14. The chapter "Œdipe: L'engagement politique," in Eric Marty's *André Gide: Qui êtes-vous?*, 115–27, is helpful on these questions.

15. Ah! pouvoir échapper à moi-même! Je bondirais par-dessus la contrainte où le respect de moi m'a soumis . . . Je veux ne plus marcher, mais bondir; d'un coup de jarret repousser, renier mon passé; n'avoir plus à tenir de promesses : j'en ai trop fait! Avenir, que je t'aimerais, infidèle! (*Nouvelles Nourritures*, 179).

> says the legend, burst suddenly into the room where the experiment was being
> carried out and, falsely guided by maternal fears, thrust aside the goddess at her work
> of forging the superman, pushed away the embers, and, in order to save the child,
> lost the god. (vii)[16]

Most evidently to be read here as a criticism of the way the Soviet Union was
abandoning the true revolutionary course, this parable occurs in a different context
in Gide's journal entry for October 8, 1929, a part of his journal that first became
public in volume XV of his *Œuvres complètes* in 1939.[17] In Gide's journal entry for
October 7, 1929, we read the following:

> I can write in this notebook nothing of what touches me most closely at the moment;
> for that reason there will be no trace here of the adventure of Constantinople which
> has occupied my thoughts so frequently in the past three months and which I cannot
> yet consent to believing finished. . . . I cannot believe that Emile D. would accept
> being forbidden to write me. Better to say nothing of it than to say too little.
> (*Journals,* 3:66)[18]

Having in fact said too little one day, Gide, slightly more upset, says too little more
the next day; and says it so that it seems life imitates his own fiction—in this case,
placing Emile in the role of *Les Faux-Monnayeurs'* Olivier, Gide in Edouard's.

> I should nevertheless like to be sure that the dear boy hasn't killed himself. In the
> state of exaltation he had reached he was capable of doing so if he suddenly met a
> blind, absurd opposition from his parents, who, if he did kill himself, pushed by
> them into despair, would certainly hold me responsible for his death . . . just as they
> have already held me responsible for everything that worried them . . . for every-
> thing in him that escaped them and in which they could no longer recognize
> themselves. They were terrified to see their son "become too fond of me." Even if he
> were, as his mother wrote me, "in perdition," if anyone was capable of understand-
> ing him, holding out a hand to him, saving him . . . it was me. But Metaneira
> reappears in almost every mother, as Ceres, here, lives again in me. (3:67)[19]

16. J'imagine la grande Déméter penchée, comme sur l'humanité future, sur ce nourrisson radieux. Il supporte
l'ardeur des charbons, et cette épreuve le fortifie. En lui, je ne sais quoi de surhumain se prépare, de robuste et
d'inespérément glorieux. Ah! que ne put Déméter poursuivre jusqu'au bout sa tentative hardie et mener à bien son
défi! Mais Métaneire inquiète, raconte la légende, fit irruption dans la chambre de l'expérience, faussement guidée
par une maternelle crainte, repoussa la déesse et tout le surhumain qui se forgeait, écarta les braises et, pour sauver
l'enfant, perdit le dieu (13–14).

17. Maurer points out this parallel without commenting on it (*André Gide et l'U.R.S.S.,* 126, n. 59).

18. Je ne peux écrire dans ce carnet rien de ce qui me tient le plus à cœur; c'est ainsi qu'on n'y verra pas trace de
l'aventure de Constantinople, qui, ces trois derniers mois, a tant occupé ma pensée, et que je ne consens pas encore à
croire achevée . . . Je ne puis croire qu'Emile D. accepte qu'on lui défende de m'écrire. Mieux vaut n'en rien dire
plutôt que d'en parler trop peu. (*Journal 1889–1939,* 939)

19. Je voudrais pourtant être sûr que ce petit ne s'est pas tué. Au point d'exaltation où il était, il en était capable,
rencontrant tout à coup une opposition aveugle, absurde, des parents qui, s'il venait à se tuer, poussé par eux au
désespoir, me feraient certainement responsable de cette mort . . . tout comme ils me faisaient déjà responsable de
tout ce qui les inquiétait, de tout ce qu'ils ne comprenaient pas dans leur enfant, de tout ce qui, de lui, leur échappait
et où ils ne se reconnaissaient plus eux-mêmes. Ils s'épouvantaient de voir leur fils « m'aimer trop ». En admettant
qu'il fût, comme me l'écrivait la mère, « en perdition », si quelqu'un était capable de le comprendre, de lui tendre la
main, de le sauver . . . c'était moi. Mais Métanire reparaît dans presque chaque mère, comme Cérès, ici, revit en moi
(940).

Gide has in fact distorted the hymn slightly (in his typically antimaternal way) by having Metaneira sweep away the coals and expel the goddess. The hymn tells us that Metaneira's timidity and concern so annoyed Demeter that she gave her own experiment up (having ruined the child for his earthly nursemaids) and had a temple built for herself instead.

Now this personal encounter recounted in the journal casts an erotic aura over the opening of the *Retour de l'U.R.S.S.*, leading us to associate a drawing back from revolutionary possibilities with a drawing back from sexual nonconformity, to associate the homophobic efforts of parental policing with Stalinist betrayal of revolutionary hopes. This very blurring of the boundaries between the political, the personal, and the erotic might seem to lend credence to claims such as de Man's, that Gide harbors a hidden confusion "between the other human being considered as a conscious, moral person and as an object for erotic gratification." But perhaps Gide is at his most political just when he sets about confusing realms that for the likes of de Man are neatly disjoined. I wonder to what extent the political import of Gide's writing might lie in his ability to disquiet in ways such as this, in a sort of queer activism that insists (however quietly, however slyly) on a disrespect for the boundaries that usually control where discussions of erotics take place—that insists on a revolutionary future that could be queer.

I use the word "slyly" to indicate that in his *Retour de l'U.R.S.S.* Gide is not exactly as forthright about his sexuality as he could be, as we have seen him in *Si le grain ne meurt,* for instance. Conceivably he did closet himself as he wrote "political" texts such as the *Retour de l'U.R.S.S.*, letting his sexuality annoy those it would annoy through the indirectness of its expression rather than through more direct confrontation. He could write considerably more directly when he chose to. In the journal from a 1939 trip to Egypt, for instance:

> No, I no longer greatly desire fornication; at least, it is no longer as pressing a need as it was in the happy days of my youth. But I need to know that I could if I wanted to; can you understand that? I mean to say that I won't find a country pleasant unless numerous possibilities for fornication present themselves. Even the most beautiful monuments in the world can't replace that; why not admit it frankly? (*Carnets d'Egypte*, 1052)[20]

A page or two later he further illustrates his frankness by telling of a chance encounter with a certain Ali. They go off to a secluded place together, where Ali "lifted up his long tunic, dropped his knickers, revealing the charming lower part of his body and, without further ado, offered me his backside" (1054). As we might suspect, Gide refused this particular offer. But no offers of any kind are recorded in his account of his trip to the Soviet Union. Indeed, in some of the

---

20. Non, je n'ai plus grand désir de forniquer; du moins ce n'est plus un besoin comme au beau temps de ma jeunesse. Mais j'ai besoin de savoir que, si je voulais, je pourrais; comprenez-vous cela? Je veux dire qu'un pays ne me plaît que si de multiples occasions de fornication se présentent. Les plus beaux monuments du monde ne peuvent remplacer cela; pourquoi ne pas l'avouer franchement?

more scurrilous attacks on his *Retour de l'U.R.S.S.*, it was suggested that his disappointment with the country was due to his difficulty finding occasions for sex there. In *Ainsi soit-il*, Gide decides to respond to such charges, saying that, despite the new Stalinist laws against homosexuality, he had no problems: "All I can say is that I was hardly aware of [these laws], and that in no other country did I ever find such indulgence and connivance in that regard. . . . But I could not insist on this point without giving far too indiscreet details. Decidedly, I was right not to note anything down" (105/1212). This difficult negotiation between necessary discretion and a desire for frankness in sexual matters creates the sly approach to sexuality we find in the *Retour de l'U.R.S.S.* and underlines some of the difficulties and frustrations Gide seems to have been experiencing in his efforts not to separate sexuality and politics entirely.

Interrogating Gide's Communism

We can observe another instance of Gide's quiet, almost frustrated queerness, another sly confluence of sexuality and politics, at a public debate at the *Union pour la Vérité* (January 23, 1935), in which Gide took part shortly before his trip to the Soviet Union. There he faced a panel of critics to discuss his conversion to communism. The sometimes not so hidden (even if unmentioned) subtext of most of the debate would in fact be his unrepentant homosexuality. "Whatever happens," says the director of the Union opening the session, "out of all the multiple aspects of André Gide's message, this one [his conversion to communism], the most recent, is the one which seems to engage most with the sensibility of our time. It is therefore with it, in all likelihood, that the bulk of our conversation will be concerned."[21] The first speaker to follow the director was Ramon Fernandez, a critic from *La Nouvelle Revue Française*, friendly to Gide and (for a brief period including this particular evening) a supporter of the Soviet Union. Already in this initial, seemingly sympathetic statement we can see Fernandez almost unwillingly bringing homosexuality into the discussion by trying to distance himself, Gide, and communism from it. Fernandez' "friendliness" to Gide seems to consist in his effort to suppress Gide's homosexuality, a suppression that only makes that sexuality and the discomfort it provokes more evident.

Fernandez poses two initial questions: "Do Gide the artist and Gide the moralist find harmony in the communist synthesis? Does communism integrate the moral message of Gide as it emerges from his work?" What Fernandez is doing is trying to portray Gide's move toward communism as something that makes him safe. Already, Fernandez asserts, Gide's role as an aesthetician, can be taken as "rassurant" ("reassuring"):

21. The speaker is Georges Guy-Grand. A transcript of the proceedings was published as *André Gide et notre temps*. See p. 10 for this citation.

His influence as a critic, as an arbiter of good taste, is much more considerable than his influence as a novelist. He has defended with a continual exactness sound values, the classical tradition. . . . Even if you did not like this or that book of Gide's, it would still have to be placed within the French literary tradition (*The Counterfeiters*, for example, an exemplary part of the critical evolution of the novel). (12–13)[22]

As we have seen, much of the criticism of *Les Faux-Monnayeurs* has followed Fernandez' lead. It is not unusual to discuss the entire text as an influential aesthetic construct (perhaps not so entirely "classical" as Fernandez asserts), while ignoring the homosexual subject matter. Principles of classical style and the importance of literary history thus strain to excuse an "aberrant" content.

Morally, Fernandez has to admit, Gide, rather than being "rassurant," has been "inquiétant," not, of course, because of his sexual behavior, but because of his "negative" moral effort: "Gide hasn't formulated a positive moral code. His work, in the moral realm, is analogous to the negative part of Descartes' work. He has taught people to free themselves from a rigid scholastic system, and opened the way toward a rich [féconde], wide and undetermined life" (13).[23] A suppressed awareness of homosexuality might lurk ominously in the background of words such as "féconde" or in the concept of an "undetermined life," but Fernandez has even more reassurances up his sleeve for those not sufficiently calmed by the analogy to that indispensably French thinker Descartes. For Gide has now stopped being such a *negative* moralist. His communist conversion has made him a *positive* thinker. "He believes he has finally encountered a positive moral system in communist morality." And so to his own burning question, "Does communism integrate the moral message of Gide as it emerges from his work?", Fernandez answers a tentatively reassuring yes: "Other moral attitudes might have come out of Gide's work, but communism is in no way contrary to his thought. . . . Gide could accept a healthy and viable discipline after having struggled to rid himself of a discipline which seemed to him ossified, dead" (14).[24] It would probably not do too much damage to Fernandez' intent to translate the adjective *saine* (healthy) as "straight," as if communism as a politics could somehow sanitize or render respectable Gide's sexuality. Gide, in his response to Fernandez, quietly accepts the adjective *viable*, passing over *saine* in polite silence. He is adamant, however, in refusing to disavow his "art":

22. Son influence comme critique, comme correcteur du goût est plus considérable que son influence comme romancier. Il a défendu avec une continuelle justesse de touche les bons principes, la tradition classique . . . Même si on n'aimait pas tel livre de Gide, il faudrait l'intercaler dans une tradition de la littérature française (par exemple *Les Faux Monnayeurs*, représentatif de l'évolution critique du roman).

23. Gide n'a pas formulé de morale positive. Son travail, dans le domaine moral, est analogue à la partie négative du travail de Descartes. Il a appris aux gens à se débarrasser d'une scolastique et ouvert la voie vers une vie féconde, large et indéterminée.

24. D'autres attitudes morales eussent pu sortir de l'œuvre de Gide, mais le communisme n'est nullement contraire à son esprit . . . Gide pouvait accepter une discipline saine et viable, après avoir lutté pour se débarrasser d'une discipline qui lui paraissait sclérosée, morte.

> He spoke of my acceptance of a *discipline*, wherein he sees a culmination. I consent readily. When he adds, a *viable* discipline, I consent . . . but barely. But if it is a question of a viable discipline *for the work of art*, I become so reluctant that I must offer an explanation. . . .
>
> The most important thing to me is my art.
>
> That an alliance between art and communist doctrine is possible, I would like to believe. But I am forced to admit that this point of accord and of fusion is one that I haven't been able up to now to obtain—something partly due to habits fixed long ago. That's why I have produced nothing in the past four years. (14–15)[25]

Gide wants to imagine a society where disciplining police agents can viably embrace prodigal sons, but to do so he feels a need to remain an outsider. What room would there be for his art there, he seems to wonder, and already he seems to acknowledge that even this effort at imagination has stifled some artistic impulse. Art for Gide, even the most classical, must somehow flirt with transgression at the same time as it flirts with discipline. Possibilities for artistic production beyond this "point d'accord et de fusion," the point where transgression is no longer necessary, or even possible, do not seem to present themselves readily. Within the text of the *Retour de l'U.R.S.S.*, he returns to this same point:

> I believe that a writer's value is intimately linked to the force of the revolutionary spirit that animates him—or to be more exact—to the force of his spirit of opposition. . . . For the question arises: what will happen if the transformation of the social State deprives the artist of all motive for opposition? What will the artist do if there is no reason for him to go *against* the current, if all he need do is to let himself be carried by it? (51–52)[26]

Gide is struggling here with a certain closeting effect produced in him by this political "discipline" to which he has submitted. What kind of exigencies would force Gide back into "discretion" about his sexuality, and at what point would this discretion, however sly, become too compromising?

There were many Catholics sitting around the table at the (itself Catholic) *Union pour la Vérité:* Jacques Maritain, Gabriel Marcel, François Mauriac, Henri Massis. It was Henri Massis, constant critical thorn in Gide's side, who, in fact, most clearly articulated the links between Gide's "artistry" and his political position, Massis who almost cleared the air by bringing sexuality into the discussion:

---

25. Il a parlé de mon acceptation d'une *discipline*, où il voit un achèvement. J'y consens volontiers. Quand il ajoute : une discipline *viable*, j'y consens . . . tout juste. Mais s'il s'agit d'une discipline viable *pour l'œuvre d'art*, j'entre dans une telle réticence qu'il faudra que je m'explique là-dessus . . .

La chose à laquelle je tiens le plus, c'est mon art.

Que l'entente de l'art et de la doctrine communiste soit possible, je veux le croire. Mais il me faut avouer que le point d'accord et de fusion, je n'ai su jusqu'à présent l'obtenir — en raison aussi de longues habitudes prises. C'est pourquoi je n'ai rien produit depuis quatre ans.

26. Je crois que la valeur d'un écrivain est liée à la force révolutionnaire qui l'anime, ou plus exactment . . . à sa force d'opposition . . . Car la question se pose : qu'adviendra-t-il si l'Etat social transformé enlève à l'artiste tout motif de protestation? Que fera l'artiste s'il n'a plus à s'élever contre, plus qu'à se laisser porter? (63–64).

> Mr. Fernandez seems to me too easily reassured. Any thought of Gide's which finds expression on the aesthetic level has an equivalent on the moral level, and if M. Gide has, for example, chosen classicism as his mode of literary expression, there entered into his choice as many moral intentions as specifically artistic concerns. . . . When he threw over romanticism it was because there is something in romantic grandiloquence that is repugnant to his stealthy heart. When he opted for classicism, it was because he saw there the most apt style for sealing up his secrets. Today, in adhering to communism, again it is his secrets that he indirectly protects, it is again that withheld part that he believes he is subtracting from moral ostracism. For that, he doesn't hesitate to pose the whole problem of mankind and of civilization—and we know the solution that he has chosen. (26–27)[27]

His secrets, his ambiguities, his insinuations, inclinations, aberrations: Massis makes what he is discussing as clear as he believes it needs to be. In his response to Massis, "I find this exposé remarkable, and I approve of it in general," Gide is thankful, perhaps, for Massis' *indiscretion* in linking Gide's sexuality to his communist politics, however offensive and reductive Massis' thought might be.

classicisme / communisme = formalismes cachant et permettant des transgressions [handwritten annotation]

"Melons for Delight"/Foreign Imports

Let us examine a few more examples of how Gide seals his secrets within his classical style in *Retour de l'U.R.S.S.* In that text Gide mentions homosexuality more or less directly on two occasions. The most direct is in a footnote to a passage about the way the Soviet Union has backtracked in certain aspects of its campaign to reorganize and reimagine the division of labor within society. Specifically, Gide's attention is drawn to the recent reassertion in the U.S.S.R. of the traditional family, the reinstitution of laws of inheritance, which allow some members of the working class to achieve a more satisfactory level of material existence than others. A footnote to this section of the text comments on the "consternation" caused by the recently promulgated law against abortions, a consternation notably felt by those workers already too poor to contemplate raising a family, now threatened with deeper poverty. In the *second* paragraph of this footnote about the new law against abortion, Gide comments:

> Can this law be to a certain degree justified? At any rate, it was occasioned by some very deplorable abuses. But from a Marxist point of view, what can one think of that

27. Il me semble que M. Fernandez se rassure un peu vite. Toute pensée gidienne, qui s'exprime sur le plan esthétique, a son équivalence sur le plan moral; et si M. Gide a, par example, élu le classicisme comme mode d'expression littéraire, il est entré dans son choix autant d'intentions morales que de soucis d'art proprement dits . . . Quand il a repoussé le romantisme, c'est qu'il y a dans sa grandiloquence quelque chose qui répugne à son cœur insinuant. Quand il a opté pour le classicisme, c'est qu'il y a vu le style le plus apte à sceller ses secrets. Aujourd'hui, en adhérant au communisme, ce sont encore ses secrets qu'indirectement il protège, c'est encore cette part réservée qu'il croit soustraire à l'ostracisme de la morale. Pour cela, il n'hésite pas à poser tout le problème de l'homme et de la civilisation — et l'on sait la solution qu'il a choisie.

other, older law against homosexuals? That law, which assimilates them to counter-revolutionaries (for *non-conformism* is prosecuted even in sexual matters), condemns them to a sentence of five years' deportation, which can be renewed if they are not reformed by exile. (38–39)[28]

Gide had known about this law for a few years, having apparently heard about it from Magnus Hirschfeld. The law had been announced on December 17, 1933. Simon Karlinsky writes that it was "made compulsory for all the republics of the Soviet Union on March 7, 1934." The law:

> outlawed sexual relations between men and prescribed five years of hard labor for voluntary sexual acts and eight years for using force or threats and for sex with a consenting minor. Maxim Gorky, true to form, hailed that decree on the pages of both *Pravda* and *Izvestiia* as a "triumph of proletarian humanitarianism" and wrote that legalization of homosexuality had been the main cause of Fascism. (Karlinsky, 361)

Gide tells Maria Van Rysselberghe that the Soviets "seem to think that homosexuality is due uniquely to leisure, to snobbism, to the blasé and vicious side of bourgeois society" (*Les Cahiers de la Petite Dame, 1929–1937,* 418).[29] Karlinsky confirms Gide's impression, by telling us of the statements made in 1936, the year of Gide's trip, by the Commissar of Justice, Nikolai Krylenko. Krylenko said

> that there was no reason for anyone to be a homosexual after two decades of Socialism, and that those who persisted in remaining homosexual must be "remnants of the exploiting classes" and, as such, deserved five years of hard labor. No one from the working class could possibly be homosexual, so the people who hang out "in their vile secret dens are often engaged in another kind of work, the work of counterrevolution." (Karlinsky, 362)

Gide's footnote would seem to assert that there is another, more adequately *Marxist* way of conceiving homosexuality, although having made this provocative assertion, he doesn't pursue it. The context of his remarks suggests that he envisions some Marxist critique of bourgeois family structure and imagines gay male sexuality as participating in this critique.[30] Gide, rather than pursuing such a critique

---

28. Encore cette loi, dans un certain sens, se justifie-t-elle? Elle répond à de très déplorables abus. Mais que penser, au point de vue marxiste, de celle, plus ancienne, contre les homosexuels? qui, les assimilant à des contre-révolutionnaires (car le *non-conformisme* est poursuivi jusque dans les questions sexuelles), les condamne à la déportation pour cinq ans avec renouvellement de peine s'ils ne se trouvent pas amendés par l'exil (52).

29. Here seems the proper place to include a comment on the metonymic path Gide takes to get to the final paragraphs of his footnote, from family and financial considerations in the main text, to attitudes toward abortion, to laws on homosexuality. Again Gide's uneasy relationship to female sexuality (what are those "very deplorable abuses"?) for some reason leads naturally to questions of homosexuality. The quotation we are about to see ("Women for duty, boys for pleasure, melons for delight") will repeat the same metonymic structure. I hope this path is recognizable as the same one I tried to trace in the chapter on *Corydon*.

30. In the French context, Guérin would be one person who makes some effort to follow out such a critique. Later in the century, Guy Hocquenghem would tackle a similar theoretical problem, this time from a Deleuzian perspective, in his *Homosexual Desire* (1972).

as a tool against his detractors, seems intentionally to try to provoke attacks of the Krylenko or Barbusse variety.

This question of snobbism and of vicious bourgeois counterrevolutionaries brings us to the most interesting reference to homosexuality in *Retour de l'U.S.S.R.*, a passage where we can see Gide's famous—or infamous—lucid, classical style being as deceptive as ever. "I would have liked," he comments about a visit to a Moscow department store, "to bring home a few 'souvenirs' to some friends; everything is frightful. Still, in the past several months, they tell me, a great effort has been attempted, an effort towards quality." He continues:

> The effort towards an improvement of quality is particularly directed to food. Much still remains to be done in this area. . . . The vegetables and fruit in particular are, with a few rare exceptions, if not actually bad, at any rate mediocre. Here, as everywhere, the exquisite gives way to the ordinary, that is, to whatever is most abundant. A prodigious quantity of melons—but they are tasteless. The impertinent Persian proverb, which I have only heard cited, and would only cite, in English, "Women for duty, boys for pleasure, melons for delight," would be misapplied here. The wine is often good (I remember in particular some delicious vintages of Tzinandali, in Kakhetia); the beer is passable. Certain smoked fish (in Leningrad) are excellent, but they don't travel well. (19–20)[31]

Gide has, of course, been criticized by some who have read this passage "straight": "his disappointment in the quality of shop goods, in his search for souvenirs to take back home, is that of any Western bourgeois tourist" (Marshall, 44).[32] Gide may well occasionally have felt like a Western bourgeois tourist, although it seems probable that his overly helpful hosts could have found him some suitably up-market souvenirs had he wanted them. What the passage in question reveals is that Gide could *write* like a leisured, blasé, and vicious bourgeois tourist when he chose to. It makes most sense when read as a perverse attempt to offend, a flaunting of exactly the decadence and deviant sexuality critics would be looking for. But the passage clearly destabilizes that criticism in that it anticipates it, parodies the very tone it also willingly assumes. Gide could write just as well in the opposite vein, as in this passage (equally problematic in tone) from *Les Nouvelles Nourritures:*

31. Cet effort vers la qualité porte surtout sur la nourriture. Il reste encore dans ce domaine fort à faire . . . Les légumes et les fruits en particulier sont encore, sinon mauvais du moins médiocres à quelques rares exceptions près. Ici, comme partout, l'exquis cède à l'ordinaire, c'est-à-dire au plus abondant. Une prodigieuse quantité de melons; mais sans saveur. L'impertinent proverbe persan, que je n'ai entendu citer, et ne veux citer, qu'en anglais : « *Women for duty, boys for pleasure, melons for delight* », ici porte à faux. Le vin est souvent bon (je me souviens, en particulier, des crus exquis de Tznandali, en Kakhétie); la bière passable. Certains poissons fumés (à Leningrad) sont excellents, mais ne supportent pas le transport (35–36).

32. Compare the remarks made by Romain Rolland in indignation at Gide's book: "It is clearly visible that Gide, a very weak man, fell under the influence of the Trotskyist opposition in France. . . . He is also an Alcibiades, who doesn't make fashion, but perpetually runs after it. The U.S.S.R. is no longer in fashion, so Gide can no longer pass as the *arbiter elegantiarum* by remaining attached to it. The U.S.S.R. has become vulgar (in the sense of the vulgate—that which belongs to anyone)" (cited in Hebey, *La "Nouvelle Revue Française" des années sombres, 1940–1941*, 154).

As for myself, I feel an aversion to every possession that is exclusive. . . . I shall not be left with much in hand for death to rob me of. The most I shall be deprived of are those dispersed, natural goods, inappropriable and common to all. . . . As for the rest, I prefer a meal in an inn to the best furnished table, the public garden to the most beautiful garden enclosed by walls, the book I am not afraid to take with me on a walk to that most rare edition, and, if I had to be the only one able to contemplate a work of art, the more beautiful it was the more my sadness would overwhelm my joy. (198)[33]

Even within his *Retour de l'U.R.S.S.* itself, Gide's voice can shift in tone from perverse to prudish. Thus, in the first section of the book, discussing his impressions of the "culture parks" he visited during his stay, the straight-laced Gide is happy to be able to report on the propriety of the young people's comportment: "These crowds of young men and women behave with propriety, with decency; not the slightest trace of stupid or vulgar foolery, of rowdiness, of licentiousness, or even of flirtation. The whole place is pervaded with a kind of joyous ardour" (5).[34] Honest, dignity, decency—here and there impromptu professors give lessons in the park and everyone takes their effort seriously, listens, and learns—no one makes any fun of anyone. Gide's prose strives for the piety it finds in the scenes it describes. But then comes a footnote to call the tone into question:

"And you think that a good thing?" cried my friend X, when I told him this. "Mockery, irony, criticism are all of a piece. The child who is incapable of making fun will turn into the credulous and submissive youth whom later on you, my dear mocker, will criticize for his *'conformism.'* Give me French cheekiness—even if I'm the one to suffer from it." (7)[35]

The instability in tone created by such a footnote resembles the instability induced by the Persian proverb quoted in English, and it is an instability Gide is cultivating as best he can—a way of pushing the limits of the discretion with which he has burdened himself. These coordinated shiftings in tone reveal many things: that Gide remains conscious of carrying his culture with him, that he remains conscious of how his sexuality is necessarily read through cultural lenses, that he was not above an occasional camp gesture, that he saw in the camp gesture a potential for the politics of sexuality to point up a retrograde aspect of Soviet social policing.

Another question about that proverb: why would Gide cite it in English? An

---

33. Pour moi j'ai pris en aversion toute possession exclusive . . . et la mort ne me retirera des mains pas grand-chose. Ce dont elle me privera le plus c'est des biens épars, naturels, échappant à la prise et communs à tous . . . Quant au reste, je préfère le repas d'auberge à la table la mieux servie, le jardin public au plus beau parc enclos de murs, le livre que je ne crains pas d'emmener en promenade à l'édition la plus rare, et, si je devais être seul à pouvoir contempler une œuvre d'art, plus elle serait belle et plus l'emporterait sur la joie ma tristesse (193–94).

34. Dans cette foule de jeunes gens, hommes et femmes, partout le sérieux, la décence; pas le moindre soupçon de rigolade bête ou vulgaire, de gaudriole, de grivoiserie, ni même de flirt. On respire partout une sorte de ferveur joyeuse (23).

35. « Et vous trouvez que c'est un bien? » s'écrie mon ami X . . . , à qui je disais cela. « Moquerie, ironie, critique, tout se tient. L'enfant incapable de moquerie fera l'adolescent crédule et soumis, dont plus tard vous, moqueur, critiquerez le "conformisme". J'en tiens pour la gouaille française, dût-elle s'exercer à mes dépens. » (25).

answer to that question is long, and it relates to the campiness of the gesture. I would like to begin my excursion toward an answer by observing the way foreign languages operate not only within that passage but within the *Retour* in general.

We have already seen, in the appendix on the *besprizornis*, Gide's embarrassment about not knowing any Russian. Not only did it prevent him from understanding the Russians speaking to one another; it also prevented him from controlling translations of his own speeches and writings. Questions of linguistic competence haunt a reader throughout the *Retour* not only in Gide's camp gesture of quoting the Persian proverb in English. He is also dismayed by the education of the school-age Soviet children:

> French had been completely abandoned. It is English and especially German that they are supposed to know. I am surprised to hear them speak so badly; at home a second-year student knows more.
>
> One of the students we questioned gave us the following explanation (in Russian and Jef Last translated it for us):
>
> "A few years ago Germany and the United States still had something to teach us on a few points. But now we have nothing more to learn from foreigners. So why should we speak their language?" (30)[36]

We might also insert here a comment from a footnote in the *Voyage au Congo*, filled with colonialist anxiety, added to a passage about French language instruction in the colonies:

> What a tragedy to see, everywhere in the colony, such eager and attentive students, so poorly served by such inadequate teachers. If only, at the very least, they could be sent appropriate teaching materials! But of what use is it to teach these children from these equatorial regions, as I heard being done at Nola, that "slow combustion furnaces are extremely dangerous," or that "Our ancestors, the Gauls, lived in caves?" (passage left out of the English translation)[37]

It is clearly not just the *utility* of foreign languages that is at stake in scenes such as these but also cultural privilege and cultural power and their embodiment in languages. This consideration must be factored into our reading of the use of foreign languages in the *Retour de l'U.R.S.S.* as well.

Consider another interesting moment, accentuating the irony of Gide's situation—unable to express his concern about linguistic competence because of

---

36. Le français est complètement délaissé. C'est l'anglais, c'est l'allemand surtout, qu'ils sont censés connaître. Je m'étonne de les entendre le parler si mal; un élève de seconde année de chez nous en sait davantage.

De l'un d'entre eux que nous interrogeons, nous recevons cette explication (en russe, et Jef Last nous le traduit):

— Il y a quelques années encore l'Allemagne et les Etats-Unis pouvaient sur quelques points nous instruire. Mais à présent, nous n'avons plus rien à apprendre des étrangers. Donc à quoi bon parler leur langue? (45).

37. Il est vraiment lamentable de voir, dans toute la colonie, des enfants si attentifs, si désireux de s'instruire, aidés si misérablement par de si insuffisants professeurs. Si encore on leur envoyait des livres et des tableaux scolaires appropriés! Mais que sert d'apprendre aux enfants de ces régions équatoriales que « les poêles à combustion lente sont très dangereux », ainsi que j'entendais faire à Nola, ou que « Nos ancêtres les Gaulois vivaient dans les cavernes » (199).

his own incompetence in Russian. This moment occurs during a debate Gide has with a Russian painter. The subject is avant-garde art, and Gide is arguing that accessibility need not always be a virtue in an artwork. Popularity sometimes comes long after initial incomprehension. Gide chooses Beethoven to support his position. As if by accident, a helpful citation falls to hand: "And holding out to him a book I just happened to have on me: Here read this:

> "In Berlin gab ich auch (c'est Beethoven qui parle), vor mehreren Jahren ein Konzert, ich griff mich an und glaubte, was Reicht's zu leisten, und hoffte auf einen tüchtigen Beifall; aber siehe da, als ich meine höchste Begeisterung ausgesprochen hatte, kein geringstes Zeichen des Beifalls ertönte." (65/53)

In case Gide's French reader wasn't fortunate enough to have the linguistic competence one hopes his interlocutor had, a footnote provides the French translation of that handy volume (*Goethes Briefe mit lebensgeschichtlichen Verbindungen*, vol. II, p. 287). Beethoven gave a concert that he thought represented the high point of his inspiration only to find his audience silent and unappreciative.

The use of a Persian proverb in English suggests that knowledge of foreign languages permits snobbish, offensive, and camp gestures, but ones with a critical edge; the lack of knowledge of Russian on Gide's part, of any foreign language on the part of the Soviet youth, suggests that lack of competence in a foreign language can be a severe political handicap or perhaps also a radical political gesture of disavowal. But what of the quotation in German? Is this more camp snobbery, or should we perceive Gide here as giving undeviating support to the ideal of a traditional education in European languages as necessary for a healthy culture?

Benjamin and Gide I

Gide as decadent, as independently wealthy, as a friend of Oscar Wilde, as an occasionally extravagant dresser; Gide as austere, classical, culturally conservative, concerned about the loss of cultural and linguistic prestige: which image (and certainly these are not the only two, nor are these two distinct and internally coherent) should we try to keep in focus? Certain voices we have noted—Adorno, Barbusse, Krylenko, for example—might recall to our attention an intellectual trend that would link Wilde (and his homosexuality) through bourgeois decadence to 1930s and 1940s fascism. This possible linkage is operative within the discourse of the moment of Gide's trip to the Soviet Union and becomes especially palpable around the concerns about cultural prestige that mark the uses of foreign languages we have been considering. Walter Benjamin was interested in these questions and wrote about them in his article, "André Gide und sein neuer Gegner."[38]

38. This article has been translated into French as "André Gide et ses nouveaux adversaires" in *Œuvres II: Poésie et révolution*, trans. Maurice de Gandillac (Paris: Denoël, 1971), 211–24. Page references here are to the German version. For an account of Benjamin's relation to Gide, see Claude Foucart, "André Gide dialogue avec la nouvelle génération allemande: La rencontre avec Walter Benjamin en 1928."

The new adversary Benjamin refers to in his title is Thierry Maulnier, who also participated in the discussion at the *Union pour la Vérité*.[39] Benjamin's article should help remind us of the important function even Gide's *sly* presentation of his sexuality could be said to have in a variety of ideological contexts. We have already arrived on the terrain of Benjamin's essay, which is concerned with the kind of support culture does or doesn't need; the relations between high culture, popular culture, and education; popularity and accessibility. Part of Benjamin's effort in this essay, the part I want to recapitulate here, was to show how Gide's position toward society and high culture could be seen as radical and as antifascist.

A collection of Maulnier's journalistic pieces was published in 1936 under the title *Mythes socialistes*. Benjamin sees in Maulnier an aristocratic fascist, one who is already somewhat behind the times in continuing to imagine that fascism will have any use for aristocratic intellectuals: "There is no way he [Maulnier] could avoid being rapidly forgotten. For as fascism gains strength, it has, of course, less need for intellectuals with the specialized qualities of Maulnier. It offers more opportunities to more subaltern types" ("André Gide," 485). But Maulnier's belief, says Benjamin, is that there is a necessary alliance to be formed between the cultured few and a politics of repressive violence. "What makes Maulnier a fascist is the knowledge that positions of privilege can now only be maintained through violence. To represent the sum of their privileges as 'Culture'—this he sees as his particular task" (486). Benjamin then goes on to cite a particular passage that reveals Maulnier's links to a decadent, aesthetic tradition:

> Civilization . . . is the creation and the discipline of those artifices, of those pre-
> tenses necessary to all human interaction, the system of salutary *conventions*. . . .
> Civilization is lying. . . . Whoever cannot accept that this *antinatural* effort of civili-
> zation against the spontaneity of instincts, that this magnificent lie of civilization is
> the very condition of all human progress and of all human grandeur, that person
> takes sides against civilization itself. Between civilization and sincerity a choice must
> be made. (Maulnier, 210, cited by Benjamin, 486–87)

Benjamin comments that Maulnier, in attempting to formulate brilliant paradoxes, has Oscar Wilde and Wilde's "Decay of Lying" as a precursor, and goes on to contrast Gide and Maulnier based on their different uses of the Wildean tradition.

> One can here first of all observe what different fruits the seed of the same life may
> have from time to time. This same man [Wilde], who finds fascism taking over his
> aestheticism, the most putrefied part of his production, also, and at the same time, by
> opposing himself to society (for which he had perpetually been a source of amuse-
> ment) as its scorner, provided a model which determined the young Gide's future
> life. Secondly, one should recognize how deeply indebted fascism is to decadence
> and aestheticism, and why it finds, in France as well as in Germany or Italy, pioneers
> among the extreme artists. ("André Gide," 487)

---

39. A brief account of Maulnier's career can be found in Paul Serant, *Les Dissidents de l'Action Française*, 211–44. For a discussion I have found immensely helpful of Benjamin, fascism, and the French context of the 1930s, see Kaplan, *Reproductions of Banality*, esp. 3–35 and 41–55. Kaplan mentions Maulnier on p. 44, Gide on pp. 48–49.

What fascists such as Maulnier take from Wilde's aesthetic art, says Benjamin, is a pose of decadent arrogance and snobbery. What they leave behind is the potential of Wildean scorn, of ironical critique, of what Ed Cohen, for instance, has called Wilde's "counterhegemonic positioning."[40]

Benjamin continues: "Fascism is interested in limiting the functional character of art in such a way that it won't have to fear from art any modifying action on the situation of the proletarian class" (488). Aesthetes such as Maulnier, says Benjamin, see art as something only capable of being appreciated by an elite. Both the aesthete and the fascist, Benjamin claims, really fear the possibility of the masses having an active relationship to the work of art, a situation that would unsettle the view they both apparently espouse of culture as entirely ineffectual. Gide upsets Maulnier by not keeping this particular aesthetic faith, by renouncing the belief that art is purely for the aesthetic enjoyment of the cultured few. Benjamin's final words are these:

> For Maulnier, even more disturbing than the fact that the East contains a public of 170 million readers is that in France there live writers who think of that public. André Gide dedicated his last book, *Les Nouvelles Nourritures*, to the young readers of the Soviet Union. Here is its first paragraph:
>> You, dear one, who will come when I no longer hear the sounds of the earth and my lips no longer drink its dew—you who, later, perhaps, will read me—it is for you that I write these pages; because perhaps you are not astonished enough at being alive, you don't admire enough the astounding miracle of your life. It sometimes seems to me that you will drink with my thirst, and that that which inclines you over this other being whom you caress, is already my own desire. (494)

Benjamin thus concludes his essay citing the opening paragraph of *Les Nouvelles Nourritures*, one we have examined. It is an oddly sensual ending for an article favoring functional art over decadent art, politically effective art over art that is refined and withdrawn. Such an ending forces us to rethink exactly what Benjamin means by functional, what possibilities there are for linking scornful deviance to revolutionary intent. This might well bring us back again to thinking about Wilde, and in particular about his sexuality and its complicated relation to his aestheticism and his political potential.

"In Moscow," Benjamin tells us in his essay on Surrealism, "I lived in a hotel in which almost all the rooms were occupied by Tibetan lamas who had come to Moscow for a congress of Buddhist churches."

> I was struck by the number of doors in the corridor that were always left ajar. What had at first seemed accidental began to be disturbing. I found out that in these rooms

---

40. See Cohen's *Talk on the Wilde Side*, esp. chapters 5 and 6. For other examples of this kind of reading of Wilde, consult Neil Bartlett, *Who Was That Man? A Present for Mr Oscar Wilde*, Regenia Gagnier, *Idylls of the Marketplace: Oscar Wilde and the Victorian Public*, and Jonathan Dollimore, *Sexual Dissidence*. For another account (by one of Gide's traveling companions on his trip to the U.S.S.R.) of Gide's relationship to Wilde, see Jef Last, "D'Oscar Wilde aux *Nouvelles Nourritures*."

lived members of a sect who had sworn never to occupy closed rooms. . . . To live in a glass house is a revolutionary virtue par excellence. It is also an intoxication, a moral exhibitionism, that we badly need. *Discretion* concerning one's own existence, once an aristocratic virtue, has become more and more an affair of petit-bourgeois parvenus. ("Surrealism," 180, my emphasis)

By ending his essay "André Gide und sein neuer Gegner" with a quotation about Gide's desire, we might conjecture, Benjamin indicates that his interest in Gide arises not only out of Gide's statements of interest in the Soviet project but also— and perhaps even more importantly—out of Gide's constant ability to take us aback (rather like the Tibetan Lamas) by displaying what is normally coded as private, secret. "Has not Gide incarnated in himself the ideal character that his journal entry for March 28, 1935, presents, that of the *inquiéteur*—the one who makes us troubled?" ("André Gide," 492).[41] For Benjamin, Gide disquiets when he is indiscreet. He disquiets, as Wilde did, because his sexuality adds another axis along which to think his political commitments. This axis, one seems to read between the lines of Benjamin's text, is where Wilde's potential for political radicalism lies. Benjamin suggests, through his closing citation of the paragraphs from *Les Nouvelles Nourritures,* that Gide's own example repeats the same lesson.

At another point in the "Surrealism" essay, Benjamin comments, "Characteristic of this whole left-wing bourgeois position is its irremediable coupling of idealistic morality with political practice" (186). Much of Gide's attraction for Benjamin, and his success at disconcerting his Soviet hosts, left-, and right-wing bourgeois critics, Maulnier, Massis, and others, appears to arise precisely out of his critical effort to break that coupling. It appears to arise out of the moments where he manages to suggest a scandalous association between politics and a politically unassimilable sexuality. These moments, where the image of Gide as a communist, but a queer one, flashes through, are the moments where he seems most ideologically upsetting.

How far it is possible to *sustain* this intermittent image of Gide assuming a radically queer position toward his own or Soviet society remains to be seen, especially given his tendency in the *Retour de l'U.R.S.S.* toward discretion. I would like to address this problem further by continuing to examine Gide's relation to culture and cultural privilege and by returning again to the question of foreign languages.

Benjamin and Gide II

In a letter of January 31, 1937, Benjamin wrote to Max Horkheimer: "I had Gide's book in front of me when I received your reference to it. The part concern-

---

41. "Belle fonction à assumer," Gide reflects in that journal entry, "celle d'*inquiéteur*" (*Journal 1889–1939,* 1224). "A good function to take on, that of one who *disquiets*" (*Journals,* 3:318).

ing religion is outstanding, probably the best in the book—I have no clue as to the present events in the [Soviet] Union" (*Briefe 2*, 728).[42] Benjamin here commends another appendix to *Retour de l'U.R.S.S.*, this one entitled "La Lutte anti-religieuse" (The Struggle against Religion). The appendix describes Gide's visits to several former churches that had been converted to museums for the purpose of educating Soviet citizens out of religious faith. Like Gide, Benjamin was interested in the status of churches in the Soviet Union. Both the diary he kept during his two-month visit to Moscow (Dec. 1926–Jan. 1927) and the essay he wrote on his return describe the changes the churches were undergoing.[43] They represented for both Gide and Benjamin a perfect locus for examining the way in which the Soviet Union would struggle to transmit, preserve, or transform bits of Western (or traditional Russian) culture in the new Soviet society. Benjamin describes churches as combining the most and least sophisticated forms of art, thereby serving as interesting places to observe what will happen to aesthetic sensibility in the new Soviet Union: how it will cope with new combinations of "high art" and low, tradition and modern taste:

> From the trashily painted ceiling hangs a crystal chandelier. Nevertheless the room is always lit only by candles, a drawing room with sanctified walls against which the ceremony unrolls. The large pictures are greeted by making the sign of the cross and kneeling down to touch the ground with the forehead. . . . Before small, glass-covered pictures lying in rows or singly on desks the genuflection is omitted. One bends over them and kisses the glass. On such desks, beside the most precious old icons, series of the gaudiest oil paintings are displayed. ("Moscow," 127)

Benjamin considers here that gaudy art juxtaposed with ancient icons might represent a new aesthetic regime whose contradictions merit consideration. Gide will attribute (somewhat speciously) the weakness of the art *he* sees in the ex-churches to the feeble cultural position of the intentionally mystifying religion that had been practiced there:

> From the outside the cathedral [St. Isaac in Leningrad] is very beautiful, but the inside is frightful. The big religious paintings which have been kept there might very well launch blasphemy on a successful career; they are really hideous. The museum itself is much less impertinent than I had feared. It was designed with the idea of confronting religious myth with science. Obliging cicerones come to the rescue of lazy visitors who are not likely to be sufficiently convinced by optical instruments and astronomical, biological, anatomical, and statistical tables. Decencies are preserved and there is nothing very outrageous. It savors of Reclus and Flammarion rather than of Léo Taxil. (*Retour de l'U.R.S.S.*, 78)[44]

42. Rolf Tiedemann mentions this passage in "Historical Materialism or Political Messianism? An Interpretation of the Theses 'On the Concept of History'." See especially pp. 98, 107 n. 58.

43. See both "Moscow" and *Moscow Diary*. Benjamin also singles out the *besprizornis* for attention in his essay. See "Moscow," 102–5.

44. L'aspect extérieur de la cathédrale {St. Isaac in Leningrad} est très beau; l'intérieur est affreux. Les grandes peintures pieuses qui y ont été conservées peuvent servir de tremplin au blasphème : elles sont hideuses vraiment. Le musée lui-même est beaucoup moins impertinent que je n'aurais pu craindre. Il s'agissait d'y opposer au mythe

It's more a respectable scientific enterprise (Reclus and Flammarion) than a scandalous, profit-seeking effort to expose a swindle within the church. (Léo Taxil was a self-serving publicist who struggled to spread the news of a scandal involving the Vatican and the Free-Masons, a scandal that provided some of the material for Gide's novel *Les Caves du Vatican*.[45]) Bad paintings are still bad paintings and need to be presented and appreciated as such.

The disdain Gide expresses here for anything that smacks of "du Léo Taxil," anything vulgar and artificial, brings us back to the question of the way in which acceptable bits of Western culture were to be transmitted to the Soviet Union. It brings us back to a letter Gide wrote to Louis Aragon in 1933, in which the same phrase occurs. The Soviet Union was thinking of making a film of *Les Caves du Vatican*, one of the newfound fellow-traveler's best known works, and Aragon writes to Gide from Moscow, telling him he is working to have the project approved. His efforts could be helped if Gide would write back agreeing that the screenplay be written in Moscow and that the screenwriters have the freedom to reinterpret the text a bit politically. Apparently one of the possible changes Aragon mentions in his letter is that the characters in Gide's novel who were swindling while dressed as priests actually *be* priests in the film. In his response to Aragon, Gide describes himself as "too surprised, first of all, and amused by the proposition . . . to think of it seriously." He continues, with a mix of politeness, firmness, and something we might call ironical naivety:

> I understand . . . the reason [for the proposed change] and that what is comic about *Les Caves*, its iconoclastic side, is directed at hypocrisies from which our comrades in the U.S.S.R. no longer have to suffer. From that arises the desire to enlarge and transpose. But what you have proposed here deforms the book too much. It becomes a bit of Léo Taxil. Better just to admit that the book isn't suitable. (*Littérature engagée*, 31–32)[46]

Could we say that Gide finds Aragon's suggestion frankly vulgar? Whenever Gide somehow queers the pitch in his writing, there is usually a simultaneous effort at some form of elegant containment, some pretense of dignity to offset any possibility of vulgarity. Vulgarity is a stylistic choice he rarely more than toys with. Deviance is fine up to a point. In the battles against what is wrong with Western culture, certain standards of decency—perhaps even the "sound values" ("les

---

religieux la science. Des cicérones se chargent d'aider les esprits paresseux que les divers instruments d'optique, les tableaux astronomiques, ou d'histoire naturelle, ou anatomiques, ou de statistique, ne suffiraient pas à convaincre. Cela reste décent et pas trop attentatoire. C'est du Reclus et du Flammarion plutôt que du Léo Taxil (77).

45. For a discussion of Taxil's position in Gide's work, and another discussion of Gide's importance to Benjamin, see Mehlman, esp. 72–76, 86–89. For discussions of Taxil's career, see Jean-André Faucher, *Les Francs-Maçons et le pouvoir*, 140–46, or Eugen Weber, *Satan Franc-Maçon: La mystification de Léo Taxil*.

46. Je comprends de reste sa raison d'être et que le comique des *Caves*, le coup de fronde, porte sur des hypocrisies dont n'ont plus à souffrir les camarades de l'U.R.S.S. De là le désir de grossir et de transposer. Mais le propos ci-dessus dénature par trop le livre. Ça devient du Léo Taxil. Mieux vaut reconnaître aussitôt que le livre ne convient pas.

bons principes") to which Fernandez referred—are to be observed. In "La Lutte antireligieuse" Gide also describes seeing a Russian priest of the worst kind by the side of the road, suitable to be used as a scarecrow, he says, to show people what they had been supporting by supporting religion. Such a priest would be part of the feeble culture that produced the hideous religious paintings Gide saw in St. Isaac's. But Gide balances this image with another, of a monk serving as a guardian of another church they visited, a monk dignified, noble, proud but resigned: "What dignity in his bearing! What nobility in his features! What a sad and resigned pride! Not a word, not a sign from him to us; not an exchange of glances" (79).[47] Again, a moment of silence, of failed communication, of frustrated identification, one might imagine, another of the missed opportunities punctuating Gide's trip, marking the stages of his disillusionment. From all this he draws a lesson about culture:

> The ignoring, the repudiation, of the Gospels and all they have given rise to cannot fail to impoverish humanity and culture in the most lamentable way. I should be sorry for people to be suspicious of me in this respect and to scent here some whiff of my early education and convictions. I should speak in the same way about the Greek myths, which have also, I think, a profound and permanent teaching value. It seems to me absurd to *believe* them, but equally absurd to refuse to recognize the element of truth that informs them, and to think they can be treated with sufficient respect by a smile and a shrug of the shoulders. (80–81)[48]

If we remember the terms of the discussion at the *Union pour la Vérité*, we can again appreciate the difficult corner into which Gide has painted himself. He wants to challenge certain political and sexual presumptions of Western society and hopes to find help in doing so from the Soviet Union. Yet, in his acceptance of his left-wing "discipline" he finds himself giving way to discretion in situations where he might not otherwise exercise it. Further, he finds himself wanting to defend bits of Western culture at various moments when it seems to him that the cultural path of the Soviet Union is going astray. It is as if he would, in certain domains, police the unnecessary excesses he observes. One shouldn't throw out the gospels and Greek myths, he feels obliged to insist, and then has to add: I hope no one will think I'm sounding conservative, lead-footed. It is a question of proper reception —or perhaps proper translation. And sure enough, yet again Gide brings up the problems of translation explicitly, as if they were somehow relevant to his observations about the Soviet Union's overly quick dismissal of certain parts of Gide's culture:

47. Quelle dignité dans son allure! Quelle noblesse dans les traits de son visage! Quelle fierté triste et résignée! Pas une parole, pas un signe de lui à nous; pas un échange de regards (78).

48. L'ignorance, le déni de l'Evangile et de tout ce qui en a découlé, ne va point sans appauvrir l'humanité, la culture, d'une très lamentable façon. Je ne voudrais point que l'on me suspectât ici et flairât quelque relent d'une éducation et d'une conviction premières. Je parlerais de même à l'égard des mythes grecs que je crois, eux aussi, d'un enseignement profond, permanent. Il me paraît absurde de *croire* à eux; mais également absurde de ne point reconnaître la part de vérité qui s'y joue et de penser que l'on peut s'acquitter envers eux avec un sourire et un haussement d'épaules. (79)

The Germans have an excellent image for which I have tried in vain to discover a French equivalent, and which expresses what I find it difficult to say otherwise: *someone threw out the baby with the bathwater.* . . . That the water was dirty and smelly is very likely . . . so dirty, in fact, that without paying any attention to the child, the whole lot was thrown away regardless.

And now if I am told that the church-bells are being recast out of a spirit of conciliation and tolerance, I greatly fear that it may be merely a beginning, that the bath will soon be filled again with dirty water—while the baby will be missing. (81–82)[49]

Gide has returned complexly to the Demeter/Metaneira story again, overlaid both with Christian imagery and with the concern about foreign languages that has been troubling him throughout this text (though here sexuality and camp codes of performance seem rather distant): unlike "das Kind mit dem Bade ausschütten" in German, "jeter l'enfant avec l'eau du bain" doesn't seem to him natural (or perhaps of sufficient classical elegance) in French. We should also notice that the cultural roles here have become more ambiguous, Gide playing Metaneira—the culture police—to Aragon's (or the Soviet Union's) vulgar Demeter. Demophoon, that magical child who was to provide access to a new, dealienated future (a future that was to be both *culturally* and *sexually* different), thus finds himself tugged away from the heat of change *by Gide*—by Gide, because of his simultaneously anticlerical and yet culturally appreciative stance toward religion, a stance he is not sure the communist society he has visited will be able to assume in all its nuances. Gide's predicament is to find himself unable to articulate all at once and in a coherent voice, in a unifying image, his political commitments, the commitments of his sexual politics, and those of his cultural politics.

Foreign Words

I would like to draw some of these threads a bit more closely together, specifically the concerns we have seen about education and the transmission of culture and the uses we have noted of citations from foreign languages. Theodor W. Adorno has written on this subject in two essays: "Words from Abroad" and "On the Use of Foreign Words."[50] Adorno characterizes the use of words from other languages as an instantiation of the alienation of *both the educated and uneducated* from the language they speak. We tend to believe, he says, that the use of a foreign word is the privilege of a cultured education. Adorno insists instead that their use does not

49. Les Allemands usent d'une image excellente et dont je cherche vainement un équivalent en français pour exprimer ce que j'ai quelque mal à dire: *on a jeté l'enfant avec l'eau du bain* . . . Et que l'eau du bain fût sale et puante, il se peut . . . tellement sale même que l'on a tout jeté d'un coup sans contrôle.

Et si maintenant j'entends dire que, par esprit d'accommodement, par tolérance, l'on refond des cloches, j'ai grand-peur que ceci ne soit un commencement, que la baignoire ne s'emplisse à nouveau d'eau sale . . . l'enfant absent. (80)

50. See also Thomas Y. Levin, "Nationalities of Language: Adorno's *Fremdwörter.*"

really depend on a traditional education but simply on knowledge or recognition ("It is really not education but knowledge [Erkenntnis] that decides on its correct use" ["On the Use," 290]). Adorno's claim is that the diverse areas of speech in which these words crop up (Gide's English/Persian proverb being a perfect example) indicate more the way language itself resists the demands of the cultured. By way of the very contexts in which they occur, Adorno implies, foreign words refuse the cultured the privilege of being alone in understanding them; they thereby reveal language itself as a document that bears somewhere within it the record of a class struggle:

> Foreign words should not be protected as one of the privileges of education [Bildung]. Even today their use is no longer determined by education or the claim to it. A worthy task for folklore would be to examine how foreign words operate beneath the sphere of culture [Bildungssphäre] but without fusing with the body of language —at the deepest level of language, in political jargon, in the slang of love, and in an everyday way of speaking that from the standpoint of organic language and linguistic purity would have to be called *corrupt,* but in which we may see the contours of a language to come that cannot be understood either in terms of the idea of the organic or in terms of education. (290, my emphasis)

Adorno's description can help us to account for Gide's linguistic difficulties and his use of foreign words in his *Retour de l'U.R.S.S.:* the Persian proverb, Beethoven's German, the baby in the bathwater, the neglect of French, Gide's ignorance of Russian. Certainly, there is often in Gide's usage a *display* of culture, but, as Adorno hints, such usages always exceed the purposes of this display and suggest precisely something that fails to merge with language perceived as part of *Bildung,* of acculturation. They might, to follow up one of Adorno's suggestions, indicate something corrupt (*verderbt*) or unpatriotic. In "Words from Abroad," Adorno narrates briefly an episode from his own childhood that captures precisely this twofold aspect in the use of foreign words: the superficial level of intellectual snobbery, the second level of a defense of something culturally or politically illicit. Adorno tells of himself and his friend Erich using foreign words during World War I to offend their Gymnasium teachers:

> Using *Zelotentum* or *Paränese* was so enjoyable because we sensed that some of the gentlemen to whom we were entrusted for our education during World War I were not quite sure what those words meant. . . . [We] felt that with our esoteric foreign words we were shooting arrows at our indispensable patriots from our secret kingdom. . . . Foreign words constituted little cells of resistance to the nationalism of World War I. ("Words from Abroad," 186)

Political resistance hidden within schoolboy snobbery, this is the scenario Adorno enacts, and his initial examples in this essay focus heavily on snobbery. He tells how, as a child, he was verbally assaulted on a streetcar by a neighbor for the way he spoke:

> "You goddamned little devil! Shut up with your High German and learn to speak German right." . . . [This neighbor] was the first to teach me what *Rancune* was, a word that has no proper native equivalent in German, unless one were to confuse it with the word *Ressentiment,* a word currently enjoying an unfortunate popularity in Germany but which was likewise imported rather than invented by Nietzsche. In short, it is a case of sour grapes: outrage over foreign words is to be explained in terms of the psychic state of the one who is angry, for whom some grapes are hanging too high up. (186)

Positively Gidean, we might exclaim about this passage, positively camp in its scornful (resentful?) gestures, even as it sets out to provide some analytic clarity, some political content to the situation—content of which Adorno, as a child, would hardly have been aware. Adorno suggests, in fact, that something *else* might be pushing him as a child (and perhaps as an adult) toward these politically structured scenes of foreign words. That something else seems to be eroticism.

> When my friend Erich and I took some delight in using foreign words at the Gymnasium, we were acting as though we were already the privileged possessors of the grapes. . . . Of course [our teachers] could warn us with red marks to avoid unnecessary foreign words, but otherwise they could do nothing more to us than they did when Erich chose "Dear Habakuk" as the salutation for his essay "My Summer Vacation: Letter to a Friend," while I, more cautious and more staid but equally unwilling to divulge the name of my real friend to the head teacher, used the precocious phrase "Dear friend" in my essay. (186)

Acting as if they possessed cultural privilege, in fact, Adorno suggests, they were propelled by something else, a sense of a secret bond whose basis was what? "The pressure to think along prescribed lines forced resistance into deviant and harmless paths [drängte den Widerstand ins Abseitige und Gefahrlose], but in times of crisis gestures that are in themselves trivial often acquire disproportionate symbolic significance" (186–87). *Das Abseitige:* the perverse or the esoteric. What is perverse/esoteric, what is harmless, what trivial, in "Dear Habakuk" or "Dear friend?" What is precocious in "Lieber Freund?" Why should the name of the real friend need to be a secret kept from the teacher? In this telling the young Adorno's perhaps religious and perhaps erotic complicities with his dear friend undergird what he portrays as nascent political resistances. Adorno asserts the erotic basis of these emergent resistances a few sentences later:

> But the fact that we happened upon foreign words in particular was hardly due to political considerations. Rather, since language is erotically charged in its words, at least for the kind of person who is capable of expression, love drives us to foreign words [so treibt Liebe zu den Fremdwörtern]. In reality, it is that love that sets off the indignation over their use. The early craving for foreign words is like the craving for foreign and if possible exotic girls; what lures us is a kind of exogamy of language [es lockt eine Art Exogamie der Sprache], which would like to escape from the sphere of what is always the same, the spell of what one is and knows anyway. At that time foreign words made us blush, like saying the name of a secret love. (187)

One of the Gidean things about this passage is its curious way of insisting on the work of language and the work of love *on* the subject. "Love drives us to foreign words," Adorno says: "So treibt Liebe zu den Fremdwörtern." We might choose to translate: love is the pulsion that punctuates our speech with foreign words. In our foreign words our sexuality occasionally speaks through us, "like saying the name of a secret love," "Wie die Nennung eines verschwiegen geliebten *Namens.*" Could we say: like the naming of a love that dare not speak its name? "Lieber Freund." "Ebensowenig willens, *den Namen* meines wirklichen Freundes dem Oberleher preiszugeben," "just as unwilling to surrender to the headteacher the name of my real friend." Thus hidden in this text of Adorno's we might in fact find a position of resistance to the theorizing we observed him performing at the outset of this chapter as to the "unconscious homosexuality" that aids and abets the formation of the archaic bonds of fascism. For in the context of "Words from Abroad," the *political* effect of the *erotically* driven bond between the two boys with a love for foreign words is the creation of an antinationalist oppositional stance in the face of World War I.

There is another phrase from this last Adorno passage with a Gidean ring. The wonderful impersonality of "es lockt eine Art Exogamie der Sprache," an impersonal "there is luring by a kind of exogamy in language," reminds us of Gide's consistent posture of writing "sous le coup de la sexualité," in the impersonal hands or under the impersonal and curious influence of sexuality. Unlike Gide, Adorno (at least explicitly) heterosexualizes ("exotic girls") this pulse of sexuality in language (thereby almost denying any eroticism one might choose to see him simultaneously tracing in his relationship with his school chum Erich), but this theorizing suggests what we might observe in Gide's foreign usages: an unspoken testimony to some kind of difference, an escape, as Adorno says, "from the sphere of what is always the same," a testimony that insists and persists despite whatever claims to cultural privilege burden those same queer usages.

Adorno, Benjamin, and Gide thus perhaps share (although it is sometimes hard to imagine them agreeing to recognize any common ground) the conviction that language and the position of a writer with respect to language are subjects for political interpretation and that sexuality plays here a central role.

For Adorno, this attention to sexuality seems infrequently foregrounded. The closing image of his essay "On the Use of Foreign Words," for instance, seems to have left sexuality far behind. Foreign words, he tells us, are citations:

> But while the writer [using foreign words] still always thinks that he is quoting from his education and from special knowledge, he is actually quoting from a hidden language that is unknown in the positive sense, a language that overtakes, overshadows, and transfigures the existing one as though it were itself getting ready to be transformed into the language of the future. For the old organic words are like gas lights in a street where the violet light of an autogenous welding apparatus suddenly flames out; they stare into it, inconsolably past, prehistoric and mythological. (291)

We might think about such a passage in relation to Gide's attempts, for instance, in the passages from *Les Nouvelles Nourritures* we examined, to imagine a revolutionary future. Gide tried to imagine that future as a projection of his own desire: "It sometimes seems to me that you will drink with my thirst, and that that which inclines you over this other being whom you caress, is already my own desire." To the extent that we might say Gide knew his desire to be the locus of his alienation, we might also say Gide understood that it was in his alienation that his radicalism was to be found. Adorno here claims that radicalism for language itself. Alienation is inscribed in language, and a possible rupture in that alienation makes itself felt in the use of foreign words. Here it does not seem to be a particular artist who plays the role as *inquiéteur*, nor is any relation to sexuality apparent. Adorno ascribes the critical role to language itself, no matter who the user. Old, aura-filled words are like gaslights, lighting a street in a familiar way, suddenly startled by the new light on the block, the foreign word one lets slip, whether accidentally or intentionally. Comparing foreign words to a welding apparatus, Adorno makes it seem as if these strange words (doing more than any individual writer ever thought they might do) would provide a more effective, one might say more cruel, light in which to perceive previously hidden rapports between a present language and its concomitant social dispensation on the one hand, and radical future possibilities on the other.

The choice of a technological image to shock the reader into a new relation to language is a stylistic preference Adorno shares with Benjamin. A passage well worth reading alongside Adorno's would be this one, from Benjamin's essay on Karl Kraus, where the "monster" plays the role of foreign word:

> [A dilettante's] work is innocent and pure, consuming and purifying masterliness. And therefore the monster stands among us as the messenger of a more real humanism. He is the conqueror of the empty phrase. He feels solidarity not with the slender pine but with the plane that devours it, not with the precious ore but with the blast furnace that purifies it. The average European has not succeeded in uniting his life with technology, because he has clung to the fetish of creative existence. ("Karl Kraus," 272)

In these passages from Adorno and Benjamin, we could choose to see an irrevocable divergence from Gide. Gide's metaphors never included a devouring plane, and the monstrosities he creates in his use of foreign words do not seem meant to reveal doubts about the idea of a creative existence. The intellectual as functionary is not a phrase that one imagines suiting him. Yet Gide's ability to let his sexuality—in all its social contradictions—find expression through him, his ability to make his writing be a place where such an expression could take place, is an ability that carves out a space for certain critical possibilities. Adorno's image of a welding apparatus in "On the Use of Foreign Words" might seem a long way from the complex yet "trivial" erotic innuendoes of his more autobiographical "Words from Abroad"; yet, Gide's strange way of using such words might help us conceive a nontrivial relation between Adorno's two critical efforts. Let us make one last juxtaposition of Gide and Adorno. Think of the Persian proverb quoted in English (as a foreign language): "Women for duty, boys for pleasure, melons for delight." Let it be the illustration for these sentences from Adorno:

> With the foreign word [the writer] can effect a beneficial interruption of the conformist moment of language, the muddy stream in which the specific intention drowns. The hard, contoured quality of the foreign word, the very thing that makes it stand out from the continuum of the language, can be used to bring out what is intended but obscured by the bad generality of language use. Further, the discrepancy between the foreign word and the language can be made to serve the expression of truth. . . . Every foreign word contains the explosive material of enlightenment. . . . In this way foreign words could preserve something of the utopia of language, a language without earth, without subjection to the spell of historical existence, a utopia that lives on unawarely in the childlike use of language. ("Words from Abroad," 189–92)

"Lieber Freund." "Toi qui viendra." "Boys for delight." Not that the expression of sexuality is the expression of some truth. Rather, it is the quality of interruption that marks Gide's writing of sexuality, often the interruption of an ideology that passes for truth, an interruption that refuses truths about sexuality, that offers a perhaps unattainable politics of sexuality "itself" as a possibly curious, radical openness. Produced within the classical writing so quintessentially Gidean, this experience and expression of sexuality exceeds the classical writing as it exceeds Gide. His strange control in expressing whatever in sexuality is beyond him, in capturing the experience of sexuality that preoccupies and yet exceeds him, remains part and parcel of his particular, continually astonishing bent.

EPILOGUE: QUEER TEARS

Doch im Erstarren such ich nicht mein Heil:
Das Schaudern ist der Menschheit bestes Teil;
Wie auch die Welt ihm das Gefühl verteure,
Ergriffen, fühlte er tief das Ungeheure.
                    —Goethe, *Faust*, Part II, 6271–74.

[Yet I do not seek my salvation in fearful paralysis.
Sublime tremblement is the best part of Man;
however rare the world renders that emotion, when
moved, he experiences deeply the tremendous.]

I n his *Journal* in 1927 Gide stingily refuses to acknowledge that he had been *essentially* influenced by anyone. Dostoevsky, Nietzsche, Blake, Browning, he could have missed out on any of them and still written what he had to write. The only influence that really marked him (and even that influence perhaps was not *entirely* essential) was that of Goethe.[1] In *Si le grain ne meurt* Gide chooses a particular word from the second part of Goethe's *Faust* to characterize one of the central experiences of his childhood: *das Schaudern*. In the course of these memoirs he recounts three instances of this experience of "an indefinable anguish," "a tremor," "some enormous presence—a religious, a panic terror" (111/160) ("une angoisse indéfinissable," "un tresaillement," "quelque chose d'énorme, de religieux, de panique" [132/193]).[2] The longest description of *das Schaudern* in *Si le grain ne meurt* might suggest to us that it is an experience we have noticed elsewhere in Gide's writing:

> I have done my best to describe the kind of overpowering suffocation, accompanied
> by tears and sobs, to which I was subject, and which, in its first three manifestations,

1. See his journal entry for November 4, 1927. For a lengthy presentation of Goethe's importance to the young Gide, see the chapter entitled "Préméditations" in the second volume of Delay's *La Jeunesse d'André Gide*, 244–72.
2. On *das Schaudern* in Gide, see Marty, *André Gide: Qui êtes-vous?*, 17–19. See also two chapters from Delay, *La Jeunesse d'André Gide*, vol. 1: "Crises d'angoisse," 171–76, and "Le troisième « Schaudern »," 321–29.

surprised me so greatly. But to those who have never experienced anything of the kind, I am afraid it will remain utterly incomprehensible. Since those days I have become acclimatized to the attacks of this strange aura; they are far from being less frequent, but are tempered now, controlled, and so to speak tamed, so that I have learnt to be as little afraid of them as Socrates of his demon. Drunkenness without wine, as I was soon to realize, was no other than the true lyric ecstasy, and the happy moment in which I was shaken by that divine madness was the very one in which Dionysus visited me. But, alas, for him who has once known the god, how forlorn, how despairing are the languid hours in which he withholds his presence! (161–62)[3]

Recall the elderly African porter with camera on his back, overtaken by a *crise de lyrisme;* recall Gide, freshly back from Africa, sobbing in front of Roger Martin du Gard; recall Gide, thinking of the homeless Soviet children, again sobbing, this time in front of Maria Van Rysselberghe; recall Olivier, in *Les Faux-Monnayeurs,* emerging from underneath the table in a state of drunken dispossession, ready to strike Dhurmer: "He seemed to be moving in a dream. . . . Olivier's hand met nothing but empty air"; recall the young Gide listening to the passionate noises being made by Delphine and Marie: "a melancholy chant, interrupted spasmodically by sobs and cluckings and cries . . . the expression of something more powerful than decency or sleep or the darkness of the night." These are all moments constituted by an encounter with subjective dispossession. In many of them we find tentative, surprising, hesitant, temporary—indeed, impossible— identifications that strive to lay the ground for new kinds of allegiances across political and sexual divides: the elderly Gide to the elderly African porter, Gide to African and Soviet children, Olivier to Bernard and Edouard, the young Gide to two female servants, and those two servants between themselves, on their last night of lovemaking. Many such moments (in which sexuality and politics are necessarily imbricated) have punctuated these pages; these moments establish a tremulant, pulsative consistency in Gide's experience of the relation between subjectivity and sexuality, between subjectivity and political positioning, especially in his experience of sexuality as it takes on form, as it coalesces into a socially inflected representation with necessary political constraints.

As we might glean from the long passage in *Si le grain ne meurt* just cited, the disruptive experience Gide calls *das Schaudern* has a difficult relation to pleasure. On the one hand, this Dionysiac delirium is described as an ecstatic drunkenness. On the other hand, it is almost inevitably a moment of anxiety, a loss of self-

---

3. J'ai décrit de mon mieux cette sorte de suffocation profonde, accompagnée de larmes, de sanglots, à quoi j'étais sujet, et qui, dans les trois premières manifestations que j'en eus et que j'ai redites, me surprit moi-même si fort. Je crains pourtant qu'elle ne demeure parfaitement incompréhensible à qui n'a connu rien d'approchant. Depuis, les accès de cette étrange aura, loin de devenir moins fréquents, s'acclimatèrent, mais tempérés, maîtrisés, apprivoisés pour ainsi dire, de sorte que j'appris à n'en être effrayé, non plus que Socrate de son démon familier. Je compris vite que l'ivresse sans vin n'est autre que l'état lyrique, et que l'instant heureux où me secouait ce délire était celui que Dionysos me visitait. Hélas! pour qui connut le dieu, combien mornes et désespérées les périodes débilitées où il ne consent plus à paraître! (194–95).

control, indeed a dissolution of selfhood—a Gribouillesque confusion of freedom
and death, a panicked dispossession:

> We are not yet born.
> We are not yet in the world.
> There is no world yet.
> Things are not yet made.
> The reason for being is not yet found. ("Antonin Artaud," 137)[4]

Gide, writing in 1948, cites Artaud and his recursive disavowals of all ground on
which subjectivity might take place as an exemplary instantiation of dispossession,
of "un lyrisme forcené," a crazed lyricism. He is writing about Artaud's famous last
performance at the Vieux-Colombier on January 24, 1947: "We had just seen a
miserable man, shaken frightfully by a god, as if he were at the threshold of a deep
grotto, secret den of the sibyl, where nothing profane is tolerated" ("Antonin
Artaud," 137–38).[5] Artaud is the incarnation of a perpetual *Schaudern;* he has
become nothing but that lyric trembling.

Alongside this extreme and fearful Dionysiac experience, we might remember a more peaceable Apollonian one, one we noted in the Introduction, from *Si le
grain ne meurt.* There, a recuperating Gide gaily stretched out on the sand in a
state of expectant somnolence after a dip in some body of water:

> For it was not the bath alone that I loved, but afterwards the expectant, the myth-
> ological waiting for the god's naked and enfolding flame. My body, shot through with
> rays, seemed to enjoy some chemical benefaction; with my garments I laid aside
> anxieties, constraints, worries, and as my will evaporated, I felt myself becoming
> porous as a beehive, and let my sensations secretly distil the honey that flowed into
> the pages of my *Nourritures.* (264)[6]

This is, as it turns out, a Goethean moment,[7] marked by a gentle permeability, a
quietly pleasurable experience of the pressure of sensation on the structures of
subjectivity. Unlike the shock of the confrontation with Artaud, this passage and
the encounter it describes are full of classical *equilibrium,* that quality Gide most
closely associates with Goethe:

---

4. Nous ne sommes pas encore nés.
   Nous ne sommes pas encore au monde.
   Il n'y a pas encore de monde.
   Les choses ne sont pas encore faites.
   La raison d'être n'est pas trouvée . . . (146).
   5. L'on venait de voir un homme misérable, atrocement secoué par un dieu, comme au seuil d'une grotte
profonde, antre secret de la sibylle où rien de profane n'est toléré . . . (146–47).
   6. Car ce n'était pas seulement le bain, que j'aimais, mais la mythologique attente, ensuite, de l'enveloppement
nu du dieu; en mon corps pénétré de rayons, il me semblait goûter je ne sais quel bienfait chimique; j'oubliais avec
mes vêtements, tourments, contraintes, sollicitudes, et, tandis que se volatilisait tout vouloir, je laissais les sensations,
en moi poreux comme une ruche, secrètement distiller ce miel qui coula dans mes *Nourritures* (318).
   7. Cf. Gide's journal entry for September 13, 1893, or also his discussion of Goethe and Nietzsche in the
"Feuillets," the "Recovered Pages" of his journal for 1937.

> Goethe's very universality and the equilibrium in which he keeps his faculties are only possible given a certain moderation and temperance. Or rather, only moderation allows for this happy equilibrium, one Nietzsche is about to refuse. Dionysus will triumph there. Goethe mistrusts intoxication a bit, preferring to allow Apollo to dominate. His work, permeated by rays, does not contain those mysterious recesses where that supreme anguish and its shadows take refuge. He can shed gentle tears; *he is never heard to sob.* ("Goethe," 159, my emphasis)[8]

How strange, then, that the word from Goethe that Gide will appropriate to his own experience should be *das Schaudern:* shudders, shivers, tremblings. How strange that Gide's experience of *das Schaudern* inevitably involves sobbing: "Maman me prit alors sur ses genoux et tâcha de calmer mes sanglots"; "tombant entre les bras de maman, sanglotant, convulsé"; "tout secoué de sanglots"; "[il] éclate bruyamment en sanglots." Sobbing on his mother's knees, in his mother's arms; shaken by sobs; bursting out into sobs in front of his friend Martin du Gard, what could be Apollonian, classical, about this strange loss of balance?

To the extent that we choose to associate classicism with a measured, stable sense of a writing subject's relation to the world, the multiple forms of the experience Gide chooses to call *das Schaudern* call that sense and that subject into question. Those moments of tremulance with which Gide seeds his own peculiar "classicism" clearly have great anxiogenic potential; they also, as moments where curiosity might take charge, glimmer with other potentials, with a productive openness to new, unimagined allegiances, to new social dispensations.

Michel de Certeau has in "The Laugh of Michel Foucault" described one feature that helped constitute Foucault's evasive receptivity, the mobility of his thought. "No, no, I'm not where you are lying in wait for me, but over here, laughing at you," de Certeau quotes Foucault saying. Then he comments,

> He visited books just as he went around San Francisco or Tokyo, with exact and vigilant attention, poised to catch, at the turn of a page or a street, the spark of some strangeness lurking there unnoticed. All these marks of otherness . . . were for him citations of an unthought. . . . When he discovered them he would roll with laughter. Sometimes an irrepressible laugh like the one he mentions apropos a text by Borges, which "when read shatters all the familiar landmarks of thought—our thought, the thought that is of our age and our geography." (de Certeau, 193–94)

"No, no, I'm not where you're looking for me, but over here, sobbing inappropriately in the corner." Rolling with laughter or heaving with sobs—I'm not sure I know how to elaborate on the significance of the difference in the affect being revealed. Nonetheless, I feel inclined to ask: Could it be that the tremulant Gide's irrepressible and queer sobs, seizures, and convulsions—sobs always com-

---

8. L'universalité même de Goethe et l'équilibre où il maintient ses facultés ne vont pas sans une sorte de modération, de tempérance. Ou plutôt : seule la modération permet cet équilibre heureux, auquel bientôt Nietzsche se refuse. Dionysos ici triomphe. Goethe se méfie un peu de l'ivresse et préfère laisser dominer Apollon. Son œuvre, imprégnée de rayons, n'a pas de ces replis mystérieux où s'abrite l'angoisse suprême et ses ténèbres. Il peut verser de douces larmes; *on ne l'entend jamais sangloter* (172–73).

ing from who knows where—contain some of that same potential for openness? That they might accidentally open a space for active, inventive thought? It is with an ear toward those excessive, uncharacterizable sobs that Gide's texts are, for me, most appealingly read. I would share those tears, precisely to the extent that they limn continually nascent, continually unauthorized sexual and political possibilities.

WORKS CITED

Abel, Elizabeth. *Virginia Woolf and the Fictions of Psychoanalysis*. Chicago: University of Chicago Press, 1989.

Adorno, Theodor W. "Freudian Theory and the Pattern of Fascist Propaganda." In *The Essential Frankfurt School Reader*, ed. Andrew Arato and Eike Gebhardt, pp. 118–37. New York: Continuum, 1982.

———. "On the Use of Foreign Words." In *Notes to Literature*, vol. 2, ed. Rolf Tiedemann, trans. Shierry Weber Nicholsen, pp. 286–91. New York: Columbia University Press, 1992.

———. "Words from Abroad." In *Notes to Literature*, vol. 1, ed. Rolf Tiedemann, trans. Shierry Weber Nicholsen, pp. 185–99. New York: Columbia University Press, 1991.

Allégret, Marc. *Carnets du Congo: Voyage avec Gide*. Introduction by Daniel Durosay. Paris: Presses du C.N.R.S., 1987.

Alloula, Malek, *The Colonial Harem*. Trans. Myrna Godzich and Wlad Godzich. Minneapolis: University of Minnesota Press, 1986.

André Gide et notre temps. Paris: Gallimard, 1935.

Anglès, Auguste. *André Gide et le premier groupe de "La Nouvelle Revue Française": Une inquiète maturité, 1913–1914*, vol. 3. Paris: Gallimard, 1986.

Apter, Emily S. *André Gide and the Codes of Homotextuality*. Stanford, Calif.: Anma Libri, 1987.

———. "Female Trouble in the Colonial Harem." *differences* 4 (Spring 1992): 205–24.

———. "Homotextual Counter-Codes: André Gide and the Poetics of Engagement." *Michigan Romance Studies* 6 (1986): 75–87.

———. "La Nouvelle *Nouvelle Héloïse* d'André Gide: *Geneviève* et le féminisme anglais." In *André Gide et l'Angleterre*, ed. Patrick Pollard, pp. 95–99. Birbeck College, London: Le Colloque Gide, 1986.

Banks, Sarah. "Pris au Jeu (ou au *je*): The Impossible Game of 'I' in Gide's Journals." French Department, University of California, Berkeley, photocopy.

Barbedette, Gilles, and Michel Carassou. *Paris Gay 1925*. Paris: Presses de la Renaissance, 1981.

Barthes, Roland. *A Lover's Discourse: Fragments*. Trans. Richard Howard. New York: Hill & Wang, 1978.

Bartlett, Neil. *Who Was That Man? A Present for Mr Oscar Wilde*. London: Serpent's Tail, 1988.

Benjamin, Walter. "André Gide und sein neuer Gegner." In *Gesammelte Schriften III*, ed. Hella Tiedemann-Bartels, pp. 482–95. Frankfurt: Suhrkamp, 1972.

———. *Briefe 2*. Ed. Gershom Scholem and Theodor W. Adorno. Frankfurt: Suhrkamp, 1978.

———. "Karl Kraus." In *Reflections*, pp. 239–73.

———. "Moscow." In *Reflections,* pp. 97–130.

———. *Moscow Diary.* Ed. Gary Smith. Trans. Richard Sieburth. Cambridge, Mass.: Harvard University Press, 1986.

———. *Reflections: Essays, Aphorisms, Autobiographical Writings.* Ed. Peter Demetz. Trans. Edmund Jephcott. New York: Harcourt Brace Jovanovich, 1978.

———. "Surrealism." In *Reflections,* pp. 177–92.

Bersani, Leo. "Death and Literary Authority: Marcel Proust and Melanie Klein." In *The Culture of Redemption,* pp. 7–28. Cambridge: Harvard University Press, 1990.

———. "Is the Rectum a Grave?" *October* 43 (Winter 1987): 197–222.

Blanchot, Maurice. "Gide et la littérature d'expérience." In *La Part du Feu,* pp. 208–20. Paris: Gallimard, 1949. Translation: "Gide and the Concept of Literature as Adventure." In *Gide: A Collection of Critical Essays,* ed. and trans. David Littlejohn, pp. 49–62. Englewood Cliffs, N.J.: Prentice-Hall, 1970.

Boswell, John. "Battle-Worn." *The New Republic* (May 10, 1993): 15, 17–18.

Brosman, Catharine Savage. "« Le Peu de réalité » — Gide et le moi." *André Gide 9, La Revue des Lettres Modernes* 1033–1038 (1991): 29–46.

Brunschwig, Henri. *Mythes et réalités de l'impérialisme colonial français, 1871–1914.* Paris: Armand Colin, 1960.

Butler, Judith. "Critically Queer." *GLQ: A Journal of Lesbian and Gay Studies* 1 (1:1993): 17–32.

———. *Gender Trouble: Feminism and the Subversion of Identity.* New York: Routledge, 1990.

———. "Lana's 'Imitation': Melodramatic Repetition and the Gender Performative." *Genders* 9 (Fall 1990): 1–19.

———. "The Lesbian Phallus and the Morphological Imaginary" *differences* 4 (1:Spring 1992): 133–71.

Caillois, Roger. "La Mante religieuse." In *Le Mythe et l'homme,* pp. 37–85. Paris: Gallimard, 1938.

———. "Mimétisme et psychasthénie légendaire." In *Le Mythe et l'homme,* pp. 86–122.

———. "Mimicry and Legendary Psychasthenia." Trans. John Shepley. *October* 31 (Winter 1984): 17–32.

Caute, David. *Communism and the French Intellectuals.* London: André Deutsch, 1964.

Cobbett, William. *A Grammar of the English Language* (1818, 1832). Delmar, N.Y.: Scholars' Facsimiles and Reprints, 1986.

Cohen, Ed. *Talk on the Wilde Side: Toward a Genealogy of a Discourse on Male Sexualities.* New York: Routledge, 1993.

Copley, Antony. *Sexual Moralities in France, 1780–1980: New Ideas on the Family, Divorce, and Homosexuality.* London: Routledge, 1989.

Coquery-Vidrovitch, Catherine. *Le Congo au temps des grandes compagnies concessionnaires, 1898–1930.* Paris: Mouton, 1972.

Crimp, Douglas. "The Boys in My Bedroom." In *The Lesbian and Gay Studies Reader,* ed. Henry Abelove, Michèle Aina Barale, and David M. Halperin, pp. 344–49. New York: Routledge, 1993.

———. "Mourning and Militancy." *October* 51 (Winter 1989): 3–18.

Darras, Jacques. "Le Voyage en Afrique." *Esprit* 128 (July 1987): 1–12.

Dean, Tim. "The Psychoanalysis of AIDS." *October* 63 (Winter 1993): 83–116.

de Certeau, Michel. "The Laugh of Michel Foucault." In *Heterologies: Discourse on the Other,* trans. Brian Massumi, pp. 193–98. Minneapolis: University of Minnesota Press, 1986.

Delay, Jean. *Discours de réception de M. Jean Delay à l'Académie Française et réponse de M. Pasteur Vallery-Radot.* Paris: Gallimard, 1960.

———. *La Jeunesse d'André Gide.* Vol. 1: *André Gide avant André Walter, 1869–1890.* Vol. 2: *D'André Walter à André Gide, 1890–1895.* Paris: Gallimard, 1956, 1957. An abridged translation exists as *The Youth of André Gide,* abridged and translated by June Guicharnaud (Chicago: University of Chicago Press, 1963). I have made my own translations from the complete French edition.

de Man, Paul. "The Resistance to Theory." In *The Resistance to Theory,* pp. 3–20. Minneapolis: University of Minnesota Press, 1986.

———. "Whatever Happened to André Gide?" In *Critical Writings, 1953–1978,* ed. Lindsay Waters, pp. 130–36. Minneapolis: University of Minnesota Press, 1989. Originally in the *New York Review of Books* 4 (May 6, 1965): 15–17.

Desplantes, Fr. *Les Explorateurs français du continent noir.* Limoges: Eugène Ardant et Cie, n.d.

Dollimore, Jonathan. *Sexual Dissidence: Augustine to Wilde, Freud to Foucault.* Oxford: Oxford University Press, 1991.

Dugas, Guy. "André Gide et Athman: Le Roman d'une amitié vraie." *Cahiers de Tunisie* 30 (1982): 247–69.

Edelman, Lee. "The Mirror and the Tank: 'AIDS,' Subjectivity, and the Rhetoric of Activism." In *Writing AIDS: Gay Literature, Language, and Analysis,* ed. Timothy F. Murphy and Suzanne Poirier, pp. 9–38. New York: Columbia University Press, 1993.

Ellmann, Richard. "Corydon and Ménalque." In *Golden Codgers: Biographical Speculations,* pp. 81–100. London: Oxford University Press, 1973.

Faucher, Jean-André. *Les Francs-Maçons et le pouvoir.* Paris: Librarie Académique Perrin, 1986.

Fernandez, Ramon. *André Gide.* 1931. Reprinted as *Gide ou le courage de s'engager.* Paris: Klincksieck, 1985.

Foucart, Claude. "André Gide dialogue avec la nouvelle génération allemande: La rencontre avec Walter Benjamin en 1928." *Bulletin des amis d'André Gide* 44 (October 1979): 3–32.

Foucault, Michel. *The History of Sexuality.* Vol. 1: *An Introduction:* Trans. Robert Hurley. New York: Vintage, 1990.

———. *Histoire de la sexualité.* Vol. 2: *L'Usage des plaisirs.* Paris: Gallimard, 1984. Translation: *The Use of Pleasure.* Trans. Robert Hurley. New York: Vintage, 1986.

Fouillée, Alfred. "La Psychologie des sexes et ses fondemens physiologiques." *Revue des deux mondes* 119 (1893): 397–429.

Freud, Sigmund. "A Child Is Being Beaten." In *Sexuality and the Psychology of Love,* ed. Philip Rieff, pp. 107–32. New York: Collier, 1963.

———. "From the History of an Infantile Neurosis." In *Three Case Histories,* ed. Philip Rieff, pp. 187–316. New York: Collier, 1963.

———. *The Interpretation of Dreams.* Trans. James Strachey. New York: Avon, 1965.

Gagnier, Regenia. *Idylls of the Marketplace: Oscar Wilde and the Victorian Public.* Stanford, Calif.: Stanford University Press, 1986.

Gelder, Ann. "The 'Retour' of the Native: Film and Repetition in Gide's African Travel Journals." French Department, University of California, Berkeley, photocopy.

Gide, André. *Ainsi soit-il ou Les Jeux sont faits.* In *Journal, 1939–1949, Souvenirs,* pp. 1161–1243. Translation: *So Be It, or The Chips Are Down.* Trans. Justin O'Brien. New York: Alfred A. Knopf, 1959.

————. *Amyntas*. Paris: Gallimard, 1925. Translation: *Amyntas*. Trans. Richard Howard. New York: Ecco Press, 1988.

————. "Antonin Artaud." In *Feuillets d'automne*, pp. 145–47. Translation: In *Autumn Leaves*, pp. 136–38.

————. *Carnets d'Egypte*. In *Journal, 1939–1949, Souvenirs*, pp. 1047–77.

————. *Correspondance André Gide–Dorothy Bussy, II: janvier 1925–novembre 1936. Cahiers André Gide* 10. Paris: Gallimard, 1981.

————. *Correspondance André Gide–Roger Martin du Gard, 1913–1934*. Introduction by Jean Delay. Paris: Gallimard, 1968.

————. *Correspondance avec sa mère, 1880–1895*. Ed. Claude Martin. Paris: Gallimard, 1988.

————. *Corydon*. Paris: Gallimard, 1924. Translation: *Corydon*. Trans. Richard Howard. New York: Farrar, Straus and Giroux, 1983.

————. "Crise du Français." In *Œuvres complètes d'André Gide*, vol. 9, ed. L. Martin-Chauffier, pp. 161–72. Paris: nrf, 1935.

————. *L'Ecole des femmes suivi de Robert et de Geneviève*. Paris: Gallimard, 1936. Translation: *The School for Wives, Robert, Geneviève*. Trans. Dorothy Bussy. Cambridge, Mass.: Robert Bentley, 1980.

————. *Et nunc manet in te*. In *Journal, 1939–1949, Souvenirs*, pp. 1121–60. Translation: *Madeleine*. Trans. Justin O'Brien. New York: Knopf, 1952.

————. *Les Faux-Monnayeurs*. Paris: Gallimard, 1925. Translation: *The Counterfeiters with Journal of "The Counterfeiters."* Trans. Dorothy Bussy. New York: Vintage, 1973.

————. *Feuillets d'automne, précédés de quelques récents écrits*. Paris: Mercure de France, 1949. Translation: *Autumn Leaves*. Trans. Elsie Pell. New York: Philosophical Library, 1950.

————. "Goethe." In *Feuillets d'automne*, pp. 161–73. Translation: In *Autumn Leaves*, pp. 147–59.

————. *Interviews imaginaires*. New York: Jacques Schiffrin, 1943. Translation: *Imaginary Interviews*. Trans. Malcolm Cowley. New York: Knopf, 1944.

————. *Journal, 1889–1939*. Paris: Gallimard, 1951.

————. *Journal, 1939–1949, Souvenirs*. Paris: Gallimard, 1954.

————. *Journal des Faux-Monnayeurs*. Paris: Gallimard, 1927. Translation: *Journal of "The Counterfeiters."* Trans. Justin O'Brien. In *The Counterfeiters with Journal of "The Counterfeiters."*

————. *The Journals of André Gide*. 4 vols. Trans. Justin O'Brien. New York: Knopf, 1947–1951.

————. "Les Juifs, Céline et Maritain." *La Nouvelle Revue Française*, April 1, 1938, pp. 630–36.

————. *Littérature engagée*. Paris: Gallimard, 1950.

————. "Ma mère." In *Journal: 1939–1949, Souvenirs*, pp. 1099–102. Translation: "My Mother." In *Autumn Leaves*, pp. 32–36.

————. *Les Nourritures terrestres suivi de Les Nouvelles Nourritures*. Paris: Gallimard, 1917–1936. Translation: *Fruits of the Earth and Later Fruits of the Earth*. Trans. Dorothy Bussy. London: Secker & Warburg, 1952.

————. *Oscar Wilde*. Paris: Mercure de France, 1913.

————. "Preface." In *Catalogue de livres et manuscrits provenant de la bibliothèque de M. André Gide*. Paris: Edouard Champion, 1925.

————. "Préface à *Armance*." In *Œuvres complètes*, vol. 11, ed. L. Martin-Chauffier, pp. 67–84. Paris: nrf, 1936. Translation: "Preface to *Armance*." In *Pretexts: Reflec-*

tions on Literature and Morality, ed. Justin O'Brien, trans. Blanche A. Price, pp. 260–74. N.p.: Meridian Books, 1959.

———. *Prétextes: Réflexions sur quelques points de littérature et de morale*. Paris: Mercure de France, 1919.

———. *Retour de l'U.R.S.S. suivi de Retouches à mon Retour de l'U.R.S.S.* Paris: Gallimard, 1936 and 1937. Translation: *Return from the U.S.S.R.* Trans. Dorothy Bussy. New York: Knopf, 1937.

———. *Romans, récits et soties, œuvres lyriques*. Paris: Gallimard, 1958.

———. *Si le grain ne meurt*. Paris: Gallimard, 1955. Translation: *If It Die . . .* Trans. Dorothy Bussy. London: Penguin, 1977.

———. *Voyage au Congo, suivi de Le Retour du Tchad*. Paris: Gallimard, 1927. Translation: *Travels in the Congo*. Trans. Dorothy Bussy. New York: Knopf, 1929.

Gould, Stephen Jay. "Only His Wings Remained." In *The Flamingo's Smile: Reflections in Natural History*, pp. 40–55. New York: Norton, 1985.

Goulet, Alain. *André Gide, "Les Faux-Monnayeurs," mode d'emploi*. Paris: Sedes, 1991.

———. "Sur une figure obsédante — Vers une origine de la création littéraire." *André Gide 9, La Revue des Lettres Modernes* 1033–1038 (1991): 47–60.

———. "Le Voyage en A.E.F. dans *L'Illustration*." *Bulletin des Amis d'André Gide* 13 (July 1985): 31–58.

Gourévitch, Michel. "Eugénie Sokolnicka: Pionnier de la psychanalyse et inspiratrice d'André Gide." *Médecine de France* 219 (1971): 17–22.

Goux, Jean-Joseph. *Les Monnayeurs du langage*. Paris: Editions Galilée, 1984.

———. "The Phallus: Masculine Identity and the 'Exchange of Women.'" *differences* 4(1) (Spring 1992): 40–75.

Green, Richard. *The "Sissy Boy Syndrome" and the Development of Homosexuality*. New Haven: Yale University Press, 1987.

Guérin, Daniel. "André Gide et l'amour." In *Shakespeare et Gide en correctionnelle*, pp. 57–68. Paris: Les Editions du Scorpion, 1959.

———. *Le Feu du sang: Autobiographie politique et charnelle*. Paris: Grasset, 1977.

———. "Préface" to Charles Fourier, *Vers la liberté en amour*, pp. 7–44. Paris: Gallimard, 1975.

Halperin, David M. "Plato and the Erotics of Narrativity." *Oxford Studies in Ancient Philosophy*. Suppl. vol. 1992: *Methods of Interpreting Plato and His Dialogues*. Ed. James C. Klagge and Nicholas D. Smith. (1992): 93–129.

———. "Two Views of Greek Love: Harald Patzer and Michel Foucault." In *One Hundred Years of Homosexuality and Other Essays on Greek Love*, pp. 54–71. New York: Routledge, 1990.

Hebey, Pierre. *La "Nouvelle Revue Française" des années sombres, 1940–1941*. Paris: Gallimard, 1992.

Hocquenghem, Guy. *Homosexual Desire* (1972). Trans. Daniella Dangoor. Durham, N.C.: Duke University Press, 1993.

Hollier, Denis. "Mimesis and Castration 1937." *October* 31 (Winter 1984): 3–15.

———. "On Equivocation (between Literature and Politics)." *October* 55 (Winter 1990): 3–22.

Howard, Richard. "1911: From Exoticism to Homosexuality." In *A New History of French Literature*, ed. Denis Hollier et al., pp. 836–42. Cambridge, Mass.: Harvard University Press, 1989.

Janet, Pierre. "Les Troubles de la personnalité sociale." *Annales médico-psychologiques* 2(2) (July 1937): 149–200.

Kaplan, Alice Yaeger. *Reproductions of Banality: Fascism, Literature, and French Intellectual Life*. Minneapolis: University of Minnesota Press, 1986.

Karlinsky, Simon. "Russia's Gay Literature and Culture: The Impact of the October Revolution." In *Hidden from History: Reclaiming the Gay and Lesbian Past*, ed. Martin Bauml Duberman, Martha Vicinus, and George Chauncey, Jr., pp. 347–64. New York: New American Library, 1989.

Kaufmann, Vincent. "Michel Leiris: « On ne part pas »." *La Revue des sciences humaines* 90(214) (April–June 1989): 145–62.

Klein, Melanie. "Early Stages of the Oedipus Conflict." In *Contributions to Psycho-Analysis, 1921–1945*, pp. 202–14. London: The Hogarth Press, 1948.

———. "The Oedipus Complex in the Light of Early Anxieties." In *Contributions to Psycho-Analysis, 1921–1945*, pp. 339–90.

———. "The Origins of Transference." In *Envy and Gratitude and Other Works, 1946–1963*, pp. 48–56. New York: The Free Press, 1975.

———. *The Psycho-Analysis of Children*. New York: The Free Press, 1975.

Kristeva, Julia. "Place Names." In *Desire in Language: A Semiotic Approach to Literature and Art*, trans. Thomas Gora, Alice Jardine, Leon S. Roudiez, pp. 272–94. New York: Columbia University Press, 1980.

Lacan, Jacques. *Ecrits*. Paris: Seuil, 1966.

———. *Ecrits*, vol. 1. Paris: Seuil (Points), 1966.

———. *Feminine Sexuality: Jacques Lacan and the* école freudienne. Ed. Juliet Mitchell and Jacqueline Rose. Trans. Jacqueline Rose. New York: Norton, 1985.

———. "L'Instance de la lettre dans l'inconscient ou la raison depuis Freud." In *Ecrits*, vol. 1, pp. 249–89. Translation: "The Agency of the Letter in the Unconscious or Reason since Freud." Trans. Alan Sheridan. In Ecrits: *A Selection*, pp. 146–78. New York: Norton, 1977.

———. "Jeunesse de Gide ou la lettre et le désir." In *Ecrits*, pp. 739–64.

———. *Le Séminaire*, vol. 3: *Les Psychoses*. Paris: Seuil, 1981.

———. *Le Séminaire*, vol. 11: *Les Quatre Concepts fondamentaux de la psychanalyse*. Paris: Seuil, 1973. Translation: *The Four Fundamental Concepts of Psycho-analysis*. Trans. Alan Sheridan. New York: Norton, 1978.

Lacoue-Labarthe, Philippe. "Diderot: Paradox and Mimesis." In *Typography: Mimesis, Philosophy, Politics*, ed. Christopher Fynsk, trans. Jane Popp, pp. 248–66. Cambridge: Harvard University Press, 1989.

———. "Typography." In *Typography: Mimesis, Philosophy, Politics*, ed. Christopher Fynsk, trans. Eduardo Cadava, pp. 43–138.

Lang, Jonathan C. "Some Perversions of Pastoral: Or Tourism in Gide's *L'Immoraliste*." *Genders*, forthcoming.

Laplanche, Jean, and Pontalis, Jean-Bertrand. "Fantasy and the Origins of Sexuality." In *Formations of Fantasy*, ed. Victor Burgin, James Donald, and Cora Kaplan, pp. 5–34. London: Methuen, 1986.

Last, Jef. "D'Oscar Wilde aux *Nouvelles Nourritures*." *La Revue des Lettres Modernes*, 223–77 (1970): 122–35.

Lejeune, Philippe. *Exercices d'ambiguïté: Lectures de "Si le grain ne meurt" d'André Gide*. Paris: Lettres modernes, 1974.

Levin, Thomas Y. "Nationalities of Language: Adorno's *Fremdwörter*." *New German Critique* 36 (Fall 1985): 111–19.

Licari, Anita. "Lo Sguardo Coloniale: Per una analisi dei codici dell'esotismo a partire dal

Voyage au Congo di Gide." In Anita Licari, Roberta Maccagnani, Lina Zecchi, *Letteratura, Esotismo, Colonialismo,* introduction by Gianni Celati, pp. 29–62. Bologna: Capelli, 1978.

Littlejohn, David, ed. *Gide: A Collection of Critical Essays.* Englewood Cliffs, N.J.: Prentice-Hall, 1970.

Lottman, Herbert R. *The Left Bank: Writers, Artists, and Politics from the Popular Front to the Cold War.* Boston: Houghton Mifflin, 1982.

Marshall, W. J. "André Gide and the U.S.S.R.: A Re-appraisal." *Australian Journal of French Studies* 20 (1983): 37–49.

Marty, Eric. *André Gide: Qui êtes-vous? Avec les entretiens André Gide–Jean Amrouche.* Lyon: La Manufacture, 1987.

———. *L'Ecriture du jour: Le* Journal *d'André Gide.* Paris: Seuil, 1985.

Marx, Karl. *Capital,* vol. 1. Trans. Samuel Moore and Edward Aveling. New York: The Modern Library, 1906.

Massis, Henri. "L'Influence de M. André Gide." *La Revue universelle* 7 (15 November 1921): 500–509.

Maubon, Catherine. "Sguardo e scrittura in *Voyage au Congo.*" *Il Verri* 9–10 (1986): 61–89.

Maulnier, Thierry. *Mythes socialistes.* Paris: Gallimard, 1936.

Maurer, Rudolf. *André Gide et l'U.R.S.S.* Berne: Editions Tillier, 1983.

Mehlman, Jeffrey, " 'Jewish Literature' and the Art of André Gide." In *Legacies of Anti-Semitism in France,* pp. 64–82. Minneapolis: University of Minnesota Press, 1983.

Moore, Ann M. "Women, Socialization, and Language in *Les Faux-Monnayeurs.*" *Stanford French Review* 11(2) (Summer 1987): 211–28.

Moutote, Daniel. *André Gide: L'Engagement, 1926–1939.* Paris: Sedes, 1991.

Offen, Karen. "Depopulation, Nationalism, and Feminism in Fin-de-Siècle France." *American Historical Review* 89 (1984): 648–76.

Painter, George D. *André Gide: A Critical Biography.* New York: Atheneum, 1968.

Peters, Arthur King. *Jean Cocteau and André Gide: An Abrasive Friendship.* New Brunswick, N.J.: Rutgers University Press, 1973.

Pollard, Patrick. *André Gide: Homosexual Moralist.* New Haven: Yale University Press, 1991.

Pratt, Mary Louise. *Imperial Eyes: Travel Writing and Transculturation.* London: Routledge, 1992.

———. "Mapping Ideology: Gide, Camus, and Algeria." *College Literature* 8 (1981): 158–74.

Proust, Marcel. *A la recherche du temps perdu,* vol. 2. Paris: Gallimard, 1954. Translation: *Remembrance of Things Past,* vol. 2. Trans. C. K. Scott Moncrieff and Terence Kilmartin. New York: Random House, 1981.

———. *Lettres à André Gide.* Neuchatel: Ides et Calendes, 1949.

Roof, Judith. *A Lure of Knowledge: Lesbian Sexuality and Theory.* New York: Columbia University Press, 1991.

Rousseau, G. S. "Apologies for Interdiction: The Homosexual Question." *Journal of the History of the Behavioral Sciences* 26 (July 1990): 225–40.

Sand, George. *Histoire du véritable Gribouille* (1850). Paris: Albin Michel Jeunesse, 1987.

Schlumberger, Jean. *Madeleine et André Gide.* Paris: Gallimard, 1956.

Schneider, William H. *An Empire for the Masses: The French Popular Image of Africa, 1870–1900.* Westport, Conn.: Greenwood, 1982.

Sedgwick, Eve Kosofsky. *Epistemology of the Closet.* Berkeley: University of California Press, 1990.

———. "How to Bring Your Kids Up Gay." *Social Text* 29 (1991): 18–27.

Sedgwick, Peter. "Out of Hiding: The Comradeships of Daniel Guérin." *Salmagundi* 58–59 (Fall 1982–Winter 1983): 197–220.

Serant, Paul. *Les Dissidents de l'Action Française.* Paris: Copernic, 1978.

Shattuck, Roger. "Having Congress." In *The Innocent Eye: On Modern Literature and the Arts,* pp. 3–37. New York: Washington Square Press, 1986.

Signorile, Michelangelo. *Queer in America: Sex, the Media, and the Closets of Power.* New York: Random House, 1993.

Silverman, Kaja. "The Lacanian Phallus." *differences* 4(1) (Spring 1992): 84–115.

———. *The Subject of Semiotics.* New York: Oxford University Press, 1983.

Sjövall, Björn. *Psychology of Tension: An Analysis of Pierre Janet's concept of « tension psychologique » together with an historical aspect.* Trans. Alan Dixon. Studia Scientiae Paedagogicae Upsaliensia, IX. Stockholm: 1967.

Smith, John H. "Abulia: Sexuality and Diseases of the Will in the Late Nineteenth Century." *Genders* 6 (Fall 1989): 102–24.

Smith, Olivia. *The Politics of Language, 1791–1819.* Oxford: Oxford University Press, 1984.

Steakley, James D. "Iconography of a Scandal: Political Cartoons and the Eulenburg Affair in Wilhelmin Germany." In *Hidden from History: Reclaiming the Gay and Lesbian Past,* ed. Martin Bauml Duberman, Martha Vicinus, and George Chauncey, Jr., pp. 233–63. New York: New American Library, 1989.

Steel, D. A. "Escape and Aftermath: Gide in Cambridge, 1918." *The Yearbook of English Studies* 15 (1985): 125–59.

———. "Gide et Freud." *Revue d'histoire littéraire de la France* 77 (1977): 48–74.

Suret-Canale, Jean. *French Colonialism in Tropical Africa, 1900–1945.* Trans. Till Gottheiner. New York: Pica Press, 1971.

Tiedemann, Rolf. "Historical Materialism or Political Messianism? An Interpretation of the Theses 'On the Concept of History'." *The Philosophical Forum* 15 (1983–1984): 71–104.

Van Rysselberghe, Maria. *Les Cahiers de la Petite Dame, 1918–1929. Cahiers André Gide* 4. Paris: Gallimard, 1973.

———. *Les Cahiers de la Petite Dame, 1929–1937. Cahiers André Gide* 5. Paris: Gallimard, 1974.

Walker, David H. *Modern Novelists: André Gide.* New York: St. Martin's Press, 1990.

Walsh, Michael. "Reading the Real in the Seminar on the Psychoses." In *Criticism and Lacan: Essays and Dialogue on Language, Structure, and the Unconscious,* ed. Patrick Colm Hogan and Lalita Pandit, pp. 64–83. Athens: University of Georgia Press, 1990.

Weber, Eugen. *Satan Franc-Maçon: La Mystification de Léo Taxil.* Paris: René Julliard, 1964.

Weightman, John. "André Gide and the Homosexual Debate." *The American Scholar* (Autumn 1990): 591–601.

Winkler, John J. "Laying Down the Law: The Oversight of Men's Sexual Behavior in Classical Athens." In *The Constraints of Desire: The Anthropology of Sex and Gender in Ancient Greece,* pp. 45–70. New York: Routledge, 1990.

Žižek, Slavoj. "Rossellini: Woman as Symptom of Man." *October* 54 (Fall 1990): 19–44.

———. *The Sublime Object of Ideology.* London: Verso, 1989.

Zoctizoum, Yarisse. *Histoire de la Centrafrique,* vol. 1: *1879–1959.* Paris: L'Harmattan, 1983.

INDEX

N.B.: Unless otherwise noted, all works are by Gide.

Abel, Elizabeth, 45
Aberration, de Man's concept of,
    185–87, 197, 199
Adorno, Theodor W., 181–82, 204,
    211–16; and foreign languages, 189,
    211–16
Adoum (Gide's attendant in Africa),
    154, 155n, 173
"Adresse aux jeunes gens de
    l'U.R.S.S.", 192
Aesthetics and politics, 197–99, 206
Africa, 50, 190; Algeria, 50, 57, 61,
    63–64, 146; Bangui, 150; Biskra,
    59–60, 62–66, 146; Brazzaville,
    149–52, 157, 176; as an escape,
    146; Gide's problem of vision in,
    149–51, 157–64, 179; Massa, 160;
    problem of history in, 161–62, 164;
    and sexual relations between
    European men and African women,
    63; temporality in, 154; transport in,
    174–80; and Tuareg, 50–51; and
    Tuarag spears, 49–51, 146; and
    'Uled-Nayl women, 60–62. See also
    French Equatorial Africa; North
    Africa
AIDS, 39n, 72, 74, 88
Ainsi soit-il (So Be It), 3n, 5–6, 14,
    15n, 34n, 173, 196
Alienation, 190, 193, 215; Lacan's
    concept of, 19, 167–73, 179
Allegiances, 190, 218. See also Sexuality:
    allegiances in
Allégret, Marc, 12, 149, 151, 176;
    Carnets du Congo, 12n, 148; filming
    the Massa, 160

Alloula, Malek, 61
Amyntas, 34n, 51, 153, 158
Anglès, Auguste, 11n
Antisemitism, 3n, 92, 105
"Antonin Artaud," 219
Apter, Emily S., 7n, 13n, 28n, 92n,
    106n, 188n
Aragon, Louis, 209, 211
Artaud, Antonin, 219
Athman (Ben Salah) (Gide's servant in
    Algeria), 12n, 53, 59, 63–67,
    117–18
Automatism, 81, 87–88

Balzac, Honoré de, 11
Banks, Sarah, 66n, 99n
Barbedette, Gilles, 16n, 182n
Barbusse, Henri, 182, 201, 204
Barrès, Maurice, 79
Barthes, Roland, 34–36
Bartlett, Neil, 12n, 206n
Baudelaire, Charles, 9–10
Beethoven, Ludwig van, 204, 212
Benjamin, Walter, 189, 204–8, 205n,
    214, 215; letter to Horkheimer,
    207–8
Bent, Gide's, 4–5, 20–21, 186–87, 216
Bersani, Leo, 21–22, 45n, 38–41,
    88–90
Besprizornis (vagabond children), 19,
    189–93, 203, 208n, 218
Blanchot, Maurice, 185n
Blum, Léon, 145; Du mariage, 92
Boswell, John, 90n
Boy with Arms Akimbo/Girl with Arms
    Akimbo (activist group), 22–23

231

Brouardel (Gide's childhood doctor), 49–52
Brosman, Catherine Savage, 111n
Brothel, 92
Brunschwig, Henri, 155n
Bussy, Dorothy, 164n
Butler, Judith, 46n, 84n, 89n, 135n

Caillois, Roger, 84n, 85–89, 102
Carassou, Michel, 16n, 182n
Carnets d'Egypte, 195
Castration anxiety, 46–47, 49–51, 85–87; in Freud, 134; postponement of, 135; of Wolf Man, 130
Caute, David, 188n
Les Caves du Vatican (*Lafcadio's Adventures*), 3, 11, 209; Proust and, 11
Céline, Louis-Ferdinand, 3n
Choang-tsu, 128–30
Claudel, Paul, 6, 8, 11
Closeted identity, 71, 195, 198
Cobbett, William, 102–3
Cocteau, Jean, 98
Cohen, Ed, 206
Colonial tourism, politics of, 156–57. *See also* Gide, André: relation to tourism
Colonialism. *See* Gide, André: relation to colonialism
Compagnie Forestière, 156n, 177
Conrad, Joseph, 147, 175
Consequence and consistency in sexuality in *Les Faux-Monnayeurs,* 116–17, 120–22, 129, 130–31, 133–35, 139–42
Copley, Anthony, 72n
Coppet, Marcel de, 176, 177n
Coquery-Vidrovitch, Catherine, 145n, 176
Correspondance André Gide–Roger Martin du Gard, 143–44, 145n, 147
Correspondance avec sa mère, 52, 63–66
Corydon, 68–95 passim, 105–6, 109n, 111, 120, 145, 200n; and decadence, 32; and openness about sexuality, 11, 14–17, 108; Proust and, 9–10

Crimp, Douglas, 24n, 72n
"Crise du Français," 96–98

Darras, Jacques, 152n, 160n
de Certeau, Michel, 220
de Man, Paul, 8, 183–87, 190, 195; *Allegories of Reading,* 185
Dealienation. *See* Separation, Lacanian concept of
Dean, Tim, 39n
Decadence, 31–32, 34, 36–37, 39
"Défense de la langue française," 99
Delay, Jean, 18, 53, 55–56, 112, 115–21, 124–25, 133, 143, 145, 217n; analysis of homosexuality, 120–21, 133; on Gide's relation to the maternal, 67n, 165–66
Deleuze, Gilles, 200n
Delphine (Gide's cook), 56–57, 166, 218
Demeter and Metaneira, myth of, 19, 193–95, 211
"La Détresse de notre Afrique Equatoriale," 145, 148n, 155
Devirilization, 85–86, 88–89
Diderot, Denis, 81n
Difference, sexual, 85–87
Dispossession, 18; of the subject, 218–19. *See also* Sexuality: dispossession in
Dollimore, Jonathan, 8n, 9n, 11–12n, 15n, 22n, 30n, 64n, 121n, 158, 206n
Douglas, Alfred, 12n, 67n
Dreams: and repose, 126–29; and representation, 128–29. *See also* Representation, repose from; Sexuality: and sleep
Drieu la Rochelle, Pierre, 100
Drumont, Edouard, 105
Du Bos, Charles, 6, 11
Dugas, Guy, 64n, 66n
Durosay, Daniel, 12n, 149n, 151–52, 156, 160n, 176

L'Ecole des femmes (*The School for Wives*), 17, 91, 92n, 96, 103–7, 137n

Edelman, Lee, 39n, 46n
Ellmann, Richard, 8n
Emerson, Waldo, 163
Et nunc manet in te (*Madeleine*), 12n

Fabre, J.-H., 84n
Fantasy, 26, 30, 40, 51; of annihilation
    in sexuality, 89; of castration, 85;
    colonial, 61–62; of dealienation in
    tourism, 173–74; of death and
    disappearance, 19, 164, 169–70,
    172–73, 175, 178; in Freud, 131; of
    Gribouille, 165; infantile, 45,
    47–48; normativity of, 52; political
    and cultural, 48, 50–51; relation of
    personal to political, 170; of
    self-punishment, 165–66
Fascism, 181, 189. *See also* Gide,
    André: relation to fascism
Faucher, Jean-André, 209n
Les Faux-Monnayeurs (*The
    Counterfeiters*), 77, 108–17, 121–24,
    126n, 133–48, 153, 169; as canonic
    novel, 197; de Man and, 187; and
    openness about sexuality, 11, 14,
    17–18, 194
Fernandez, Ramon, 31–33, 36, 196–97,
    199, 210
Le Figaro, "Anti-Littré" column in, 101,
    107
"Find the good fag" game, 109n,
    110–11
Foreign languages and expressions:
    competency in, 4–6, 189–92,
    202–4; use of, 201–3,
    211–17
Foucart, Claude, 204n
Foucault, Michel, 30n, 38, 40, 57n,
    124n, 220
Fouillée, Alfred, 82n
Fourier, Charles, 182n
French Equatorial Africa, 143–65
    passim, 172–80 passim
Freud, Sigmund, 24, 25n, 26, 42,
    48–49, 126, 127n, 130–31, 134;
    Gide's knowledge of, 124n; and "the
    homosexual," 134n; theories of
    sadism and masochism, 165; *Three*

Essays on the Theory of Sexuality,
    132
Frustration, 161–62, 164, 179–80; and
    the desire of the other, 168; of Gide
    in writing, 151; and Gide's Soviet
    trip, 189; and grammar, 163–64; of
    nonseparability and division, 167
    (*see also* Self: split); and the
    personal as inextricable from the
    political, 170; of pleasure, 154, 157,
    163, 175; and pulsion, 174; and sly
    sexuality, 196; relation to subjectivity,
    19; of vision, 160, 162

Gagnier, Regenia, 206n
Gautier, Théophile: "Albertus ou l'âme
    et le péché," 93–94; *Mademoiselle de
    Maupin*, 93
Gelder, Ann, 149n, 151n, 160n, 163n
Gellner, Ernest, 64n
Geneviève, 91, 92n, 95, 103, 137n
"Goethe," 219–20
Gide, André: and aestheticism, 183–87,
    196–97; antisemitism of, 3n, 92n;
    book sale, 14–16; and Catholicism,
    8–9, 12–13, 198–99; classicism of,
    12–13, 150, 157, 161, 197,
    198–99, 201, 204, 211, 219–20;
    critics of, 8, 10–17, 71–74, 108–17,
    181, 183, 185, 189–90, 196,
    198–99, 201n; "decadence" of, 204,
    206; entomological vision of,
    159–64, 172, 176n, 177–78; erotic
    utopias of, 193; and "essentialism,"
    11–12n; and exoticism, 160,
    162–63; and feminine writing, 96;
    and German occupation, 100; and
    homosexuality, 8, 27–28; openness
    about homosexuality, 9–14, 16, 19,
    68–69, 108, 199; origin of political
    interests, 152–54; politics of, 3, 145;
    racism of, 154–55; relation to Africa,
    6, 13, 17, 19, 37, 42; relation to
    colonialism, 3, 14–15, 17, 28, 30,
    36–37, 39, 46, 51–52, 61–67,
    144–165 passim, 175–80 passim,
    190, 203; relation to communism, 3,
    6–7, 14, 19, 153n, 181–82, 185,

Gide, André (*continued*)
187–90, 192–203 passim, 207–11;
relation to fascism, 189, 205;
relation to his mother, 17, 43,
46–48, 52, 54–59, 64, 66–67,
93–94, 97, 137n, 165–67, 174–75,
195, 220; relation to religion, 29n,
207–11; relation to tourism,
177–78; and sexual pleasure, 7;
snobbism of, 201, 204; and Vatican
ban, 6, 8, 10; works by, 16, 192n,
194. *See also under individual
works*
Gide, Juliette (née Rondeaux, mother),
43, 49–50, 54–56, 59n, 62–67,
93–94, 137n, 166; sexuality of,
52–53, 57–58, 81–82, 93. *See
also* Gide, André; relation to his
mother
Gide, Madeleine (née Rondeaux)
(cousin and future wife), 12, 66–67
Gide, Paul (father), 49–50, 52
Goethe, Johann Wolfgang von, 217,
219–20
Gould, Stephen Jay, 84–85
Goulet, Alain, 109–11, 139n, 160n
Gourévitch, Michel, 124n
Gourmont, Remy de, 80, 84n, 91
Goux, Jean-Joseph, 110–15, 134n, 135
Grammar: and chastity, 102–3; and
comparatives, 104; in English,
101–3; and first person, 9–11, 13;
and imperfect, 35–37; mixing of
present and future tenses, 192; and
nationalism, 101–2; and preterite,
35–36; and present, 40–41, 164n;
relation to politics, 102; and "si"
clauses, 34n; and subjunctive, 34,
96–99, 101–3, 106; in translation,
163–64; of women, 98–99, 105–7;
of working-class men, 103n; of
working-class women, 96–98;
writers' mistakes in, 101
Green, Richard, 116n
Gribouille (character), Gide's fantasy of,
164–66, 168–73, 219
Guérin, Daniel, 18n, 182, 200n
Guy-Grand, Georges, 196n
Gynaeceum, 91, 94–96, 99, 103, 137n

Halperin, David M., 70n, 90n
Harem, 92–94
Hebey, Pierre, 100n, 201n
Heterosexuality: coerced, 134; and
desire, 84–85; and instinct, 80; and
marriage, 92
Hirschfeld, Magnus, 200
Hocquenghem, Guy, 200n
Hollier, Denis, 85–86, 88
Homophobia, 3n, 32, 36, 64n, 67n,
74n, 114n, 115; and AIDS, 72, 74;
and anal intercourse, 39n; in
Corydon, 69–71, 81; in criticism of
Corydon, 17, 70, 73–74; and
"deficit" in homosexuality, 134n; de
Man's, 185, 187; and developmental
models of sexuality, 133; and
mimesis, 73, 76–77, 85; and
parental policing, 195; relation to
misogyny, 17, 88, 90, 92, 94,
110–11; and sincerity, 109–11, 124;
and tourism, 173. *See also* Phobia
Homosexuality, 41; Adorno's analysis of,
181–82; and class, 182n;
criminalization of, 199–200;
"decadence" of, 182, 204; "deficit"
in, 112, 114–16, 118; and desire,
118; legal status of, 75, 89–90; and
masculinity, 90; and military, 89–90;
"narcissism" in, 115, 120; openness
about, 196–99, 204 (*see also*
Sexuality: openness about; Sexuality:
sly presentation of); origins of,
76–79, 116–17, 132–33 (*see also*
Sexuality: origins of); penchant for,
79; "priority" of, 79; relation to
mimesis, 94; relation to politics, 65,
132, 181, 186–87, 192, 196 (*see
also* Sexuality: relation to politics);
temporality of, 29, 78, 118, 131–33,
141 (*see also* Sexuality: temporality
of); and Wolf Man, 130–31. *See
also* Gide, André: and homosexuality
Horkheimer, Max, 207–8
Howard, Richard, 70, 76

L'Immoraliste (*The Immoralist*), 3, 146,
187
Instinct, 79–81, 84–87, 94

Interviews imaginaires (*Imaginary Interviews*), 101–4
Invention, 78–79; relation to mimesis, 77–78

Jammes, Francis, 6, 11
Janet, Pierre, 85, 111–13, 117–19, 139
Jouissance, 22, 25, 40–41, 165
The Journals of André Gide, 68n, 95–96, 100–102, 207n, 217, 219n; and openness about sexuality, 16, 68–69, 194–95; and Proust, 9–10
Journal des Faux-Monnayeurs (*Journal of "The Counterfeiters"*), 112n, 139n
"Les Juifs, Céline et Maritain", 3n

Kaplan, Alice Yaeger, 3n, 205n
Karlinsky, Simon, 200
Kaufmann, Vincent, 150n
Kingsley, Mary, 158n
Klein, Melanie, 44–46, 47n, 48–49
Kraus, Karl, 215
Kristeva, Julia, 44n, 46n
Krylenko, Nikolai, 200–201, 204

Lacan, Jacques, 5, 18–19, 45n, 55–56, 108, 117–21, 124, 125–35, 166–73; hypothesis of mirror stage cited by Edelman, 46n; on Gide's relation to the maternal, 165; and knocking dream, 125–26; and sardine can story, 171–74, 177; on separation and alienation, 167–71
Lacoue-Labarthe, Philippe, 81, 87n
Lang, Jonathan C., 146n
Laplanche, Jean, 25–26
Last, Jef, 203, 206n
Leiris, Michel, 150n
Lejeune, Philippe, 24n, 29n
Lesbianism, 55–56, 58, 95; in *Corydon*, 79–81; in Gautier, 93; in *Geneviève*, 95, 106
Levin, Thomas Y., 211n
Licari, Anita, 150n, 152n, 155
Linné, Carl von (Linnaeus), 156
Littérature engagée, 153, 155, 209
Lottman, Herbert R., 14n, 188n

Lyford, Amy, 16n
Lyricism, crisis of, 178–79, 218–19

"Ma mère" ("My Mother"), 47, 54–55
Mala (African boy), 6–7, 14, 173–74
Mallarmé, Stéphane, 143
Marcel, Gabriel, 198
Les Marges, inquiry into literary homosexuality by, 19n, 182
Marie (Anna Leuenberger) (domestic in Gide household), 56–58, 59n, 67, 93, 166, 218
Maritain, Jacques, 3n, 198
Marshall, W. J., 188n
Martin du Gard, Roger, 117, 143–45, 148, 177n, 180, 190, 218, 220; *Les Thibault*, 147
Martin-Chauffier, Louis, 16n
Marty, Eric, 13n, 15, 16, 24n, 153–54, 193n, 217n
Marx, Karl, 110n
Masculinity, 90. *See also* Homosexuality: and masculinity
Massis, Henri, 13, 198–99
Maubon, Catherine, 160n
Maulnier, Thierry, 189, 205–6
Maurer, Rudolf, 188n, 192n, 194n
Mauriac, François, 198
Mehlman, Jeffrey, 3n, 13n, 92n, 106n, 209n
Melas, Natalie, 150n
Memory, 32–35, 37, 70–71, 78, 129, 164; relation to ecstasy, 162; relation to vision, 163; of Wolf Man, 131
Mimesis, 70–71, 75–81, 85–89; and aesthetics, 184; in animals, 91; and homophobia, 73, 76–77; and masculinity, 90; relation to homosexuality, 80–81, 94
Misogyny, 17, 69–70, 85; in *Corydon*, 79, 81, 90; relation to homophobia, 88, 90, 93–94, 110–11
Mitchell, Juliet, 45n
Moore, Ann M., 137n
Moutote, Daniel, 14n, 145n

Nachträglichkeit (deferred action), 24–25, 34, 40, 118, 121
Nietzsche, Friedrich, 219n, 220

North Africa, 24n, 27n, 28–30, 33–37, 42–67 passim, 72, 100, 148
Les Nourritures terrestres (*Fruits of the Earth*), 7–8, 31, 34, 36, 191–92, 219; de Man and, 183, 186; Wilde and, 9
La Nouvelle Revue Française, 11, 16, 100
Les Nouvelles Nourritures (*Later Fruits of the Earth*), 192, 201–2, 206–7, 215
Nudity, 28–29, 31

Oedipus complex, 48, 54. *See also* Sexuality: anti-Oedipal; Sexuality: Oedipal and pre-Oedipal
Offen, Karen, 82n
Out, 8–13, 77. *See also* Gide, André: openness about homosexuality

Painter, George D., 3n
Paludes (*Marshlands*), 118, 183–84, 186
Pederasty, 72–74, 77, 80–81, 90
Perversion, 78
Phobia, 130–31, 135; Gide's use of, 185; object choice and, 131; of recognition, 130; violence of, 111. *See also* Homophobia
Plato's *Symposium,* myth of androgyny in, 134
Poe, Edgar Allan, and "The Gold-Bug," 83
Pollard, Patrick, 75n, 109n
Pontalis, Jean-Bertrand, 25–26
Porterage, 151–52, 156, 159, 162, 173–75, 177–79
Pratt, Mary Louise, 150n, 151n, 156, 158
Praying mantis, 82–89, 91, 93–94
Prétextes, 38
Prins, Yopie, 192n
Prostitution, 59–61, 88, 92, 110
Proust, Marcel, 8–11; *A la recherche du temps perdu,* 9–11, 16n, 97–98; and homosexuality, 99
Psychasthenia, 85–86, 112–15, 117–19, 128, 139
Pulsion (Lacanian concept), 18, 170–73, 218; of aggression, 175; and foreign words, 214; and frustration, 174

Queer: activism, 195; allegiances, 17, 81, 89, 107; communism, 207; frustration, 196; gender identification, 49; noises, 57; origins, 120, 132–33; outbursts, 190; pitch, 209; portrayal by Proust, 10n; psychoanalysis, 46n; pulse, 171; reading, 89; resistance, 110; revolutionary future, 195; sexual potential, 67; sobs, seizures, and convulsions, 220; subjectivity, 70, 135; swerves, 187; tears, 144, 217; theory, 5, 46

Régnier, Henri de, 14
Representation, repose from, 126, 128. *See also* Dreams: and repose; Sexuality: and sleep
Le Retour de l'enfant prodigue (*The Return of the Prodigal Son*), 191
Retour de l'U.R.S.S. (*Return from the U.S.S.R.*), 15n, 68, 185, 187–204 passim, 207–11 passim; and mixture of sexuality and politics, 14; and openness about sexuality, 19
Le Retour du Tchad. See *Voyage au Congo*
Robert, 91, 95, 103, 107
Rolland, Romain, 201n
Roof, Judith, 46n
Rousseau, G. S., 72–74

Said, Edward, 64n
Sand, George, 164–65, 169–70. *See also* Gribouille
Das Schaudern (Goethean term), 217–21
Schlumberger, Jean, 12n, 153, 155
Schneider, William H., 50n
Sedgwick, Eve Kosofsky: *Epistemology of the Closet,* 10, 71n, 74n; "How to Bring Your Kids Up Gay," 116n
Sedgwick, Peter, 18n, 182n
Seduction, 28, 30, 35

Self: boundaries of, 7–8, 39–40,
43–44; split, 113, 117–18, 123,
136, 149, 167–68, 172
Separation, Lacanian concept of,
167–71, 173; and dealienation, 174
La Séquestrée de Poitiers (*The Sequestered
Woman of Poitiers*), 95
Serant, Paul, 205n
Sex, just, 21–23, 27, 37–38, 40
Sexual acts, 3, 6, 21–22, 24–26,
38–40, 134n; anal intercourse, 22,
37, 39, 88–89; of animals, 80–81,
91; of insects, 84–85; invention or
imitation of, 78; the love-bite, 87;
masturbation, 48–49, 51–52, 140;
offered, 195; reciprocity of, 76; and
sexual economies, 64n; witnesses to,
25–27, 31–32, 36
Sexuality: allegiances in, 93, 95;
anti-Oedipal, 56, 65; conservative
ideology in, 71; delay in, 117–19,
121, 125; dispossession in, 123–24,
136–39, 141–42; in drag, 84, 88;
female, 17, 42–43, 53, 67, 81–94
passim; in foreign words, 213–14,
216; Gide's openness about, 2 (*see
also* Gide, André: openness about
homosexuality); of insects, 82–85;
intervallic, 120, 124–26, 132–33;
itself, 4, 27, 41 (*see also* Sex, just);
Jewish, 92; male, 83–84; marginal,
93–94; narrative models of, 18;
Oedipal and pre-Oedipal, 44–47,
49–53, 58, 62; origins of, 24–25,
35, 37, 43, 47–48, 130 (*see also*
Homosexuality: origins of; Sexuality:
temporality of); pulsation of, 120,
132 (*see also* Pulsion); radicalness of,
71; relation to politics, 1–2, 4–5,
19, 22, 27, 30, 37–42, 90, 145,
154, 181–83, 186–89, 193,
195–96, 199, 202, 206–7, 211,
213–14, 216, 218, 220–21; and
reproduction, 92; and sleep, 18,
115n, 122–26, 138–39, 141–42,
219; sly presentation of, 13–14, 19,
195–96, 205; *sous le coup de* (*see*
Sexuality: under the influence of);
temporality of, 25, 27, 32–33, 35,

40, 46–48, 119–20, 132, 135n (*see
also* Sexuality: origins of; Sexuality:
temporality of); Western, 92; under
the influence of, 3, 121, 138, 142,
214
Shackleton, Anna (Juliette Gide's
governess and friend), 53–56, 166
Shattuck, Roger, 14n
Sheridan, Alan, 64n
Si le grain ne meurt (*If It Die*), 12n,
21–38 passim, 43–44, 47–66
passim, 109n, 117, 119, 120n,
124n, 137n, 139n, 217–19; and
Gribouille, 165; and openness about
sexuality, 7, 11, 14, 17, 108, 195;
and origins of Gide's politics, 145,
153; Proust and, 10; and temporality
of sexuality, 78, 81–82
Signorile, Michelangelo, 10n
Silverman, Kaja, 134–35
Sincerity, game of, 11n, 18, 109–13,
116, 121n, 122, 124, 142, 205
Sjövall, Björn, 112
Sleeping Beauty (patient), 113, 139,
141
Sly depictions of sexuality. *See* Sexuality:
sly depictions of
Smith, John H., 112n
Smith, Olivia, 103n
Sobbing, 217–18, 220–21
Sodomy, 22, 39
Soviet Union. *See* Gide, André: relation
to communism
Stalinism, 195–96
Steakley, James D., 75n
Steel, D. A., 12n, 124n
Stendhal, 123–24
Stevenson, Robert Louis, 151
Subjectivity: disappearance of, 169;
intervallic, 129; and sleep, 129; and
vision, 164
Suret-Canale, Jean, 155, 158n
Symptom, Lacanian concept of,
119–21, 129, 141

Taxil, Léo, 208–9
Tiedemann, Rolf, 208n
Trauma, 126–27, 129–31, 172

Union pour la Vérité, 153n, 196, 205, 210

Van Rysselberghe, Maria, 189–90, 200, 218
Vision, problem of, 172–73. *See also* Africa: problem of vision in; Gide, André: entomological vision of
Voyage au Congo (*Travels in the Congo*), 11n, 17–19, 66, 143, 145n, 147–65 passim, 174–80 passim, 193, 203; and openness about sexuality, 7, 14
Le Voyage d'Urien (*The Voyage of Urien*), 143

Walker, David H., 112–13, 116n
Walsh, Michael, 120n
Ward, Lester F., 83n, 84n

Weber, Eugen, 209n
Weightman, John, 73–74, 77
Wilde, Oscar, 9–12, 32–33, 37, 67n, 71, 74n, 112, 121, 204, 206–7; and antiessentialism, 11–12n; "The Critic as Artist," 81n; "The Decay of Lying," 205–6, 81n; *Phrases and Philosophies,* 12n; *The Picture of Dorian Gray,* 12n; "The Soul of Man Under Socialism," 206n
Winkler, John J., 90n
Wolf Man, 129–31
Writing: camp gestures in, 202, 204, 211, 213; practice of, 3–4; relation to sexuality, 41, 192

Zizek, Slavoj, 120, 128n, 167–68
Zoctizoum, Yarisse, 155n, 156n, 158n